Walkers Between
the Worlds

Walkers Between the Worlds

*The Western Mysteries
from Shaman to Magus*

Caitlín and John Matthews

Inner Traditions
Rochester, Vermont

Inner Traditions International
One Park Street
Rochester, Vermont 05767
www.InnerTraditions.com

Library of Congress Cataloging-in-Publication Data
Matthews, Caitlín,
  Walkers between the worlds : the Western mysteries from Shaman to Magus / Caitlin and John Matthews.
    p. cm.
Rev. ed. of: The Western way.
Includes bibliographical references and index.
  ISBN 0-89281-091-2 (pbk.)
  1. Mysteries, Religious. 2. Occultism. I. Matthews, John, 1948- II.
Matthews, Caitlín, 1952- Western way. III. Title.
  BL610.M377 2004
  299'.93—dc22

                            2003024337

Printed and bound in the United States at Lake Book Manufacturing, Inc.

10 9 8 7 6 5 4 3 2 1

Text design and layout by Priscilla Baker
This book was typeset in Sabon, with Diotima and Avenir as display typefaces

To Dolores Ashcroft-Nowicki and to all who believe in the possibility of bringing things back from Faeryland; and to Gareth Knight and all who seek to rectify the hidden stone.

You are all one, under the stars.
—MERLIN,
JOHN BOORMAN'S FILM *EXCALIBUR*

Contents

Part 2 ◆ The Hermetic Tradition

Foreword

*H*ere is a book that answers a great need of our times—and it answers it very well.

That need is for a rational and informed description of how to apprehend the forces that form the structure of the "inner worlds," those hidden forces that underpin and mold the outer world, which we know through our physical senses, for a realization of the need to come to terms with these other dimensions of reality is fast coming upon Western man.

Those who have not yet understood this need are at times dismayed by what they see as a flight from reason. However, we ought to realize this flight for what it is. It is not a mindless rout of the irresponsible but the winging pinions of an informed intuition no longer content with an intellectual preoccupation with surface appearances.

Others decry what they choose to describe as "dabbling in the occult," which they consider either idly foolish or perversely misguided. While we, too, would not wish to encourage the occult dilettante, those of us who have spent more years in this research than we care to remember feel, with all due humility, that we have gained rather than lost in wisdom and human fulfillment.

There is no shortage among us of able, responsible citizens—even if those less well informed may sometimes gasp incredulously when confronted with our view of truth. We who know understand it to be no facile escapism, but a hard and testing—though infinitely rewarding—struggle toward the truth of what we ourselves are, what our place in the universe is, and what our duties are before God and the rest of creation.

Stock political, scientific, and religious answers to these questions today leave many people unsatisfied. Seeking within for the deeper issues may be one way out of a nuclear or ecological crisis—although ultimately it is more profound even than that! Crises pass, or come to pass. Man's relationship to eternity lasts forever.

John and Caitlín Matthews bring to the subject not only erudition, balance, and common sense, but also a wide practical experience. I have shared in some areas of that experience, and so I confidently recommend that individuals place themselves in the guiding hands of the writers of this book. They will not be led astray.

Furthermore, the authors have a breadth of knowledge and wisdom that puts many more strident occult pundits to shame. They are as much at home at the angelic heights of Christian mysticism as with the "lordly ones" in the depths of the hollow hills. And theirs is a living experience, not mere "book knowledge," though, as readers will soon gather, their literary resources are profound.

This is an instruction book for the present and the future. The old-time occult groups, with their body of doctrine and rigid esoteric structure, are fast becoming a thing of the past. Their good has been done. Their weighty volumes of doctrine remain as monuments and milestones along the way. They may still help us now, but the esoteric students of the present and the future will be ones who take what they can find, in eclectic freedom, for the immediate purpose at hand. Their training will be no less rigorous for being more open and unstructured, their working groups no less powerful despite their relatively transitory, even ad hoc, nature.

John and Caitlín's *Walkers Between the Worlds* provides an Ariadne's thread to help a new generation of seekers find their way through the labyrinth, and goes some way toward enlightening less adventurous souls as to what the maze we call this world is all about.

—GARETH KNIGHT, AUTHOR OF
A PRACTICAL GUIDE TO QABALISTIC SYMBOLISM

Preface to the
New Edition

*S*ince the publication of *The Western Way* in the early 1980s, there has been an immense explosion of interest in the spiritual path. Weekend courses, books, and training programs proliferate wherever we look. They range from the earth-based Pagan and shamanic to the mystical and magical, including a fusion of ancient and modern traditions termed, sometimes opprobriously, New Age. Most interest, however, remains in the popular middle ground. Traditional esoteric discipline and progressive training tend to take second place to self-improvement and self-help that may pave the way to spiritual development, but which can just as easily remain complacently self-serving. As the results of a number of self-improvement plans illustrate, concern with physical health and well-being sometimes displaces care of the soul or a sense of service.

The post-religious twenty-first century is in a spiritual muddle. Having thrown out orthodoxies as outmoded and restrictive, dubiously condemned most mystical methods as "cults," and cast doubt on the sanity of any spiritual practice, we in this century nevertheless aspire to see ethical standards reflected in our society, then wonder where the standards went and why no one is upholding them! Instead of religions, mystical orders, and ordinary spirituality to inspire and guide us, we now have politically correct watchdogs, governmental bodies, and Big Brother surveillance cameras to police our lives. The Orwellian state is no substitute for the Republic of the Spirit.

Many people are now born and brought up with no spiritual focus at all, but they still yearn for the nurture of soul food that gives true life. Hugh Paston, the dilettante hero of Dion Fortune's esoteric novel *The Goat-Foot God,* perfectly expresses this yearning: "I don't want anything spiritual, it isn't my line, I had an overdose of it at Oxford. What I want is that something vital which I feel to be somewhere in the universe, which I know I need, and which I can't lay my hand on."(163)

How we lay hands on the vitality of life itself—which has been called the Pearl, the Hidden Stone, the Grail, or life eternal—is what the Western mystery traditions are all about. There are many paths toward it, many approaches, and every one of them is valid. Instead of looking for a way of entry, we may do better to look within, considering our needs, motivations, and aspirations. Where our heart's desire leads us is usually a good starting-off point for our spiritual journey.

Whatever it is that draws our deep interest and stimulates our yearning, whenever and where our soul goes out to be met, then and there we will find the markers for our path. Though these may not take the orthodox or esoteric forms found in textbooks, they will act as stations along the way, assuming forms that may change and mature as our understanding matures. The louche young musician who drew our eyes as a teenager may lead us to the powerful voice of Orpheus in our adulthood; the tree that we leaned against in the wood months or years ago may at a later date show us the verdant mysteries of the Green Man; the alluring portrait of a woman in a gallery may, on second or third study, reveal the way to the altar of the Goddess of Life. Such simple, unremarkable beginnings can lead us to the spiritual path beneath our feet. We will find our treasure wherever our heart is. The more we meditate upon our heart's core desire, the closer we are to finding our spiritual path.

Beauty draws us, but spiritual practice will maintain our journey. The *Corpus Hermeticum* (Book 7, verse 5) tells us, "If you seek after God, you also seek after beauty. There is one way leading to that beauty: devotion with knowledge." (640)

Shamans, magicians, and mystics gain spiritual knowledge through soul craft and practical application. Transformative change and patience are the means of devotion. In this study of the Western Mysteries we hope that you may follow the way of beauty, by devoted service, to arrive at the knowledge that you seek. As thrice greatest Hermes says, "Knowledge . . . provides the origin of what is to be known. Let us therefore take hold of the origin, and pass over everything else with speed; for it is a path full of tangles, when leaving the familiar and present, to return to the ancient and original." (640) We hope that by returning "to the ancient and original," you may find your way through the tangle of our present time to discover and understand your spiritual inheritance that is the Western Mysteries.

Twenty years have passed since this book first appeared and much has changed in our world in that time. This new edition has been recrafted, rewritten, and updated to make a more communicative text for this era, although we have changed little of the central drive of our argument. In addition, while those who heard we were making these changes to the text were most afraid that we would lose the practices at the end of each chapter, instead we have edited them to reflect the fruits of our own increased experience and to clarify and open the paths leading to the Western Way. In fact, two new practices have been added to create a sequence of twenty-one "steps" that can help you find and walk the Way. Like the Fool in the Tarot who journeys through the Major Arcana from Magician to the World, may your feet be led to experience the rich spectrum of this ancient tradition.

Preface to the
1993 Edition

*T*his book was written as an overview of the Western mystery traditions at a time when the full spectrum of the indwelling spirit had begun to reveal its ancient glory. That light has not dimmed but rather has spread its rays abroad to rekindle personal spiritual practice, illuminating the places that nurture our roots and helping all to find effective ways to manifest their revelation in the world.

After the first publication of the two volumes that now make up parts 1 and 2 of this book, Eileen Campbell, our original editor, asked us to write a third volume to complete the story of the development of the Western Way. We agreed to do so, but only if delivery was acceptable in three incarnations' time, when we might be reborn to complete our study, because there were still so many spiritual movements that had not reached their full flowering.

Since this book was written there have been subtle changes in the way we view the world. There is greater awareness of our environmental responsibility, of the necessity for appropriate spiritual nourishment. But wherever we turn, a collective loss of soul threatens our world. A sense of disorientation exists everywhere, derived from a rejection of the creative, mystical, and spiritual dimensions that have always sustained humankind. A literal-mindedness that ignores the mystical dimensions of life has pervaded our culture, fostering a narrow and fearful spirit that turns to fundamentalist "certainties" for support. In this corridor of creative repression and growing fundamentalism, it seems even more essential to reaffirm our spiritual belonging and practice, to find the connections between our own story and that of this planet. This is how traditions are upgraded by each subsequent generation: by considering how ancient wisdom can be applied most effectively to our time.

It is thus that the Mysteries enter a phase of chaotic readjustment that challenges all we have held as fixed and immovable. At such times the necessity for spiritual reeducation and supportive community becomes more urgent. Many idealists envision the skillful weaving together of generations, social structures, and ancient wisdom, yet this cannot come about until outworn patterns of racism, consumerism, poverty, and war are overcome. We are still far from universal social justice because the spiritual principles underlying the Mysteries are not being applied by governments. Nevertheless, each individual who maintains his or her spiritual practice with impartial compassion widens the way to this possibility.

The two traditions we have written about in these pages are complementary and their wisdom is now receiving widespread recognition in quite unexpected ways. The enduring power of the native tradition, the ancient earth wisdom of indigenous peoples, is at last being acknowledged as an essential guide to living wisely upon the planet. Similarly, the alchemical map of the Hermetic tradition is being traced in theories of chaos physics and the newer science of complexity, showing us that the antique formulas of spiritual progress do indeed reflect the subtle and creative connections of the universe. There are many energetic vehicles at work restating and bringing forth the wisdom of the Western traditions. Any container of a tradition becomes the tradition in due course; only time will tell which vehicles are most effective.

In the meantime, the seeker must be vigilant in order to steer a course around spiritual materialism, to avoid poorly trained teachers promising immediate results for cash, and to escape the rootless trend of "mystical tourism" that pervades training courses. No one can walk the Western Way in an afternoon's workshop. The Mysteries call initiates of many kinds to their service in every age and the dues are always paid in the currency of total commitment. To be worthy of our hire, we must work with integrity.*

To keep our practice supple and effective, we need simple rituals that link the inner and outer life in respect and honor, training programs that

---

* An updated list of groups and organizations offering responsible training in the interrelated branches of the Western Mysteries can be found in the resources section on pages 397–399.

encourage a better integration of esoteric principles in practical ways, a lively imagination, regular meditative and contemplative periods, and a compassionate heart for all living beings.

The Mysteries cannot die, be diminished, or be lost while there are people keeping the sacred path open. Our ancestors have walked the Western Way; those now living walk it; and it will be trodden by children yet to come—whose ancestors we will be. Our task is to keep the pathway clear by walking it with honor, thereby enabling the mystical rose to bloom once more upon the tree of tradition.

Acknowledgments

We would like to thank all those with whom we have worked over many years. Special thanks go to Basil and Roma Wilby; R. J. Stewart; Marian Green; Naomi Ozaniec; Vivienne O'Regan; the late, great Dick Swettenham; Tony Willis; Wolfe and Johan van Brussel; Dolores Ashcroft-Nowicki; Nuinn; Joscelyn Godwin; Adam McLean; Kathleen Raine; Anthony Rooley; Deirdre Green; Phillip Clayton-Gore; Felicity Wombwell and all at the Domus Sophiae Terrae et Sancte Gradale and the Company of Hawkwood; also to Geoffrey Ashe, Delenath and all at Chanctonbury, and to all those who have opened up the pathway between the worlds.

The illustration on page 303 is reproduced with the kind permission of T. and T. Clark Ltd., Edinburgh.

The native and Hermetic landscape

PART ONE

The Native Tradition

The mythic truth is the whole truth.
—P. L. Travers

Introduction to Part One

The Inward Spiral

[Our task is to be] the Secretaries, the interpreters and preservers of the memorials of our ancestors.
—WILLIAM STUKELEY

Mankind, more than is realised, is an expression of the part of the earth upon which he subsists. A rose of the West should not aspire to bloom like a lotus of the East.
—GARETH KNIGHT, *THE ROSE CROSS AND THE GODDESS*

Threading the Labyrinth

*I*n 1968 a book appeared called *The Western Mystery Tradition* (232). Its subject matter was the bedrock of ancient myth and beliefs upon which most systems of Western magic are based. Its author, Christine Hartley, was a member of one of the leading esoteric schools of the time and she was thus uniquely placed to comment from within on the magical tradition. While her book is still valuable for its insights and perceptions, it leaves many questions unanswered. It does not, for example, attempt to relate the more ancient native Mystery traditions with those of the later, so-called Hermetic schools. Yet the Hermetic tradition could scarcely have existed without the native tradition, and an important relationship still exists between them. *Walkers Between the Worlds* attempts to bridge this gap, as well as to disprove the old adage that you cannot bring back anything from the world of faery. There is indeed much to be brought back that can be of value to us now in our perennial quest for a transcendent reality. Above all, it is our intention to present a practical and conceptual view

2

of the Western Mysteries rather than a theoretical and chronological one, and to provide a map to the powerful mystical traditions that are our birthright.

At the outset, let us define the term *Western Mysteries* itself: It refers to a body of esoteric teaching and knowledge constituting a system of magical technique and belief that dates from the beginning of time. From the Foretime, when our ancestors first began to explore the inner realms of existence, these Mysteries have evolved into a variety of practical ways to explore the sacred continuum of life. They have been handed down primarily by oral means and have been remembered and practiced by those who are called to act as the memory of the group, who show the way or act as the soul or spiritual consciousness of the tribe.

Our focus here is on the Western Mysteries, rather than on the many Eastern systems and concepts that have found so strong a foothold in the West. It often has been assumed that the West had no sophisticated or mystical view of the cosmos before Eastern disciplines provided us with a ground plan and expert language. We hope to disprove this assumption here.

Eastern spiritual traditions have given a great deal to the West, offering us precise terminology for concepts unfamiliar to most European languages: *Avatar, dakini, karma, nirvana, sakti, mandala, yantra, mantra*—all these have become established words in esoteric practice. But though Eastern religious and esoteric techniques are certainly relevant to us in the West, we too have a native lore and wisdom. It is important to remember that in esoteric circles there are no rival traditions, only different ways of approaching the same goal. The East is a place of beginnings, while the West is a place of manifestations. The two are not competitors but are part of the same whole. The sun tracks from east to west across the heavens and esotericism reflects this movement. In the East religious devotions are practiced at the day's beginning: bathing in Mother Ganga, offering hymns to the sun, performing morning *pujas* in answer to generations of belief. In the West the devotional practices come at the day's end with vespers, evensong, and the greeting of the Sabbath. The Mysteries themselves belong to no one culture, tribe, or nation, but are part of a universal wisdom that is our inheritance.

Another important phrase, *walker between the worlds,* is used throughout this book to denote any person, whether seeker, initiate, or adept, who passes from the world of everyday reality into the world of spiritual reality and back again. This is accomplished through the practice of meditation, magical rituals, and ceremonies through which our everyday world and the Otherworld are comprehended as one reality.

The mystery traditions—both Western and Eastern—are concerned with keeping open the door between the worlds and mediating the energies that pass through from the Otherworld to our world. In the West's materialist and consumerist culture, we can easily lose sight of the spiritual purpose of life, but an ever greater number of people are searching for something more profound and spiritually sustaining than the quick-fix solutions of the contemporary way of life. We should remember, though, that we have not always had a choice of paths in our personal spiritual quest. Until only a short time ago in the West, this spiritual search had to begin and end within the liberation or limitation of religion.

By appraising the traditions that are our birthright, we learn that they have coexisted alongside the official religions of the West but have been either overlooked by these religions or marginalized by being termed "unauthorized." Religions themselves have arisen from ancient mystery traditions but have chosen to discard their magical practices, which has created in the West an unnatural division between the religious and the magical that is not present in other parts of the world. Religious prohibitions against studying our magical mystery traditions still remain deeply embedded in the Western consciousness, playing on our fears and disempowering our spiritual progress. By examining the nature of mystical reality, by aligning ourselves through simple daily practice, we can learn how false this division really is. The Western Mysteries have maintained the bridge between the two sides of reality, a Western Way that we can still walk.

Imagine, then, that you are about to embark on a journey to an immeasurably distant and strange country. Who will act as your companions and guides? If you are wise, you will turn to those who know the way and are familiar with the terrain. In the same way, if you journey to your own inner landscape, peopled by those from your cultural background and tradition, you should seek those along your path who can help you, familiarizing yourself with what they will say to you and the symbols they will show. You must also learn the words that you must say to open significant doors and how to address those who guard them.

And of course you will need maps. One such map is the labyrinth, and though you will meet with many other recurring images throughout this book—the tree, the circle, and the cross, to name only three—the labyrinth is one of the most important. The unicursal labyrinth as a symbol of the path of initiation is found at many mystery sites throughout the world. It is a living glyph of the Western Mysteries through which all must pass in pursuit of their spiritual destiny. The way in is also the way out—but in order to get out, we must first go in. The spiral journey inward takes us to the center, where we return to our roots and beginnings, honoring the ancestral wisdom. The spiral journey outward takes us to the periphery, to the place of emergence where we can explore the cosmos while referring to the self-knowledge gained on our inward journey.

The inward spiral   The outward spiral

Fig. 1. *The inward and outward spiral of the labyrinth. Its path leads up into the originative depths, changes us, and brings us forth again.*

In our exploration of the Western Mysteries, we will first go back to our beginnings and explore the native tradition, from its origin in the Foretime to its present-day manifestation in the reemergence of paganism. Then, having visited the place of our origins, we will explore the Hermetic tradition—named after its supposed founder, Hermes Trismegistus—from its beginnings in classical antiquity to its current renaissance found in the work of contemporary magical schools and the alchemy of soul making.

We treat the native and Hermetic traditions with equal respect here. The native tradition draws upon ancestral wisdom, with its instinctive respect for the earth, and is focused upon the microcosm. Through the tribal lore of the collective it acknowledges the feminine and the power of story and it listens to the vision of the shaman. The Hermetic tradition, with its emphasis on the pursuit of knowledge and oneness with the godhead, focuses upon the macrocosm. Through the heightened consciousness of the magus it looks to the stars and planets for influences upon our world.

The Hermetic way is grounded in the perennial philosophy—that treasury of cumulative wisdom that remains continuously applicable to the human condition in every age and culture—while the native tradition is grounded in the Otherworld. The deity is seen in terms of elemental forces in the native tradition, while the Hermetic perception shifts from "God out there" to God within the self. The evolution of consciousness is encompassed by both traditions. Just as the Hermetic tradition cannot exist without the foundations of the native tradition, neither can the native progress without the projection of the Hermetic. They are the roots and branches of the tree of the Western Mysteries, providing us with a blueprint for every possible vision.

Christine Hartley points out in her pioneering study of the Western esoteric tradition that "the original working of the Mysteries looked first backwards, and then forwards; and upon their basic teaching we may found the traditions and mysteries of our Western schools." (232) The two-way journey into and out of the labyrinth is a continual spiral of discovery: We go inward to come out again, and when our thread is wound out fully we must return inward to take stock, to gather our findings, and to rest. This is the pattern we must follow if we desire to learn.

Western Folk Weave

While most people consider the "real" Western Mysteries to reside in the Hermetic tradition, others are coming to see them in the context of their foundations. Those who look to the major civilizations of the Middle East and Mediterranean for insight into the Mysteries fail to see the ancestral wisdom all about them. A tradition, like a prophet, is often without honor in its own country; other grass seems greener and more succulent, and so it will ever appear. In considering the native tradition, we have drawn largely upon examples from the British tradition not because it is the only representative of the Western Way, but because it reflects our own experience, ancestral memory, and heritage.

The native traditions of other Western cultures can be drawn upon in this exact same way.

How, then, do we define *Western* in Western mystery tradition? Geographically, we are considering the area from the Middle East westward. Culturally, the margin is less easy to define. None of us is really a native of anywhere any longer. Even those families who have lived in, say, Scotland for generations, were originally Norse, Pictish, or Gaelic invading stock with perhaps a few drops of indigenous blood. There are no pure bloodlines. What occurred long ago in the British Isles has now occurred in the United States and elsewhere: Immigrants have entered America in successive waves from every continent on earth. Those involved in this cultural hodgepodge tend to maintain their own native traditions in their new homeland for at least a few generations. These traditions were once upheld for even longer periods, but the influence of global communication on the homogenization of cultures is greater now than ever before. The last two centuries have uprooted many people, exiling them from their homes as refugees or immigrants in strange lands that no longer know their own cultural identities. Yet for all this, it is doubtful that humanity will have only one skin color, one culture, and one language in the future. Differences do matter and home is still best.

We human beings are territorial animals who want our own plot of land and our own customs. If, however, we cannot achieve our own "plot of land," our cultural being becomes even more important. Native folk traditions and religious practices become even more precious when they are our only possessions; as we know from history, we will practice them under the most rigorous tyranny. Yet even in nonreligious, totalitarian states, the folk soul is rarely jettisoned; it can even become a way of controlling the nation, as we saw in Hitler's reversion to Teutonic mythology during the rise of the National Socialist Party. Whether through indigenous myth or religious or political ideology, the folk soul can be harnessed to one manic individual's vision with terrible results. But while it is true that following the native tradition too closely can result in a counterproductive atavism, native culture itself is not inimical. The folk soul can be powerfully cohesive in times of crisis and war; it can serve to anchor the confused or unhappy and can provide a sense of belonging in the face of exile or loss.

In a time of rapid globalization, however, regional cultures and traditions can often revert to an atavistic nationalism that is fundamentally tribal. Such deeply rooted nationalism can lurk beneath a veneer of seemingly sophisticated civilization and religion, becoming the instrument of oppression or repressive colonialism. Folk traditions and religious beliefs, as well as cultural values, can then be imposed upon one people by another, as in the case of European Americans upon American Indians, Dutch settlers upon black South Africans, or British immigrants upon Australian Aborigines. We will be dealing with the backlash from colonial repression for generations to come, attempting to make restitution for our mistakes.

But while Western cultural imperialism has spread all over the globe, creating terrible imbalances, this is not the path of the Western Mysteries. In fact, if we had been listening to our ancestral wisdom, to our profound spiritual sources, things would have been different. Those who attempt to use the Western Mysteries for repressive and fundamentalist ends are not true walkers between the worlds. Let us remember that genetic research tells us that all peoples now alive derive their ancestry from Africa. Before modern humans emerged, our ancestor species themselves evolved from different forms of life. We are all animals who have our roots in even earlier forms of life. From the first microbial beginnings of the primal soup of life to the dust of extinguished stars, we are all deeply related, whatever our land of birth or cultural coloring.

The Mysteries themselves transcend the divisions of race and country, but our way into them is very much paved by cultural predisposition. We have to start our spiritual journey from home. We each have our sense of belonging to a tribe, a nation, a people, and this is how it should be. It is possible to foster national pride yet to reject racism and any kind of supremecism, to balance our love of the past with our responsibility for the future. We must ask ourselves if we want to belong to the earth on which we walk or to be cut off forever from our roots, bereft of a sense of greater belonging.

Our intention in studying the native tradition in the West is to seek the roots of our consciousness, to track our development in relation to the needs of humankind. Our native tradition is, after all, where our genetic impulse has been coded, the place from which our hereditary memory first springs. But to go beyond our roots, not to remain among them, is the intention of this book. We must live wisely today and not attempt to inhabit a spiritual past.

Since we crossed the bridge of time into the third millennium, there has been a more urgent interest in our beginnings, in the history of how we came to be where we are now. Instead of assuming that our ancestors were poor, ignorant savages, archaeologists and historians are learning a new respect for the resourcefulness of our forebears. They are realizing that in order to understand ancient cultures, it is essential to learn something of their spiritual viewpoint, religious customs, and ceremonies. It is evident that in the Foretime of prehistory, landscape and cosmos were formative sacred influences and people had an understanding of reality's two sides—of both everyday consciousness and that unseen but no less real Otherworld inhabited by the dead and other spirits.

But how can we come to understand such concepts from our own standpoint? What sources will authentically put us in touch with the same spiritual contacts? If the Western Way has its roots in the Foretime, what assurance do we have of uninterrupted descent from that time to our own? Certainly, if we are looking for some kind of apostolic succession, we are going to be disappointed. There may exist families whose lifestyle has altered little over hundreds of years, who have retained their intimacy with nature and have handed down a collection of wise lore and belief, but they are surely rare (see chapter 5). How can we share knowledge to which we have never had physical access? Given that the continuity of tradition is to some extent severed, how, for instance, can we learn why certain ancient stone circles were erected and what rites were performed there?

The ability to enter the eternal present of the Otherworld is the task of the shaman, who is the prime guardian of the native tradition. The information that the shaman brings back is not always verifiable by empirical scholarship. The evidence of such visions is distrusted by those who rely wholly upon the text and who do not experience the sacred continuum of life as accessible by many other means. Some methods of recalling and entering into that continuum are presented in this book so that you may experience it for yourself. This is our sacred heritage within the native tradition: to be aware of the timeless present through the focus of meditation and ritual; to learn that the tales and traditions of our homeland are ours in a more immediate and intimate sense, that the contacts, allies, and guides who work with us are not figments of our imagination. We are not talking about playing archaeologist and visiting our own past or fashioning a romantic and cozy fiction out of half-understood histories or pleasant daydreams, but rather we refer to a willingness to perceive with our inner as well as our outer senses the true nature of reality.

What esotericists call reality, empiricists call dream, vision, or nonsense because they see only one side of reality. To perceive both sides of reality and know which is which is the task of the walker between the worlds. Experience, instinct, intuition, and common sense will show how to distinguish truth from wish fulfillment. As with all experiments, we must judge by results. Insights come in many guises and at many different levels of time and experience. For example, we may learn about the reality of Atlantis from writers such as Dion Fortune (167) and Helena Blavatsky (48), or from the writings of Plato (480). All three experienced and wrote about the nature of Atlantis at a deeper level than most. While their approaches are individually different, the results create an interesting composite picture.

Maps of the Otherworld are as rare as maps of Treasure Island. Somehow we have lost our road markers on the way to civilization and must rediscover where we are in the cosmos. Esoteric vision may be subjective, but definitions of Otherworld reality become clearer as the evidence of our meditations reveals more and more. As we reach for the reality behind our definitions, like explorers who begin to experience the reality of a map by entering the unknown landscape in person, suddenly much more is revealed. Whether we speak of the sacred continuum of the universe in terms of God or Goddess, Mother Earth or Father Sky, or some other term, we begin to understand how different explorers experience the central intelligence of the universe.

It requires patience to retrieve wisdom by these means, but the knowledge that the way has been walked by others before us is comforting. They have left the path clearer for us, and their knowledge is available for our guidance, living on not only in the oral traditions of song and story, but also within the very cells of our bodies and in the earth beneath our feet.

The folk soul itself, the group soul of each nation, which exists in the blood and memory of its people, forms a collective wellspring of imagery and belief. A legend that lives on or a tradition that survives holds the clues we must seek. Although the fragmentary nature of such clues renders them frustratingly elusive, truth will surface from deeper levels that our normal consciousness cannot appreciate—and through various techniques, including the practices included here, we can encourage the emergence of this truth. Many of the myths and stories of our native traditions can enable us to engage in the magic of walking between the worlds. The anthropologist Bronislav Malinowski maintained that myth is not a dead product of past ages but is instead a living force, constantly surrounding magic with new testimonies. Magic moves in the glory of past tradition, but it also creates its atmosphere in ever-nascent myth. Just as the body of legends exists, fixed, standardized, and constituting the folklore of the tribe, so there is always a stream of narratives linked to mythological time. Because magic is the bridge between the golden age of primeval craft and the wonder-working power of today, its formulas are full of mythological allusions, which, when uttered, unchain the powers of the past and cast them into the present (363).

The Sacred Arts

It is across the bridge of magic that the ever-living powers we have thought of as lying in the past can flow into our lives today. This is why we begin walking the Western Way by first returning to our ancestral roots. Neglected by many as childish or primitive, the clear and primal wisdom of the Foretime is alive within the timelessly active present of the Otherworld. By contrast, the New Age has seen many come to grief through reaching for "higher" things through a forced assumption of unrealized spirituality and idealistic mysticism. It is easy to become ungrounded by seeking elevation of spirit. If we neglect the roots of the tree in order to reach for the fruit of the branches, we may find that the fruit has not set because the roots have not been nourished. Fervent would-be mystics arrive all too often at an unbalanced good that causes unaccountable suffering to both themselves and others mostly because they have not attended to their roots.

Not only must we start from our beginnings, but we must also build stamina as we go. The techniques of the shaman, magician, and mystic are founded upon continuous practice and repeated effort informed by spiritual dedication and are focused by ethical intention. This is the Way of the initiate, who is able to walk between the worlds and be streetwise in both. The sacred arts of the Western Mysteries begin with such unglamorous practices as repetitive meditation, training the mind, honing perception, and searching the soul. Some have been misled into thinking that this is yet another system to grant quick riches or cosmic knowledge, but the Way is often long and hard, requiring great discipline and dedication. Those who imagine this is a commercial enterprise that will afford them money or status will meet with great disappointment.

The shaman, magician, and any others who practice the sacred arts have low status in the Western world because our society marginalizes rather than honors all who engage in spiritual transaction and show the way. Shamans and magicians have long been outlawed from the mainstream and labeled as charlatans, heretics, and deceivers by those with religious vested interests. But the schism between magic and orthodox religion has left many scars. The fog of suspicion and superstition has clouded our understanding, while fear and distrust of the Otherworld and those who attempt to go there has created a barrier around the sacred arts. In fact, fear of the "supernatural" and of "dabbling in the occult" is attached to all who attempt to walk between the worlds.

Because so much of our society is governed by central institutions, many people expect there to be some executive board or central authority governing the Western Way. Yet the truth is that it has no church, no pope, no "king of the witches," despite claims to the contrary. Instead there are disparate movements and groups that take its path and bear its seal, some of which do not associate together very happily. All those who wear this seal can recognize their fellow travelers, and though human pride and bigotry or fear and uncertainty may mask this recognition, it is somehow always apparent, indicating the common kinship that binds together the Western Mysteries.

The Western Way indeed has had many societies and associations that have taken the place of the mystery schools of ancient classical tradition, but these organizations have never governed the Mysteries themselves. During times of persecution they have operated in necessary secrecy. Some have been enlightened and humanitarian in focus, while others have been merely self-serving coteries for the fashionable occult dilettante. The good schools have seeded the world with ideas and concepts around which life can reconstellate in harmonious ways, but many of them now seem rather creaky and aged as new forms and disciplines carry forward the Mysteries. In our own lifetime, closed spiritual disciplines and inwardly ruminating esoteric groups have been largely discarded in favor of open seminars, public rituals, and personal meditation. The sacred arts have become accessible through books that range from helpful and informative guides to ludicrous attempts to confer initiation or enlightenment in a week's time.

One of the secrets to learning the sacred arts is that though we can read, study, and practice on our own, we need others to act as catalysts to our sacred education. Much confusion can arise from solitary work when it is neither checked nor witnessed; our commitment can falter when our enthusiasm flags. While the true guides are our spiritual contacts, allies, and helpers, we who are learning to walk between the worlds need others to walk beside us, fellow travelers who may have walked the way before us, who can act as sounding boards and mentors.

The Western Way does not advocate a retreat from the real world. Western esotericism has always integrated the spiritual and material worlds into one unit: The way of the *sadhu, sannyasin,* and monk has always been a specialist one. Though the shaman and magician have taken Hermetic retreats in order to be solitary for short periods of meditation and communion with spiritual allies and guides, they each return to engage the world. We need a group of peers to help us explore the road and at least one mentor so that our path doesn't remain merely theoretical and bookish.

The time for dynamic reappraisal has come. We live in an era in which we do not have to be secretive in order to keep the sacred arts alive. Now, as never before, the world is engaged in a great rediscovery of its spiritual heritage, and though few are aware of their part in this process, more are learning and seeking. We believe that we know everything, that the world has been cataloged and explored. Nothing remains but to seek the mystery of ourselves and our place in the sacred continuum of life. Having lost any sense of spiritual perspective, we turn once more to the sacred arts of the shaman and magician and to our inner journey.

The product of this journey is the recovery of our own traditional wisdom, often revealed by symbols during dreams or insights received through meditation. The time is approaching for the symbols and systems to be regenerated by an influx of new yet ancient material arising from within the group soul and hereditary memory of ordinary people. The work of recovery has already begun on many levels and within many disciplines. Of course, we are not all equipped to become shamans, mystics, magicians, healers, or wise women; yet by virtue of living our lives in the West, we are inheritors of the Western Way. While there will always be special mediators, we can now take personal responsibility for our inner path. The practices included in the following chapters offer the means of contact with the principle archetypes and spiritual forms of the Western Mysteries.

This book does not set out to convert anyone to any particular path, but it may be that what we have written will reveal your own path to you or show you in a clearer light the path you have already been walking. Because so many people today have fallen away from or never belonged to a tradition, understandings that were once common can no longer be assumed. We hope that if you are already following a defined path, this book will help to increase your commitment to it or prompt you to consider how well your path is meeting your needs. We hope that if you are struggling to clarify your path, you will find the clarity you seek perhaps not as a result of reading this book but maybe in reaction to it. We ask you to incorporate from it whatever is personally useful in order to individualize the material in the practices while respecting the specific instructions of each.

Chapters 1–3 address the beginnings of the Western Mysteries, those first stirrings of the religious impulse that led our ancestors to focus their attention on the elements: the earth beneath their feet, the sky above them, the stones and trees and rivers that were, to them, living beings capable of independent action and thought and with whom they shared the inheritance of their Mother Earth. The Western Way holds many of the secrets of our kinship with the earth. As chapter 2 shows, the earth guards the knowledge of who we really are and can confer the keys of our true heritage.

In chapter 4 we make the journey to the Otherworld. Those who have traveled the road to and from it have formed their own place within the borders of our world. They are the "secret people" who build and maintain the inner realm in the heart of every land (278) and who stand at the center of the labyrinth, looking backward and forward. With them we follow the movement from tribal consciousness to individual consciousness. After chapter 5, having reached the center of the labyrinth, we pause to assess our progress before beginning the outward journey, where we will see how native and Hermetic traditions flow into each other.

Our native tradition is still very much a living force whose guardianship passes on, as it always has, to the next generation. You, the readers of this book, are its new guardians at a time when we seek a closer affinity with tradition. It is your generation that holds the threads of the great tapestry making up the Western Way, and it is for you to continue the weaving of the pattern of tradition.

Fig. 2. The lintel stone at New Grange in the Boyne Valley, Ireland. Marking the opening to a pre-Celtic passage grave, the stone is carved with interwoven spirals that remind us of the labyrinthine path we must walk in the pursuit of wisdom.

Notes on the Practices in This Book

Please read this section before attempting any of the practices in this book. A recording of some of the practices, along with two practices not available in print, is available from the Foundation for Inspirational and Oracular Studies (for address and Web site information, please see the resources section on page 397).

Each of the practices in this book includes its own instructions, but a few general remarks here may be helpful to the inexperienced practitioner. We believe that the Western Mysteries are a living path, not a theoretical concept, and that you, the reader, have a right to experience the journey on this path. As with a good cookbook, every exercise here has been tried and tested. The provenance of the techniques varies: While our own work within the Western Mysteries has provided us with their basis, we have drawn liberally on oral tradition, written lore, and others' experiences for their substance. We have tried to be broad in our choice of material—the Western Way is diverse, combining pagan, Christian, and kabbalist with priest, witch, magician, and other gentle souls from a range of New Age groups. The exercises have been designed for a single practitioner who has little or no experience, but each is adaptable for use in groups and can be "stepped up" judiciously for those who know the ropes. Though some practices have prerequisites of sorts—exercises that should precede them—generally no attempt has been made to order the practices. If, however, they are performed in the order of their appearance, a logical progression through the Mysteries will emerge.

Unless otherwise stated, all the practices can be performed while seated comfortably in an upright chair at a time and place free from interruption, so take your phone off the hook and warn your family that you are not to be disturbed for an hour. Of course, some of the outside exercises, especially at sacred sites, are likely to be fraught with interruption. Remember that although it is difficult to tune into a sacred earth center in the midst of the tourist season, it is still possible, given a modicum of common sense and a great deal of concentration. Regardless of your location when performing the practices, be aware of the importance of quiet, rhythmic breathing and physical relaxation. Without these two essentials, which are often stressed but seldom applied, the results of your performance will be negligible.

The meditations in this book can be handled in two ways: You can read through the instructions and memorize them before beginning each practice or you can record the instructions and perform the practices while listening. Pathworkings, as meditations are often called these days, stem from the kabbalistic method of working upon the paths of the Tree of Life and should not be confused with the guided imagery techniques used by psychologists. The meditations given here are based upon traditional pathways that will bridge you with the Otherworld. Guided imagery meditations, on the other hand, are mostly invented scenarios. The more often a path is walked, the stronger it becomes. If you decide to record the meditations, remember to leave sufficient pauses in between parts of the text where you may need to visualize or engage with the material. The technique of pathworking is easily learned; it is like listening to a story, only you are the protagonist. Instead of seeing yourself as on a television screen, look out through your own eyes at the scenes before you; be there with all the clarity of your visual powers instead of simply observing yourself doing something, which can indicate that you are not in alignment with the meditation. As the esotericist Dion Fortune says, "What you contemplate, you touch. What you enter into in imagination, you make yourself one with." (166)

Immediately after meditating, and indeed after each practice, write down your impressions. Like dreams, they will escape otherwise. Having a record of your work is a useful check for the future, when you may wish to branch out into other areas of exploration. But though your notebook is a companion and reminder, remember that it is not holy writ. You will eventually reach a stage in which you won't need to take notes; you are instead living the Way. Until then, however, allow the practices to expand your understanding of the sacred continuum of which you are a part.

Repeat each exercise several times. Apart from noting your realizations, you will also discover how you react and change. The more you walk the path, the clearer it will become.

Many who begin esoteric work or a meditation practice that involves the exploration of the Otherworld will find useful the following basic rules of travel. We will expand upon them later, but these pointers will enable you to practice safely and without fear:

- Seal off your aura.
- Retain clear motivation and common sense on whatever level you operate.
- Establish clear boundaries between your ordinary life and your meditational practice by using words or signs to both open and close each session.
- Use your clan totem as a passport to other realms and call upon spiritual allies, guardians, and guides to accompany your otherworldly journeys. Keep good connection with them and ask their help when you need it rather than taking all steps alone and unaided.
- Do not expect fear distractions and terrors; do not follow them or become entangled with them.
- Respond courteously to those you meet on your travels. Discern whether or not they are present to speak to you. Remember that in everyday life, not everyone you meet on the street wants to give you advice, nor would you wish to ask it.

Meditation is a means for you to explore your inner world, which borders the Otherworld (see chapter 4). The reality you meet in the Otherworld is consistent within its own boundaries and if you observe its code, you will be safe: Follow the way set down for you, respect the guardians, and be alert for landmarks. Meditate with serious intent, but keep your sense of humor. If you take a wrong step, if you meet with something you don't expect or are reminded of some terrible past event in your life that is painful to contemplate, don't panic. Meditation tends to bring up aspects of our personality that we have not fully integrated, but remember that the theme of the Mysteries is "Know thyself." Learn not to run away but to face up to your shortcomings; if you start bearing responsibility for your personal development, your spiritual growth will continue steadily.

Remember that your experiences will be unique from anyone else's, so while it is sometimes helpful to compare notes with fellow travelers on the path, it can be confusing and detrimental to your progress to attempt to speak about your findings to someone who is not involved in similar work; everyone must experience for him- or herself the realizations implicit on the path. However much you love other human beings, you cannot attain enlightenment on their behalf; they must find their own way, make their own metaphor, and engage in their own realizing.

We each aim to potentize our individual capabilities and perceive more clearly our relationship with the spiritual evolution of our planet not out of a desire for self-aggrandizement, but in order to coordinate our bodily, psychic, and spiritual vehicles, enabling them to be effective instruments in the work of planetary service. This pattern of service underlies the work of the Western Mysteries and should be considered by those who have any qualms about exercises that may seem self-centered. To know yourself is the first task. Any measure of control you gain over yourself has a positive effect on the world around you.

In meditation it is useful to have some kind of device to mark the start and close of your practice. Such a device can be helpful in avoiding confusion between physical and spiritual consciousness and in establishing both mental adjustment and right intention. Here we offer some suggestions, but if none appeals to you, you can come up with your own; they will doubtless work much better for you than adopting ones that are not comfortable to you.

To start a meditation, imagine that you are a pilgrim about to pass between the worlds. Say the following:

> *I stand at the door with staff and pack,*
> *May God [or the gods] protect me there and back.*

Protecting yourself in this way does not necessarily indicate that you expect devils and dangers, but instead shows that you undertake your inner journey with intention—which is probably its most important requirement. You can substitute the name of your spiritual protector and incorporate your personal or clan totem (see practice 1, Finding Your Clan Totem) in the following chant:

> *From light to light,*
> *From this world to the Otherworld,*
> *Through the thresholds,*
> *In the name of [your protector],*
> *I come bearing the [your own symbol or totem].*

To return from meditation, you can repeat your entry chant with the intention of returning to where you began or, as you strongly imagine your personal symbol, you can modify the first line of the second chant to:

> *From the Otherworld to my world*

To begin and end a meditation, many people employ the simple device of opening and closing a pair of imaginary doors or curtains.

Regardless of the method you use to start and close your practice, it is important at the end of any exercise to consciously close off from the rest of your life the esoteric work you have done. This is common-sense psychic hygiene that is often neglected, but if you have ever tried to get a good night's sleep after going over your accounts or having a flaming row with a friend, you will understand the importance of this step. A quick sealing-off gesture made with intention takes only a few seconds and is preferable to leaving your psyche running like a car engine.

For each exercise, follow the instructions carefully and use your common sense. Journey with the same street wisdom you would employ in daily life. Any technique that develops little-used abilities can be initially disorienting; expect a certain upheaval of consciousness in the first few weeks and accept that you are new to these experiences. Any technique also can wreak havoc when practiced by those who consider themselves experts on everything. For a fine example of this, read Franny's experience of the Orthodox Jesus Prayer in *Franny and Zooey*, by J. D. Salinger (518). As a general rule, you should practice each exercise until you understand how it works. The Western Mysteries will wait, so be patient with yourself and take time to master each technique. There are no instant results and no "right" answers. You alone possess the key to each exercise, for without your participation, the practices are worthless.

As a follower of the Western Way, you should focus on becoming aware of your own potential as one who opens the way, who walks between the worlds of spirit and matter, who inherits and wields traditional wisdom within the human scheme of existence, and who lightens dark places within the human consciousness. The point of these practices is not to lift you from the planet, but to help you discover how your realizations can enable your spiritual vocation as a human being.

As you become more deeply involved in inner work, so will you begin to sensitize your being to the workings of both inner and outer worlds: Life lessons will come up more frequently as you participate in the earth's own subtle changes and disturbances. This may be disconcerting at first, but gradually you will learn to cope with the kind of inner pressure that sometimes builds. Minor headaches are to be expected from time to time in this work. If you are ill, depressed, or otherwise under the weather, leave the practices alone until you feel better. Because they are intended for practical application in your everyday life, if your daily living is under pressure and your circumstances are emotionally fraught, then the exercises become a burden that you can do without. Likewise, be aware of using the Otherworld, your inner landscape, as an escape from life's traumas. Be aware of the hazards of doing too much. If you are pushing both your outer and inner selves, your physical vehicle can become quite depleted in vitality, resulting in a paper-thin etheric body that can offer little protection. The only cure is regular rest, relaxation, and a complete break from inner work. Read harmless novels rather than improving literature, watch television, or do the gardening, but don't step up the inner work.

Do not attempt these exercises if you use mind-altering drugs. Hallucinogens may seem to offer a quick route to enlightenment, but rather than providing a real shortcut, they more often result in short-circuiting the system. Whatever your path, the truth is the same, and you can get there only under your own steam. While medicinal drugs can, to some extent, correct imbalances in the body that result from inner disturbances, they often do not penetrate to the root cause of the illness.

We owe a debt of gratitude to those who have helped us in our testing of each practice and technique over a long period, and to our other supporters, both outer and inner. But even more, we owe a debt to those who have walked the Western Way before us and have left signposts along the road for us to follow. By working with these vital images, it is possible to trace the pattern of the maze inward and then outward again toward the future.

Walking the Western Way can be a lonely business at times; nevertheless, there is a genuine companionship among its travelers that transcends time and space. The landmarks on the path and the guardians whom you encounter along the way have been recognized by and known to others before you, as they will be again by those who come after you. We wish you a happy and empowering journey into your heritage.

1

The Old Religion

The cult-man stands alone in Pellam's land . . .
he can fetch things new and old . . .
the things come down from heaven together
with the kept memorials.
—DAVID JONES, ANATHEMATA

In the old days when we were a strong and happy people,
all our power came to us from the sacred hoop of the
nation, and so long as the hoop was unbroken, the people
flourished. The flowering tree was the living center of the
hoop and the circle of the four quarters nourished it.
—JOHN G. NEIHARDT, BLACK ELK SPEAKS

Rite and the Foretime

"*O*nce upon a time, there was no time, and it was then that . . .*"
This is the traditional opening of a Breton storyteller's tale
and it immediately places the teller's audience in another
realm of existence. It is to this "once upon a time" that we must go to
find the first traces of the Western Way, for to start our story within
recorded history would be to leave out the most important of beginnings. It is in this "no time" that we find the Otherworld—a dimension
where the gods still live in the inner landscape of our spiritual home.
The Otherworld, the Western equivalent of the Australian Aborigines'
Dreamtime, is neither a memory of the past nor a remnant of some
golden age, but instead a living and eternal present in which past and
future meet and mingle.

In part 1 of this book we move within the world and work of the shaman, the original walker between the worlds. Shamans and their lineal descendants are the keepers of the native tradition, working within the primordial framework that has evolved from the earliest levels of tribal consciousness. The upsurge of interest in native tradition has tended to focus the events and beliefs of the Foretime in a spotlight of reverential awe. Present-day Pagans who have reconnected with the native tradition and drawn upon it for their inspiration sometimes adopt a rosy or romantic view of shamanic rites and the practices of the Foretime. They may forget that life in the Foretime was difficult, and that spiritual practice was not a self-improving pastime, but rather a necessary way of life. Magic was not separate from everyday life; it was part of it: Features of the universe had not yet been departmentalized as supernatural, normal, or scientific. Life in the Foretime was infused with the numinous nature of gods and spirits who were acknowledged daily. Animism was the first religion, the Old Religion.

Fig. 3. One of the earliest images of the shaman, the prehistoric antlered figure from the cave of Les Trois Frères in southern France

The Western Way has evolved from tribal, animistic consciousness. Symbolic truth is as true now as it was in the Foretime, yet the means of that truth, conveyed by image and symbol, myth, song and story, has changed as the consciousness of humanity has evolved. The language of metaphor is the first language; the subtle conveyance of meaning through the allusions of song and story is the first brushstroke of image and symbol. At any one historical cross section of linear time, symbolic truths are revealed by the metaphors that resonate with the prevailing consciousness of the time. While it is now very difficult for us to read and understand the images executed upon cave walls by our ancestors in the Foretime, for people at the time of their creation, the meaning would have been plain. The development and evolution of human consciousness provides the motivation in the Western Way; it is the impulse that sets upon the path those seekers, whether shamans or scientists, who are determined to find the unifying factors in physical or outer life and spiritual or inner life. The capacity to understand and equate these factors is dependent upon the level of consciousness brought to bear on this search.

Our first steps upon the Way are taken within the native tradition, in which tribal or collective consciousness prevails. Out of the tribe emerges the shaman, who engages with the deepest otherworldly wisdom in order to translate the symbolic language that informs the next step on the evolutionary road of the spirit: individual consciousness. By recognizing, meeting, and identifying with the numinous gods and spirits, and by synthesizing this experience and transmitting it in an appropriate form to the tribe, the shaman educates the people. Not all take the step to individual consciousness at the same time. It is the result of an evolution that takes many generations and is partially achieved through the presence and work of the shaman and a growing body of initiates who have already begun to effect the transition within the tribe.

The native tradition of any country takes its people on this long journey from tribal consciousness to individual consciousness, just as its Hermetic or esoteric tradition attempts to lead people from individual consciousness to cosmic consciousness, in which evolved humanity will perceive its collective responsibility (see fig. 4).

The task of spiritual traditions, both now and in the Foretime, has been to hasten this evolutionary process through whatever means they have at their disposal. Their varying success can be gauged by a quick mental assessment of your own life experience to date. Consciousness

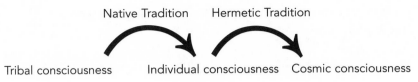

Fig. 4. The evolution of consciousness

can evolve only at the pace of those who are slowest to develop, however. Even in the third millennium there are atavistic aspects of tribal consciousness that the Western world is still struggling to throw off as it wrestles with regional differences and extreme forms of nationalism and racism. Ancient fears of merging with, surrendering to, or being invaded by unfamiliar concepts, alien cultures, or different religions result in a kind of fundamentalism that causes spiritual evolution to become petrified.

In the Foretime this evolutionary search for individual consciousness was begun by means of contact with the mineral kingdom and with the earth's vital energies, which led to an understanding and personification of these energies with god forms. The earth itself was a numinous spirit, a sacred living being. The native tradition has never abandoned, forgotten, or neglected this immediate and familiar relationship with the earth. It remains an important means of understanding the universe. Upon this firm foundation the Hermetic tradition was able to perceive the relationship between the earth and the macrocosm that motivates the universe, and to identify the operation of each within both elemental and sophisticated god forms, as we shall see in part 2.

Those who today turn with renewed respect to the native tradition for their inspiration seek to work with the essential seed ideas and ancient knowledge of the Foretime, discarding forms and practices that are inappropriate for the modern world. This is done primarily via the Otherworld journey (see chapter 4 and practice 8, The Two Trees), in which the primordial wisdom yet lives. But before we can follow the way of the earth and the gods, before we board ship for the Otherworld, we must enter the world of the Foretime, the "once upon a time" of our ancestors.

The nineteenth-century poet "A. E." wrote:

There is an Everliving in which past, present and future are one, and when we brood upon the past it may be that our intensity brings us to live in that which we brooded upon. It is not only in vision that we revisit the past; our hearts may sink into it and know what others have known. (514)

To "know what others have known" is never easy, and when we make excursions into the prehistory of the Foretime, we need atavistic sensitivity in order to see with the eyes of our ancestors and perceive with their consciousness. Imagine a time when feeling and sensation were a means of perception: when people shared a common conscious-ness and communicated in subliminal ways, as sensitive to changes in weather as animals are, aware of the seasonal round, and so deeply con-nected to the land that there could be no disconnection from it. These were the Firstborn; the terms Neanderthal and *Homo erectus* are but convenient hooks on which to hang old bones. All cultures have had their Foretime—indeed, some traditional societies are still living through theirs—and what is written here may be true of many periods of time that existed when landmasses, which we know today as conti-nents, were connected and when present national divisions had not yet evolved.

The first intimations of the sacred were a subtle blend of many understandings—among them, of the earth energies whose currents crystallized into natural features of hill, stream, and tree; and of the ever-present power of the ancestors before the ancestors. It was a name-less, sensuous evolution at first, little more than a realization of what made stone something other than wood and both something different from flesh or bone. The immobility of stone and the quick, liquid gush-ing of water took on individual characteristics and qualities. Fire, air, earth, and water were the elder brethren of humankind, energies to be recognized and greeted with respect and the elementals of life that endowed the earth with power.

It was in the Foretime that these elementals were named and rec-ognized. Before developed concepts of deity, the earth was already understood to be female—the Mother, the one who brings forth, the provider. The sky was discerned to be male—the Father, the one who rains and thunders. Eventually, the names and the images combined to formulate the seeds that would grow from meaningful metaphor into the gods. The ability to bestow names, together with the art of visuali-zation, distinguished the shaman from the rest of those in the tribe. The first stirrings of imagination are perceptible in an individual's ability to create a "picture" in his head. William Golding's *The Inheritors* (187) gives insight into the consciousness of the Foretime and the way in which such pictures were tentatively shared.

In the native tradition of the Foretime, place was of the utmost importance. Unlike today, when people may draw upon the spiritual sources of cultures that are not their own, native tradition was generated from the land and customs of a specific location. Further, rather than communicating with transcendental spirits, shamans were in contact with spirits related to hunting, agriculture, fishing, the earth, sun, moon, and stars. They looked to the symbols that appeared in the natural world as guides to action and as resonant metaphors of the spirit world.

A modern Australian Aboriginal woman of the Pitjantjara tribe helps us to understand this sense of belonging to a particular place when she says that the moles, warts, and skin discolorations on her body are the same as the marks left by her ancestors upon a particular rock at her birthplace (422). Although we still acknowledge the importance of our place of birth, experience the frisson of power at a sacred site, or even yearn for some remote place that we feel is our spiritual home, very few of us in the West intimately know the network of influences at work on a site that has been continuously occupied over many generations. The natural features of such a place take on characteristics that are familiar and friendly to its inhabitants, eventually coalescing into spiritual forces: the *genius loci,* or spirit of the place. Today, ancient spiritual forces can still be encountered at old wells, on hills, and in woods. Though few people still make a wish, or tie a prayer rag from a branch at these places, the genius loci remains.

In the Foretime the tribe was a unit; its members, an extended family, were focused on maintaining themselves and surviving. To be part of the tribe was to be one of the family; to be cast out was almost certain death. To be subject to the tribe's customs, laws, and privileges was to participate in the tribal consciousness that had been built up over many generations until a group soul began to operate. This group soul subscribed to a common symbolism and understanding that was upheld by domestic custom and transmitted through the traditions of ritual behavior. Ritual is a method of formalizing and therefore remembering things, a way of codifying the functions of humanity within a spiritual sphere of reference so that the deeds and responsibilities of ancestors can be transmitted to the tribe. It is a way of connecting everyday reality to otherworldly reality so that Otherworld beings can witness changes in our world, or so that we can witness the powerful changes of the spirits.

Tribal consciousness, concentrated in the here and now, was concerned with the body's magnetic relationship to the earth and with the mingling of the earth and the ancestors. This focus is reflected in tribal rites such as the cult of the severed head, the veneration of ancestors' bones, and the ritual of pouring the blood of sacrifice upon the stones (64). The recurrent rhythms of life and death were the tribal reality, and from these stem the ancient historical or religious promptings that still sway our opinions today. The early encodings of tribal ritual are yet with us, sometimes enshrining irrational and aberrant beliefs and other times giving us access to the group soul and potent wisdom of our people.

Because these rituals are based in earth, it might be easy to deride their efficacy for our own time, but we must remember that "[t]he heavy matter through which we move is not the antithesis of cosmic consciousness but its densest and most inert expression." (511) The first stirrings of consciousness may appear crude and barbaric to us, but within the context of their times they were the valid attempts of a people to relate to the realities hidden behind appearances. They are the foundations of spiritual belief.

At the heart of the Old Religion was *animism*, the belief that every thing as well as every living organism has a soul. The term Old Religion has been used in diverse contexts, in some instances by those of one group who wish to define themselves in relation to those of a group that has descended from them. For instance, in countries where Catholicism was outlawed after the Reformation, members of the Catholic Church applied this term to their belief system in order to differentiate it from Protestantism; likewise, present-day witches use the term with regard to their own ancestral beliefs. In the context of this book, we apply the term Old Religion to the earliest native animist beliefs. The Old Religion here covers the vast period from the Foretime right up to and including the beliefs of the Celts, who welded their own practices onto older native patterns.

Such is the variety inherent in the Old Religion that we cannot trace every single factor in its makeup. Some of its earliest forms come down to us as folk customs and prayers, as simple ways of acknowledging the tasks of life rather than as formal expressions of worship. We can understand this by looking to the traditional sayings and prayers collected from the islands and Highlands of Scotland by Alexander

Carmichael in the *Carmina Gadelica* (78). No aspect of life is too humble to have its own special saying and blessing—from smooring (covering) the fire at bedtime and blessing the seed corn for sowing to invoking against the evil eye and offering charms for travelers. The woman who weaves the cloth on her loom, ever aware of the vital interdependence of the animate and inanimate, sings:

> *May the man of this clothing never be wounded,*
> *May he never be scathed.*

The *Carmina Gadelica,* collected in the late nineteenth century, gives a clear impression of how even household gear and weapons participated animistically in their users' lives. The particular blessing for each everyday activity could not be omitted without inviting danger, and rhymes and songs were sung to ease ongoing work. In orthodox Judaism, prescribed blessings of thanksgiving are still recited when performing daily actions. Even today the protection of saints, angels, and fairies is still sought. Places of accidental or violent death have been memorialized not in stone but in songs of lamentation and sad remembrance. Of the dead themselves there is little mention because their realm overlaps the realm of the living. The gateway is always open to the world of the ancestors, and they live potently in story and song.

The first forms of deity thus arose from recognition of the genius loci, which was the first germ of the idea of a god or gods. The second germ grew from the cult of the ancestors. The dead were both buried and cremated in the Foretime, but if burial was called for, the preparation for entombment was carried out with great care and exactitude, even to the inclusion of food and personal equipment in the tomb, as though death were but another form of life, which was exactly how it was understood. The ancestors—those who had gone before—were considered the go-betweens from the Otherworld, which was itself a continuation of this world. In life they had helped establish the fundamental shape of tribal existence by acting as links in the chain of tradition and by transmitting tribal wisdom. Reverence for ancestors is by no means extinct today. Many still celebrate the great festival of the dead on Halloween or on All Saints' and All Souls' Day, notably in Mexico, where candles are placed over ancestral graves, and in other parts of the world, where it is customary to offer news of the family to the deceased (65).

In the Foretime the deeds of ancestors were related to the next generation until eventually some of these individuals grew in stature to resemble gods or goddesses. Sometimes such retellings show how the behavior of the ancestors helped to codify tribal laws and precedents. The Irish historical chronicle the *Book of Invasions* sets many such precedents: the first adultery, the first fire kindled, the first fair assembled. These are all activities in which the ancestors participated in the tribe's distant past, memories encapsulated and sung (321). These early tales seldom feature ancestors experiencing happy family life, but instead are rife with violence, chaotic relationships, and bloody slaughters. In the *Welsh Triads,* bardic mnemonics in which the ancestors and their deeds are celebrated in threes, we read of the three famous shoemakers, the three amazons of Britain, and the three unfortunate assassinations (602). Such tales provided a way for members of the tribe to share in the exploits of the dead who did not die.

Though everyone had ancestors who could be contacted and who could give aid, it required a specialized member of the tribe to interpret the realities of the Otherworld. In the shaman, the priest, the walker between the worlds we find the third germ of the god idea and a beginning of formal religious practice.

Walkers Between the Worlds

Every one of us is an earth walker; however, only certain people—the psychics, the mystics, the dreamers—are called to perform the shamanic function. In our society we exclude such people from the circle of community life out of fear or ignorance; for us they seem to have no useful purpose. Yet in the Foretime a tribe without a shaman was a tribe without a spiritual representative. Someone had to be able to go to the thresholds of the worlds and transact the tribe's spiritual business with ancestors, spirits, and gods.

The shamans were the first guardians of the Western Way, the first keepers of tradition. Although the word *shaman* belongs properly to Siberia, it is more applicable to the Old Religion than is *witch, magician,* or *priest,* for the shaman fulfilled many roles: keeper of tribal lore, healer, prophet, diviner, and ceremonialist as well as ambassador to and interpreter of the gods. A shaman was born, not made, and was trained or guided only by another shaman. In an initiation, the shaman candidate went to an isolated place and, often near death from rigorous ordeals, made his or her first formal encounter with the Otherworld to meet a protector or mentor and the tribe's ancestors or totem. If this initiation was successful, the candidate returned to the tribe to be inaugurated into the shamanic function by the elders (318).

The shaman was literally a walker between the worlds, one whose attunement to both tribal consciousness and the gods was so fine that he or she could slip between the hidden parallels of life and death, between this world and the Otherworld. The shaman affected the quality of the group soul on levels not immediately appreciable to normal consciousness. His or her vision informed, shaped, and changed the tribal unit. If we look to the ages after the Foretime, we can find mystics of many religions—the Christian Saint John of the Cross, the Jewish Nahman of Bratislav, and the Muslim Rumi—who carried the group soul forward through their silent witness and intimate contact with the spiritual realities of their faiths and through their intensive meditation upon the symbols of their religions in ways that made these images strongly evocative for others. The shaman's role was even more crucial because his or her personal revelation shaped the tribal consciousness and formulated and named the gods. As Joan Halifax explains in her book *Shamanic Voices:*

> This special and sacred awareness of the universe is codified in song and chant, poetry and tale, carving and painting . . . it gives structure and coherence to the unfathomable and intangible. By "making" that which is the unknown, the shaman attains some degree of control over the awesome forces of the mysterium. (223)

It was upon the shaman's revelation and visualization that the Old Religion was built and from which subsequent god forms and spiritual practices were derived. While tribal members had only a vague notion of the threshold dividing the worlds, the shaman not only could divine through observation of the spirits of nature and of elemental forces, but was also supremely sensitive to the will of the ancestors, the first gods. The first stories of the gods arose from a weaving of the relationships among such animistic powers.

The shaman also maintained a close relationship with the tribe's luck, the ancestral totem. Certain Highland clan chiefs in Scotland still retain their clan's luck today: The MacLeods, for instance, possess the Fairy Flag, an otherworldly banner with the power to protect the clan from peril (424). The form of the tribal totem varied: If the tribe depended upon an animal, then an animal skin or horn might be worn by the shaman in great ceremonies. Or the totem might take the form of a stone or implement to be wielded, an emblem of the office of shaman or tribal ruler. The stories attached to the tribe's luck were bound up with the beginnings of the tribe itself and can often be traced within the genealogies of certain families.

In the Foretime, the shaman was responsible for the spiritual balance of the tribe and the tribal ruler concerned himself with its daily governance. Sometimes the functions of shaman and ruler were combined in one person or family, which led to a close identification of that family with otherworldly entities or the gods. In this we see how some kings were said to descend from gods—the peace kings of Sweden from Freya, the Saxons from Woden, and the emperors of Japan from the sun goddess Amaterasu—while others were believed to have descended from animals, such as the Macfies, who were descended from a seal woman, and the French Lusignan line (whose later descendants became kings of Jerusalem during the Crusades), who were descended from Melusine, a water goddess or mermaid (137).

In some senses the shaman was also an early form of herald, bearing the arms or symbols of his tribe on its behalf. Armorial emblems or coats of arms representing people or groups of people can act as a substitute for a person, even after his or her death (424). Because we are all intimately related through a handful of common ancestors, we each have some share in a tribal symbol. Although we may not be eligible to bear arms, certain symbols or mascot images—the shaman's animal ally and the animal familiar of the witch, for instance—crop up everywhere and are still powerful spirits belonginging to each of us. A technique for establishing such a shamanic or tribal totem is offered in practice 1, Finding Your Clan Totem. Clan totems like these, initiators into the Otherworld, are still powerful allies in walking the Western Way.

The shaman functioned not only as the spiritual representative or herald of the tribe, but also as its memory. Journeying between the worlds gave him or her a familiarity with both sides of reality. Most of us have lost the facility to pass from everyday reality into the Otherworld, but artists, priests, and initiates still have this ability. *Analepsis,* or the process of remembering and recovering forgotten knowledge—a technique used by poets, historians, mediums, and others—is, as you will see, an inheritance available to all of us who succeed our shamanic ancestors. While analepsis is skillfully discussed by Robert Graves in chapter 19 of *The White Goddess* (194), the following two examples show how it functions.

Just after World War II James Fraser, a cartwright in Beauly, Scotland, told in such detail a recurring dream in which he witnessed the Battle of Blar-na-Leine that his listeners did not doubt that he had seen the fray. However, this battle between the Frasers and the Clanranald, in which nearly all the Frasers were killed, occurred in 1544. James Fraser's description of the clansmen's dress, equipment, and methods of fighting could be verified only by some obscure sources unavailable to him (424). If one of Fraser's ancestors had survived that battle, could this be some form of hereditary memory?

Many theories have been put forward to explain this phenomenon, such as Jung's theory of the collective unconscious (280), reincarnation memory (239), and access to the ancestors (424). Each of these hypotheses uses an idiosyncratic metaphor for a single understanding. If we accept the Otherworld as a reality that is always available and is not subject to linear time, we begin to see how analepsis may be one of the keys to the Western Dreamtime. A technique for developing far memory is given in practice 2, Analeptic Memory, at the end of this chapter.

A second example of analepsis concerns Alfred Watkins, the nineteenth-century antiquary who "rediscovered" ley lines, or those energetic paths connecting ancient sacred sites. He spoke of an experience in which he was beset by a "flood of ancestral memory" when he first saw ley lines etched upon the countryside (639). Such sudden recall can allow an age-old facet of our tradition to be retrieved and thereby enlighten our own time. Whatever terms we choose to use for analepsis—communications from beyond the grave or from another space rather than from ancestors or the Otherworld—we each possess the means to use this technique.

Nothing is ever truly lost, and this is the joy of the Western Way. Recurrent themes crop up in a seemingly isolated way in individuals and, when synthesized, these form a body of knowledge that has lain forgotten for centuries. The shaman ensured that such knowledge was not left to chance. Each tribal member's initiation into adulthood was a collective version of the shaman's own otherworldly initiation; candidates were introduced to the symbols, spirits, and totems of the tribe in a memorable ceremony. It might be said that initiation into arcane knowledge has now been transferred to the examination process at universities, and that students, as candidates, still set themselves apart for a certain period of time, seeking the required response. This is itself a shadow of an older form of lengthy training and memory testing in which the initiate had to recall lost knowledge, a process that was the preserve of the shaman's successors: the druids.

We can see the bridge between the Foretime shamans and the druids if we look at the Irish *Book of Invasions* (321). Here we read how one chief druid, Mide, kindled the first fire upon the hill of Uisnech, causing the "indigenous" druids to complain bitterly because he was usurping their function. Mide then brought them together, had their tongues cut out, buried the tongues on Uisnech, and then sat upon them—a suitable parable demonstrating the power struggle between the old and the new shaman, and how the powers and knowledge of the old ones were appropriated by the new.

The druids did not simply arrive, fully fledged, with the Celtic invasions, but instead shared the function and position of the old shamans. As links in the chain of succession, the druids were the strongest guardians of the Western Way. Yet even in the classical accounts of druidism they do not constitute a priesthood as we understand it today. The words of Strabo, Caesar, and Tacitus (71, 586) give us a slanted view of a society that was at odds with Rome; these witnesses are concerned not with the religious character of a priesthood but rather with the political threat posed by druidic powers of council. Parallels have been drawn between the class structure of classical India and that of the Celts (503). Druids and kings were brahmins, aristocrats of Celtic society, following the usual association between the ruling and priestly clans. A druid ranked above a king and was attached to the royal household as both shaman and learned divine, being adviser, teacher, and prophet in one.

The Romans sought to extirpate druidism; yet, ever mindful of the power of a land's genius loci and gods, they retained the native god forms for their own use and encouraged the overt similarities between native and Roman deities—just as, five centuries later, Pope Gregory the Great advised missionaries to convert old pagan sites in Britain to Christian worship in accordance with the locally established genius loci and interpenetrating geodesic axes (511; see also chapter 2). The power of the aristocratic shaman may have been crushed or temporarily diverted during the Roman occupation, but Rome did not succeed in suppressing the group soul of the people. Nor did it quell their systems of law-giving as established by the druids or ever penetrate or conquer

Ireland, where, as the ancient literature shows, druidism and all its functions remained intact.

In the Irish story "The Siege of Druim Damhgaire," Mog Ruith, a West Munster druid, dons a bull's hide and the *enchennach,* or bird dress, and soars above the heads of the opposing army to bring back details of the troops' disposition. This is clearly an early example of astral flight, with his costume resembling the standard shamanic dress for such activities (388). In another tale the king of Ulster's druid, Fingen, looks at people's illnesses and injuries and gives them remedies (388). And in the *Táin Bó Cúalnge* (588) the royal woman Ness asks Cathbad, a passing druid, "What action is auspicious for this hour?" He prophesies, "It is good for getting a king on a queen." Seeing no other male handy, she takes him to bed with her on the spot. Here we have an example of the druid as both shaman, prophet, and progenitor of kings. Besides these functions, the druids acted as judges, administrators, and philosophers. While Continental druidism may have developed differently, we begin to see that the role of shaman was subject to specialization within druidism. No "colleges of druidism" emerge from the evidence, however, though children were sent to a druid to be fostered by his wife, raised with his children, and taught his craft.

We are told that Ireland liked Christianity so much that it converted quietly and without fuss when, in actuality, Christianity adapted itself so well to druidic elements that it was accepted without question. As the missionaries of Ireland set out to convert Scotland, Wales, and northern England, elements of druidism were incorporated into the new faith, giving Celtic Christianity its own distinct flavor: that of native tradition Christianity.

At the coming of Christianity in Ireland, many of the specifically nonreligious druidic functions fell to the poets, or *fili.* In Ireland we see that instead of an all-purpose shaman, there came to be a number of specialized experts: the *brehon,* or judge; the *seanchai,* or professional storyteller, historian, and genealogist; and the poet, who had the equivalent of a small library in his head. The knowledge of each of these experts was marked by an equivalent to our university degrees of bachelor, master, and doctor. While each of these learned men and women shared the shamanic function of walker between the worlds and each was concerned with the passing on of traditional knowledge and deep learning, the poet retained the longest into the Christian era both shamanic and druidic ability (385).

Throughout the corpus of Celtic literature we come across poems in which the poet boasts the impossible. The Irish Amairgen says:

> *I am a hawk on a cliff,*
> *I am a tear of the sun,*
> *I am a turning in a maze,*
> *I am a salmon in a pool.* (389)

Likewise, Taliesin, the Welsh poet and priest, says:

> *I have borne the banner before Alexander.*
> *I was at the place of the crucifixion of the merciful Son of God.*
> *I have been in the firmament with Mary Magdalene . . .*
> *I shall be until the day of doom on the face of the earth.* (404)

In these boasts we see the seeds of analeptic memory at work, remembrances of other lives, times, and places, as well as an intimate acquaintance with the nature of the Otherworld. These boasts indicate knowledge gained in initiatory rites, hidden within metaphorical poetic utterance. These poems are often intense compressions of symbolic concepts that enter the understanding of the listener with the penetration of an invisible arrow. For the poet there is no distance between reality and metaphor, for he has experienced these conditions and states on his journeys in the Otherworld; he has embodied these qualities.

Poetic training was long and arduous, lasting at least twelve years and requiring the candidate to memorize the history of the race, the genealogies of kings, secret languages, the complexities of meter and prosody, and the laws and customs of the people. A poem was never invented; it was instead brought from the Otherworld by means of the spirit journey and was the result of personal experience—of being one with the nature of a bird or a fish, of sharing the revelation of a hero or a god. The poet's initiation, like that of the shaman, was a journey through the labyrinth, and the mysteries met upon the way were codified and assimilated by the initiate. Like Taliesin, the Irish sage Tuan mac Cairell (388) experiences successive transformations into a deer, a boar, an eagle, and a salmon, at which point he is eaten by the wife of King Cairell and is reborn through her. Tuan was the sole survivor of the invasion of Ireland by Partholon many centuries ago and, through both reincarnation and memory, was able to survive to chronicle the events of passing generations for the benefit of later ages.

Though we are merely earth walkers, with training we may yet succeed to the heritage stored up for us by the walkers between the worlds. Druids and poets were polymaths as great as any living during the Renaissance. Indeed, they may be considered greater because they memorized their learning without reference to either books or writing. Our modern aids—the tape recorder, the CD-ROM, the notebook—are useful, but they have left us with lazy brains. Yet it is still possible to hone our senses and mental faculties, if not to razor-sharp druidic standard, then at least to a greater awareness of the Western Way and its treasures. The use of the creative imagination and the cultivation of analeptic recall can put us in touch with the Mysteries that are our heritage. Though the role of shaman, druid, and priest is scarcely recognizable in our society, we still have need for guardians of the Mysteries. Now more than ever, when the links are tenuous, do we need to become walkers between the worlds, finding the way over the threshold to interpret for our own generation the Mysteries we discover there. There are no longer shamans or elders to initiate us into these Mysteries today; however, we have provided one very old method of initiation in practice 8, The Two Trees, which will give you access to the Otherworld and to your own vision.

Mysteries and Initiation

The Mysteries are gateways, thresholds between this world and the Otherworld, the meeting place of gods and people. As symbolic truths, they appear removed from the mundane world, difficult for the uninitiated to approach. From the viewpoint of the Otherworld, the Mysteries are a language in which spiritual concepts can be communicated and stored, just as the Christian Eucharist uses the mundane elements of bread and wine to express the presence of Christ, or as the tribal ruler dresses himself in oak leaves to mark himself as the living embodiment of the oak tree, the indwelling god of the forest and a totem of the Green Man (397). As the Mysteries formalized, a structured priesthood emerged to guard and dispense the keys to the teaching of these truths. We shall be speaking further about the development and work of the mystery schools in part 2.

The word *mystery* comes from the Greek *myein*, to keep silent. The overtones of secrecy and elitism attached to the Mysteries have alienated many who approach the Western Way for the first time. Yet it is in the nature of the group soul to preserve its own Mysteries and guardians even as it welcomes respectful strangers. To enter the Mysteries is to participate in the nature of the gods. As Joan Halifax writes:

> The Altaic shaman describes his or her adventures through the ecstatic and theatric action of trance. He or she physically performs the journey while undertaking it on the spiritual plane. The interior state is revealed, made known, and then ultimately exorcized through performance. The venerated images of the awakened psyche are communicated as living symbols in the process of inner spiritual transformation. (223)

These Mysteries cannot arbitrarily be open to all, if only for the sake of individual safety: They must be guarded and communicated with caution. Even for those born into the tribe, initiation into the Mysteries was an earned privilege won by suffering, sacrifice, and ordeal, not an automatic right. But the true secret of the Mysteries is that they cannot be communicated by one being to another. The mystery guardian can give guidelines and keys to knowledge, not the actual knowledge itself, which is revealed to the initiate only through his or her personal experience and revelatory realization. The impact of participating in the Mysteries has been largely discounted today by those who appreciate them in solely an intellectual rather than symbolic manner, but to those who stood revealed to the personified energies of the gods and naked to the group soul of the ancestors, the experience was terrifyingly unforgettable as well as deeply nourishing.

Whatever our training, whatever we have been prepared for, our personal experience of the Mysteries is revealed only to those of us who step over the threshold, for it is there that the otherworldly teachers meet initiates to take them forward. Otherworldly allies and mentors build upon the theoretical map of spiritual constructs and systems that an initiate has already learned, but more immediately, they weave a tapestry of meaning from the fabric of an initiate's unique cultural experience. One person's metaphors and spiritual relationships are utterly different from another's, although both may share a cultural background. The only means to the Mysteries are each individual's personal contacts and bridges made between this world and the other.

In the Foretime, the Mysteries tended to fall into a three groups: personal, seasonal, and tribal. The personal Mysteries were concerned with rites of passage: birth, life, and death. The three stages of life were closely connected to the Otherworld, and each was marked by a ritual of initiation to indicate the transition from one state to the next, as an individual died to the old stage and was born to the new. In our own society we have no formalized rites of passage to ease the young into life and the old out of it again into the wider Otherworld.

Initiation does not itself confer great powers or show how knowledge is to be used. It is merely the planting of a seed that life's experiences will help germinate, depending on the resources of the initiate. It stimulates the latent potential of the candidate, enabling him or her to share in the patterns of life at a deeper level. In the Foretime a newborn child who had recently come from the Otherworld did not have a strong grip on this world's reality. It could be stolen or returned to the Otherworld. Hence, rituals were performed on the baby's behalf. It was protected by salt and iron, two substances inimical to the Otherworld (see chapter 4). A tree might be planted to link the life of the child with that of the earth (411). Charms were recited over the child and talismans were tied around its neck. The shaman might prophesy the child's life pattern and bind some *geis,* or prohibition, upon the infant, forbidding it to kill or eat a certain animal, for instance, that was its tribal or personal totem.

The seed planted by this initiation at birth was reinforced by initiation at puberty, a time when everyone stands on the threshold of the worlds and is sensitive to otherworldly energies, when the childhood personality is set aside in order to make way for the new, responsible member of the tribe. In many parts of the world today where tribal consciousness is analogous to the Foretime, the women still ritually weep in acknowledgment of their children's "death" as young adolescent candidates are led away to suffer the ordeal that will make them adult. These young people are kept in seclusion, subjected to many prohibitions, and told the ancestral lore; and they suffer circumcision or the painful marking of the flesh with ritual tattoos and scarification in preparation for their appearance at the ceremony in which they will reenact the mysteries of the gods (65). In one ritual parallel to the shaman's initiation, the candidate for adulthood was left among the tombs of the ancestors in caves or underground chambers, signifying the descent to the Underworld. Indeed, it was a daring step to cross the threshold of the worlds and a dangerous journey to wrestle with the dead, but the initiate's return was greeted with joy, for it signified the emergence of a new adult tribal member.

Although the keys to the Mysteries are given to the initiate of the Western Way, all must still find the way through the darkness by the light of personal intuition. To enter the chambered passages and caves of ancient initiation scenes today, to grope in the labyrinth and find the finger holds and ledges once grasped by earlier initiates of the Western Way can still be a revelation. Suffering and pain are just one part of the process: At the heart of the maze is freedom and mastery over the elements of life.

The final initiation at death scattered the pattern. The body was left to disintegrate in the air before burial, or it was burned and the ashes were placed in an urn. The gear of the deceased was sometimes smashed to indicate that it was henceforth relegated to Otherworld use (64). Chants were sung to help the spirit's transition to the ancestral realm. Death was merely a threshold between the worlds and was not feared as it is today.

The seasonal rituals were concerned with the cultivation of the land and the interdependence of animals, crops, people, and the elements. Modern farming methods, the importing of foreign food, and the ability to freeze our food have severed us from our dependence upon seasonal changes for our daily bread (though such changes are still determining factors between plenty and starvation in the Third World). The fertilizing of the soil, winter sowing, lambing, spring sowing, cultivation, and harvest followed each other in a constant round of activity shared by the whole tribe. The influence of the lunar and agricultural calendar can still be discerned in the later Celtic festivals of Samhain, Imbolc, Beltane, and Lughnasa, celebrated on the eves of November 1, February 1, May 1, and August 1, respectively. These were the times when people felt the Otherworld to be particularly close. In practice 3, The Festivals as Hidden Doorways, we have suggested ways in which these festivals can still serve as hidden doorways through which we can pass. In England and Scotland the solar calendar days are still used by universities to determine term times and by courts of law as the times for the sittings and circuits of judges, an inheritance from druidic practice and from the Foretime in which the equinoxes (March 21, Lady Day, and September 21, Michaelmas) and the solstices (June 21, midsummer, and December 21, midwinter) were important, as research of standing stones, megalithic circles, and earthworks shows (56). Of all the rituals from the Foretime, those relating to the seasons are most approachable, combining as they do both high mystery and tribal enjoyment (203). They are still a good excuse to stagger, as a modern folksong has it,

> *from the Old Half Moon to the Rising Sun,*
> *with our pint-pots in our hands.* (465)

Something of the communal celebration and joy of life can be captured if we participate in the surviving seasonal rituals enacted today. However obscured by time, they stir deep-seated memories and offer us access to the Foretime.

Long-ago tribal rituals involved the whole clan in great ceremonial assemblies while secular gatherings were accompanied by games, music, and dancing. But whether held to enact the god stories or to inaugurate a new leader, all such assemblies served to reinforce the group soul. Something of this feeling of communal cohesion can be seen in modern Highland clan gatherings in Scotland. Dame Flora MacLeod of MacLeod has spoken of the bond of affection and obligation that she and her clan owe to each other, which "in all the airts of the world is indeed a living tie that neither mountains nor a waste of seas can divide . . . the spiritual link of clanship embraces them all." (424) However blasé the British may be about their own national cohesion, the potent and ancient ritual of the coronation of a monarch is still an event surrounded by numinous awe, bridging the ages with its pageantry, exhibition of heraldic totems, exchange of promises, and rituals that marry the sovereign to the land (39). The inauguration of a president in the United States, although a diminished form of the royal ritual, shares similar status as a great tribal event, with the rivalry and competition during an election campaign serving as an echo of the Foretime, when rival chieftains confronted each other in deeds of arms for the privilege of becoming tribal leader.

In the modern coronation rite many early ritual practices are enshrined, but the marriage of monarch to the land is the most fundamentally important. Because the tribe had its being from the earth that bore it, it was necessary that the ruler, as chief representative of the tribe, be closely linked with the earth energies. In many parts of the West the genius loci became personified as the Goddess of Sovereignty, the Lady of the Land, seen as a royal spirit–queen of great bounty who, either symbolically or in the person of a woman, was married to the king. She was the mother of the people, and the king was her consort and steward. He administered the land as her gift and by her right (378).

But while the king aged, Sovereignty did not; if his vigor did not equal hers, the king was replaced, often meeting voluntary death to become an ancestral guardian (575). Here the kingly and priestly roles overlapped. The union with the land was ruptured if the king was maimed or blemished—an important feature of the Grail legends (390). A wounded king personified a wasted land, and the obligation of such a king to step aside and be replaced was very great. In terms of the Western Way, this spiritual concept is important today: Only by the close meshing of shaman and ruler and the earth can the land achieve its fulfillment and the people themselves be made whole (see practice 5, The Terrestrial Zodiac).

The location where the king was made was often an ancestral place. The kings of Argyll in Scotland were inaugurated by stepping onto the royal footprint engraved in the rock at the hill of Dunadd—they literally shared the footsteps of the ancestors. The stealing of the Stone of Scone—the ancestral inauguration stone of the kings of Scotland, and said by some to be the ancient Irish Lia Fail—by Edward I in 1296 was an attempt to purloin the sovereignty of Scotland. Its illicit return to Scotland from Westminster Abbey's coronation chair in 1951 was greeted with shrieks of fury in England and cries of glee north of the border, for a people does not give up its native heritage very quickly. The sacred stone, however, was returned to London in time for the inauguration of Queen Elizabeth II, the lineal successor to the Scottish kingship (39), and it has since been returned to Scotland once again, to lie in state with the Honors of Scotland at Edinburgh Castle.

Loyalty to ancestral and cultural patterns is still very deeply seated within us. The domestic propitiations, the seasonal rituals, the ancestors and their power remain. These are the roots of the Old Religion and a few leaves from the traditional family tree can still be seen today. By themselves such rituals and prayers are powerful, but without the inspiriting intention of their practice, they are nothing. We must look to the symbols of our native tradition, its archetypes and myths from our own culture, as living scions of that tree—and beyond them we must look to the god forms. The surest way to approach them is through the sacred sites and temples of the old earth magic.

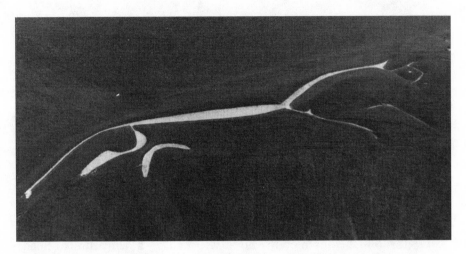

Fig 5. *The white horse at Uffington, carved into the chalk hills of the Berkshire Downs in southern England, dates from the Bronze Age. Some of the theories as to its origin and purpose include the possibility that it was some sort of tribal symbol or an homage to a goddess related to Epona, horse goddess of the Celts.*

PRACTICES
❧ *1. Finding Your Clan Totem* ❧

Along the Western Way it is usual for the practitioner to adopt some motto, device, or secret name, just as Christian candidates for confirmation or the monastic life take the name of a saint or ancestor. Symbols can be acquired, but the clan totem is a symbol of your belonging to the ancestors, the collective family that has followed the Western Way before you. The number of people alive in the world only thirty generations ago is theoretically exceeded by the number of ancestors we each would have if we counted our two parents, four grandparents, eight great-grandparents, and so forth until we reached a total of 1,073,741,904 people. We are therefore intimately related to one another and share a common set of ancestors (113). Our ancestral families each had their unique clan totem or symbol, which, by right of blood, we share. Your family may bear arms of its own, in which case you have a ready-made heraldic totem. But most of us cannot trace our genealogies with any certitude and have no knowledge of what this totem might be.

In this practice we bypass rational knowledge and instead use sleep as a way of learning that which is not consciously knowable. The ancients used incubation—induced or "temple" sleep—to help cure sicknesses of mind and body, as well as to help resolve deeply rooted problems (469). Sleep transports us to the Otherworld very speedily, and it is there that we shall find what we seek. Alternatively, you can perform this as a meditation and use your waking consciousness to find your totem.

Method

If you follow this technique during the day or you don't want to stay asleep for long, lie down on the floor with a cushion beneath your head. Otherwise, go to bed as you normally do at night. Curl up on your right side and repeat the meditation's entry chant ("I stand at the door with staff and pack, / May God [or the gods] protect me there and back"; see Notes on the Practices in This Book, page 15). Feel yourself getting heavier and heavier until you experience the pleasant sensation of slowly and gently sinking through the floor or bed until you reach the earth and begin to descend farther. You are descending the trunk of your family tree inside its bole, like Alice down the rabbit hole. Sink as far as you are able until you reach the bottom of the trunk. Don't be frightened of going too far. You land gently at the bottom, stand up, and pass through a door in the trunk.

You may already have fallen asleep by this point, but don't worry; practice makes perfect. On the trunk at eye level is the totem or symbol you are looking for. (You may have been aware of seeing other symbols as you gently fell down the tunnel inside the tree, but these are not the ones you are looking for.) Your family tree towers above you, its branches disappearing into the far distance of the heavens. Its leaves are green and its trunk is a living thing, full of the vital sap that it draws from the green earth beneath it. Though you may want to, don't begin walking and exploring. Instead, look carefully at the symbol on the tree and make the strong intention to bring it back in your remembrance.

Discovery

Your clan totem may be an object, an animal, a plant, or an emblem. As you repeat your practice, you may find that the totem ceases to be merely symbolic and appears to you as a living being that joins you near your family tree. Ask it if it is your clan totem. It may answer in speech, speak to you through body language, or communicate with you directly through heart or mind. Visit it often, get to know it better, create a personal and trusting relationship with this totem. It is your direct link to your ancestral wisdom.

If you are performing this practice as a sleep incubation, you may find that you wake in your bed the next morning with little or no remembrance at all. Don't be deterred; keep practicing. As with a dream, you may find that the day's activities will free your remembrance from its fetters. A symbol can remain in the psyche a long time before it is recognized, but you will begin to notice the continual recurrence of a theme or image pushing itself forward in your consciousness. Don't dismiss the trivial or the bizarre—you may not yet have sorted out the finer points of your totem, for the brain often stores things in a kind of shorthand that is your true metaphor or language. If you keep getting, say, a kettle, then a kettle it probably is: perhaps a cauldron translated into modern imagery. The cauldron would make a good clan symbol; it cooked the tribe's food and it is still called a kettle in some parts of England today—as in "a kettle of fish," a pot that hangs over the fire. It is the ancestor of the Grail symbol itself, and a host of imagery lies hidden here. Or perhaps you find that the neighborhood dogs have started to take a friendly interest in you and congregate around you when you appear on the street. Could it be that a dog is your clan totem?

In this first practice you may be fearful of deceiving yourself and making things up. At first, it is difficult to tell when you are perceiving an image that is present and when you are consciously putting it there. Because we have separated our imagination from our mind and because of our long history of leaving spiritual transactions to experts, we naturally distrust ourselves and feel disempowered. Only experience will teach you the difference between perceiving and creating. When you begin working with the symbols that have revealed themselves, however, you will feel and know with your bodily awareness and instinct whether a clan totem is yours; it will express that same pulsing vitality found in the trunk of the tree. If it feels lifeless to you, then try this practice again, asking for the help that you need. Call out to your ancestors to send you a clan totem that will be a living key to wisdom.

How will you work with the clan totem when you have found it? On your journeys to the Otherworld it will serve as your calling card, your passport brought to you from the very root of the tree of Western tradition. It is also your guide, leading you surely, helping you when you become confused, and granting you certain "clearances" when you meet difficulties. You can use it as a visual meditation device by painting, drawing, or embroidering it. Re-creating it in this way makes it yours in this world. The clan totem is your symbol of belonging and when you work under its aegis you are directly in touch with your ancestors who have walked the Western Way before you.

Keep your totem secret and safe. If you learn, however, that someone shares your token, it may indicate a deep link between you. We belong to the human race as well as to our clan; don't let your symbol divide you from human fellowship with those on whose behalf you tread these paths, for if you cannot apply what you learn in these pages to your own circumstances and condition, the path you walk will be a dead end.

❖ 2. Analeptic Memory ❖

This practice enables you make a request in order to retrieve knowledge from your deep memory. All journeys to the Otherworld require a clear purpose and intention. Use this practice when you need to clarify or understand aspects of the Western Way. You might, for example, ask to be shown or taught some aspect of ancestral wisdom that will help you in your life at this time. As a rule of thumb, choose to ask questions out of need rather than curiosity. If your request is motivated merely by curiosity, it may be denied. Worse still, if you ask something that is beyond your ability to understand and accept, you will forever after have to bear responsibility for that knowledge. Frame your request clearly as a question. Write it down and scrutinize it—does it ask what you really want to know? Spend time on this part before rushing into the meditation. The longer you take to arrive at the right question and its wording, the more you will learn.

As with practice 1, repeat the first part of this meditation until you are acquainted with the way and have recognized the guardians. Be respectful of them and don't forget to thank them. Courtesy is the hallmark of all walkers between the worlds.

Method

The first time you perform this practice, enter your family tree as in practice 1, taking with you your clan totem as guide and passport.

Instead of stepping out where the trunk meets the ground, continue on down the tree and emerge underground, among its roots. A clear pathway is before you; follow it until it opens out into a cavern, where you find a large lake. On the left side of the lake is a wellspring beside a whitened, rotten tree stump. Do not drink from this water that flows away from the lake into the ground, for it is the water of forgetfulness. On the right side of the lake is another wellspring. This one, the well of memory, feeds the lake, and behind it stand the guardians. As you meditate, these guardians will form themselves in your imagination. They appear different to everyone. Ask those who reveal themselves whether they are the guardians of memory. If they are not clear to you at first, repeat the meditation from the beginning until you have a better sense of them. They may not always show their faces. Ask for the help of your clan totem at any point when you need it.

You have come here in order to retrieve the memory of something you have either lost or that has not been accessible to you in this life. Perhaps this knowledge has not been available for many centuries. Whatever you seek to know and remember, be sure you have properly formulated your request for it beforehand, for when you face the guardians, they will require that your request be clear. Approach the well of memory when they instruct you to do so. You will not be allowed to drink until you speak the following password:

> *I am a child of Earth and of the Otherworld,*
> *But my race is of Heaven alone.*
> *I thirst for the living waters.*
> *In the name of the three worlds,*
> *Give me to drink of the well of memory.*

The guardians will dip a crystal cup into the waters of the well where they spring from the rock and give it to you to drink. Although it is only springwater you are drinking, its coldness and clarity sparkle in your veins like iced wine.

At this point you have a choice. You can remain seated in meditation, quietly absorbing the water throughout your being and examining the thoughts and images that arise in connection with your request; or you can go to sleep, as you did in the first exercise, allowing the images to arise in your dreams. Both methods are effective. At first you may get no clear results from either one, but as we have already said, these practices often work in circuitous ways. There may not be a flash of revelatory awareness so much as a quiet, rising intuition pushing at the back of your thoughts or a feeling or sensation waiting to be perceived.

Discovery

What happens when you get results? Knowledge that remains theoretical is no use to anyone. Analeptic memory of arcane and abstruse matters is likewise worthless if it goes no further than mere possession of facts. If you keep drinking from the well of memory and retrieving further information that will lie unused, you might just as well drink from the well of forgetfulness. Whatever you have been given you have been made guardian of, and therefore you are responsible for it. Incorporate your realizations into your own life, especially if you have asked for help with personal issues. If the wisdom has a wider application, make some attempt to apply it, share it, or work with it. This is respectful of both the source of knowledge and the wisdom you have remembered. Continue to meditate on these memories and their actual usefulness in everyday life. Do your own research, following up on whatever evidence there may be.

This method can be used at an advanced level for reincarnation recall. However, if you do use this practice as a means of past-life retrieval, be ready for the results, which can sometimes have a shocking effect if the full flood of memory releases pain and emotional trauma. And remember that though memory can he excessively painful, it can be used as a positive means for identifying current life problems. Above all, it is important to live the life in the body you now occupy, rather than to daydream and drift in the tides of yesteryear. Avoidance of certain recurrent life lessons is a refusal to grow.

For this practice, it is important to remember that we may not drink from the waters of forgetfulness while we are here in this world. These waters are for the dead who die to Middle Earth and are reborn into the Otherworld, for they must forget the world of physical reality in order to progress in their new place. When we are born of our physical mother, we "die" to the Otherworld, and when we die physically, we are born into the Otherworld.

This practice should not be repeated often. If you get no results after about two weeks, leave it alone for a few months before trying again. Analeptic recall is not easy for some people. More important, do not use the time your body needs for rest and sleep as a springboard for psychic experience or meditation. Your sleep patterns will become disturbed if they are being constantly interrupted by a preprogrammed exercise. If you are interested in the Western Way, it is likely that your training has already begun under the aegis of sleep. You will be aware of places that you visit often in dreams, or of certain kinds of instruction that you receive. The fact that little or no remembrance of this teaching rises to the surface of your consciousness is not important. Some of the practices in this book may stimulate remembrance and others will give shape and purpose to vague longings that are seldom pursued because they remain unrecognized at the conscious level.

It is not necessary each time to take the journey in this practice right from the beginning. When you know your way around, simply visualize the lake before you and the two wells and take it from there. Those who know their classics may well recognize this landscape as part of the mystery instruction given to Orphic initiates, which we have adapted hardly at all; it is part of the native Underworld tradition in another guise. The well of knowledge also appears in the Celtic Otherworld tradition, sometimes as a well and sometimes as a cauldron or Grail. But the underground waters of this exercise, bubbling up from the roots of the earth, are the same waters our ancestors drank.

❧ 3. The Festivals as Hidden Doorways ❧

The native seasonal festivals are popularly seen as excuses for nothing more than indulgence in quaint folk custom and rural junketing, but these celebrations can be approached on a deeper level. It is not within the scope of this book to give exhaustive lists of such festivals, but the following suggestions can be applied to any festival in your part of the world.

Method

First, choose your festival and meditate on its inner meaning: Is it primarily religious (Christmas or Passover, for instance); agricultural (Lammas); solar (the equinoxes and solstices); from primal folk tradition (Pace Egging) or historical commemoration (such as Thanksgiving or Oakapple day, commemorating Charles II's hiding in an oak tree)? Obviously, the historical and commemorative festivals will not have the powerful spiritual force of the others, but these can be used to gain helpful insights into national consciousness. Some celebrations now have saints as protectors replacing the old god forms—such as the patronage of Saint Brigit at Candlemas—but though the forms change, the inner protective energy remains the same (203, 400, 401).

If you have no religious or folk festivals because you follow no particular tradition or because you have made your home in a land that is not yours by birth, you might adopt the yearly round of the Celtic calendar, which is now celebrated among English-speaking groups throughout the world. Although a festival may be assigned to a particular date, shifts in the calendar and seasonal inclemency should be taken into account when deciding the right time to celebrate. The right time is more important than the right date. Those living in the southern hemisphere will already be well aware of this. If this is where you live now, please celebrate seasonal festivals according to their harmonious placement in your seasonal calendar. For instance, if you want to celebrate a spring festival that in the northern hemisphere occurs in March, you should transfer it to the southern hemisphere's September, rather than celebrating spring during the autumn!

After you have chosen your festival, find out all you can about its origins. Celebrate it with the kind of rejoicing that suits it—with the fruits of the harvest or by rising early to greet the midsummer sun. Meet with friends, being all the time aware that you are capable of mediating the spiritual energy of this festival to those present as well as to others in your community—not by verbal teaching, but through deep meditation on the forces involved, by example, and through inner attention. As the festival approaches, begin to plan and meditate each day. Visualize the coming celebration as an inner impulse striving to be born. Consider the quality of the festival: Is it joyful, reflective, life-giving? Consider your own life in relation to these qualities, freely using the gifts of each festival to develop yourself.

Discovery

In following this practice, the festivals can indeed become hidden doorways in your life, allowing the influx of inner vitality and fostering sensitivity to the important psychic tides that energize the world. This is how festivals were always intended to work, but their contemporary celebration has tended to obscure these purposes. You can make of this practice what you will; it may not look very dramatic on paper, but it is applicable to any tradition. Its full effect will be experienced by those who work hardest at it. Festivals are times of rejoicing, yet their origin designates them as holidays—literally, holy days—as times set aside for physical recreation and spiritual uplifting, not as excuses for self-indulgence.

This practice can also be used in conjunction with other techniques outlined in this book. Festivals are those times when the door to the Otherworld stands open. They are celebrations out of time, subtle demarcations that provide openings in linear time. They have been hidden for too long. You will learn which times are best for contacting certain forces, for visiting the Otherworld, for retreating. We each create our own doorways, but while some entrances may shift, the festivals themselves remain embedded in our national or religious folk year, ready to be opened by those who know how.

2

The Magic Earth

Stand ye in the ways, and see, and ask for the old paths,
where is the good way, and walk therein.
—Jeremiah 6:16

Human life was enriched by means of a force activated
through the correct geographical relationship
of sacred centres.
—John Michell, *New View Over Atlantis*

Sacred Space

The earth is alive, and because of this there is no place on it that has not been holy to someone. Our proper relationship with the environment is one of total harmony, though we seldom, if ever, attain it, for we do not always know how to relate to our surroundings. Too often we are selfish, neglecting quality of life in favor of quantity—we always want more than we have. Our ancestors, the Firstborn, knew better. They were skilled in husbanding the power and life force of the earth. They knew themselves to be the children of a great Mother whose body they trod upon daily, who nourished and fed and sheltered them as a mother should. With this understanding came a sense of the earth's energies flowing in their own bloodstream, and this gave them a feeling of oneness with the rest of creation and a belief in a vital force linking all matter in a great rhythm of becoming.

So far in this book we have looked at the beginnings of the spiritual impulse, the reactions of the Firstborn to the world in which they found themselves. In this chapter we shall deal with the earth as something to which we can respond on a personal level. But it is essential first to understand the nature of the rapport our ancestors had with the great storehouse of energy beneath our feet, and why, as followers of the Western Way, we must reestablish that rapport for ourselves.

The land we walk upon is like a great book in which the history of our race is recorded, layer upon layer, age upon age. Archaeology, the scientific reading of the land, can tell us a great deal about the past and the kind of people who lived then, but there are other ways of reading it, and some of these can open to us the secrets of our ancestors, including how, where—and perhaps who—they worshipped.

But first we must reconstruct within our own mind and with our own imagination the landscape of the Foretime. It was filled with strange and frightening things that could easily either create or destroy with their power—and every part of this world was uniquely holy: "The image of the earth as mother, producing from her womb not only crops, cattle, men and women, stones, minerals, and forests, but also the knowledge to make all these fruitful and useful, may be considered the dominant symbol in the holy places." (11)

It was from this understanding that there grew the idea of the *temenos,* the sacred place where the life force of the earth's energies was focused and where those who were properly trained in the Mysteries could, for a time, become one with that vital essence. This understanding was open to all through the agency of shamanic priests, whose task became to guard the collective heritage of the tribe. To ensure that the holy places would never be desecrated, forgotten, or lost to view, these shamans decreed that the sites should be marked in such a way that they would always be clearly defined and recognizable. Today, even though the knowledge of their use has died, we still recognize these sites as full of sacred power.

Certain places where the lifeblood of the planet ran closer to the surface than elsewhere had always been distinguished, at first by no more than lines scratched in the earth or a few scattered stones placed to indicate the sacred boundaries. But some time in the megalithic period of history people began marking them more permanently with stone monoliths carved and decorated with patterns that conveyed their sacred function.

Because the circle had always been a natural shape—evolving from the threshing floor or the site of ritual dancing or the rotation of the stars—these stones were set in circular formations within which the ground was sacred. Here people could worship the elemental forces of the living earth that were to become their gods.

At some time during this period—more than four thousand years ago—when the first stone circles were constructed, their builders discovered that through an exact orientation of different kinds of stone, shaped and cut to a particular design and varying in size and volume, the primal currents of energy within the earth could be tapped, amplified, and directed, as they were through trance or ceremony, and that the resulting energy could be drawn upon by both individuals and the group as a whole. How this realization came about we shall probably never know, but from this moment the stone circles were no longer simply places of worship; they became storehouses of vast and unique energies that would fuel the religious and magical activities of mankind for thousands of years—perhaps even to today.

Of course, the use of stone circles in this way did not come about overnight. A lengthy period of experimentation followed the initial discovery of their power. Various other configurations were tried, though builders always returned to the circle, whether of stones or of trees, as the most effective formation to focus the magic of the earth. As Peter Vansittart, author of *Worlds and Underworlds,* writes: "Sophisticated engineers erected Avebury, the three Stonehenges, the 20,000 barrows and smaller stone circles signalling to a sky thick with gods. Salisbury Plain was . . . embossed with temples, palaces, sprayed with avenues and roads." (612) We can see just how long it took for some kind of fixed pattern to evolve by looking at the examples of larger sites such as Stonehenge, where archaeological investigation has found evidence of an almost continuous state of growth extending over a huge span of time as knowledge of the earth Mysteries increased. The addition of a bank and ditch around the perimeter of the circles helped to seal the energies within the site, and the observation and measure of the changing heavens from such places became part of the discipline of the priesthood.

Great importance was attached to star lore as a visible and measurable correlative to daily life. The moon's connection with tides and with the cycle of human fertility was recognized, and the fructifying sun, with its passage across the sky and the mystery of its nighttime journey (during which it was said to visit the Underworld), was allotted great attention. Sophisticated techniques for measuring and recording the mysteries of the heavens and the ways in which they related to those of the earth gradually evolved into an exact science (57).

The laws governing the siting and layout of such holy places and the shaping of the landscape around them are called *geomancy*, and it was once a worldwide discipline. In recent years a great deal of research has been done in this area by writers such as John Michell, Nigel Pennick, Paul Devereux and Ian Thompson, and Paul Screeton, who, with the aid of a legion of known and unknown helpers, have begun to map out the sacred geometry of Britain (419, 467, 129, 534). Many of those who have walked some ancient path between one sacred site and another have experienced a sense of enlightenment, a subtle awareness of the links between these holy places, and have been able to plot them with a map and compass to allow others to follow their lead. This has extended our knowledge of such sites and has revealed an increasingly detailed pattern.

Only recently, with the work of scientists like Alexander Thom (594) and Euan Mackie (348), has it been possible to see just how accurate these ancient systems of alignment really are—though many have refused to accept such findings. Yet it is now possible to show that there once existed a system of sites linked by countrywide paths of energy. From this it is only a small step to believing in a global network, a vast energy grid, that once connected sites as far apart as Scotland and Australia. Perhaps most extraordinary of all, each of these structures found around the globe seems to have been built more or less independently—and yet we find the same kind of siting and the same carving of patterns and symbols at sites in America, China, Egypt, Norway, and the British Isles (511). It is as though a single impulse rose simultaneously in the consciousness of temple builders all around the world, even in its farthest corners.

Alfred Watkins, first to use the term *ley lines* (see chapter 1, page 33) for those paths connecting sacred sites, spoke of an almost visionary experience in which he saw the landscape revealed in a new light: the hills and tumuli, stone circles and megaliths were all connected by shining paths, golden veins standing out amid the green and brown of the land (639). Such visionary glimpses, strongly akin to the analeptic mindset of the Foretime, are part of the earth Mysteries and often come unbidden to transform the world around us. By following the shining paths that crisscross the land, we can recover ancient sites long lost to view and begin to perceive the overall plan our ancestors used to interpret and later encode the mysteries of the world surrounding them.

Equally as important as the megaliths are the world's great barrows, round and oblong mounds of earth that covered the bones of sacred ancestors, or that later became caves of initiation and enlightenment entered by the seeker only after long and arduous tests (553). Carved within these barrows, on the stones used to support the weight of the earth, are mazelike, spiraling patterns and shapes meant to be read and understood by those who penetrated the Mysteries—or perhaps by the dead who were laid there. More than two thousand barrows have been excavated in Britain alone, and many more are known to exist. They too are part of the all-embracing pattern, the magical diagram of the life force, the bloodstream of the earth.

> No wanderer in enchanted barrow-land, among those forsaken shrines of dead heroes mightier in their dissolution than in the springtime of their lives, can doubt that such piles of sacred earth were raised of a proud and set purpose to dominate the scenes they do. Our barrows were reared where they could contemplate the world without and beneath them and, like the deified lords resting within them, lived in a mid-world between earth and heaven. Seen along the skyline, they are indeed the stepping-stones of the Gods. (349)

Nor are these death houses or the stone avenues built on alignments of the sun, the moon, and stars the only such stepping-stones. Even greater arrangements of terrestrial geography are believed to exist.

At Glastonbury, in Somerset, recent research has detected the presence of a vast terrestrial maze coiling around the tor that has been called "this holiest earth." (18, 508) Some individuals, notably the Elizabethan magus John Dee (123) and Katherine Maltwood (365) in the 1930s, have detected the outlines of a vast zodiac laid out in the landscape around Glastonbury. Whether this is actually present or a memory within the land of older mysteries remains a vexing question. There are now some half dozen such zodiacs under investigation, and more will doubtless be uncovered in the future (652). Practice 5, The Terrestrial Zodiac, at the end of this chapter, offers an exploratory voyage that can be adapted to fit other sites that contain these zodiacs in the land. It also asserts the importance of the Arthurian impulse: the latest example of the rising of earth energy combined with the cultural myths of the country.

In recent years the traditional technique of dowsing has been extended and refined to include the measurement of energy fields at sacred sites that emanate from both individual stones and larger group-ings. Varying degrees of measurable magnetic force have been detected and at times they have been strong enough to be off the scale of ordi-nary instrumentation. The precise nature and cause of this energy has yet to be established, but researchers have noted that many of the stones possess a magnetic current that changes their polarity from male to female and back again during the time between one new moon and the next (245).

In connection with this polarity, the ithyphallic nature of certain stones becomes important, for though the earth has been generally seen as female and the sky as male, these attributes subtly reverse themselves at times so that the exchange of life force between the earth and sky can take place. Such unions between earth and sky seem to be a mysterious extension of human birth patterns. While people have long believed that we are influenced by the stars under which we're born, perhaps our place of birth and the phase of the moon at the time are of equal or greater importance. It's possible that in many early cultures women sought out certain ancient sites when it came time to give birth in order to "tune in" to the very energies of creation (444). The children born under such circumstances would have special abilities, and they may even have been revered as potential shamans. Certainly the image of the labyrinth is apposite here. What else is the womb but a labyrinth, with the umbilical cord an Ariadne's thread leading to new life?

In this perhaps we have the origin of folktales connecting certain sacred sites with fertility rituals. Whether or not such rites took place at these sites, they may have been symbolic of a far greater exchange than that between men and women—in fact, they may have been sym-bols of exchange among the elements themselves. Thus the Maypole, a comparatively recent manifestation in the history of mystery celebra-tions, can be seen as a symbolic linking of earth and heaven, with those who dance around it holding colored ribbons—red and green for earth, blue and yellow for sky—being bound to the pattern of birth, life, and death that lies at the heart of the maze of the Mysteries.

Theories such as the ley lines system and the terrestrial zodiacs are frequently dismissed as pure fantasy by skeptics—and indeed, many such hypotheses are based on "received" evidence that cannot be sub-jected to normal definitions of proof. But it is not necessary to subscribe to these ideas in order to feel the mystery and power of ancient sites. Whether we see them as accidental formations of the landscape or as freakish mementos of forgotten religion or as part of a universal pattern of belief, worship, and Western magical practice, we cannot ignore the often profound effect they can have on our psyche.

The sheer scale of the ancestral vision indicates both the ability of our forebears to interpret natural forces and the importance they attached to them. All we ask of prospective followers of the Western Way is that they keep an open mind and heart and that, when visiting such sites, they try to feel for themselves the flow of energy. This magical force that springs from deep within the earth can affect us very powerfully if we let it. It can open doors to the past, as well as demonstrate that these energies are still present, giving life and vitality to everything, and imparting to us the wisdom to interpret the mystery of the land and our relationship to it.

Paths of the Dragon

One particular symbol became associated with the earth Mysteries over time: the Dragon, or winged serpent. The reasons are not hard to see: In the Foretime the snake represented life, death, and renewal. It lived in the ground, which made it sacred to the Mother, and it shed its skin, emerging renewed. Creation myths in which the World Snake gave birth to the egg of generation, warming and hatching it as actual reptiles did, were widespread. We shall meet with this symbol again in the Gnostic and Orphic Mysteries discussed in part 2.

The myth of the dying and rising god has at its heart this same belief in the magical power of the serpent. Like the serpent, the god went into the earth (or below the horizon) and came forth renewed. This is the basis of most if not all initiation rituals, which often enact the "death" of the uninformed spirit and its rebirth in a new, wiser form. In the Mysteries of Osiris the god was often represented by a vessel carved with the likeness of a coiled snake and filled with Nile water. As the Jungian Marie Louise von Franz remarks: "This snake is the numen who guards the tomb and protects the transformations of the God [sic]. Psychologically it symbolizes the deepest levels of the collective unconsciousness, where the transformation of the god-image occurs." (625)

This is basic to all initiation, which takes us to the profoundest depths of the human psyche. To plunge deeply into the fabric of our universal awareness is to sharpen the senses to a degree almost beyond expression. Here changes occur that alter the very construction of the soul. The world grows thin, allowing the voyager to see beyond the patterns of normal understanding. In this state visions are real and the earth sends her dreams to lodge in our minds like arrows. Our blood sings with the energy of the dragon and we are truly changed.

The numen that guards the transformation of the god has its parallels in the outer world: It was common to find temples of the classical period and before guarded by pet snakes that were fed on milk by the priests and priestesses and encouraged to take up residence nearby.

The Dome of the Serpents at Rouffignac, in France, may be the earliest known illustration of the magical power of the serpent. Dating from many thousands of years before the more famous Lascaux murals (probably around 7000 B.C.E.), it consists of a multitude of coiling forms covering the roof of a cave cut deep into the ancient rock. One recent investigator has suggested they were painted there as a form of protection against the unknown, but a far more likely hypothesis is that they are simply glyphs of the energy that courses through the body of the earth like a snake within its nest (641). Even archaeologists, generally wary of committing themselves, have suggested that some of these earliest cave paintings may represent water cults because they seem to depict the flow of earth energy often linked with actual underground springs and rivers. Many such cave paintings may represent the shaman's entranced vision.

Among the Warramunga tribesmen of Australia the serpent is a sign of manhood and is painted on the back and breast. A part of their sacred ceremonies consists of crawling into a hollow that has been scooped out of the earth beneath a huge rock in order to view the picture of the sacred snake, Yarapi, painted on the underside of the stone (430). Yarapi is clearly reminiscent of the carved spiral and mazelike forms found inside tombs and mounds in the Celtic world, where only the dead (or those temporarily suspended by an initiatory drink) could see and understand their significance.

The fact that the snake was also sacred to the moon goddess is well known and has been preserved in the astronomical terminology for the points at which the orbits of the earth and moon coincide: The ascending node, where the moon's orbit first passes through that of the earth, is called the dragon's head, and the descending node, where the two intersect again, is called the dragon's tail. The line drawn between the two is called the dragon line, and the time between the moon's passes through the same lunar node is termed the dragon's month. If this were not remarkable enough, the symbols used to represent these intersections are quite similar to the decorative patterns worn by the Warramunga, as seen in fig. 6.

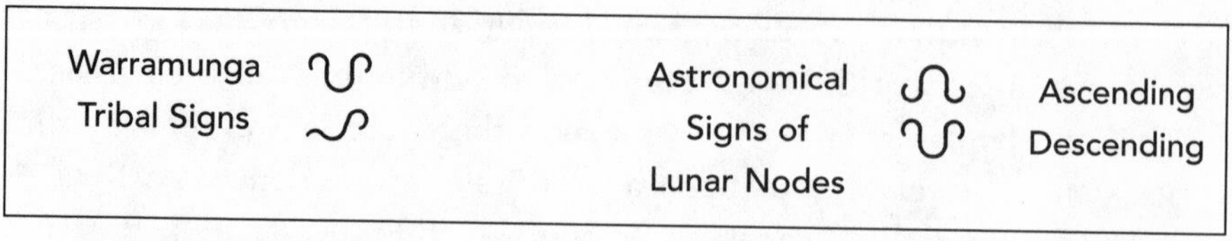

Fig. 6. *The Aboriginal Warramunga symbols on the left are remarkably similar to the dragon's head and tail, the astrological terms for the lunar nodes, or points at which the orbits of the earth and moon intersect.*

As Joseph Henderson points out in *The Wisdom of the Serpent*, having remarked upon the universality of the snake as a symbol of renewal:

> This lies essentially in mankind's having projected into this . . . creature his own secret wish to obtain from the earth a knowledge he cannot find in waking daylight consciousness alone. This is the knowledge of death and rebirth forever withheld except at those times where some transcendental principle, emerging from the depth, makes it available to consciousness. (241)

The dragon energy was just such a transcendental principle, emerging from the depths to illuminate and transform mankind's relationship with the earth.

So far we have looked chiefly at the terrestrial power of the dragon, which reflects the energy of the earth, its shining coils linking the sacred sites in a network of vital force. But it was believed to perform a similar function in the heavens. The dragon was identified with the constellation Draco, whose chief star, Draconis, was once the Pole Star of the ancient West. The heavens revolved around Draconis, protected by the coils of the dragon, prompting the Italian astronomer Sabbathai Donolo (c. 940 C.E.) to write: "When God created the two lights [the sun and the moon], the five stars [the planets] and the twelve signs [the zodiac], he also created the fiery dragon, that it might connect them together, moving about like a weaver with his shuttle." (42)

In Australia, where the Aboriginal culture still contains much that parallels the Foretime, the vital force that animates the land is still recognized. It travels roads laid down by the gods themselves in the Dreamtime. These pathways are cast in a mirror image of the star paths and are recorded in a glyph known as a *tjuringa,* a small stone carved with patterns of lines and circles encoding the paths of the earth force. Tjuringas can be used for orienteering and enable their wielders to travel great distances across the trackless Australian bush (419).

More than one researcher has noticed the similarity between the marks found on tjuringas and those found at megalithic sites, in particular the curious cup-and-ring markings discovered at a large number of sacred places but never satisfactorily explained (217). It becomes clear, however, that such marks are far more than representations of geographical formations; they are also guides to the Otherworld. A shaman wishing to make contact with the hidden vitality of the land contemplates the tjuringa, using it as a gateway to the inner realm.

Everywhere around them our ancestors saw signs of the forces that guided and inspired them. Here was a hill that gave access to the Otherworld; there a stream where the gods of summer and winter fought for the hand of the Spring Maiden. But there were other, more potent signs. It is still quite common to come across curiously striated hills, roughly conical in shape but with flattened tops, and to find in connection with them an accompanying folktale of the Great Worm in which, meeting its fate at the hands of a local hero or saint, the serpent squeezed the hill in its coils, imprinting the land with the shape of its agony.

Embodied in tales like this is the great change that overtook the dragon power and its relationship with mankind. It may seem a long way from the dragon priests to the heroes remembered as dragon slayers, yet the two groups are closely related to the pattern of change and decay that overcame the native Mysteries. The step from dragon priest to dragon slayer is small when considered in the light of the Christian adoption of ancient sites as places to build their churches.

The ancient priests stood as interpreters and purveyors of earth energy, but the new religion brought condemnation of the old ways. Dragon energy and its related symbolism were outlawed and later became identified with the serpent in Eden, a creature to be crushed beneath the heel of its slayer, usually Saint Michael or Saint George, whose role is recorded in the dedications of churches built in their honor at places once associated with dragon power.

But the importance of the old serpent mounds remains. They indicate the presence of the dragon energy that may be invoked by climbing them (which is best not done without some prior intention). The main significance of the serpent, however, lies in its relationship to the maze.

The image of the maze is one we have encountered before in this book. It is no surprise, then, that it is strongly connected with the Mysteries of the earth. The serpent, as we have seen, is a symbol of the earth's magic power, and its sinuous form is a subtly changing, living maze closely associated with initiatory experience. In the mythology of the Hopi Indians of Arizona, these two associations come together. For the Hopi, the maze symbolizes the Mother and represents a passage through different levels of understanding (638). It points the way to actual experience through symbolic truth—the way of the serpent is synonymous with the way of the earth, and both represent the initiation of the maze.

Hills possessing a serpentine shape, such as Glastonbury Tor and the Herefordshire Beacon and the great mound of Silbury Hill, which lies adjacent to Avebury, one of the most important temples of serpent power in Britain, are all associated with earth Mysteries. Geoffrey Ashe has suggested that the Glastonbury Tor was intended as a ritual site that, when walked in procession, gave admittance to an interior world (17). And Silbury, despite all attempts to explain it, remains an enigma unless it is seen as a spiral dragon hill.

The importance of the serpent in the Foretime can even be seen in the shapes adopted by the temple builders of that age, who laid out many of the great stone edifices to conform to the pattern of the earth force. Thus at Avebury, whose serpentine form was first recognized in the eighteenth century, the circle is crossed by a serpentlike avenue, while at Carnac, in Brittany, whose name derives from *cairn hac,* "hill of the serpent," the coiling shape assumed by the many hundreds of stone avenues is an image of both the serpent and the maze.

But perhaps the most sensational construction of this kind is found in the United States, in Adams County, Ohio: a vast serpentine earthwork, over 1,254 feet in length, arranged in seven coils and ending in a triple-coiled tail. In its jaws the serpent holds an egg, a symbol of creation. It combines the expression of both maze and spiral in a single form. Built by some of the earliest inhabitants of the North American continent, it is one of the strongest representations of the native tradition to be found. Coupled with the maze symbol of Hopi mythology, it makes a clear statement of the universality of the cult (539).

The oldest way of raising the power of the serpent was the labyrinth dance, performed as a path to enlightenment and to joining with the gods. Traces of the dance floors of turf and stone used in this ritual have been found as far apart as Germany, Greece, Australia, and Britain, where relics of several hundred labyrinths can still be detected (299). To enter the labyrinth is to walk the passage of death, to emerge is to be reborn—a pattern that still bears meaning for us today. In the labyrinth, as in the carved spirals of the tomb builders, the serpentine coils through which the initiate moved or danced toward his birth were representative of both the womb and the seed that passed through it: From both, and from the energy of creation carried through the earth by the power of the serpent or dragon, came new life.

Like the labyrinth, the barrow mounds—Maes Howe in the Orkneys, La Houge Bie in the Channel Isles, Brugh na Boyne in Ireland, West Kennet in Wiltshire—were all, to some extent, images of the earth womb. Painted red to signify the life force, the blood of the tribe, the bones of the dead were laid in the fetal position to await rebirth in the Otherworld, a reminder of the way back into the earth that all must one day take.

The final period in which dragon power was actively used and recognized was marked by a steady decline that all but obscured knowledge of the lines of force and the ancient sites they vivified. During the Foretime the shamans focused the energy felt by all, but after it, a change took place. Gradually, the priesthood came to stand between the people and their gods, becoming increasingly the guardian of a secret knowledge intended only for the few. By the advent of Christianity there were few who remembered the old ways well enough to offer opposition. Those who did were either killed or held up as objects of ridicule by the followers of the new way. It was a pattern that would be repeated throughout the ages, even in our own time.

Though obscured, the mystery of dragon power and its sites remained largely untouched by the passage of years. In time, Alfred Watkins and the ley line enthusiasts—many of whom worked in ignorance of the real significance of what they had stumbled upon—rediscovered them, as have a few Hermetically trained magicians of our own time, who have begun to see dragon energy as a source too long neglected.

Though it is no longer possible to see the entire picture of this aspect of the Foretime as it once was, there still exist enough fragments of knowledge that, combined with the evidence of the sites themselves, enable us to restore much of it. Reports by such eighteenth-century antiquaries as John Aubrey (23) and William Stukeley (580), who saw many of the sites virtually intact (and, incidentally, praised their "classical" design), give evidence of their original form. Other evidence is hidden in folklore (447), where the dragon appears regularly as a creature of fearsome character and fiery breath—and as a guardian of immense treasure, a half-conscious harking back to the treasure of life and energy it once symbolized.

None of this, of course, can substitute for a personal visit to one of the ancient sites. They are still largely neglected, for speculation about their purpose has obscured the fact that they are there to be experienced and that within them lies a source of contact with the native tradition.

Wisdom of the Earth

We have spoken of the first magics, of the passionate awareness of the living being upon which we walk, and of the way the earth's people discovered how the energies flowed through the ground. The symbol of the dragon represented those energies until it fell into disrepute. But no matter how we perceive the energies of the earth, we must learn to accept responsibility for what has been held in trust for us for thousands of years. The wisdom of the earth is ours for the seeking, but we have to be careful how we go about the search. Nowadays we have grown away from the earth and out of step with her rhythms. Where once we acknowledged her influence in our lives, cared for her, and garnered her riches, we now rape and destroy her, greedily snatching all she has to offer in food and resources, leaving her barren and ruined. We no longer have a relationship of sharing with the environment, one in which we give back the food and nourishment needed by the living earth.

When the scientists Lovelock and Epton developed their theory of the globe as a living entity (511), they named her Gaia at the suggestion of the novelist William Golding, thus echoing her classical and preclassical worshippers who predated ecological science by many thousands of years. As Theodore Roszak, commenting on this, noted: "There clings to the image something of an older and once universal natural philosophy that quite spontaneously experienced the earth as a divine being animated by its own moods and intentions, the primordial Mother Earth." (511) It is this universal philosophy that lies behind the stone circles and dragon paths, the serpent power and initiation dreams of the mound builders. Within the earth lay all secrets: the way to the Otherworld and the ancestors. But more than this the earth was a dwelling place for personified energies, the first shapers of the world who labored long over its perfection and who, in time, came to be bound beneath it.

The classical myths of the Titans are the clearest representation of this. They can offer us a profound message about the way we treat the earth and what may happen if we fail to restore the original state of balance that once existed between ourselves and our environment. The clue lies in the use of the word *titan,* originally meaning "lord" but now more often applied to the most awesome energies of the earth: the *titanic* force of the volcano, the whirling wind, the ocean.

The Titans, children of Gaia and Uranus, Earth Mother and Sky Father, sided with their mother against the cruelty of Uranus, who had banished their elder brothers to the underworld of Tartarus. Choosing Cronos for their leader, they laid siege to their father, and Cronos castrated him with a flint sickle. The blood from his wounds fathered the Erinyes, the Furies, who are bound to avenge crimes of family bloodshed. On Uranus's death, Cronos assumed his father's power (192, 294).

These were the first whose deeds were immeasurably savage, whose stature was huge. But the next generation of gods were neither savage nor towering. Cronos married his sister Rhea, another Earth Mother. But because Uranus and Gaia had prophesied that he would be dethroned by one of his children, Cronos devoured every child born to him by Rhea. Rhea, however, secretly bore another child—Zeus—and hid him away, substituting a stone for her child, which Cronos duly swallowed. When he was grown, Zeus returned to his father as cup bearer and gave Cronos a poisoned drink that acted as an emetic. Cronos disgorged all of Rhea's children, who were restored whole to her, and Cronos himself was banished—some say to the British Isles, where he sleeps still. It is Zeus and his siblings who formed the Olympian pantheon, and the Titans were chained beneath the earth.

While these legends tell us much about the power struggle that took place between succeeding Greek races, the archetypes resonate with our own times. In one sense, nothing has changed: We are still the children of Gaia and her energies are still ours to free or harness according to our needs. As is all too obvious, however, we are not in complete control of them, and the titanic energies that spilled over into violence in myth threaten to do so in reality.

The forces of nature have always been rightly feared and human-kind's relationship to them has always been a changing one. In one sense it has always been a struggle to combat and protect ourselves from them. Fear of giants and monsters, perpetuated by these early Greek models, recurs again and again in the mythologies of other lands. It was this fear that resulted in the transformation of the dragon of the Foretime into the serpent of the Judeo-Christian Fall, the Beast of the Apocalypse in Revelation 12 that was overcome by the Woman Clothed by the Sun (45). Today Titanic forces are manifested in the shape of nuclear energy. Gaia's children rise again and one above all dominates the scene—Uranus. One of the minerals to which the Titans gave their names has been in the forefront of human consciousness for the last few decades: uranium, the major component from which the world's most destructive weapons are made.

Left in the earth, uranium is a positive source of energy. It, like other minerals, is one of Gaia's children, the personifications of her energies without which all would be barren. But in our modern age we have not had much respect for mineral life. If we treated the minerals we mine from the earth as living entities, we would at last be showing responsibility toward the forces we seek to master. As followers of the Western Way, we are the guardians of the earth's energies. In beginning to consider and respect her dynamic power, we begin to reach an under-standing that all energy has its own flow to be misapplied or used appropriately.

Stories of the Titanic forces of the earth have not remained static. They have grown and changed with time. Ultimately all stories of giants derive from memories of a projected golden age during which immense energy was seen as beneficial rather than destructive. But as with all memory of perfect states, it began to blur with time. The Titans were replaced by quarrelsome and all-too-human gods and god-desses, and so on until they were finally reduced to the faery folk, the dwellers-under-the-hill. Paradise, the Realm of the Shining Ones, became the Otherworld and the people of the Golden Age became its inhabitants.

The Titanic archetypes, however, have left their images on the land-scape itself. The vast shapes incised on the plains of Nazca or in the chalk hills of southern Britain are testimonies to the way in which the Firstborn saw the originators of our race: the gods before the gods (82). Echoes of Atlantis, of a time when evil, sickness, and death were virtually banished, remain at the deepest levels of our consciousness. From Plato to Tolkien, the archetype of the Golden Age continues to fascinate, and behind this fascination lies an awareness of the old earth magic in its earliest form. These ancient chthonic powers have remained unchanged and gradually have been rising from immeasurable depths until, in our own time, they have begun to return to the surface again. Many of the old gods may thus be said to walk abroad again, while others sleep, seeking their renewal. (574)

All of us are the unknowing possessors of a lost landscape of circle and stone, pathway and mound. If we are once again to be in tune with the earth energies still living in our landscape, we must visit them, get up early and find them in the dawn or even earlier, when the silence is complete and they are close at hand. Wherever we approach the numinous places of their existence in the spirit of respect, we will find awesome powers lying just beneath our feet. Remember that you tread on sacred ground and that you have already taken the first step toward a relationship with the Mysteries. You may invoke the old powers of the Western Way that sleep lightly under the surface of the earth. Cernunnos, the horned god, or Wayland, smith of the gods, or forms that are even more primeval may rise to greet you from the green hillsides.

The task we set ourselves is one of spiritual ecology, seeking our personal contact with the spirit of the earth, whether we find this in the image of the dragon, through walking the labyrinth, or by following the outlines of a stone circle. There are many hundreds of sacred sites in our homelands, awaiting your visit. Many are in ruins or are totally destroyed; others are still active. Remember that some sites are dormant, made purposely inoperative while they renew themselves. It is best not to stir up these places before their time of reemergence. But at the sites that are awake it is possible to learn how the vital energy of a single center can send out ripples to every part of the land.

Once you have discovered this for yourself, you may indeed find that you "stand in a place that is holy ground and . . . breathe the intoxicating exhalations as did the sibyls of old." (514) And neither you nor the land will again be the same.

PRACTICES

❧ 4. The Shimmering Way ❧

As we have said, the best way to experience firsthand the power of the earth energies is to visit one of the sacred sites. When you approach such a place, whether a stone circle, a chambered tomb, or a serpent mound, try to do so via one of the sacred track ways that lead to this site. Many are described in the writings of Watkins (639), Michell (419), Devereux and Thompson (129), Screeton (534), or Pepper and Willock (469). However, the question still remains of what to do when you arrive. Given the right circumstances, there are many possibilities, some of which you may discover for yourself. Two are offered here as ways into the world of the earth Mysteries.

The first practice is for use in relation to one of the old tracks or paths, and may be applied to any ancient pathway that still retains serpent energy. It comes from the great assemblage of native myth and lore known as the *Mabinogion,* and concerns the figure of Sarn Elen, or Elen of the Roads, the goddess who opens the ways and dream paths (378). To invoke her and walk one of these ways from dusk to dawn is to open the inner landscape of your country to your waking eye. The pathworking that follows is part of her story, which invokes the most ancient laws of dream and mystery. Use it with care and in a proper frame of mind, remembering that these spirits of place are some of the most potent energies underlying our life and being. If you treat them with respect, they will respond, but if you enter their presence in a spirit of disrespect or levity, you will not experience anything.

Method

As you relax with eyes closed, gradually let your surroundings fade. You find that you are standing at the top of a hill—not a high one, but one that nonetheless permits you to see for a considerable distance across the countryside around you. Facing west you see before you a faint but well-trodden path leading down from the hill and out across flatlands. On every side stretches a checkered pattern of fields, and as you look down at them they move and whisper, stirred by a warm breeze from the south. They look for all the world like a many-colored sea. But in the midst of them, the path leads away into the distance, vanishing at last into a haze of mist that may, perhaps, hide higher ground.

Starting down the hill, you begin following the path. Insects hum around you and there is a sound of distant birds, but otherwise the world seems silent and still, as though it had only recently awakened from a long sleep. For a long while you walk onward, always following the faint track. Gradually the sun begins to descend in a fiery glow and dusk advances toward darkness. As the daylight fades you become aware that the path is rising again and that it is faintly glimmering with a light of its own.

Still you follow it, climbing steadily all the while now, until you find yourself at the beginning of a range of hills leading toward a soaring bulk of mountainous country. The moon has risen and now floods the scene with silvery light. You marvel that you do not feel tired and you press on, climbing higher through the cool evening air scented with nighttime flowers and a feeling of growing and burgeoning life.

At length, after climbing for some time, you round a shoulder of the mountains and see before you the entrance to a narrow valley filled with moonlight and shadows. Pausing for a moment, you see that at the head of the valley there is a wide shelf of rock at the foot of more mountains. There stands a circle of ancient, weathered stones, wreathed in coils of white mist. The path you have been following leads straight to the circle. Hurrying now, you press onward, for this is your destination.

Arriving at the circle, you find that the stones are far greater in size than you realized. They tower over you, casting long shadows on the ground. But they are not threatening; you are welcome here and you press forward without fear.

At the center of the circle is a great monolith lying lengthwise on the earth. Seated upon this, as though in a natural chair, is the slender figure of a woman. Her hair is long and glinting and her gown is a rich red edged with gold. Over it she wears a blue cloak fastened at the left shoulder with a round brooch of intricate workmanship. Her face is so beautiful that you know she cannot be mortal, and you bow low before her in awe and wonderment.

For several moments you remain kneeling before the golden lady until at last you hear words that seem to form themselves within your mind: "What do you seek here?"

You must answer truthfully and without hesitation: "I seek Sarn Elen. I seek a key to the Shimmering Way."

"Sarn Elen you have found. Why do you seek the Shimmering Way?"

"That I may come to learn the mystery of the land."

"Then you are welcome."

Silently the Lady, whom you now know to be Elen of the Roads, rises from the stone and beckons you to follow. As you do so, you notice that both the central stone and all the rest of the circle are intricately carved with spirals and lines, like huge maps. Try to remember some of the marks you see, for you may need them later.

You follow the Lady to the western edge of the circle and find that you are standing as though at a gateway. Before you the ground falls away rapidly toward a great plain that stretches to the horizon. Crisscrossing it are many faintly glowing lines interspersed at certain points with spirals of light. You realize that the designs on the stones of the circle are related directly to these, and that what you are seeing is a network of ancient tracks connecting stone circles and standing stones across the whole country and beyond.

As you watch, the Lady raises her arms, and at her command the lines of light burn brighter until you can hardly bear to look at them. You feel the energy coursing up through the land and into your feet and then rising through your body until it reaches the crown of your head and spills out over you. You feel yourself bathed in light, and though you dare not look directly at the Lady, you know she shines like a great beacon or star in the night.

Slowly the light begins to fade until there is once more only a faint glimmer on the moon-washed land. Turning away, you find that Elen of the Roads is no longer at your side, nor indeed anywhere in the circle, and that the sky is beginning to be flushed with the first rose of dawn. As you stand amid the circle of great stones, the scene slowly fades and you find yourself once again seated where you began the journey. Let yourself return slowly to normal consciousness.

Discovery

Now the Shimmering Way is open to you to visit at any time. When you next walk one of the ancient ways, you will be aware of the energy and life that are a part of them—and that are now a part of you.

❧ *5. The Terrestrial Zodiac* ❧

This practice is primarily intended to give you a deeper understanding of the nature of the terrestrial zodiacs. Although it is based upon what is known of the example at Glastonbury, it can, with only a little adaptation, be applied to other sites, such as the serpent mounds found in the United States and Mont-Saint-Michel in Brittany. This exercise does not require that you have visited any of these sites—though, of course, to have done so would be useful. It would be best of all to base your meditation on a sacred site or landscape near where you live.

Method

You are standing at the top of a rise looking toward the shape of a great hill. It is night but there is a full moon and you have no difficulty in seeing. The hill is surrounded by water upon which small light craft ply to and fro in the moonlight. Mist rises from the earth on all sides so that you seem to be standing on an island in more senses than one. You can see people moving about on the side of the hill that is nearest you. They are dressed in long robes and carry torches that flare and smoke in the damp air, adding to the miasmic quality of the scene. At the top of the hill is a great trilithon of ancient stones, and as you look, a brilliant glow begins to shine from within them. It grows brighter and brighter until the whole scene is bathed in light and a great ball of fire rises from the hill and climbs heavenward, where it hovers, casting a brilliant glow over everything. From it rays of light shine forth, falling on the tops of hills on every side, some close by, some far off. Answering gleams of light come from the hills, and you become aware that a great host of people is gathering around you on all sides, though you cannot see them. Your eyes are again drawn to the hill and there you see a great figure whom you know to be the king climbing the last stretch of the hillside, bearing across his outstretched arms a great sword in a sheath of red and gold.

At the summit of the hill, just beyond the edge of the trilithon, stands a figure clad in shimmering robes. This is the lady of the hill, and though she seems no taller than the king, she is somehow larger than life, invested with titanic stature and majesty. At her shoulder stands a great white horse, its coat gleaming in the light, its eyes flashing as it tosses its head. The king advances and exchanges a symbolic greeting with the lady of the hill. He then mounts the great steed and raises the sword, still sheathed, above his head. From the darkness around the stones, which seems impenetrable, twelve figures appear, each with a sign of the zodiac painted on his brow. In addition, each bears a symbol, some of which you may be able to see. These are the twelve treasures of the year linked with the inner life of the land, and the figures are their guardians. The guardians form a circle, raising their symbols toward the lady and the king. Then they turn until they are facing outward, and they begin to move, faster and faster until they form a bright ring of light. The king and the lady remain still at the center, the axis of the turning wheel. Soon the light grows too bright for you to see the figures clearly any longer. They become a whirling wheel of light that now rises from the hill and ascends toward the glowing light still hovering overhead. The two lights meet and become one, burning even brighter for a moment before beginning to fade and disperse outward to the stars. Slowly the scene returns to normal; the hilltop is deserted and only the light of the moon shines serenely over all. Awake slowly to your own place, but try to remember as much as possible of what you may have realized.

Discovery

You have the opportunity to work with one figure of the zodiac every month, as the wheel of the year turns. Visualize the wheel surrounding your land and people, and mediate the energies of the requisite sign outward. In times of national crisis, focus upon the king and the lady of the hill as the axial balance of the wheel, for they are the symbolic guardians of the land.

3

Meeting the Gods

An innate knowledge of the Gods is coexistent with our
very essence.
—IAMBLICHUS, *DE MYSTERII*

All the gods are one god; and all the goddesses are one
goddess, and there is one initiator.
—DION FORTUNE, *ASPECTS OF OCCULTISM*

Native Myths and God Forms

*E*very country has its native myth cycles that hold the dynamic power patterns of the land. Because of this, it is very important for us to be familiar with the mythology of our own place. Anthropologists like Ken Wilber (648) and John Layard (319) and mythographers like Joseph Campbell (75) and Robert Graves (194) can help us understand where our land's particular mythology fits in the overall myth patterns of the West. Entering the core myths of our land allows us to meet the dynamic powers that inhabit them. Because it is not possible to deal here with all the powers, beings, and scenarios making up native myths, we have drawn upon a selection of British and Irish legends to illustrate how to explore a mythology.

The first step in accessing the power of myth is to familiarize yourself with the legends of your land of occupation and with those of your family's place of origin, if these are different, for while harmony with the earth begins where you live, the myths of your cultural background are invaluable. If you have a Germanic background, for instance, but are living elsewhere, you might explore the world of the Siegfried myths

73

incorporated into the *Nibelungenlied* (449) as well as the legends of your newer home. Likewise, if you are Celtic in heritage, you would turn to the Ulster Cycle or the Arthurian mythos as well as the myths of your new home. Those with a Scandinavia background might benefit from a familiarity with the Finnish *Kalevala* (286), and those of central European or Latin ancestry might look at the French Charlemagne cycle (89) or the Spanish epic *El Cid* (98), respectively. Whether you are a native of the Americas or part of a family that has immigrated to the United States, Canada, or Central or South America, you can explore the earth magic of the Hopi Indians (638), or the grim mythology of the Aztec and Toltec cultures (323), or the stories of the Lakota or Cree along with those of your ancestral culture. The more we explore, the more we learn that each myth cycle covers familiar magical territory: the earth's creation, the quest for fire, the naming of the gods, the rites of passage, and the discovery of agriculture and animal husbandry, as well as the process that metamorphosed the genius loci into anthropomorphic forms.

The immense stretch of time has confused and darkened the lines of the mythic universe, combining deities of the sun and the moon, the earth and the stars, dividing those of corn and wine, lightning and rain, intermingling form with form, until it takes a considerable effort of mind to separate them into their original shapes and descriptions. Because of the scarcity of written records, it is not easy to see the outlines of the early Celtic deities. Caesar, to whose account we owe most of our contemporary information about the ancient Britons, is not very reliable (71). But the transcriptions of early British and Irish material from medieval scribes give us a clearer picture. Remember that if you cannot read about your new or ancestral culture's ancient gods, you can grow to be aware of them in other ways, recognizing the individual qualities of native god forms from the land itself.

Once, every tree, stone, and spring in Britain had a tutelary spirit that could be contacted by anyone who wished to communicate with it. In a larger sense the whole country's national identity was embodied in the genius loci, the spirit of the land. The wrinkled faces of ancient stones were the faces of the gods, and the brooks and streams were their voices. We have largely forgotten the names of these personifications, though they may still be detected in the names of those places where our ancestors once worshipped. The forces whose powers were much more vast than those of local spirits lived on through the stories and

Fig. 7. A triplicity of Celtic mother goddesses from a Romano-British temple in Gloucestershire

poems that grew up around them. Such tales paid homage to these greater powers, embodying some of their mystery as their actual worship faded with time.

These great forces were the gods, and their children were the figures in fairy tales and hero stories. There was the bear god Artos, whose cult was once widespread in Britain, but who became absorbed into the cycle of stories about a national hero—Arthur of Britain. Similarly, Arianrhod was once a goddess of poetic initiation, but in the medieval stories of the *Mabinogion* (343) she becomes a semi-human character, with the only vestige of her original role being her name, which means "silver wheel."

So the gods changed form, and their old names were either forgotten or took on new meanings. But the gods themselves did not disappear;

their worship continued in isolated areas long after the coming of new ways and beliefs. Eventually, some were absorbed by new deities. Others dwindled until they became the dwellers of the Hollow Hills—the faery folk of whom so much has been written and so little understood. Their names and natures were enshrined in memory, but the deities themselves grew old and weary. Some went away, but others adapted, retreating into the deep places of the earth or passing into timeless sleep.

In time, however, some people began again to seek out these ancient denizens of the inner world, to acknowledge their heritage as rulers of the earth and sky. Medieval witches, for instance, recognized the mystery of the natural elements and continued to worship them as their ancestors had done, following the natural cycle of birth, decay, and rebirth. Those who travel the Western Way find that the old gods and goddesses are not dead but remain potent forces in archetypal guise.

Studying the selective list of deities that follows will help you to recognize the faces of the gods as you follow the native Mysteries. Some of these beings can become part of your daily meditation, especially if you meet with them through practice 8, The Two Trees. This is the first step toward a deeper appreciation of the gods. As our ancestors well knew, meeting the powers enshrined within certain god forms is one of the most profound mysteries of the Western Way. It reestablishes our harmonic link with the ever-living reality of the Otherworld. To our ancestors, the earth's first children were the gods, and their children were the heroes, although in the blurring that occurs in the immense distance of time separating us from our forebears, it is often hard to tell where god or goddess ends and hero or heroine begins. The figure of Bran in the Welsh pantheon is clearly a god, and Gawain, in the Arthur cycle, is a hero who happens to assume the sun mantle of midsummer godhead. But who, or what, is Merlin? No god, perhaps, but certainly a great tutelary guardian of the mythic realms. There are many answers to such questions, for the gods wear many garments and have many names. We can make no attempt to separate them into ranks of mortal and immortal, but we can recognize the functions of the gods by their deeds and qualities—Thunderer, Shiner, Watcher over the Land. The lord or the lady of the moon is known in all lands, as are the tutelary spirits of river, tree, and stone.

In more contemporary time, much has been written about the gods, especially those of the classical world, but few writers ever go beyond simple delineation of type and character—Bacchus was the god of wine and Poseidon was a god of the sea. Yet the gods were no mere abstractions to those who worshipped them. If we read Iamblichus (262) or Plutarch (485) or Apuleius (14), we can see that the people of the ancient world had a theology that was as complex and meaningful as any held today. The gods permeated everything; they had then, as they still have, a power that is sufficient to fill all things. As the Neoplatonist Iamblichus (250–325 C.E.) says:

> The power of the Gods is not partibly comprehended by any place or partible human body . . . but is wholly everywhere present within the natures that are capable of receiving it. . . . Moreover, existing itself prior to all things, by its own separate nature, it becomes sufficient to fill all things, so far as each is able to partake of it. (263)

We are drawn to learn the most about those gods and beings that reflect our own characteristics. When we first work esoterically with ancient beings and god forms, we can immediately tell when our kindred feeling is reciprocated: We might experience a sense of lively communication, a physical sensation of well-being and love, and then a regenerative change throughout our whole being. Traditionally, practitioners of the Western Way explained this true sense of relationship and exchange as "being contacted." It results from a relationship of mutual respect rather than devotional worship, although individual practitioners may indeed venerate their closest gods with rites, ceremonies, and offerings. Through identification and subsequent affiliation with god forms, the initiates can begin to mediate the transformative energies of these deities into their everyday lives.

Once we accept the possibility of mediation, we are able to understand the full significance and efficacy of the signs known as the faces of the gods. Iamblichus calls these *synthamata,* inexplicable images, and accords them an individual power to work within the framework of creation:

> We do not perform these things through intellectual perception; since if this were the case, the intellectual energy . . . would be imparted by us . . . [Instead] when we do not energise intellectually, the synthamata themselves perform by themselves their proper

work, and the ineffable power of the Gods itself knows by itself, its own images. (263)

The realities we recognize outwardly have their own inner correlatives, whether we call them gods or archetypes. We cannot summon them at our pleasure. We cannot cause them to appear to us through any amount of theoretical study on our part. They come of their own volition when we are able to be receptive to them. They take their own forms and use their own signs; by means of our senses and imagination, they will constellate in ways that we can understand.

The Faces of the Gods

This selective list and description of gods and heroes includes both places associated with them and particular "doorways" through which they can be contacted. There are many ways of entering into communion with a god form, and the suggestions below represent just a few of them. We do not always ask for help or clarification from the beings we encounter, but when we seek appropriate allies and spiritual companions, asking is often a good way to understand their functions. Because the essential courtesies of any relationship apply even more so here, gratitude, remembrance, and inclusion should be an important part of your practice.

Arianrhod

Arianrhod is the goddess of poetic initiation. Her legend appears in the *Mabinogion,* in the story "Math, Son of Mathonwy." Like Ceridwen, with whom she has much in common, Arianrhod is an enchantress and initiator. She is a hard, stern mistress of destiny, setting heavy *geasa* (prohibitions) upon the candidate. Taliesin says that he spent three periods in the prison of Arianrhod, referring to his initiation at Caer Arianrhod, her ever-spinning castle in the Celtic Otherworld—the castle of both death and rebirth. In Welsh, Caer Arianrhod is the name for the *corona borealis,* the Crown of the North. There seems to be a link between Arianrhod and the Greek Ariadne, who received a crown from Dionysus that became known as the *corona* in subsequent myths. If you wish to learn from Arianrhod, seek out the turning tower of her fortress and ask her to teach you.

References: The *Mabinogion* (343), Gruffydd (211), Ross (510), C. Matthews (379)

Arthur

Arthur is the son of Uther Pendragon, king of Britain, and Igraine, the daughter of Custennin. Taken by the enchanter at birth to be brought up in secret and trained in the arts of kingship, war, and magic, Arthur subsequently achieves the mystery of the Sword in the Stone, proving by this his right to rule. He founds the Round Table of knights, dedicated to bringing order to the land. He marries Guinevere, who represents the sovereignty of Britain and who, through her love for Lancelot, brings about the downfall of Arthur's kingdom. He passes to Avalon— one of the many names for the Otherworld—to be healed of his wounds by Morgan le Fay after a final battle in which he first is wounded by his son Mordred and then slays him. He sleeps in Avalon, waiting for the time when he is needed. Arthur himself has appeared in many incarnations, ranging from the battle lord of the Dark Ages to the medieval king. Many places are associated with him, such as Cadbury Castle in Somerset, Alderley Edge in Cheshire, and Glastonbury in Somerset. As the tutelary protector of Britain, he may be encountered at almost any site if the heart and will of the seeker are truly focused on discovering him. Enter the hall of the Round Table and ask to be seated there.
References: Malory (364), Geoffrey of Monmouth (178), the *Mabinogion* (343), *Trioedd ynys Prydein* (The Welsh Triads—602), Loomis (336), Morris (427), Ashe (18), Knight (311), J. Matthews (392), Matthews and Matthews (386)

Bran the Blessed

Bran is a titanic god of the Celts. So great in size is he that when his followers want to cross the ocean, he wades through the water, towing their ships behind him. His story can be found in the *Mabinogion,* but the deepest mystery associated with him concerns his instruction upon his death: He commands that his head be struck from his body and carried thereafter by his followers. It continues to communicate with them for some time and leads them at last to a mysterious island (sometimes identified as Bardsey, off the southern coast of Wales), where the Company of the Noble Head finds lodging and is fed and entertained by Bran's head in an endless state of joy. Finally, though, one of the company opens a forbidden door that faces west and with this action they are all reminded of their mortality and of the passing of time. Thereafter a few of the company (one of which is Taliesin) carry the miraculous head to the White Mount (now called Tower Hill, in

London) and bury it there. It is said that while it remains undisturbed, no enemy could ever conquer the land, but Arthur digs it up in the belief that no one but he should protect the country of Britain, and after this, it is lost.

There are many aspects of the story and character of Bran that make him a prototypical Grail contact, his links with the fate of the land being the most obvious. He is also a Cronos figure whose influence may still be felt at certain places: Dinas Bran, in Wales, has strong associations with him, though like Arthur, his presence is diffuse and may be felt at many sites throughout Britain. Take a voyage to the withdrawn island and join the Company of the Noble Head, asking to hear the story that you need to understand.

References: The *Mabinogion* (343), Ross (510), MacCana (344), Newstead (448), C. Matthews (379)

Brighid/Brigantia

Brighid is a figure who is found in every part of Britain and Ireland and has been identified as "the British Minerva" by several classical writers. Irish Brighid, daughter of the Dagda of the Tuatha de Danaan, is the goddess of poets, healing and smithcraft and protector of flocks, dairy production, women in childbirth, and the domestic hearth. She is remarkable in that her cult bridges pagan and Christian centuries, much of it passing into the cult of Saint Brigit of Kildare (525 C.E.). The Christian shrine at Kildare was maintained by nineteen nuns. A sacred fire was kept burning in the middle of a sanctuary that was forbidden to men, only to be extinguished at the Reformation, but the fires have recently been relit as many women have taken up Brighid/Brigit as their matron. Saint Brigit's feast day is February 1, or Imbolc, when invocations to both her pagan and Christian aspects are best made. In Britain she is associated with the figure of Brigantia, the local goddess of the Brigantes, a Celtic tribe of northern England. A statue of Brigantia was found at Birrens, where she bears the emblems of Victory and Minerva in Romano-British guise. Her places are (for Saint Brigit) the shrine at Kildare, County Kildare, and (for Brigantia) the whole of the West Riding, which has strong natural associations with her. As you light a fire or a candle, ask her to protect your household.

References: Ross (510), Rees and Rees (502), Carmichael (78), *Oxford Dictionary of Saints* (460)

Cailleach Beare, or Bheur the Carlin

The Cailleach Beare, or Hag of Beare, is a titanic goddess of the British Isles. *Cailleach* means "hag," though in polite Gaelic it is still used to refer to an old wife or grandmother. References to her remain in folklore, but rarely in textual sources. She is the primeval goddess of southwest Ireland and, like her Scottish equivalent, the Cailleach Beare leaps across mountain ranges that have been formed from stones dropped from her apron. She pursues her son, although the story is sometimes reversed so that she is the quarry, and mother and son take part in a chase in which she (winter) and summer compete for mastery.

Like the Middle Eastern goddess Tiamat, the Cailleach has many associations with water dragon stories. Although she appears as a withered hag, she has the ability to show herself as a young maiden. The folk rituals accompanying the feast of Saint Brigit hint that this transformation is accomplished at the transition from winter to spring. In Scottish Lowland folklore the Cailleach becomes the Gyre Carlin, sometimes also called Nicnevin, or Daughter of the Bones, who resembles the Indian Kali, which suggests that she is scarcely the most comfortable of archetypes to work with. There are numerous places associated with the Cailleach, including the many mountains in Ireland and Scotland called Sliabh na Cailleach; the old rocks of the Beare Peninsula, County Cork, Ireland; and the glacial outcrops of northwest Scotland. When you need an overview of your situation or more stability, visit her in her mountain fastness for piercingly accurate advice.
References: Mackenzie (347), Ross (510), C. Matthews (375)

Ceridwen

Ceridwen is the goddess of inspiration. The supreme initiator, the mistress of the Mysteries, she is described in the *Welsh Triads* as one of the three most beautiful women on the Island of Britain. Ceridwen possesses the Cauldron of Rebirth, the earliest prototype of the Grail, and in it she brews an initiatory drink that Taliesin accidentally tastes, thereby receiving all knowledge. She is a shapeshifter, appearing in many guises to the candidate for initiation. As a guardian of wisdom, she can assume frightening shapes, such as that of the sow goddess, but her purpose is to inculcate responsibility for knowledge and its uses. Echoes of her personality are to be found both in Morgan le Fay and the Celtic battle goddess known as the Morrigan. Her roots are deep in the earth, of which she is mother, and thus she is best encountered at earth mounds or the more ancient sacred sites. She is especially associated with Llyn Tegid, Bala, in Wales. If you would serve her, tend the fire under her cauldron and place within it whatever needs to be transformed. **References:** The *Mabinogion* (343), Matthews and Matthews (404), Spence (555), R. Graves (194), Ashe (17)

Cernunnos/Herne

Cernunnos is master of the animals, god of green and growing things, huntsman, and spirit of the earth and masculinity. He is most often pictured sitting cross-legged, with antlers sprouting from his brow, as on the Gundestrup Cauldron (148)—see figure 8. Sometimes he is seen as the consort to Ceridwen, with whom he is tutelary deity of many witch covens. As Herne the hunter he is depicted leading the Wild Hunt—a pack of white hounds with red ears—much like Gwyn ap Nudd, or Arawn. He seeks out injustices that are beyond human appeal or solution. His stomping grounds include Windsor Great Park, though the tree generally referred to as Herne's Oak is not the best place to seek him. Indeed he is best not sought at all; he will certainly come of his

Fig. 8. The Gundestrup Cauldron, a votive offering found in a Danish bog, depicts many Celtic divinities, such as Herne the Hunter.

own accord once he has scented activity in his neighborhood. For a powerful and primordial contact who can opens your eyes to the deepest levels, wait for him in the depths of the forest, in a clearing where a great tree grows.

References: Spence (552), Ross (510), Markale (366), Petry (474), Mottram (428), J. Matthews and Green (403)

Cronos

Oldest and first of the primitive gods, Cronos is associated with Britain. He is reported by Diodorus Siculus (130) to be bound in eternal and unchanging bondage deep within the earth of the British Isles (see chapter 2). Thus he becomes the oldest of the many sleeping-god archetypes, which also include Arthur and Bran. As a tutelary spirit he is extremely powerful and should be approached with caution. It is his destiny to wake in some future age, and because he is said to have ushered out the last great Golden Age of humanity, his eventual waking may be the signal for a return to the ways and beliefs of that time. As a god of the earth and time, his presence can be felt only in the timelessness of a cave or earth mound. When you seek to enter into the living present and pass beyond time, go to Cronos's cave and learn from him.

References: Ashe (18), R. Graves (192), Powys (492), C. Matthews (379)

Gawain/Cuchulainn

Gawain and Cuchulainn are heroic figures who share many aspects of the solar deities while retaining their own individuality. Both are noted for a fiery temper, red hair, and the waxing and waning of their strength throughout the day. Cuchulainn, also called the Hound of Ulster, of Irish myth, is the more primitive figure of the two, though we may catch glimpses of an earlier Gawain in the Welsh texts, where he is called Gwalchmai, the Hawk of May. Over time he is Christianized as his character develops, until, in the great medieval poem *Sir Gawain and the Green Knight,* he has become an exemplar of the Christian virtues set against the evil magic of Morgan le Fay and the Green Knight, a far older and darker figure akin to Cernunnos. Gawain displays only dim echoes of the battle madness of Cuchulainn, who undergoes a physical transformation during a fight. As solar beings, both have a freshness and strength that are easily felt in the open air under a hot, midsummer sky, which make them excellent companions on the

Way. To some, Gawain represents the ancient Hibernian Mysteries reaching back into Pictish times, and his association with the Orkney Islands suggests an Otherworld connection, for the Orkneys have been regarded as a gateway to the Shining Lands. Cuchulainn's presence in Ulster cannot be denied. When you need a strong protector or to learn how to live with courage, seek out Gawain or Cuchulainn at the pass or the ford.

References: *Sir Gawain and the Green Knight* (543), Malory (364), *Trioedd ynys Prydein* (The Welsh Triads—602), *Táin Bó Cúalnge* (588), J. Matthews (398), Matthews and Matthews (386)

Gwyn ap Nudd/Arawn Gwyn

Gwyn ap Nudd is lord of Annwn, the Underworld, and the king of faery. Arawn is the hunter with a pack of white, red-eared hounds—the Hell Hounds, or Gabriel Hounds, that also hunt with Herne. He is mentioned in the *Mabinogion* as a companion to Arthur and is responsible for the carrying off of Creiddylad, the daughter of the god Llyr. He must fight to possess her every first of May, challenging Gwythyr, son of Griedawl, in a contest between summer and winter. This tale is a parallel to that of Pwyll and Arawn in the first branch of the *Mabinogion*. Pwyll must also fight for his bride, Rhiannon, in a yearly contest.

In the Welsh poem the *Preiddeu Annwn* (The Spoils of Annwn), Arthur voyages to Gwyn's kingdom to bring back the magical treasures of the Island of Britain, including the cauldron watched over by nine maidens—an early prototype of the Grail. In the medieval *Life of Saint Collen,* there is a meeting between the saint and Gwyn: Saint Collen enters Gwyn's palace by descending into Glastonbury Tor from the top, where Gwyn's influence is supposed to have been banished by the application of holy water.

These related gods have special powers of guardianship and responsibility for the land. As Underworld gods, Gwyn ap Nudd and Arawn may be seen as the guardians of winter with their Persephone-like consorts. They are patrons of the underside of things, of the psyche's harrowing, and may conduct the voyager into the deepest of inner realms. Gwyn's territory is Glastonbury in Somerset, Neath in Glamorganshire, and Llangollen in Clwyd; find Arawn at Arbeth, Pembroke. Go to the high hills when your land is in disarray or decay and call upon Gwyn or Arawn to cleanse it of stagnating influences.

References: The *Mabinogion* (343), Rees and Rees (502), Spence (554), C. Matthews (379)

Helen of the Roads/Elen

Known sometimes as goddess of trackways and ancient roads, goddess of the dream paths, Helen, or Elen, features in "The Dream of Macsen Wledig" in the *Mabinogion,* in which she rules over the country of dreams. Known also as the goddess of evening and morning, she performs the role of guide and instructor for those seeking the old serpent ways to the sites of arcane knowledge (see chapter 2). Perhaps one of the oldest native deities, she assumed Roman influence and became identified with Saint Helen of Colchester, the mother of Constantine the Great. One of the great trackways in Wales is known as Sarn Helen, Helen's Road. Following this on foot is an excellent way to establish contact with this particular archetype. She may assist in opening the gates to the old sites (see practice 2, Analeptic Memory).

References: The *Mabinogion* (343), Chant (86), Spence (554), Ashe (18), C. Matthews (378)

Mabon/Maponus

Mabon is the *puer aeternus* of the Celtic pantheons. He is always referred to as Mabon, son of Modron, Youth, son of Mother, and the story "Culhwch and Olwen" in the *Mabinogion* tells of his incarceration. He is the primal child who existed at the beginning, and throughout the story is sought for by Culhwch, Arthur's nephew, with this: "Do you know Mabon, Modron's son, who from his mother's side was reeved when time was first begun?" Birds and animals give clues as to where he may be found, but nonetheless this question is repeated over and over with sad, liturgical inquiry. The Mysteries of the lost child are closely related to the mother, the Matrona or Modron—the goddess of earlier times—and though no personal names come down to us, the impact of Mabon and his mother is still strong. Maponus, or "divine son," is a northern Romano-British variant often associated in inscriptions with Apollo. Gloucester is the place associated with Mabon's imprisonment and the area around Lochmaben, Dumfriesshire, with Maponus. Many inscriptions to him are to be found along the Scottish borders. To find Mabon, to retrieve lost aspects of your soul's landscape, take the journey to an old childhood haunt and ask the animal that you meet there to guide you.

References: Ross (510), the *Mabinogion* (343), Gruffydd (211), Ashe (17) C. Matthews (379)

Manannan/Manawyddan

Manannan is the master of the seas, the pilot of souls who seek the way to the Blessed Isles of the Otherworld. He is originally allied with the Tuatha de Dannan, and in later texts is incorporated into them. His title is Mac Lir, "of the sea," and he finds his Welsh equivalent in Manawyddan, who in the *Mabinogion* helps lift an enchantment laid on the land and is one of the children of Don. Both Welsh and Gaelic figures are shape-changers visiting this world in the guise of travelers and craftsmen. Manannan's horse or his glass boat bears the seeker to the Otherworld. He keeps a host of treasures in the crane bag, itself a receptacle of wisdom. His places are the Isle of Man; Emain Abhlach, or Emain of the Apple Trees, which is identified as the Isle of Arran in the Firth of Clyde; and any place of enchantment that resonates with the Otherworld. His symbol is the three-spoked wheel, or *triskel,* which may be seen in the symbol of the Isle of Man. Use the triskel as your meditation symbol to help you find him, or meditate to the sound of the sea.
References: The *Mabinogion* (343), Rees and Rees (502), Ross (510), R. Graves (194), C. Matthews (379)

Math ap Mathonwy

Math ap Mathonwy is an archetypal god of druidry and transformation. Although he has some of the characteristics of Merlin, he is a much older figure whose brand of magic is at times both just and unrelenting. He excels in the ability to transform both himself and others into the shapes of animals or birds. In the *Mabinogion* he is responsible for fashioning for the god Llew a bride made of flowers. He is guide to many Mysteries and seems to represent a druidic wisdom both older and deeper than that of most of his fellows divinities. Enter his hall of justice only after you have clarified your motivations for approaching him.
References: The *Mabinogion* (343), Spence (555), R. Graves (194), Garner (176), Gruffydd (211), C. Matthews (379)

Merlin

As one of the most important figures in Western tradition and the prime mover behind the age of Arthur, Merlin spans both pagan and Christian

Mysteries. To make contact with him is to place ourselves squarely at the center of both the ancient druidic Mysteries and the high Christian magic of the Hermetic way (see part 2). Like Taliesin, he is a contact who opens many doors: those to the Otherworld, the country of the Grail, and the druid way of which he is a part. There are many places where his influence may be felt, notably in Merlin's Cave at Tintagel in Cornwall and in the Merlin's Tump at Marlborough in Wiltshire, but nowhere as strongly as at the hilltop site known as Dinas Emrys in Wales and around the town of Caermarthan, which is named after him. Emrys is the name by which Merlin is known in certain parts of Wales and Dinas Emrys is the supposed site of his first great adventure, when he revealed the meaning of the red and white dragons that battled beneath the earth and made his first great series of prophecies. The whole story and the text of the prophecies can be found in Geoffrey of Monmouth's *History of the Kings of Britain* (178). A lord of seashore and dark cave, Merlin links many diverse forces. He can be elusive but at the most unexpected moments finds those who seek him. Merlin can sometimes be found in the woods or in his observatory tower.

References: Geoffrey of Monmouth (178), Spence (555), Markale (366), Jarman (267), Matthews and Matthews (404), Stewart and J. Matthews (578), *Vita Merlini* (621)

Morgan le Fay/Nimue/the Lady of the Lake

In many ways, this is one of the most important figures of the Western tradition. As Morgan le Fay she appears as a force of chaos and evil in the Arthurian cycle, though because the medieval stories have overwritten the earlier tales, she is also depicted as caring for Arthur when he receives his wound at the last battle of Camlan. Nimue, who is both another aspect of Morgan and the beguiler of Merlin, is present at this scene as well, when a dark boat appears to carry Arthur to Avalon. Together with the mysterious figure known as the Lady of the Lake, these women form a triplet dating back to the character of the Morrigan in Irish and Welsh myth, where this archetype is known as a battle goddess. Their roles throughout the Arthurian mythos are those of both helper and hinderer. Thus the Lady of the Lake fosters Lancelot and provides Arthur with his magical sword, Excalibur, while Morgan le Fay frequently opposes both Merlin and Arthur with her dark magic. Nimue lures Merlin and is eventually the cause of his downfall, but before this is a trusted confidante at the Arthurian court.

Behind all these figures is a far older, darker, and more mysterious figure—a mother goddess whose aspect is both fearsome and gentle, a teacher and guide, and a ruthless slayer of hopes, all at the same time. As a contact she brings with her all these aspects and thus requires careful handling. Found on open hillsides, in thorn trees, and by the banks of rivers, she appears dressed in a dark cloak and hood, sometimes keening for the souls of dead heroes, or as a bird, usually a raven, keeping watch from high trees or outcroppings of rock. When you require a time of healing or retreat so that you can order your thoughts clearly, go to the water's edge and ask for a boat to ferry you across the lake to Morgan's dwelling.

References: R. Graves (192), Spence (555), Markale (366), Malory (364), Ross (510), *Vita Merlini* (621), Knight (311), C. Matthews (378), Matthews and Matthews (389)

Nuada/Nodens

The Romano-British god Nodens has his counterpart in the Irish Nuada. Nodens is a hunter, a woodland guardian, and a guide of souls. His temple, excavated at Lydney, Gloucestershire, has facilities for incubation, where pilgrims came to sleep in order to receive messages from the god through their dreams. Nuada Airgetlam (Silver Arm) is king of the Tuatha de Danaan. His name derives from the loss of his arm in battle. Because Irish kings—indeed most ancient kings—were deemed unfit to reign if maimed or blemished in any way, he resigns his kingship and is given a silver, fully functional arm by the god of healing. When this is later replaced by an arm of flesh, he resumes his kingship. Nodens can still be consulted at Lydney. When you lie down to sleep, begin to build the temple in which your bed is set. As you fall asleep, ask Nodens or Nuada to send you a dream in answer to a deeply held question.

References: Ross (510), the *Mabinogion* (343), Rees and Rees (502), Spence (556), C. Matthews (379)

Rhiannon

Found in the *Mabinogion* in the story "Pwyll, Prince of Dyfed," Rhiannon is strongly linked with the Mysteries of Mabon and Modron, for she also loses a child, suffers a heavy punishment, and regains her former glory. She is without doubt the Welsh Persephone. Her name signifies "great queen" and her cult is connected with that of the pan-

Celtic mare goddess, Epona, which has associations with the early worship of the Greek Black Demeter. Rhiannon is also the mistress of otherworldly birds whose song brings sleep, tears, and joy to the listener. Her places are Arberth in Pembrokeshire and any site sacred to the mare, such as White Horse Hill, Uffington, Oxfordshire.

When your present state of being seems intolerable, ask Rhiannon to send her birds to heal you, whether through the discharge of sorrow, the sleep of forgetfulness, or renewed joy after hardship. She is a patient teacher to all who seek the track of her hooves.

References: The *Mabinogion* (343), Ross (510), Gruffydd (211), R. Graves (194), C. Matthews (379)

Taliesin

Taliesin is chief bard of the Islands of Britain, one of the Company of the Noble Head (see Bran, above) and a magician second in stature only to Merlin. The mystery of his birth, outlined in the *Mabinogion,* involves transmogrification through bird and animal forms and an initiation ritual that was at one time current in many parts of the world: The initiate drinks a specially prepared draft that causes him to see visions and pass through various states of consciousness. From this myth originate many of the surviving poems of Taliesin found in the *Black Book of Caermarthen* (171), which describe in riddling form a journey through all of history. These were in part unraveled in *The White Goddess* (194) and more fully in *Taliesin: The Last Celtic Shaman* (404). Taliesin has the power to conduct through many dimensions of place and time and through the elements themselves anyone who establishes rapport with him. He is the companion of all who tread the difficult, solitary way of understanding through the highest elemental contacts. Ask him to show you the metaphors that weave together your existence.

References: The *Mabinogion* (343), Nash (437), Spence (554), C. Matthews (379), Matthews and Matthews (404)

Tuatha de Danaan and the Children of Donn

These are the names given to the pantheons of Irish and Welsh deities, respectively, of the early Celtic period. The family of Donn, or Danu, was made up of the hereditary gods of an invading people. In the Irish *Book of Invasions,* the Tuatha de Danaan are the fifth body of invaders, themselves subjugated by the Milesians. Although traces of the Irish

Tuatha are appreciable within the British Children of Donn, neither they nor their stories are identical. This can be explained if we look at the known colonization of western Wales, particularly at the Pembroke coast of ancient Dyfed. Reminders of this time remain in the shape of forty ogham stones still standing in Wales today.

Danu, Anu, or Donn is a shadowy matriarch whose origins are unknown to us; she has been equated with the Indian goddess Dánu, mother of Vrtra in the Rig Veda. However we see her, she is a titanic figure, comparable to the Greek Rhea, who also founded a line of gods. Danu or Donn's children are defined by their mastery of the arts and skills of many kinds, including magic and fighting. They have no skills in agriculture; this function is relegated to the vanquished lesser gods. Danu is the mother of the gods; Dagda, the "good god," also called Ruad Rofessa (lord of great knowledge), is the god of magic. His daughter Brighid is patroness of poets, smiths, and women. Diancecht is god of healing. Nuadu is king of the Tuatha. Lugh, called Sabd il Danach or "prince of many skills," is the Tuatha's champion who finally defeats the older gods. Manannan, although older than the Tuatha, becomes one of their number and bestows many immortal gifts upon them. Both he and Lugh survived strongest in folk memory after the Milesians vanquished the Tuatha and they had been driven to the Hollow Hills. The two appear as otherworldly helpers to kings and heroes, Manannan in particular having an interest in the fosterage and care of unprotected children and women. Goibniu is the god of smiths. Ogma, surnamed Grian-ainech, or "sun-faced," is the god of poetry and writing; the invention of the magical language known as ogham is ascribed to him.

The Welsh Children of Donn are particularly distinguished for their magical skills. They appear within the story "Math, Son of Mathonwy" in the *Mabinogion*, where their influence upon events turns the world upside down. Gwydion, described as a son of Donn and nephew to King Math, is the arch mover and magician. With his brother Gilfaethwy, he starts an intrigue that kills Pryderi, Rhiannon's son. This may well indicate the suppression of an older family of gods, for Rhiannon's origins are in the Underworld and are therefore closer to the beginning of things. Gwydion's sister Arianrhod gives birth to two sons—Dylan, son of Wave, who is one with the sea, and Llew Llaw Gyffes, Lieu of the Skillful Hand, the equivalent of Lugh Lamhfada, or

Lugh of the Long Arm, in the Tuatha. Arianrhod puts upon him insuperable geasa, or prohibitions, including one that he shall not marry a mortal. As a result, Gwydion and Math make a woman out of flowers—Blodeuwedd, "flower face"—for Lieu. But she betrays Lieu, after which he, who cannot be killed outright, transforms himself into the shape of an eagle. Blodeuwedd is herself turned into an owl as punishment for her betrayal, while Lieu returns to mortal shape. To this day owls are called by her name in parts of Wales.

A convention of early Christian Ireland had members of the Tuatha appearing to monks or hermits in order to relate their deeds and be baptized so that they could pass out of the Hollow Hills into the Christian heaven. Even after their reign was supposedly over, then, these archetypes remained strong. Those who walk the inner realms of the Western Way are likely to meet with some of the Tuatha, especially if they visit a barrow or chambered tomb in their meditations.

References: Rees and Rees (502), Ross (510), de Jubainville (124), MacCana (344), Garner (176), the *Mabinogion* (343), C. Matthews (379), Matthews and Matthews (388)

Wayland/Govannon/Goibnui

These are three types of one figure: the smith of the gods. An immensely strong, deep-rooted contact, he is said to be willing to shoe your horse if you have the right payment to offer—and he may also open to you the door to the Underworld, where he is a king in his own right. Wayland's Smithy in Oxfordshire has the strongest associations with him. He is almost the only Saxon deity who has remained active, assuming the roles of earlier Welsh and Irish gods. This is an indication of the special position accorded to smiths, who were the first makers and knew the mystery of iron—the origin of the folk belief that witches and faery folk cannot cross a threshold protected by "cold iron." Wayland shares many affinities with the ancient green king, the man of the woods, who leads to the deeper levels of lore. He is also said to have made many magical weapons, including, in all probability, Arthur's sword, Excalibur. Whenever you need to be reforged, go the smithy, taking a silver coin for payment.

References: Branston (55), Hayles (238), R. Graves (194)

The Mythic Cycles

Most of the beings discussed in the previous list have a place in the great mythological cycles of the West: the cycles of Arthur or Fionn, the Ulster Cycle, and the Four Branches of the *Mabinogion*. Each of these requires considerable study and has whole books devoted to this pursuit. Here we only indicate, however partially, their essential qualities, which include some of the most profound Mysteries of the Western Way. Knowledge of these cycles is essential for anyone wishing to follow the Way; their characters and stories are gateways to other realms for the seeker to wander into and out of at will. Some tried and tested methods to do this can be found later in this chapter, but first it may be helpful to familiarize yourself with the individual cycles and their inner meanings.

The Arthurian Cycle

This is perhaps the most familiar of the cycles we discuss here. The stories of King Arthur and his Knights of the Round Table are actually a loosely knit body of myth, legend, and hero tale drawn from Celtic, and later French, background, elaborated upon by countless authors down the ages. From the height of the myth's popularity in the Middle Ages we have the image of a band of mail-clad knights going in search of love and battle and the Holy Grail, led by a mighty king who is advised by the wise seer Merlin. These knights stand for many of the noblest aspirations of human endeavor: to create harmony out of chaos, to preserve what is most worthy, to reach for the highest possible ideals. Thus the cycle as a whole contains the widest possible spectrum of human love, folly, desire, and attainment. Arthur is the noblest of men and stands for the land—indeed he *is* the land and, according to legend, sleeps beneath it in caves until he is called upon to return and succor the human race. Guinevere, rash and human in her impetuous love for Lancelot, stands for an even older feminine Mystery (313), as do many of the figures in the cycle, such as Morgan, Nimue, Lunet, Lionors, Dindrain, and Isolt. The male counterparts to these women, the great knights Galahad, Gawain, Perceval, Lamorack, Gareth—their names, like their deeds, are legion—each stand to some degree in relation to the Western Mysteries. In this respect, they can be powerful guardians, companions, guides, and exemplars on the Way.

All of these figures have become invested with timelessness by the unending interest lavished upon them, and they respond well to direct contact in meditation or dream. Once you have contacted them, you may find that a single knight or lady attaches him- or herself to you, acting as an escort throughout your daily life, both magical and mundane.

Because its basis is Celtic, Germanic, and even Atlantean, working with the Arthurian cycle can be particularly rewarding, for it may lead to one or more of the inner realities of these cultures. For those who take special interest in the Mystery of the Grail, knowledge of the Arthur stories is essential. The intimate understanding of the esoteric Grail kingdom revealed by many of the romances and adventures of the Grail seekers are superlative guides. The Mystery at the heart of the Grail is service, and each of the knights who achieves this Mystery possesses the ability to help and instruct us on our path to the place where the wounded King Arthur awaits our coming as eagerly as he always has and always will.

Arthurian source books abound, and there are several good histories and bibliographies available to illuminate Arthurian Britain. A select list can be found at the back of this book. Nor should fictional retellings be ignored; many contain great insights, and for this reason we have included some of them in our bibliography.

References: Matthews and Matthews (389), J. Matthews (393), Loomis (336)

The Mabinogion

The *Mabinogion* (343)—*mabinog* translates as "youth tales"—is a collection comprising four branches and related stories. The four branches themselves—"Pwyll, Prince of Dyfed," "Branwen, Daughter of Llyr," "Manawyddan, Son of Lyr," and "Math, Son of Mathonwy"—form a loosely woven cycle of tales written down in the ninth century but incorporating material from much earlier times. They are a rewarding source from which to quarry the myths of the land.

The remainder of the tales, grouped under the heading *mabinogi,* are more disparate, consisting of several Arthurian stories generally believed by modern scholars such as Loomis (336), Brown (60), and Bromwich (602) to be copies of medieval French poems by Chrétien de Troyes; an Arthurian tale, "Culhwch and Olwen," which contains some of the earliest material extant of the whole cycle; and two primary mythic stories, "The Dream of Macsen Wledig" (see chapter 2) and "The Dream of Rhonawby," both of which contain material of a significantly earlier kind. The collection is completed by the story "Lludd and Llefelys," relating to the dragon myths and Merlin; and the very important "Hanes Taliesin," omitted from more recent editions of the texts because of its "difficult" and fragmentary nature. It can, however, be found in the original edition by Lady Charlotte Guest and should certainly be read for its magical and initiatory content.

Unlike the Arthurian cycle, the overall bias of the *Mabinogion* is toward the heroic rather than the chivalric. Despite a thin overlay of later material, it is made up of the most primary matter of the native Celtic mythos. However the material came to be transmitted, it is manifestly older than the medieval versions that descended from it. One of the three Arthurian stories—"Peredur, Son of Evrawc"—contains the earliest form of the Grail legend, and the atmosphere found in both "The Lady of the Fountain" and "Geraint Son of Erbin" is much more magical than that of Chrétien de Troyes's elegant French versions (94).

Finally, we find correlating information within the text of the *Triads* (602). These are a form of mnemonic used by the old storytellers and bards to preserve the principal themes of their extensive repertoire. Thus the "Three Disastrous Revealings" and the "Three Golden-Torqued Bards of Britain" would immediately recall the stories associated with them. Sometimes brief, shorthand versions of the stories were appended to the *Triads,* and because many of the stories have perished, these offer tantalizing glimpses of a little-known world. Indeed, one of the best exercises we know of for becoming familiar with the native god forms is to take one of the *Triads* and use it as a theme for meditation. You may be surprised at the amount that can be recovered in this way and at the insights it can reveal in your daily life.
References: C. Matthews (379, 378), Sullivan (581)

The Fionn Cycle

The Fionn Cycle is similar to the Ulster Cycle, though lighter in tone. Fionn MacCumhal is the captain of King Cormac MacAirt's band of Fianna, or heroes. The Fianna roam the countryside of southern Ireland, and much of the cycle is taken up with their adventures. In order to be admitted to the band a man must be able to accomplish all kinds of miraculous physical feats, such as running through a forest without a hair on his head or a branch on any tree being disrupted and drawing a thorn from his foot while running without slackening his pace. The candidate was expected to be adept in the arts of poetry as well as fighting (the parallels to Robin Hood and his band are not hard to draw). As in the Ulster Cycle, a woman brings the story to a tragic close: Grainne, the intended wife of Fionn, runs away with Fionn's best friend, Diarmuid, to Scotland, where they live an idyllic, if temporary, life in the wild. Similarities with the Arthurian stories, "Culhwch and Olwen," and the Tristan and Isolt legends are also clear. Fionn himself is an initiate after the manner of Taliesin; he touches the Salmon of Knowledge while cooking it for his poet-master, which gives him immunity from his enemies (poets enjoyed exemption from attack) as well as access to the Otherworld, with which he is still connected in folk tradition. According to the story, Oisin, Fionn's son, survives right up until the Christian era, when he meets Saint Patrick and relates to him the deeds of the Fianna. Like all the more primitive myths discussed here, the heroes of the Fionn Cycle make fine companions in the investigation of the native magical sites and areas of Britain.

References: Rees and Rees (502), MacCana (344), Sutcliff (583), Matthews and Matthews (404)

The Ulster Cycle

As the Fianna are to the south of Ireland, the heroes of the Ulster Cycle are to the northern part of Ireland. Here we are still connected to the high days of the Tuatha de Danaan, but if the Tuatha represent the Golden Age, then the heroic tradition of Ulster represents the Silver Age. Its high deeds, honor, and heroic codes of behavior are reminiscent of the Trojan Wars as described by Homer. In the Ulster Cycle people are placed under severe geasa (ill-wished enchantment) that restrict their actions to such a degree that the outcome can only be tragic. Ulaidh, ancient Ulster, is ruled by Conchobar mac Nessa, whose court is at Emain Macha, near the present-day city of Armagh. In his court are the champions and heroes who together form the Red Branch Knights: Conall Cernach, Fergus mac Roich, and, most famous of all, Cuchulainn, whose exploits nearly form a cycle in themselves. The fate of Ulster is tied up with tribal feuding, particularly with the rival court of Queen Maebh of Connacht. The most famous tale is the *Táin Bó Cúalnge* (The Cattle Raid of Cooley), after which Cuchulainn is killed by the magic of the Morrighan, the primal

Cailleach whose malice stems from the time before even the Tuatha de Danaan reigned. Related stories in the cycle are "Deirdre and the Sons of Uisnech"—a parallel to "The Pursuit of Diarmuid and Grainne" from the Fionn Cycle—in which the beauty of Deirdre and the honorable and impossible geasa imposed on those about her form the basis for the subsequent tragedy of Ulster. "Bricriu's Feast" and "Mac Da Tho's Pig" are humorous interludes in which the heroes have otherworldly adventures and suffer very real humiliations. The former story contains the first instance of the beheading game that later appears in the medieval *Sir Gawain and the Green Knight* (543), featuring the Cuchulainn-type hero Gawain. The Ulster Cycle as a whole remains a work of dark vengeance and proud honor and is perhaps the most difficult cycle for us to work with today.

References: MacCana (344), Rees and Rees (510), *Táin Bó Cúalnge* (588), Sutcliff (584), Matthews and Matthews (387)

The Robin Hood Legend

Probably better known to cinema audiences than to students of the esoteric, Robin Hood, or Robin Wood, is nevertheless an important figure in the Western Mysteries. Originally a spirit of the woodlands of Britain, he is a supremely English character. His beginnings are lost in the mists of time, and have become overlaid with a doubtful historical figure known variously as Robin of Huntingdon or Robin of Locksley. A series of ballads dating from the twelfth and thirteenth centuries outline the adventures of the great outlaw of Sherwood Forest involving such picturesque characters as Little John, Will Scarlet, Allan a Dale, and Friar Tuck, while many tales involving older and darker characters are little more than dim memories by this time. Robin is very much a man of the people, an equalizer whose image still reappears in contemporary figures of the solitary masked avenger of injustice. As a contacted archetype, he opens the mystery of the woodlands and shadowy, overgrown glades. Robin Hood is inscrutably deep and quick and eager to lead upon new and surprising paths all those who follow him. With Maid Marian as his consort, he rules over the woodlands of Britain like a king of Faery.

References: J. Matthews (397), Holt (249), Child (93), Vansittart (611)

The Way of the Story

There is no authorized book of the native tradition, no holy scripture from which succeeding generations may quote or to which they may refer as an index to living. Instead there are the primal myths, densely patterned stories and themes strung together on a loose framework and exemplified by characters in the guise of gods and goddesses, heroes, and lovers. Written sacred texts such as the Bible, the Koran, the Popol Vuh, and the Rig Veda remain virtually unchanged once they are formalized; they can be referred to at any given moment in time. Myths, however, continue to grow and change because they are told, not written. In addition, they are open to endless variation and interpretation. James Joyce, for example, can make us see Ulysses anew by setting him down in modern Dublin. The seemingly endless repetition of Greek or Arthurian myths from the Middle Ages to today occurs because the themes they contain are timeless and reach the most profound depths of that same human experience that gave birth to them. These myths are the roots of story, the preserve of archetypes that trip the wire of our ancestral memory. The art of the storyteller is to reach the deepest possible level in humans, and all true practitioners of the art can be recognized because they do this and, in the process, add to the layers of meaning that each successive generation finds in the bedrock of the original story.

As we saw in chapter 1, the shamans were the first storytellers. Drawing on their immediate experience of the Otherworld and its inhabitants, they gave birth to the first myths. Thereafter, the stories and events relating to these myths became the core of religion, the Mysteries, and the tribe's place in the scheme of things. And as with any story that is told more than once, the myths acquired accretions and additions as more and more people embroidered them into complex retellings, so that while myth remained the province of the tribal shaman, the story was for everyone. Later this changed—the sacred text was written down and interpreted by priestly specialists who forbade anyone to alter or meddle with it. Many of the central sacred stories of our people have been debased, becoming legend, folktale, and, finally, nursery entertainment. No one doubts the power of the written word, but at one time the spoken word was stronger.

Ray Bradbury's famous science-fiction novel *Fahrenheit 451* (53) tells of a time in the future when books are forbidden because they stimulate the emotions and give an entirely different view of the world from that accepted by the administration. In Bradbury's story each person in a group of individuals takes it upon him- or herself to learn and remember an entire book, word for word, so that its story will not be lost. In this way each of them becomes a living book. The novel's premise may seem farfetched, yet this is exactly what the ancient storytellers did—they learned by heart a story that often lasted for several weeks in the telling, making it an important element of tribal events. This tradition continued in Ireland and the west of Scotland until recently, when the demand for such long stories was met by radio and television. A particularly sad fate for the storyteller became the lack of an audience, as Alwyn and Brinley Rees tell in their book *Celtic Heritage:*

> There came a time when it was but rarely that he had an opportunity himself of practising his art in public. So, lest he should lose command over the tales he loved, he used to repeat them aloud . . . using the gesticulations and the emphasis, and all the other tricks of narration, as if he were once again the centre of fireside storytelling. . . . On returning from market, as he walked slowly up the hills behind his old grey mare, he could be heard declaiming his tales to the back of the cart. (502)

This almost extinct tradition stemmed from the highly organized repertoire of the professional poet, whose duty was to learn up to one hundred fifty stories in the course of his training. These were classified by category—destructions, cattle raids, abductions, conceptions, visions, voyages, invasions, and so on—according to their suitability for recitation at certain events. Each story was told at an event in keeping with it and in this way its details and elements communicated themselves to the hearer. The story "The Wooing of Emer by Cuchulainn," for example, would be recited at a wedding or betrothal. The traditional blessing, curse, or abjuration of each tale that often went with its telling followed many tales into medieval literature, where the reader was warned against altering a word of the story or shortening it, and where a blessing was included to "one who hears these words and keeps them."

The words of the story are therefore words of power and must not be tampered with by the unskilled. Hence the familiar opening of many stories: "This story is a true story and I had it from X who had it from Y.

Whoever doesn't believe me had better leave this company than hear the story unbelieving." This level of power has remained in the scriptures and sacred writings of all people. Even today among Muslims, a strip of paper with a *surah* from the Koran, when used to bind a wound, is considered essential to hasten healing. The Guru Granth Sahib, the sacred book of the Sikhs, is treated as a living being and consulted accordingly, while Hindus still go to a priest in time of trouble to have some verses of the sacred writings read over them.

Today, we in the West accord stories little of this respect. The word *fiction,* when applied to a story, has come to mean it has no factual truth. Yet the lives of many are held in thrall today by the power of the soap opera, itself an immensely long story that lasts many days in the telling. When a character in a soap opera is about to marry or is killed, the audience feels delight or pain in proportion to the amount of identification shared with that character.

The story, then, still has power when it is heard, read, or enacted. The hearer may add a dimension to his or her life and character, subtly altering both according to those of the hero or heroine. And even today hearers are nurtured by stories that fill leisure hours as they once filled the long, cold, dark nights of winter, when the storyteller was a welcomed guest who was treated like royalty and given the best the household could supply, or when the old ones with long memories were called upon to tell again the stories of long ago. As Ruth Sawyer writes:

> One of the ancient wise ones of the tribe comes to take his place. Around his neck hangs the string of bear's teeth, numbering the tales he knows. He may carry his own drum or an apprentice may carry it, one who is learning the tribal tales and the act of telling them. The drum sets the rhythm for the chanting; it marks the pauses; it beats gloriously for the ending. (520)

Stories come in many shapes and colors. The literary or "high" style is embodied in the poetic lamentations of Deirdrui in Alba, the intricate descriptions of Helen of Troy in Homer, the entrelacement or weaving together of story themes much used by medieval romancers, or the multifaceted narrative of Lawrence Durrell's *Alexandria Quartet* (139). Other types are the family saga, from the *Nibelungenlied* (449) to *The Forsyte Saga;* the adventure story, whether it tells of the voyage of Bran or of the latest journey of Tim Severin; and tales of war, from the *Táin Bó Cúalnge* (588) to those of Desert Storm—all returning again and again to the same themes. There truly are only a handful of stories, and all are variations of the folktale, with its common experiences of life.

The strength of the story may well be discounted among the ranks of the wise and powerful, but its staying power will outlast them. Rulers may try to bend stories to the uses of propaganda, but the results don't last long, or they may try to ban them, but stories have a way of creeping back in, however subversively.

Stories do not die; they only change to suit the times and current folk legends. But we must be aware that those tales that are our heritage, those that have been orally transmitted for so long, may, in their original form, pass from memory. They are easily overlooked or undervalued in an age during which everything is written and stored in a computer. But they, like the Otherworld, possess a kind of endlessly unfolding and timeless reality in which the archetypes of the kind investigated by Jung (280) and Rank (500) range freely. Mythographers such as "A. E." (515), W. B. Yeats (659), George Macdonald (345), J. R. R. Tolkien (596), C. S. Lewis (328), and Philip Pullman (493) have all written from a deep understanding of this archetypal reality—hence the phenomenon of their popularity. Though some dislike such literature, the degree of their reaction depends upon the degree of their awareness of the reality from which such stories draw.

Beneath this is a very fundamental problem. Eliot (142) said, "Mankind cannot bear too much reality," while both Lewis (326) and Tolkien (597) wrote warnings of the way in which our very humanity is undermined by those who insist that to believe in anything that cannot be seen, felt, or heard is childish and demeaning. It should be said that those who bury themselves in one-dimensional reality—whether in their daily living or artistic appreciation—and who cannot bear the richer reality of their inner lives are least fit to follow the Western Way, though paradoxically they are in the greatest need of doing so. As one of the best writers of contemporary fantasy literature, Richard Monaco (423), commented:

> Some of us confuse fantasy with escape from reality. . . . Escape? But to where? Into your own mind and images, in the end. And you'll have to deal with the facts and fears, agonies, frustrations

and hopes . . . the quest that leads towards inner freedom and an intensity that brings more joy and real passion than you'll ever find in any literature of daydreams.

In entering the inner realms, we are not running away or hiding from the outer world, but rather are seeking to deepen and enrich our awareness of a multidimensional universe. Fantasy opens our lives. It is a laboratory where the alchemical possibilities are first tested and tasted. It is the magical waking of our lives. This is our quest: the search for the reality behind the gods and beings of the Otherworld. Whether you come to them through the myths of Greece or the adventures of the Native American hero Coyote or through the legends of Arthur or the strange, wild myths of the Celts, or become attuned through the modern myth-based techniques of psychosynthesis (20) or the dream workshops of Progoff, Whitmont (645), or Spiegelman (558), you will find yourself led inevitably to the realm of the Otherworld and to the figures of the gods who rule it. There are as many entrances as there are stars in the heavens—indeed, some of those stars are themselves entrances (see chapter 4).

The Way of Story is one entrance only, but an immeasurably valuable one, for through it you may have your first encounter with the landscape and characters that you will meet with again and again on your quest. Someday you may even encounter the lords of story themselves, to whom tradition gives the origin and shaping of all stories, myths, and tales told in the light of the campfire or found in the pages of an ancient book or some new saga of sword and sorcery. These lords control the destiny of the creative artist and are the guardians of experience and the shapers of beginnings and endings. To meet them is to encounter fear and joy in almost the same breath and in equal measure—not unlike the feeling of taking the first step beyond the boundaries of the "real" world into that timeless place where all adventures and quests begin and end, but where, paradoxically, there are no beginnings or endings at all, only a timeless flux in which all shapes and forms have their origin and where the Mysteries of creation itself are kept. Irish mystic and visionary "A. E." wrote of the moment "[w]hen inner and outer first mingle" as "the bridal night of the soul and body":

A germ is dropped from which inevitably evolves the character and the psyche. It is a seed as truly as if it were dropped into earth or womb. Only what is born from it is a spirit thing, and it grows up and takes its abode in the body with its other inhabitants, earth-born or heaven-born. (514)

These experiences are far from the start of the quest. Perhaps you have known them already without recognizing them; perhaps you never will. But you may be sure the search will be endlessly challenging and that though you grow weary in its pursuit, you will never really want to give it up once you have begun.

PRACTICE

❖ 6. Meeting the Gods ❖

In this practice you will establish a rapport with an otherworldly figure, either a god or a hero. Begin with a figure for whom you feel sympathy. It need not be one of those listed earlier in this chapter; for instance, it may just as easily be a saint.

Method

Regardless of whom you choose for this practice, you should begin by reading as much about him or her as possible. Become familiar with his story and, if you can, any sites especially associated with him. If there are none, try to think of the kind of place you would expect to find your chosen being: by a river or lake, on a mountain or hillside, in woodland or on cliffs overlooking the sea. But always remember that he or she can be anywhere—in your own front room as well as in a wild and desolate place in the open.

Go to that place in your meditations, accompanied by your clan totem, and call for your chosen figure to appear. It may be necessary to go there quite often to begin with, until you get the feel of the terrain. Do not be surprised or disappointed if nothing much happens at first; these things take time. Before you begin you may wish to evoke your chosen figure by creating a chant containing the name and nature of this god form, repeating it silently or aloud as circumstances permit, or you might choose to read some familiar passage, such as a poem you have written or enjoyed, which has her or him as its subject.

After a time you will begin to receive "flashes" of insight about the otherworldly character you've chosen, who may take shape and even begin to speak to you. Don't worry if his or her features are unclear. Concentrate on recognizing and remembering the feeling or quality that accompanies your god form's appearance. This is a call sign, and even if you can't visualize it very well, you will know it as surely as you can identify a piece of familiar music or the fragrance of a piece of fruit. Use all your senses when appreciating information in your meditations. It might not all be visual: What voice does the god form have? How does she dress, what does he carry? How do you feel when you meet him? Physical signs of response in your own body are as important as any other realizations and always denote a true meeting. Thus, if you are struggling with concerns that you perhaps imagined the figure you see or sense, turn your attention to your response to its presence.

Discovery

Because there is always an exchange between everyday reality and otherworldly reality, some of what you perceive in your chosen god form will have been supplied from your cultural and symbolic background and some of it will be coming from the Otherworld. Don't analyze where all of it is coming from, but merely observe and note. You will find that after a time, you've established a consistent rapport with your chosen subject and you will be guided farther into the realm of which you are a part. This can be one of the most rewarding experiences open to us today, and in fact correlates exactly to our ancestors' perception. It means that you have established a bridge or gateway between the worlds that will always be open to you.

It is also possible to meditate at a site associated with the figure, but this can be very difficult in a world where a pilgrimage to a sacred site is a major tourist activity. You will seldom have such places to yourself and may have to be content with merely visiting and, once home, meditating your way back to the site in a spirit journey. This can make for a powerful meditation, however. If you do wish to attempt meditating at a sacred site, your best chance of being alone is either very early or late in the day. Of course, this necessitates being aware of your own vulnerability: If you go to a remote location, go with a friend, and always be sure that people know where you are.

If you are contacting a god form at a sacred site, be aware that some powers do not wish to be disturbed and will let you know this in no uncertain terms. It is one thing to awaken a site and another to close it down again. Many ancient powers have been unrepresented for centuries. Some of these can bring remembrances that are helpful to our present time (see chapter 2), while others do not serve us now. These old powers have had their time and must be allowed to depart. In some instances their times were not good ones.

First contact with an ancient site may be very powerful. Whatever your spiritual tradition, whatever the energy you are used to mediating, invoke its protective influence if you feel threatened or that something is out of balance. It often happens that after initial contact and awakening at such a site, a huge rush of primeval energy is released. You should concentrate on the harmless dispersal of this energy into the atmosphere. Those who visit ancient sites often remark that the stones are lonely or that the earth feels hungry, subjectively perceiving the kind of rites once performed there. The sadness of some sites is due to the loneliness or isolation of an important energy that will be willing to cooperate with the initiate who is able to mediate it objectively. This mediation will often be felt in small, insignificant ways throughout the months after your visit. Careful meditation upon the place, its spirit, or its god form will allow you to determine its usefulness for our time.

Finally, always remember to thank your contact before you leave, and make clear your intention to return to your everyday consciousness. This can easily be done through some carefully chosen words. Never just step out of your meditation without formally closing it—you may find that you have left open a bridge or gateway that may be disturbing to others and that may make it difficult for you to distinguish one side of reality from the other.

If you have any impression that you have made an unhealthy or obsessive contact, act swiftly. You can ritually sever contact with your god form and return its energy to the earth by stating aloud your intention to be neither amenable to it nor cooperative with it. Or you can take a cleansing bath of saltwater and make contact with the most protective god form or energy you are used to working with, asking her for assistance. You can also firmly, compassionately, and with emotional objectivity ask the troublesome contact to leave you. Imagine your breath to be a circle of light that surrounds you: When you breathe in, you draw in the blue light of your protective god form; when you breathe out, imagine the contact and any other negative energy leaving your system, beyond your blue circle of light.

With these precautions in mind, you may pursue a rewarding relationship that will teach you a great deal and help you in your quest for further knowledge of the Western Mysteries. Remember that in contacting the gods, you are also contacting the energy they represent, the reality beyond the outer god form. You must work with and assimilate this reality before you can reach a full understanding of the gods. Once you have made direct contact with a ruler of the sea, sky, or earth, these elements that surround us but which are often seen as separate from our daily existence will from that time forward seem like an essential part of experience. To know them is to be initiated, in both an ineffably simple and a hugely complex way, into the Mysteries of life itself.

4

Voyages to the Otherworld

Smooth the descent and easy is the way
(The Gates of Hell stand open night and day);
But to return and view the cheerful skies,
In this the task and mighty labour lies.
—AENEID VI, 126–29, TRANSLATED BY JOHN DRYDEN

How beautiful they are,
The lordly ones
Who dwell in the hills,
In the hollow hills.
—FIONA MACLEOD, THE IMMORTAL HOUR, ACT 1, SCENE 3

The Ancestral Paradise

*A*ll along we have been speaking of the Otherworld—but what is the Otherworld? Our perceptions readily inform us about the physical reality of our world, but they are less capable of telling us much about the reality of the Otherworld. In actuality, there is only one reality, but it has two sides: our everyday realm of appearances that we apprehend with our senses and the Otherworld, which, though our ordinary senses cannot apprehend it, is just as real as our own world. Together they form one sacred continuum of life. In our everyday arena we move and exist in our physical bodies; when we enter the Otherworld, we exist in our spiritual bodies. Most important, every one of us bridges these two sides of reality, even if only in our dreams.

The phenomenon that we call synchronicity, characterized by events that seem to spontaneously occur in accord with each other, is actually an instance of an exact match between the fabric of our world and that of the Otherworld. While we normally dismiss such an occurrence as coincidental, in looking more deeply we can see the exact correspondences between one world and the other. Unfortunately, over time we have lost or neglected the ability to look more deeply, to comprehend these worlds as two sides of one reality, although the shamans of the Foretime as well as many artists, mystics, and visionaries have always bridged the worlds and affirmed this living truth. Each generation has found its own metaphor to describe the existence of the Otherworld: Ancestral place of the dead, earthly paradise, heaven, happy hunting ground, Hell, the land of faery, the astral plane, heightened consciousness, and the collective unconscious—all these terms describe the Otherworld, which has been perceived in many cultures as a place, a condition, or an after-life abode.

Because our culture has dismissed otherworldly conditions and states of consciousness, there is no common language to discuss them except the jargon arising from psychological conceptualization. Rather than using this here, we can instead define three distinct "places," or states, within the Otherworld:

1. Middle Earth, or the unseen side of our own everyday reality
2. The Underworld, or the ancestral realm of power
3. The Upperworld, or the inspirational realm of gods and spirits

These rough distinctions will help us understand the overlapping, multilayered regions where dwell ancestors, angels, gods, spirits, faeries, and legendary beasts.

In the Foretime the most potent region of the Otherworld was the realm of the ancestors, the Underworld. This chapter begins with the famous warning of the Cumaean Sybil to Aeneas as he attempts to journey into Hades to consult with his dead father in Virgil's *Aeneid*: The descent is easy, but the return is much more difficult (264). A shaman trained long years to make this very same journey to the ancestors in order to return with their advice for the benefit of the tribe. The significant features of this journey were depicted on the shaman's drum, which, like the Aborigines' tjuringa mentioned in chapter 2, was a map charting the landmarks and helpful spirits of the Otherworld. In many Western lands the Underworld was believed to have an entry bordering on Middle Earth. This might have been the mouth of a cave or a semi-dormant volcanic fissure such as the one Aeneas descends into at Lake Avernus, the birdless entrance to the classical Hades.

Given that even long ago in many Western cultures the dead were buried in the ground, it was natural for people to assume that the deceased took up residence beneath it in the Underworld. Most native cultures have their own Underworld tradition: In Norse mythology, Niflheim and Hel are two parts of a compartmentalized Underworld—and the latter part gives its name to that fearsomely potent netherworld of Christian tradition. Canaanite and Sumerian mythologies share the view of a miserable, dreary Hades full of twittering ghosts. The Welsh Underworld, Annfwn, is a chthonic, powerful place full of mighty ancestors.

The idea of the Underworld as a place of judgment for an evil life was foreign to those of the Foretime. It was merely the place to which all the dead went, unless the infringement of some tribal law condemned the deceased to wander as a lonely ghost, outlawed from the tribe even beyond death.

The powerful and effective interaction of the Underworld with Middle Earth has been persuasively argued by the writer and musician R. J. Stewart in his book *The Underworld Initiation* (575). In it he explores the Underworld tradition of Britain, and by offering a simple entry meditation, he has opened the way significantly (570) so that we may connect with our ancestors in a manner not experienced since the Foretime. The Underworld is the foundation of the Otherworld reality and the deepest stratum of native consciousness, where we meet with the most uncompromising inhabitants. Stewart prefers not to call these beings archetypes, which implies a set of psychological personae. Like the gods (see chapter 3), the Otherworld's inhabitants are real in their own world and in their own right, not the result of our imaginative state.

Otherworldly cosmology is dependent upon those who perceive and experience it. We rely on travelers' tales, the shaman's report of his or her journey. We remember that "people listened to the poets and heard the versions of those who were thought to have penetrated the veil." (264) In classical Greece, accounts of Underworld descents virtually made up a genre of their own: the *katabaseis* (264). Indeed, such accounts are present in every tradition—and the reason for visiting the

Underworld is always deeper than mere curiosity. Aeneas descends for information—Ishtar, the Babylonian goddess, like her earlier prototype, the Sumerian Inanna, descends to the Underworld to release her beloved from the realms of the dead and there undergoes herself a ritual stripping and death. Ishtar's experience is like that of the Norse Odin, who hangs nine days and nights on the ash tree, Yggdrasil, as an offering to himself:

> *Myself given to myself*
> *On that tree*
> *Whose roots*
> *No one knows . . .*
> *Into the depths I peered,*
> *I grasped the runes,*
> *Screaming I grasped them,*
> *And then fell back.* (109)

This is the experience of the shaman and it is at the heart of the Mysteries: a costly self-discovery that brings knowledge and power by means of initiation in the Otherworld. The World Tree Yggdrasil runs through each of the three levels of the Otherworld: Middle Earth, Hel, and Asgard, the place of the gods (109). During his ordeal, Odin successfully learns eighteen runes in all, giving him knowledge from each of the three levels but especially from the realm of the dead.

The Otherworld can be understood readily if, as in the Norse myths, we use the metaphor of a central tree as the axis around which otherworldly regions are situated. Its roots penetrate the nourishing soil of the earth, extending deep into the Underworld. Its trunk rises, proud and strong, through Middle Earth. Its branches ascend into the heights of the Upperworld, where its fruits ripen. The tree appears in many of the practices in this book and is a vital image for both the native and Hermetic traditions (107). It is the tree of life, death, and rebirth; the shaman's pole or ladder (222); and the kabbalist's ladder of light (198). For Christians, the Tree of Knowledge in Eden and the Tree of the Cross are of made of one wood.

A clear parallel among Odin, Ishtar, and Christ is easy to perceive: Each suffers death and transformation upon a tree, gaining knowledge of the dead or release for the dead by this means. The passport for a visitor to the Underworld is desire for another's good fortune: Love kills death. Both Gilgamesh and Orpheus journey to the Otherworld, the former to release his friend and the latter his wife. At great cost to himself, Quetzalcoatl returns from the Underworld with the bones of previous generations in order to create a new race (323, 76). In apocryphal tradition (consistent with native Underworld traditions throughout the Western world), Christ harrows Hell (13). But there can be a heavy toll for visiting the Underworld, as old Vainamoinen, the Finnish hero, discovers. He visits the dead in order to learn charms that will magically finish the boat he is building. He offers nothing about his visit but warns:

> Do not, future people,
> Do not, former people,
> set out to get charms from Death's Domain.
> . . . many have gone there, not many come back.
> . . . from the eternal cottage of the Abode of the Dead. (286)

The gods and heroes who visit the Underworld to redeem or release the dead may be seen as forerunners of the later saviors of revealed religion, but we must remember that each of these figures embodies tribal responsibility at every level of history and consciousness: Each fulfills a task outside of time that is vital for every people in every age.

Despite Vainamoinen's warning, it is important to note that traditionally the place of the ancestors is not seen in a fearful light. For the Jews, to die is to be gathered to Abraham's bosom. The native translation of this can be found in Mistress Quickly's account of the death of Falstaff, who, she says, seeks "Arthur's bosom." What's more, the ancestral abode of the dead is only one of the many regions comprising the Underworld. In fact, sleep is the first hint of otherworldly travel, while death is the final proof of that journey. Both, however, are journeys undertaken without control or volition, unlike those of the trained shaman, who travels with motivation and intention.

In the Foretime, heavenly and paradisal places were not conceived of as somewhere in the sky; they were firmly situated in the earthly sphere, in the place beyond the sunset, ever westward, where the light is always that of twilight. The way to the Otherworld is often found by means of water, especially in the Celtic tradition, in which it is possible to sail to Hy Brasil, Avalon, Annfwn, or the Blessed Isles (373). But sometimes the Otherworld lies nearby in the Hollow Hills, in the Summerland, in Faeryland—regions not so distant that it would be impossible to travel to them (19, 430). We know from folktales and mythological texts that the Celtic Otherworld tradition is particularly rich, and it is significant that the Greeks referred to the British Isles as Hyperborea—the Land Beyond the North Wind, where the Titans still lived in exile. The Greek poet Pindar spoke of these islands in connection with the initiate's journey:

> *All who have endured three times*
> *In a sojourn in either world,*
> *To keep their souls utterly clean of wrong,*
> *Go by God's road to the Tower of Kronos,*
> *Where the Airs, daughters of Ocean,*
> *Blow round the Island of the Blest.* (476)

Plutarch described the Fortunate Islands:

> *Rain seldom falls there . . . they generally have soft breezes*
> *the air is always pleasant and salubrious. . . .* (416)

And this place was enshrined forever by Tennyson in *Idylls of the King,* in which Arthur speaks these words:

> *. . . I am going a long way . . .*
> *To the island-valley of Avilion;*
> *Where falls not hail, or rain, or any snow,*
> *Nor ever wind blows loudly.* (592)

The Otherworld is a place not only where the dead go, but also where heroic mortals still live in the fullness of their powers. It is the place of traditional learning and wisdom, where springs the well of inspiration. The Celtic Otherworld has no exact geographical location; however, it is thought of as lying somewhere in the western Atlantic. But neither this nor the strong Atlantean tradition, which has exercised its fascination since the time of Plato, need imply a physical island from some historical era. It can point instead to otherworldly remembrances that have slipped from psychic understanding to earthly understanding (157, 311). Atlantis, like Eden, was a place where inspirational knowledge was always available. The myth of Atlantis, like that of the Fall of Man, is concerned far more with the end of communion with the

Otherworld than with the consequences of sinfulness. The realization that it is our essential birthright to contact this Otherworld has been the impetus for meditational exploration in every time and place, among every people. Alongside official pronouncements about heaven and hell, the Everliving Realms have always flourished within the native tradition. And if the "official" way to heaven is often shown as cold and legalistic, the native tradition has always preferred its own familiar ways to ancestral places.

Paradise and heaven, however, are not one and the same place. *Paradise* has its roots in the Persian *paerodaeza,* meaning "park" or "enclosed garden," and is a perfectly appropriate synonym for the Otherworld—an intermediate state between incarnation and bliss. The enclosed garden or island paradise is a primal state, an interior reality in which every vital component of life is in potentiality. It still has its first wildness, yet it also has its own grace and rules of governance. There is no human trickery or deception there—nor will such debased currency serve in our transactions with the Otherworld. It is a waiting place, a place of learning and nourishment.

The happy Otherworld is an earthly paradise in many legends, a place where feasting and love continue harmoniously. The Celtic Otherworld tradition is distinguished by the fact that it has no hell nor anything parallel to the classical Hades, with its gray emptiness. Although the Underworld is present in good measure, represented by the Hollow Hills, the Celtic Otherworld retains its ambience of joy. It is aptly described as the Fortunate Island, the Honeyed Plain of Bliss, the Apple Island, and the Summer Country—all set somewhere west of the sunset in the mighty ocean.

Travel to these Otherworld islands was such a noticeable feature of Celtic life that the poets coined a special genre of stories about them called *immrama,* or "voyages." The most famous of these was *The Voyage of Bran, Son of Febal* (416), which describes the travels of Bran and his companions to the Land of the Living, their arrival at an otherworldly island, and their sojourn in the Land of Women. It tells how, after a short time, one of their number becomes homesick and they prepare to go home. As they reach the shores of their land, they are hailed and asked to identify themselves: " 'I am Bran, the son of Febal,' saith he. However the other saith: 'We do not know such a one, though the Voyage of Bran is in our ancient stories.' " (416)

One of Bran's men who leaps ashore turns to dust as he once again becomes subject to the laws of time, leaving Bran and his companions to sail away. Similarly, in Keats's "La Belle Dame Sans Merci," the traveler who seeks to return from Faeryland wakes from too long a sleep "on the cold hill's side."

The greatest question we may ask is, Why did we cease such voyaging? The Otherworld did not go away, though conceptions of it narrowed or accommodated themselves to Christian cosmological patterns. We could say that the sense of the Otherworld as it was known in the Foretime went underground, sometimes fusing with the ancestral Underworld, sometimes withdrawing, as it did in Scotland and Ireland, into the Hollow Hills, where its inhabitants continued interacting on the level of the folk soul, never quite disappearing from consciousness. Voyaging and walking between the worlds continued—but secretly, to avoid persecution. The spiritual energies that had been venerated in the Foretime and which had engodded streams and hills now put on ragged clothing as disguise—but in the Otherworld they were revealed: They were the Shining Ones whose power was still respected, whose help was still sought by those who knew them. The Otherworld might shrink to the appearance of a grassy mound, and its inhabitants to rustic elementals, but the reality of Faeryland is more virile than anything envisioned by those who looked hopefully for diminutive fairies at the bottom of their garden (301). When the gods of Faeryland speak of themselves, a different picture emerges:

We are from the beginning of creation
Without old age, without consummation of earth . . .

So says Manannan mac Lir, the otherworldly king in *The Voyage of Bran* (387), speaking about the inhabitants of the Land of the Living. It is to these Shining Ones that we turn next.

The Shining Ones

I have always made a distinction between pictures seen in the memory of nature and visions of actual beings now existing in the inner world. We can make the same distinction in our world: I may close my eyes and see you as a vivid picture in memory, or I may look at you with my physical eyes and see your actual image. In seeing these beings of which I speak, the physical eyes may be open

or closed: mystical beings in their own world and nature are never
seen with the physical eyes. (642)

So speaks an anonymous Irish seer, interviewed in the early part of
the twentieth century by W. Y. Evans Wentz for his book *Fairy-faith in
Celtic Countries*. He describes perfectly the method by which
Otherworld beings are perceived. Although there is a definite interaction
or communion among those of the otherworldly realms, to "see" them
we use an inner state of perception rather than the five physical senses.
This should not imply, however, that otherworldly beings—the Shining
Ones—are unreal. As the seer says, they belong "in their own world and
nature." But what are they? There have been many theories: a folk memory of a small, native people; a remembrance of a mighty priesthood; a
remnant of forgotten gods, immortal heroes, or the ancestors.

As we have already seen, the ancestors play a great part in
Underworld belief and, like the gods, they are a force to be reckoned
with. More recent psychological theory, particularly Jung's theory of
the collective unconscious, has suggested that the Shining Ones are
nothing more than archetypes—collective, formalized energies that
inhabit our psyches. Every generation finds its own metaphor for a condition that is understandably difficult to express in human terms. We
leave it to you to find your own means of understanding, as long as it
allows for archetypes to inhabit the Otherworld as well as the psyche
and acknowledges that the Shining Ones are real in their own world
and not the inventions of a disturbed mind or a rich imagination.

We have suggested in chapter 1 that deity is formalized by a gradual building of image that grows in power and effect in relation to the
visualization of the group soul. Similarly, in our discussion of the god
forms of the native tradition, we saw the importance of the latent
power of the elements, which crystallized into signs and symbols of the
gods. Deity or pure spirit has no form; but in order for it to have any
communication with humankind, it must assume an acceptable form or
symbol. There is no way any of us can escape the language of symbolism lying, sometimes deeply hidden, within our cultural and genetic
memory. In the Foretime the world was visited and guarded by homely,
familiar spirits whose manifestations came in numerous forms and
varying gradations of intensity.

The Shining Ones range in nature and kind from the primal elemental forces of air, fire, water, and earth to distinct spirits that we

know as gods, with many variations—angels or tutelary spirits—in between. Some native Otherworld traditions have lost access to the full range of the Shining Ones through a shifting religious focus. The beings of the elemental forces are usually the first to suffer, being regarded as less "evolved." It is a truism—and one to be remembered—that the gods of an outgoing religion become the devils of the incoming one. The gods of the native tradition have suffered demonization as "unauthorized" entities.

For example, during medieval times the potent god of the hunt was associated with God's opponent, the devil, although the magnificent antlers of Cernunnos were derived from a totally different symbolic basis than those of Satan. Horns, once synonymous with power, became associated with evil (103). The divinities of the old pagan religions still took the shapes that drew upon European cultural memory— the gods and goddesses of the old forest, divinities with animal as well as human attributes. Horns were emblems of animal strength and supremacy. Shamans and their tribes survived in difficult times by aligning themselves with the cunning instincts of animals. We know that from earliest times, people have created horn headdresses for dances and ceremonies. From the Stone Age antlered headdress found in Starr Carr Cave in Yorkshire and the depiction of a man with antlers on his head in the cave painting of Les Trois Frères in southern France to the reindeer horns still carried by the Abbot's Bromley horn dancers in Staffordshire, this element of ritual homage is clearly seen. Using animal disguises, especially around midwinter, was common throughout Europe—and was forbidden by the Church because of its association with ancient pagan religion. Those who practiced such rites were thought to be in league with the devil. Eventually, native horned divinities were identified with the Christian understanding of the devil, and by the late Middle Ages, the word *devil* summoned up an image of a native horned god who possessed all the death-dealing and corrupting power of the Christian Satan.

Similarly, the female spirits of wells and springs, conceived of originally as beautiful women, became dragons, water serpents, and sirens. The guardians of the wood became malevolent ogres and the dragon, which had symbolized potent earth forces, became a representative of fire-breathing evil (see chapter 2). Whenever people neglect their dependence upon nature, this downgrading of symbolism occurs. As we lose our respect for such symbols, the elements become untamed; their relationship to human life becomes diminished to that of servant. During the Industrial Revolution, the mechanized instruments of slaughter and harvest completed the degradation of the Shepherd of Flocks, John Barleycorn, and the ancient gods of vegetation and the harvest. It is no wonder people believed that field and forest were haunted by neglected elementals and that wanderers were prey to ghosts that could not find their ancestral abode.

We find that some gods have made more successful translations to the modern world than others because their aspects and symbolism remain vital to our time. But what becomes of those god forms that remain dormant? Do their energies merely await renewed human attention? Whether sleeping or active, the energies of god forms are always available to those who familiarize themselves with their call signs and symbolism—and the Otherworld journey can help us contact the primordial current behind all god forms.

Travelers to and from the Otherworld

If the gods choose to manifest themselves to you, remember to maintain respect for yourself as well as them. Do not allow their energies to overwhelm you. When one side of reality is superimposed upon another, the traveler can become as bemused as Saint Peter was at the Transfiguration (Matthew 17: 1–13). He was taken by Christ, an incarnate god, up Mount Tabor, where they were visited by Elijah and Moses, two otherworldly beings. No wonder he was all for setting up camp for the four of them! Encountering varying levels of consciousness or different world realities can be confusing. As we have already said, the uncharted realms of the Otherworld demand a good guide or inside contact to facilitate such encounters.

The nature of your guide on your Otherworld journey will depend upon your own native tradition. Whether we call him or her an angel, spirit, guardian, or daimon, we each have access to a personal guide. Suggestions on how to contact yours appear in practice 7, Contacting the Guardian, at the end of this chapter.

We do not all aspire to become shamans, magicians, or mystics; most of us seek to fulfill our vocation through our work, home, and family. Even though there are many paths to spiritual growth, not all are suitable or practical for each person. A personal experience of the Otherworld and its inhabitants can promote spiritual growth, making us aware that we belong to the sacred continuum and giving us a sense of our spiritual family. The inner guardian is the initiator for each of us—and it need not be a monumental spiritual figure. The link for you may be someone familiar to whom you have never given a face, perhaps an inner voice or secret companion. The inner guardian is our true north, the keeper of the charts, the one who shows the way. He or she is one who has already traveled the paths we are walking for the first time and thus has a wealth of wisdom for us to draw upon.

Many ancient traditions believed that after death and a suitable number of incarnations, we progressed to the angelic condition in order to become teachers in the psychic world. Plato's *Cratylus* tells us that "poets say truly that when a good man dies he has honour and a mighty portion among the dead, and becomes a daimon, which is a name given to him signifying wisdom."(478) The word *daimon* means "he who apportions" (264)—the guardian who allots experience to each of us. But does this imply that otherworldly inhabitants have already plotted our course—that we are not free agents?

The Otherworld includes the Upperworld, from which emanates the blueprint of creation. Each individual has a destiny to fulfill, a task or spiritual purpose that is our part in the work of creation. The guardians—like the angelic hierarchies in part 2 of this book—are those who promote our creative potential, feeding us with the life experience we need to be effective human beings. But this potential is not a fixed destiny. We are free to make our own way, to neglect this potential or to achieve it. The guardian acts as an ambassador of the Otherworld in this process. His or her task is the otherworldly counterpart of the shaman's journey: to explore Middle Earth and consult with inhabitants of this world.

Contact with the Otherworld changes our lives forever, enriching us spiritually and affecting the whole sacred continuum. But before we go on to discuss how we can travel there, it is helpful to be aware of some otherworldly visitors to Middle Earth and the methods some inhabitants of our world have used to travel to otherworldly realms.

Often a special symbol or token has served as a passport to the Otherworld: Aeneas plucks the golden bough, which he must present to Proserpine in the Underworld. Similarly, Bran, son of Febal, uses the gift of a musical silver branch. Both of these are scions of the axial tree of life from which the Otherworld extends. In Irish poetic tradition the gold or silver branch was actually an item of shamanic regalia borne before a poet of high status, signifying his connection with otherworldly wisdom and teaching.

In some native traditions, a special vessel serves to ferry earthly visitors to the Otherworld. The glass boat that is frequently featured in Celtic Otherworld travel also makes an appearance in the story of an Algonquin brave whose wife dies. Like Orpheus, he determines to find her. An elder tells him, "To reach the Island of the Blessed, you must cross yonder gulf you see in the distance." (556) He finds himself in a glass canoe and his wife in another and both of them row toward a wooded isle set in the middle of the water like an emerald set in silver.

While Bran's musical branch serves to gain him entrance to the Otherworld, music also often figures in the arrival of otherworldly visitors to our world. The faery folk—potent Otherworld beings who bear no resemblance to the romantic vision of tiny fairies with butterfly wings (570)—are said to teach their mysterious faery music to those musicians who sit patiently near their dwellings in the Hollow Hills, and in British faery lore otherworldly tunes are often heard before the arrival of the faery host.

Otherworldly visitors not only play music; they also dance. In the Algonquin story of Algon the hunter, the hero finds a circular pathway on the prairie that seems to have been worn by many feet, although no footprints can be found outside this area. Then, hearing music that slowly becomes louder, he hides himself in the long grass. From there he witnesses a host of star-maidens in an osier chariot, all descending from the sky. The maidens alight and dance, and he captures one to be his bride (556).

Sometimes a journey to the Otherworld is not followed by a return to our world. In one of the Scottish border ballads, "True Thomas," or "Thomas of Erceldoune," Thomas the Rhymer meets with the queen of Elfland, the visitor and guide who conducts him to the Otherworld, pointing out the landmarks along the way. He is rewarded for being an apt apprentice to the queen:

> He has gotten a coat of the elven cloth,
> And a pair of shoes of velvet green,
> And 'til seven years were past and gone
> True Thomas on earth was never seen. (93)

But Thomas is not the only Scot to have vanished. Michael Scott, the thirteenth-century scholar, also vanished after a life of seemingly fabulous length and achievement. His posthumous reputation as a magician was so widespread that he entered the folk imagination as a type of Merlin. Likewise, a seventeenth-century clergyman, Robert Kirk, who documented the experience of seers and the faery lore of the Scottish Gaelic-speaking people, never returned from an expedition to Faeryland; although his gravestone is exhibited at Aberfoyle, there is nothing under it (301). These two were, of course, Master Men—those who had contacts with otherworldly beings and who were seasoned travelers to other realities. They were the inheritors of the shamanic tradition from the long-ago Foretime. But who are we to say that these men have disappeared? Years in our world are but days in the Otherworld. Perhaps their visits to that reality are not yet over or, like Elijah and Enoch, they have not tasted death but have instead taken the role of otherworldly helpers.

Stories of visitors to our world from the Otherworld include the legend of the Green Children: Two children with green skin were found wandering in the vicinity of a cave during the reign of King Stephen. Because he would eat nothing but green vegetable food, the boy died, but the girl learned to eat ordinary food and lived. She said that the land of their origin was a place where the sun never shone; the light was like that of twilight or sunset (57).

Sometimes, like Algon, the Algonquin hunter, humans take otherworldly visitors as lovers. The ghostly or demon lover is a theme that runs throughout world folklore. The *dybbuk* of eastern European Jewish legend, the medieval incubus and succubus, and the sealwoman of Scottish and Scandinavian story all testify to close communication between the beings of the Otherworld and our realm. The otherworldly lover and his or her earthly partner must, however, observe certain prohibitions if the relationship is to work: The true appearance of the otherworldly being must never be revealed and the earthly lover must never speak unkindly or demand that the other eat the meat of the sacred totem animal or dress in its hide. We see again and again, however, that to mix the sexuality of the physical plane with otherworldly magical polarity is to confuse the worlds, often leading to disaster (see chapter 5). In part 2, however, we shall discover how the partnership of Otherworld and Middle Earth beings can act as a positive device of visualization and power.

Passports to Inner Realms

Now we turn to the ways in which we can travel to the Otherworld. Some may wonder why we should travel at all. Such journeys may be hard to justify to the pragmatic and self-determining realist who acknowledges no world beyond Middle Earth and no other evidence than that of each of his or her five senses. There is, however, an answer to the question "Why journey to the Otherworld?": Learning to become a traveler in otherworldly realms can connect our spiritual and hereditary yearnings and can help us to cope more effectively with our experiences in our world. As we increasingly become conscious of the Otherworld, a vital link is created between tribal and cosmic consciousness, which enables a necessary spiritual evolution and allows us to receive new and helpful forms of ancient wisdom.

As traditions meet and merge, the way stands open for you to join those who have conversed with the dead, accessed the knowledge and conversation of their holy guardian angel, or been given the means to spiritual wisdom. All of this can be accomplished through meditation, through finding your own metaphor for the Otherworld and exploring your own inscape. Because each of us has a unique background and ancestry, there are as many approaches and entrances to the Otherworld as there are individuals in our world. You already possess your key or symbol (see practice 1, Finding Your Clan Totem). Practice 8, The Two Trees, will lead you farther into the landscape of the Otherworld, where you can work on getting to know the guide you have met in practice 7, Contacting the Guardian. Your journey itself will be unique and yet similar to that of others—but comparing notes may not be helpful, for every person enters at his or her own level. There is no "right" way to travel; all of us take our own risks and experience our own adventures.

On your journey you may be convinced that you are deluding yourself. In addition, guides and gods may often turn up in confusingly modern guises. You may struggle with your manner of perception at first, but aim for a waking state of consciousness and controlled breathing. With practice you will enter the Otherworld and meet with your guide and others. You will discover your destiny, your guiding theme, and your inner impulse to act creatively, all of which you can fulfill in our world, within the context of your everyday existence. At first, the images and encounters in the Otherworld may be as elusive as dreams, but soon you will learn to record and remember them. The concentration required to make contact and hold on to it can be wearying in the beginning—you may even fall asleep. Just remember that though your experience of the Otherworld may fade between sessions, this does not mean that the Otherworld is a shadow any more than familiar but far-away friends are shadows in between your visits with them.

There will be days when Otherworld travel comes easily. But at other times it will seem that the door opens only to our world. In addition, the "location" of the door may shift, but you will always find it. As the professor in C. S. Lewis's *The Lion, the Witch and the Wardrobe* tells the children:

> I don't think it will be any good trying to go back through the wardrobe door . . . you won't get into Narnia again by that route . . . don't go trying the same route twice. Indeed, don't try to get there at all. It'll happen when you're not looking for it . . . and don't mention it to anyone else, unless you find that they've had adventures of the same sort themselves. (328)

There are different doors that children use and then lose and have to find again as adults, of course. But while some ways into the Otherworld are more suitable for you than others, once you have mapped out the approach, you do not need to go through the whole customs procedure again.

Though we have described Otherworld travel in terms of meditation, it can also occur during sleep or daydreams, initiation, vision, astral travel, loss of consciousness, and near-death states. Two famous examples of this last experience—"The Vision of Aridaeus" (411) and "The Vision of Er"—are recounted in *Plato's Republic* (479). The classical Otherworlds of Hades and Elysium are described by a man who is thought to be dead but revives and shares the story of his journey. There are also many modern examples of this kind of recollection (239).

The mantle of consciousness, with all its textures, can serve as a workaday trench coat or can become an invisible cloak, depending on our needs. In contacting our native Otherworld, we do not neglect our own world, but instead sensitize ourselves to its requirements, learning to see the earth as a living entity that depends upon the Otherworld as much as we depend upon its beings, the Shining Ones. As mystics, shamans, and philosophers have been telling us for ages, and as the new science is beginning to discover, the scale of our universal sacred continuum is vaster than we ever realized.

In order to be able to cooperate fully with the Otherworld, we must first look at ourselves. The maxim "Know thyself" is of primary importance to any of us who want to walk the Western Way—and knowing ourselves is a task that will never be finished. Yet if we don't begin the task of clearing ourselves before attempting a deep exploration of the Otherworld, we will inevitably meet with our own worst qualities. Once we are capable of recognizing and working with our own worst traits, we may explore the deeper hinterlands of the inner worlds and will begin to appreciate how we fit into the scheme of things and how the guides and spirits of the Otherworld can help us to achieve our destiny. Of course, human nature being what it is, no sooner have we cleared our psychic attics of the "junk" stored there than we start accumulating more. The Augean stables will perhaps never be entirely clear, but we can at least try to keep them to manageable proportions. Some suggestions for clearing yourself can be found in practice 9, Self-Clarification.

Ultimately, the primary importance of Otherworld travel is not just to go, but to return as well. Many have been lost in the mazes of the Otherworld. It is all too common for some to be led astray by the glamour of the spiritual and the psychic (32). Unless we are well grounded in the physical plane, make our commitment to the path of the hearth fire, and organize our lives satisfactorily before approaching esoteric paths, we could have a tendency to drift off. This is why many esoteric schools insist that candidates have reached a mature age before accepting them. Unless we first develop our character here, in our world, to be an effective human channel of communication, we will be weak and easily swayed by everything we meet in Otherworld travel.

It is as important to stand up to anything that seems contrary to your own integrity in the Otherworld as it is here. Use the street wisdom you are accustomed to relying on when you travel anywhere in everyday reality. The Otherworld is populated by all kinds of beings and some will be more helpful to you than others. There is nothing sinister about this observation—the same is true here. If you stop any number of people on the street and ask them to help you, some may and some may not, depending on their ability or disposition. The help of your otherworldly guide and the use of your own common sense will ensure that you journey safely.

If travelers to the Otherworld observe certain rules, they will meet no harm. Those who fall into Faeryland by mistake are said to be saved by their possession of salt or iron, the elements of earthly life that are not common coinage of the Otherworld. On our journey, our humanity and humor are this "salt," for the Shining Ones work on a wider scale that reaches far beyond our human viewpoint.

Keeping a sense of humility will also help us to travel safely. Responding to Otherworld beings and their communications with hubris can lead to difficulty. In faery stories, incautious women who boast of their offspring's talents or beauty—gifts of the Otherworld—lose their children to the faeries, who leave behind a loathly changeling as a lesson. Attempts to avoid hard work are met with more hard work in the Otherworld—much as the elder sisters learn who wish to share their younger sister's good fortune when she returns home from Mother Holle's house covered with gold (209). Pride, curiosity, improvidence, ingratitude, and dishonesty disqualify the traveler; but obeying the rules, observing commonsense precautions, and behaving with humility and straightforward courtesy enable you to journey far. Most often the impediments to safe traveling lie with the traveler. We can recall Aragorn's sound advice to Boromir, who distrusts the idea of going to the paradisal realm of Lothlorien in *The Lord of the Rings*. Boromir complains that "few come out who once go in; and of that few none have escaped unscathed," and Aragorn replies, "Say not unscathed, but if you say unchanged, then maybe you speak the truth. Only evil need fear it, or those who bring some evil with them." (596)

Human faults are amplified by inner work and can create obstacles. Much like the hero of a folktale, we have to face and accomplish a series of dreary tasks that act as correctives to our unprepared and untrained nature before we can achieve the hand of the princess or find the treasure. But our achievements are not solely for our own benefit. The goal of our journey to the Otherworld is not to become like Galahad, the later Grail hero who, after achieving the Grail, assumes a spiritual state in the city of Sarras and dies to the world forever. Instead, our destiny is more like that of Peredur, or Perceval, the earlier Grail hero who, after his achievement, returns to the world to become a master of Grail tradition—one who teaches others. Our goal is to travel to the Otherworld and return with its gifts (390).

The idea of the Otherworld providing mortals with gifts, like the faery godmother who bestows blessings and creative propensities upon the newborn child, is a concept that points to the Otherworld's ability to recharge Middle Earth with vital and redeeming energy. We are each gifted with certain abilities or aptitudes. While some of us perfect these abilities, becoming the creative artists who fructify the folk soul of the people, others allow their aptitudes to become stale and unmanageable from neglect. Our lives are effective only insofar as we bring through energies from the Otherworld and combine them with creative effort in this world. In each generation artists make this mystical journey into themselves and return charged with new life and purpose. This is how otherworldly teaching is disseminated—not by overt teaching, but through song and story, play and film, innocuous methods of transmission that have a sweeping influence on all levels of consciousness. It is therefore imperative that such a transmission be managed by the hands of those who know what they are doing.

Within each generation there are those who transmit their art by every means of creativity known to them, and this is how the torch passes from hand to hand. The vocation of the artist is truly a holy one. Those who fulfill it with humble awareness of the debt they owe to the Otherworld—rather than those who create art that merely reflects themselves—are the true artists of our generation.

But the call of the Otherworld is for all of us to fulfill. The sudden insights that arise without our bidding, the overwhelming urge to use our abilities to create something new, and the sense of fulfillment resulting from these urgings are clear signs of our allegiance to the common work of restoring and revitalizing the sacred continuum.

> *For the gods have hidden and keep hidden*
> *What could be men's livelihood.* (242)

And it is our duty to find out for ourselves what we can best do in Middle Earth.

Paradise Lost and Regained

Without access to the Otherworld, our world becomes a sad, dead place. Today, in the West, our common perception of the Otherworld has been repressed by the dictates of both classical and Christian fundamentalist concepts: Demons, ghosts, evil spirits, and witches are the sole inhabitants of the modern Otherworld, whose joyless, soulless face can be seen almost any night in horror films of mindless evil.

This, of course, is not the Otherworld but merely a shadowland. The way between the worlds has never been entirely closed, but obstructions block it and many no longer believe it exists. Those for whom heaven is a myth and Hell is an ever-present reality are cut off from the guiding mythology of the Otherworld. Without trust and belief in the one reality made up of our world and the Otherworld, we become prey for threadbare doctrines of despair. When we have been sealed like prisoners into one side of reality, doubt and destruction follow and we live without thought of cause and effect. When we stop praying for the dead—for those in purgatory and in the ancestral places—we begin to fear ghosts and unhoused spirits (60). When we cease listening to the voice of our inner guide, we hear the temptations of our worst side. When we cease to fulfill our spiritual aspirations, God becomes devil.

Into this vacuum of doubt and uncertainty many new, seemingly otherworldly scenarios have sprung, and many of us have grasped at these despairingly, hopefully, longingly. One new metaphor for the Otherworld in our modern age seems to consist of God as an astronaut and the possibility of interstellar, supervisory visitors to our world. While this gives solace to some, others grasp at psychological discoveries that seem to parallel shamanic experience but often remain theoretical in their application to life. Some of us, grown weary of the bland Otherworlds proclaimed by church, synagogue, and mosque, look to the East to find more satisfying paradigms. But though the native Otherworld tradition seems dead in all of this, it is far from defunct.

Those who expect alien intelligences to help our world overcome its mistakes and save us from the tentacles of technological disaster may find the old Shining Ones returning. If popular imagination now defines travel to the Otherworld as space travel—the new immrama—perhaps the paradisal islands will relocate to the stars as we look outward rather than inward for help. We may consider the constellations as the star gates of the Otherworld, mediating its archetypal forces and existing with their mundane correlatives on the earth itself (see practice 5, The Terrestrial Zodiac). As for those who look to psychology for connection, it is possible that the purgative experience of psychoanalysis may again put damaged psyches in touch with their own inscapes, where they may converse with otherworldly archetypes. And for those who look to the East, there is no doubt that Eastern techniques, themselves derived from valid spiritual disciplines, can stimulate our own Western Otherworld traditions, although we ultimately must make connections with our own cultural metaphors.

Otherworldly realms and their inhabitants can translate to other countries and cultures by means of spiritual heritage and blood lineage. Celtic immigrants brought with them to America and Australia their faery folk, the People of Peace, although each of these countries has its own native Otherworld in American Indian and Aborigine cultures. The American John Crowley, in his novel about the Otherworld, *Little, Big,* says that it takes a long time for the inhabitants of ancestral Otherworlds to establish themselves:

> We as a people are too young to have cultivated stories like those told of Arthur, and perhaps too self-satisfied to have felt the need of any. Certainly none are told of the so-called fathers of our country; the idea that one of those gentlemen is not dead but asleep, say, in the Ozarks or the Rockies is funny but not anywhere held. Only the despised ghost-dancing Red Man has a history and a memory long enough to supply such a hero. (111)

Begun in the last century, the rediscovery in Britain of a folk heritage and its Otherworld tradition continues today. The movement known as the Celtic Twilight produced at one end a Never-Never Land woven of unrealistic yearnings and at the other a broad and informed picture of the Otherworld whose proponents included the great poet W. B. Yeats and the mystic "A. E." (the pseudonym of George Russell). Their genius and vision inflamed the whole Celtic world and is still the basis for many fantasy novels whose authors glimpse, through them, the gleam of paradise. In other countries folklorists collected the last remnants of native traditions before the last storytellers forgot their craft. Antiquarians and poets began to realize the importance of their heritage and that in all too short a time the living links with the past would be dead.

We must not imagine, however, that professionals and experts on folklore will record all of our world's heritage for us. The Otherworld traditions of many living cultures are in danger. In the nineteenth and twentieth centuries many native peoples lost their own links as they were hounded into extinction or second-class citizenship. The vital impulse of these traditions has, fortunately, been preserved or revived, but in the face of unprecedented opposition and systematic rooting out of cultural identity. The move is on in Australia, motivated by the Aborigines themselves, to transmit their lifestyle and their access to the Dreamtime to their people, who have no place in the white man's ecology.

Similarly, around the world the guardianship of native earth sites and holy places is taught along with transmission of the Otherworld tradition. This is heartening, but we cannot afford to be complacent about our own traditions.

An understanding of the Otherworld is essential within the context of the Western Way or, indeed, of any spiritual tradition. It is the basis from which all mysticism grows. The Otherworld focuses the spiritual experience of seers, prophets, shamans, and visionaries, who in turn inspire followers. Without a vision, the people perish, yet there is never any shortage of a spiritual vision. The rediscovery of Otherworld reality within each generation has been the impetus of spiritual life. Spiritual wisdom does have a common source, even if its otherworldly apparatus is perceived and interpreted in so many diverse ways among the world's many cultures.

Our part in this transmission of tradition is vital. We travel to the inner home to which we are silently called and from which we journey out again into our ordinary lives, bringing with us all that we have experienced. We cannot always speak about this treasure in words, but we can communicate it through attitudes and intentions that are apparent to others on levels deeper than any of us realize. Without the influence of the Otherworld, the Western Way would be a dead end, its travelers merely armchair esotericists. Many who hear the otherworldly call have no means to come to it consciously, although they visit it in dreams, daydreams, and visions and read about it and yearn for it: "Jerusalem, my happy home, when will I come to thee?" It is the longing of the heart to have a permanent home, an interior place that is bright and unfading in its delight. The longing for an earthly paradise has led many to explore the unknown Middle Earth, to stake a claim in holy places, just as Muslims, Jews, and Christians have all claimed Jerusalem as their own. But the earthly paradise cannot be secured by armies. The desire for it leads us in a totally different direction (390), and upon finding it, we offer a different kind of homage.

The native Otherworld tradition is generally overlooked as a means of spiritual realization, but its ways lie next to the ways of revealed religion and Hermetic esotericism, which we will examine in part 2. As Dante explored the three worlds of Purgatory, Hell, and heaven with his guide, Virgil, so with our guide we can pass through the seemingly complex time frames of the Otherworld, meeting ancestors, gods, angels, faeries, people dead and those yet to be incarnated.

We can exclaim, with the seventeenth-century English mystic Thomas Traherne:

> *A stranger here*
> *Strange Things doth meet,*
> *Strange Glories See;*
> *Strange Treasuries lodg'd in this fair World appear,*
> *Strange all, and New to me,*
> *But that they mine should be, who nothing was,*
> *That Strangest is of all, yet brought to pass.* (599)

The path to enlightenment and the journey outward to realization is a long, painful one, fraught with many failures. But it is a worthwhile journey. It is the only journey. Take ship for your blessed islands, go there, learn wonders and mysteries. Voyage, but come back.

PRACTICES
⟫ *7. Contacting the Guardian* ⟪

We are mentored by beings of different kinds—ancestors, spiritual teachers, guides, and spirit animals—in much the same way newborn children are guided by godparents who are appointed to them to create a loving and spiritual kinship and mutual obligation. The collective wisdom of these spiritual teachers can be contacted through practice 8, The Two Trees. The beings you will meet there are teachers whom you encounter on the road and who post you onward to the next experience; they do not assume any responsibility for you. The personal guardian that you will meet here in practice 7 serves a slightly different role. This being is perhaps closer than you think, although many people are unaware of their own spiritual contacts. We each have such a guardian—whether we call it a daimon, an inner companion, or a guardian angel—whose role is to initiate us into the kind of experience that will stretch us.

The golden age of childhood gives us our first introduction to the guardian through our creation of a secret companion whom we visualize as active during times of quiet play. In adolescence this image retreats, to be replaced by what the Jungian school calls the *anima* or *animus,* or what we see as the psychic counterparts of the female muse or male daimon, the inner beloved (377). Not everyone is aware of these influences, which are created within the imagination according to culture and experience. We find our own particular metaphors, symbols, or imaginative clothing for the guardian, although we might not refer to it by that name. Some of us are aware of an inner voice or conscience without form, or of a watcher. If you have experienced any of these within your life, you are already in touch with your guardian. But if you have not, you may use this practice to do so.

Method

Sit in meditation with the intention of finding and meeting your spiritual guardian. You see before you a full-length mirror in a frame. Approach it. Its surface does not reflect you because it is opaque, like a milky opal. Within the mirror someone is sealed away from your vision. Breathe upon the surface, seeing your breath as a flow of rainbow sparks of light. This is life-giving breath. See the frosted, milky surface slowly melt away under your breath. Within the mirror the figure of someone grows clearer. It may be male or female, old or young, but it is never an animal or nonhuman entity, nor is it someone known to you in life. If the figure is still indistinct, concentrate upon your breath and the rainbow sparks of light. You are not giving life to your guardian so much as giving life to yourself. Your guardian has always waited at this door to greet you and now, of your own volition, you create the opportunity for this. The surface of the mirror is now clear as day and the frame becomes a doorway.

Greet the one who stands before you and ask if he or she is your guardian. When this is affirmed—and it may take a few attempts to establish contact—ask his or her name. In all your dealings with the guardian you must always speak first; your guardian will not speak to you unless you first make contact. If you cannot catch the guardian's name, establish a mutual recognition sign that you can exchange on future meetings—a small hand gesture will do, or a sound, color, or symbol. In future meditations this will immediately establish the being as your own guardian and not some stray contact.

Discovery

Now that the door is open between the worlds, you can meet and talk to your guardian whenever you want. You may wish to do this privately in your room by speaking aloud or by conversing on paper. Or contact can be established by meditation and inner listening. Find your own level and be patient. As with all relationships, friendship and understanding will grow in time.

Your guardian can be a sounding board, adviser, and guide not only in the Otherworld but in this world as well. Good rapport with the daimon or muse is still considered valuable among creative people whose livelihood depends on inspiration, technique, and concentrated effort. The friendship of the guardian enables them to fulfill their destinies by interpreting Otherworld ideas into crafts, art, performances, and music. But you do not have to be a creative artist in order to live creatively at every level of life.

If you ask for advice, sound out the guardian's teaching—try some part of it if you have yet to learn to trust him or her. Don't surrender yourself to the guardian; try to be responsible for your own actions and thoughts. Nor should you worship your guardian as though he or she were a god; try instead to view him or her as an older brother or sister, a companion with more experience than you have.

Contact with your guardian is intimately personal and can take many forms. We can only broadly hint at the relationship you might have. Further contact will come as a result of practice. Both your inner and your outer life are enriched by contact with your inner guardian. From this relationship you will acquire flexibility of personality, a new self-awareness, confidence, and humility.

❈ 8. The Two Trees ❈

This meditation is a powerful initiatory entry to the Otherworld that has been transmitted orally from teacher to pupil over many generations in the native tradition of Britain. It has been guarded as a hidden treasure and has never before been written down. Because of its importance and because the native tradition is coming into the forefront of consciousness once again, it seems that now is the time to share it in this way. While practicing it, you will meet certain beings who will show you certain aspects of yourself and teach you about them. Those who don't work at it will get nothing from it. Those who work with it, however, and benefit from its practice are the ones for whom it is intended, for in oral transmission, the living spark of the teaching must seed in the heart of the hearer.

Like an unfinished story, this meditation stands as a challenge to all who have felt in their blood the vital impulse of the inner levels. There is no end to this inner exploration, no correct way, no right order of events; each of us finds the journey tailored to our specific needs. The landscapes, events, and characters vary according to our perceptions, yet from our experience and the experience of those related to us, it seems that common images do recur. Because you make your way alone, this is not an easy journey to take. And because this was intended as an oral exercise for use within a teacher-pupil relationship with at least a minimal amount of supervision, you must bear in mind certain basic instructions: If you cannot get beyond the beginning or you get stuck or encounter recurrent images, stop. The time is not right for you either to start or to continue your inner charting. An opportunity may arise later. Some may find that they do not do the meditation—it does them. This can be disconcerting but manageable if you keep a sensible balance in your life. This meditation, like much in esoteric exploration, can become an obsession, but you will find that once the initial effect has manifested, the meditation continues at a more even rate.

In many ways, The Two Trees is a compendium of the other practices in this book. Some seekers have emerged from this experience alternately shattered and enlightened. Its effect is deep, so do not approach it facetiously. Those you meet beyond the two trees may take many forms: recognizable religious figures, animals, spirit companions, and teachers and guides, as well as misleading characters who set obstacles in your road. Face up to any authorized threshold guardians that you meet, for they can have a salutary effect on those who have been avoiding personal issues or who seek to hold on to cherished and mistaken precepts. Wrestle with these guardians and play their riddling games until you come to a place of mutual respect. But have nothing to do with those who make you fearful or who have no compassion in them. Upon meeting them, call to the guardian whom you met in practice 7, Contacting the Guardian, and call up the strength of your clan totem to be with you and strengthen you (see practice 1, Finding Your Clan Totem). If you meet ancestors or troubled spirits, do not become involved and overwhelmed by their scenarios. Refer them to the help of your guardian.

Method

You are standing at the top of a low hill. Below you is a shallow valley at the center of which lies a lake. Beside it are two trees—silver birches, which are reflected upside down in the water. Walk down from the hill and around the edge of the lake until you pass between the two trees. As you do so, focus your attention on the sky well above the horizon. There you will see either the sun or the moon: Is it day or night? When you have established which it is, lower your gaze and see a figure approaching. It may be male or female, veiled or unveiled. This is your teacher. Attend to any instructions he or she gives you. Your teacher may accompany you or appoint a companion, or you may be sent on alone. Follow the way laid out for you and seek the goal to which you will be led. Ask questions of the teacher when you are unsure or you need his or her teaching.

You may return from your journey at any point that you choose, passing through the gateway of the two trees. In formal meditation sessions you need not recapitulate all your experiences; merely use the gateway of the two trees to begin your journey, and continue your visit by following its unfolding course.

Discovery

Over a period of time the images and teachings of this journey will integrate themselves into your life, becoming part of your "interior furnishing." It is good to keep a written record of your travels for future reference. When attempting to compare notes with a friend or group who are working this meditation, remember that results will be varied and that no qualitative judgments can be made on anyone's progress. Even the teacher is not in a position to judge or comment, only to help and advise in the event of difficulty.

Do not be alarmed if, after practicing for some months, the landscapes and inhabitants of this meditation resurface outside of the meditation. You will probably find that you slip in and out of the landscape of the journey at unexpected moments, and that after a lapse of several weeks or months you will find yourself taking up the journey again. Sometimes the journey may seem to continue even though you are not conscious of it, so that you reenter the landscape at a different point but in full awareness of what has passed, much like remembering and reentering a recurring dream. The landscape may surface in your dreams as well. You should understand that this inner journey may take years, possibly a lifetime, and that once begun, it will continue to reappear in your life.

5

The Secret Commonwealth

For you took what's before me and what's behind me;
You took east and west when you wouldn't mind me.
Sun and moon from my sky you've taken,
And God as well, or I'm much mistaken.
—"DONAL OG," TRADITIONAL IRISH FOLK SONG

There are nine and sixty ways of constructing tribal lays,
And every–single–one–of–them–is–right!
—RUDYARD KIPLING, *IN THE NEOLITHIC AGE*

Native Wisdom

Though the Foretime is no more, its native wisdom survives intact within the Otherworld, and in our world folk tradition and esoteric lore still retain and reflect aspects of its practice today. But those who choose to see the wisdom of the Foretime in the rosy glow of a Golden Age, rather than in the light of the secret commonwealth that it represents, do themselves a disservice. The term *secret commonwealth* was first used by Rev. Robert Kirk (301) to describe the land and secret life of the faery kind.

It is a fact that what we have not known with our own bodies, in our own world, through our own experience can easily become specious and disempowered by our fantasies—as real faeries have become today, and as native wisdom has become by virtue of those who see it in a kind of rosy, long-ago light. But in order for native wisdom to remain real, we cannot approach it from a distance; we must experience it in our own lives. Our native wisdom is literally our common wealth, the treasury upon which we can draw for spiritual nourishment. Into its storehouses goes every aspect of tradition, both pagan and Christian, old and new. If the treasury of our secret commonwealth ceases to be loved and used and becomes enshrined like a museum exhibit, then its living currency turns to dross.

Tradition is never static. It endlessly transforms, adapting itself to every generation. This miraculous ability is often overlooked by those who study native tradition from a theoretical basis, ignoring anything that is not cataloged in a museum or written in the annals. But the fluidity of traditional lore cannot be assessed by these means. We have always successfully passed down traditions by giving them free rein to change and adapt to the prevailing times and customs.

So far in this book we have shown how the traditions of the Foretime have returned: how the god forms reemerge, how the earth's energies can be contacted again, and how the Otherworld is the key to native wisdom. Tracing the course of the Old Religion (see chapter 1) from the Foretime to today is a bit more difficult. Its path has twisted and turned, and confusingly.

Pagans today claim the origin of their tradition lies in the Foretime, but most do not claim to have any apostolic or uninterrupted tradition from that time to this. For example, many modern witches in the Craft, as modern witchcraft is generally known, believe their practice descends from the Old Religion of the Foretime, at the same time denying any correspondence with what is popularly known as black witchcraft or sorcery. Witchcraft's bad press is due largely to its clash with Christianity and to the dubious evidence and "confessions" of witches extracted during episodes of torture in medieval and Jacobean times. These two factors have colored public imagination—so much so that some modern witches, who prefer the term Wiccans to differentiate themselves from the practitioners of witchcraft as sorcery, are quick to proclaim their uninterrupted lineage from the Foretime, though they may also be embarrassed to explain how their tradition has survived untainted by the accusations of cursing, child sacrifice, orgies, and devil worship that are frequently leveled against them. If there seems to be an inexplicable hiatus between the Foretime's Old Religion and the modern Craft, it is either because the links are invisible or because they were never there.

Yet if there are any successors to the tribal shaman, then the most likely candidates are the inheritors of the secret commonwealth of our native tradition—those who have remained closest to their communities. These are not the Wiccans of today, with their well-informed background reading and their hermetically influenced rituals, but those who have lived on the land, near to their roots, those who have maintained the traditional crafts and customs with their hands and their lives.

While the legend of "old families" keeping alive a dying tradition has been much embroidered, certain families and communities have transmitted the Old Religion in some form. One famous East Anglian witch, George Pickingill (1816–1909), who was consulted by Masons and Rosicrucians from Europe and America, traced his descent from Julia of Brandon, a witch who died in 1071 (610). His hereditary tradition descends through the nine covens that he founded over the course of sixty years, and thus may be said to be operative today. But if this was one possible descent of the tradition, does it tell how the tribal shaman became a witch?

As druid succeeded shaman, so priest succeeded druid. Eventually, those who entered the Christian priesthood became increasingly involved in ecclesiastical administration, theological abstractions, and tending to the spiritual needs of the people and less responsible for their physical well-being. Rites of baptism, marriage, and death could not be recognized without the Church's intervention; the people became spiritually and financially tied to maintaining the parish priest. At one level, the Old Religion and the new religion rubbed along together, with priest, people, and ruler often exercising their dual membership in both. The shaman's ritual role had been usurped by the priest, but there was no one to look after the welfare of the tribe in an official capacity—this role had to be practiced secretly. Those who remained helpful to their village or settlement were most likely those who maintained a double belief system: They were seen going to church and taking part in the everyday life of their community, but they still honored and understood the old ways. These descendants of Foretime belief could not afford to be rebels who stood out from the crowd or who openly opposed Christian belief. (275)

Wise women and cunning men who were practitioners of old tribal traditions maintained contact with the old divinities. They continued to offer the old spiritual transactions: healing, intercession, spells, both lifting and laying curses, and giving reassuring and helpful advice that assisted people in their daily lives. For physical infirmities they could offer simple herbal cures, midwifery, community support, and spiritual help from the old and trusted gods and spirits. These wise ones lived among people, knew their practical needs, and spoke the common tongue. They filled a void not addressed by the Christian clergy, who demanded tithes in return for spiritual help and whose ceremonies were spoken in Latin. While the Church reigned supreme in its authority, it was often in the pocket of the nobility, who, with their might, could coerce the people to be obedient to Church and monarch. Someone who would speak for those with no authority and give them a sense of power was therefore an important person.

Because these wise ones maintained a spiritual connection with the gods of nature and pre-Christian understanding, they were seen as evil witches, for Christianity did not tolerate unauthorized divinities or alternative practices. The Old Religion was animistic, accepting the spirits of ancestors, animals, and plants as powers and presences. As the Christianization of Europe was completed, these older understandings began to be subsumed by Christian belief. Practicing any ancient custom might be seen as heretical, especially in the fifteenth, sixteenth, and seventeenth centuries, when the struggles of religious reform swept through Europe and Protestantism began to threaten the long tenure of Catholicism.

Wise women and cunning men began to represent a blatant opposition to authority and communal well-being because, the Church argued, they pretended to have powers that could harm as well as heal. In the eyes of the Church, only God had the power to heal. For a person to pretend to have powers of healing, even by means of herbs or potions, was to usurp the role of the Divine. To understand this attitude today, we must look to fundamentalist Islam, which can view even cheering for your football team as a form of heresy. It argues that only the Divine being can bring aid and assistance according to the divine will.

During the Renaissance a new wind began to blow. The Protestant Reformation of the Church sought not only to sweep away what it saw as aberrant and anti-biblical customs, but to also sever the links with a tribal spirituality and replace it with a Christianity restated in national terms. The Reformation tried to purge the mystical and formless consciousness that medieval Catholicism had inherited from the native tradition. At the time of the Christian mission to Britain, Pope Gregory the Great encouraged missionaries to site churches on pagan centers of worship and to continue the celebration of pagan festivals, but in a

Christian guise. Folk customs—including disguising people as animals—that had continued as rites of community bonding and which had become embedded, along with ancient songs and dances, into saint's day celebrations and other holy days, were now overturned.

The deities of the Foretime—the mother and father of the tribe, the Old Religion's lord and lady whose aspects and exemplars were the gods, goddesses, and spirits—had continued to be venerated in the forms of Our Lord and Our Lady, Jesus and Mary. But under Protestantism and its offspring, Puritanism, the reverence of the Virgin was banned and the celebration of native festivals was outlawed. Those who had lived happily with dual allegiance—to the Old Religion and to Christianity—now found themselves forced to take sides. The Protestant Reformation purged the land and its people of the pollution of both pagan and Catholic influence.

The Old Religion was forced into sudden extinction. But before it died, it showed its ugly side. Revivalists like to think of the "burning times," as they are known in Craft circles, as a parallel to the persecution of the early Christians: Small, fervent bands of dedicated pagans striving to keep the old ways alive met secretly at night for fear of the activity of spies and virtuously went about their daily business, wishing ill to no one. But the reality was often far more human. To have your spirituality derided, to lose your livelihood, to see your family suffer did not inspire feelings of goodwill in the followers of the Old Religion. Those with the power to heal and hurt often chose to hurt out of a spirit of vengeance and retribution. There were few on either side of the fence, whether Christian or pagan, who practiced the highest principles of their faith. The notion of the devil as God's opponent had been propounded from both Catholic and Protestant pulpits. Under threat of persecution by their oppressors, some of the followers of the Old Religion no doubt turned to the devil for support: If God allied himself with the persecutors, let them join God's opponent.

We who live in more tolerant times—or in more tolerant parts of the world—in which many religions coexist without rancor cannot really know the turmoil of those times. The basic compatibility of pagan and Christian was overturned in a hysterical purge. Protestant Christianity, ashamed of its pagan beginnings and its superstitious Catholic past, embarked on the systematic eradication of offending members. Yet a fascination with the earlier levels of religion remained voyeuristically embedded within the hearts of Christian persecutors. It has been observed that at this time, "treatises on witchcraft came near to being a pornographic genre." (630)

The spectacle of two religious traditions fighting each other is not a pleasant one. To what degree we may look at these times as an attempt to grow out of tribal consciousness into something less institutional and more individualistic is hard to tell. They may be regarded as a clumsy step upon that road, but in an age not noted for its tolerance, it was a step that not everyone took. Yet not everyone lived in darkness.

Those who love their gods and venerate them faithfully consider themselves to be good, to be working for the benefit of all. The good that each of us requires from life does not differ from faith to faith; it is the same for all human beings. Those who embraced the old and the new gods as family members of the same tribe of life did not live in mutinous hostility and resentment of Christianity. They considered the new religion but another cloak that served the same purpose as the Old. This fact is often strenuously denied by modern Wiccans, many of whom continue to battle orthodox religion.

In his introduction to Carlo Ginzburg's *The Night Battles*, a study of pagan survival within the context of agrarian cults, E. J. Hobsbawm remarks of this sixteenth-century Italian phenomenon:

> [H]ere we have not Margaret Murray's subterranean old religion hostile to Christianity but ritual practices which had long established a symbiosis with the dominant religion—the *benandanti* (literally, "those who go well") originally regarded themselves as champions of Christ against the devil—but which are forced into opposition . . . by Church policy. (180)

These benandanti, ordinary country folk, went forth at night to do battle with those who threatened the crops. Doubtless some families continued this ancient guardianship, while isolated individuals with wits quicker than those of their contemporaries bore witness to the old ways more secretly. It was no time to hold—and to be seen practicing—double belief. Of primary importance was to survive without being arraigned for witchcraft.

The impetus of the Old Religion was thus broken and its shamans were dead or scattered. But apart from certain wise women and cunning men such as George Pickingill, there were still the storytellers, poets, musicians, and craftspeople who retained the ancient wisdom in their lore and skill and in their memory.

We can directly trace the survivors and inheritors of the ancient lore in only a few cases. During the eighteenth and nineteenth centuries, just as ancient sites were discovered by gentlemen archaeologists and the old mythologies were debated by bored divines, so the Old Religion was reinvestigated. These students of the ancient were most intrigued by druidism, which seemed to them to have connections with classical lore, biblical speculation, and secret Masonic rites. We owe a debt of gratitude to the commentators and collectors who recorded what would otherwise have been lost, for just as Pausanius recorded ancient Greek customs and religious sites before the imposition of Christianity upon the classical world (464), so did William Stukeley and John Aubrey record the British landscape before industrialization (580, 23). (What the Protestant Reformation had started, industrialization helped complete as people grew further from their land and customs.) Later on, Cecil Sharp and Sabine Baring-Gould (465) collected folk songs, stories, and dances before radio and television arrived to replace them. The ancient wisdom glittered in the hands of these collectors, even if they did not always understand it in context. But as we know from the evidence of the last two centuries, an anthropologist's discovery of or first contact with a people invariably causes them to become aware of their traditional customs, which mutate as a result. Whatever we observe, we change.

A number of theories about the survival of the Old Religion in the form of witchcraft stimulated the native consciousness from the beginning of the twentieth century. Charles G. Leland, an American folklorist and himself a descendant of John Leland, who was the Royal Antiquary in 1553, uncovered evidence of Italian witchcraft and published his findings in *Aradia, the Gospel of the Witches* (261). Around the same time, the anthropologist Margaret Murray wrote two influential books: *The Witch Cult in Western Europe* and *The God of the Witches* (433). While Leland's findings were an isolated instance of survival shared by a firsthand informant—a witch called Maddalena—and were concerned only with Italian practices, Murray's books attempted to take witchcraft seriously as a survival of the Old Religion. There were no witches to come forward and affirm her findings. Persecution had resulted in an understandably deep-dyed secrecy among them and the statutes against witchcraft were still on the books in England. Not until the Witchcraft Act of 1736—which stated that those "pretending to be witches" were subject to imprisonment—was repealed in 1951 did other kinds of evidence began to turn up (609).

Gerald B. Gardner, an amateur archaeologist and anthropologist who had formed links with a coven in the New Forest in southern England, was the one to spearhead the dissemination of this new evidence. He was subsequently initiated into the New Forest coven and, after the repeal of the Witchcraft Act, began to publish books about the Old Religion from within. *Witchcraft Today* and *The Meaning of Witchcraft* exploded the misconceptions surrounding witches and propounded a cult of shamanlike practitioners of the Old Religion who kept the old festivals, worshipped the old gods, and worked only beneficent magic (175, 174).

Gardner's claims have perturbed both those inside and those outside contemporary Paganism. Doreen Valiente, who knew and worked with him, has this to say: "The rituals he had received were in fact fragmentary . . . and to link them together into a coherent whole . . . he had supplied words which seemed to him . . . to strike the right chords in one's mind." (609) It would indeed be astonishing if anything like a coherent text had survived the oral transmission of traditional rituals. The Old Religion, never a codified whole, even in the Foretime, was without a holy text or any handbook of methodology—until Gardner assembled the *Book of Shadows,* which has acted as a core text for Gardnerian Wiccans ever since.

The tradition that Gardner contacted in the New Forest was different from those Pagan pockets that had survived in other parts of the British Isles or in Europe. Yet whatever the leaders of other covens might say, Gardner's ideas sparked the dry tinder of a seemingly dead tradition. Those who had fallen out of orthodox religion were attracted to Gardner's covens and soon a great mushrooming of neo-Paganism occurred. The Craft of the Wise, derived from the Saxon word *wicce,* or "wise," grew at a phenomenal rate. Covens soon exceeded their autonomous units of thirteen and created daughter covens, and the Craft soon crossed the Atlantic to the United States, where its growth was even greater (260).

Gardner was not alone in his attempt to spread the Old Religion; other individuals, some with inflated egos, were soon claiming witch grandmothers and special powers. Paganism had become cultist. Margot Adler discusses this phenomenon in the United States in her book *Drawing Down the Moon* (3), while *Persuasions of a Witch's Craft* details the British scene. Many of the ingredients of the Foretime's Old Religion, however, are present within the Craft: the worship of the old gods and goddesses, the celebration of agrarian and calendrical festivals, the parity of men and women.

The popular response to aspects of ancient belief has been overwhelmingly positive, even in an age when there are many spiritual alternatives available to people to replace or fill in the gaps of orthodox faiths. It seems that we are experiencing a reintegration of the native tradition. In the years since Gardner began his good-faith revival of the Old Religion, a significant pattern has been emerging (340). Certainly there are those who claim to be witches as more of a fashion statement or as an expression of individuality or those who earnestly seek to establish a nostalgic realm of Pagan peace, but there are also those who are reconnecting with the old ways through analeptic means, who are seriously practicing these ways as modern-day shamans in their communities. Rather than being called neo-Pagans, contemporary Pagans prefer the term "reconnected Pagans" because it reflects their desire to genuinely reconnect with the Foretime.

The appeal of Paganism today is due largely to the authentic search for ancestral roots and spiritual authority. Through centuries of authoritarian religion, there was no room for the individual mystic and no tolerance of those who sought their own connection to the gods. Christianity, in which each of the faithful was merely part of the congregation, did not allow for the status of the individual. But initiates in most Pagan religions eventually become priests or priestesses themselves. Another major factor, as we shall see, is the Pagan inclusion of the feminine within the divine.

Differences between our ancestors and today's Pagans involve both a sense of connection to the land and the importance of individual consciousness. Contemporary Pagans are informed by more recent attitudes about environmental concern and personal spiritual growth. Both exemplify how the native tradition addresses the needs of our time. However, whereas our ancestors would have been immersed in tribal consciousness for the well-being of the community, the emphasis in our time on personal spirituality can manifest in Pagan revivals that tend to focus on the satisfaction of the individual rather than on the community as a whole. In addition, these revivals do not always arise from an understanding of an ensouled universe because they do not emerge from an integretive tradition. It is rare, for example, to find many modern Pagans who could confidently sing the songs of their own folk tradition or who have informed themselves of the local customs and seasonal rituals that make up the spiritual lore of their particular land or locality (275).

There are many Pagan practices other than the Craft that are alive and well in the Western world and beyond. Not only are there indigenous traditions that have survived by growing through Christianity— Santería, for instance, fuses African gods and Christian saints in the New World—but druidic, Celtic, northern, Goddess, and shamanic traditions also thrive. The living practices are those that respond to the times as well as to the tradition, rather than merely seeking to re-create an ideal past, which is ultimately a wasted effort. Atavistic nostalgia does not serve the needs of our times.

But while "modern neo-mystics . . . have been drawn by . . . a rebirth of interest in mythology and especially British mythology; by the ill-defined belief in a New Age; . . . [or] by a rejection of Christianity which is not the old atheism or humanism, but a search for an alternative spirituality, often with magical and occultish aspects,"(17), they cannot altogether ignore the mystical cohesion of Christianity, which has preserved aspects of the native wisdom quite successfully along with imparting its own wisdom as a spiritual path. The way back to the Foretime lies through the territory of Christian belief, a fact that is often conveniently overlooked by reconnected Pagans.

The secret commonwealth is restored through many means, and those who mediate this restoration may not necessarily occupy shamanic or priestly roles. Ultimately it does not matter who mediates this renewal, as long as is not characterized by factionalism. We give no honor to either our ancestors or our descendants by fighting over whose tradition is more ancient or more authentic. Ultimately, the past is "neither pagan nor Christian, it belongs to no nation and no class, it is universal," (483) and we all have come from it.

The Secret People

They have given us into the hand of the new unhappy lords,
Lords without anger and honour, who dare not carry their swords.
They fight by shuffling paper; they have bright dead alien eyes;
They look at our labour and laughter as a tired man looks at flies.

And the load of their loveless pity is worse than the ancient wrongs.
Their doors are shut in the evening; and they know no songs. (91)

This quotation from G. K. Chesterton's poem "The Secret People" might well stand with that of the Irish folk song at the beginning of this chapter, "Donal Og," as an indictment of the people of the native tradition against the leaders who have lost the vision of enduring community. If you have followed us this far, perhaps you have glimpsed the reasons why the native tradition is as important as the Hermetic tradition in the formation of the Western Way. While the native tradition is rooted in tribal consciousness that cannot operate now as it once did in the Foretime, it still carries important understandings that we will need in order to weave any kind of cosmic consciousness: respect for the land, the essential connection between the work of our hands and the ideals of our hearts, and a sense of community and belonging to the sacred continuum of life. Throughout the centuries of Western civilization these values have been frequently betrayed and neglected by those who have the duty to lead and encourage. Those secure in their religious beliefs, who have fixed and reassuring views on all aspects of life, can afford to be dismissively smug about the "secret people" from whom the sun and moon, East and West, and any approachable concept of God have been derived.

In truth, we are all secret people who have been exiled from our tribe. In the Foretime the sacred continuum was maintained collectively by the tribe, with a suitable tribal representative chosen by the shaman to be the leader. The ancient responsibility of kingship was initially sacral rather than political. With the coming of Christianity, shamans had the choice of either surviving as priests or nuns and serving the establishment or remaining close to the earth and faithful to the sacred tribal vision by becoming cunning men or wise women. Tribal leaders who understood the responsibilities of sacral kingship and the ancient sacrifice required of the leader—to rule in harmony with the sacred continuum and, if necessary, to spill their blood in its defense—were swept away by successive invasions (first Romans, then Saxons and Normans).

Under Norman rule, Britain's ancient tribal ways were finally crushed under the weight of the feudal system, which was responsible for establishing a class distinction—an underclass and an overclass—whose remnants are still evident in Britain today. Instead of being managed by tribal leaders whose first care was for their people, the land was administered by foreign feudal barons who amassed wealth and land in the king's name.

By the late Middle Ages, when the descendants of the French-speaking Norman kings had become entirely enculturated as English-speaking monarchs, dynastic and religious changes altered the focus once more. Set against the background of a more prosperous and literate people, the Protestant Reformation sought to simplify religion. In overturning centuries of Christain practice in which cults dedicated to local saints, devotion to the Virgin Mary, and prayers to the dead had figured largely, it began to erase practices whose roots lay in pre-Christian times. During this upheaval, the true tribal leaders, recognized by the secret people as those who bore responsibility for the well-being of the land, paid for their convictions with their lives: "Families of priests and noblemen, blessed with family trees as old as the Creation, were obliterated" (483) with a vigor that reminds us of Margaret Murray's theory concerning the divine victim sacrificed every seven years for the good of the people (433). They died not only to defend their faith, but also in recognition of a deeper loss of faith with the land itself.

The last attempt to maintain the ancient leadership of the land can be seen in the idea of the divine kingship as promulgated by the Stuart kings who succeeded Elizabeth I and the demise of the Tudor dynasty. The Stuart dynasty, which had its roots firmly planted in the land of Britain, believed that kingship was divinely appointed. This notion was instrumental in bringing Charles I to the scaffold and plunged Britain into a Parliamentary interregnum of Puritan severity.

With the demise of the Stuart cause, however, and the eventual institution of constitutional monarchy in Britain, a diminished sense of tribal leadership prevailed. With this, the cohesion of the tribe was broken and the secret people were left leaderless or in the hands of those who cared only for their physical well-being—the "new unhappy lords" who were so out of touch with the urgency of the native tradition that "they knew no songs." Content only to administer rather than to spiritually engage, the political overlords, like the feudal barons before them, pursued wealth and self-interest. The Industrial Revolution brought prosperity to a few but took many from the land. Mechanization of labor was the starting point for the pervasive consumerism of our age; it marked the point where everything was a commodity and everyone was a wage slave. It was the final nail in the coffin for tribal consciousness.

But along with this loss of an ancient way of life and its traditional views, the foundations were laid for individual consciousness. Land and law reforms, equitable labor conditions, education for all, the repeal of slavery, the broadening of voting rights to include poorer men, and a greater tolerance for religious differences were all milestones along the way—for without these, the rights and liberties of the individual could not be upheld.

Throughout all this time of internecine dynastic struggle and political turmoil, the secret people were mostly pawns and not players. They knew that the high-sounding names of God, the alien rituals, and the political theorizing were not for them, that there was a homelier and easier way than this. Yet they often allowed themselves to be duped by a dependence on tribal consciousness and were thus manipulated to fight in foreign wars or were left hungry and landless instead of finding the essential spiritual destiny that was rightfully theirs. By the time industrialization had moved them from the land to the city, they began to lose the secret commonwealth that had sustained them, though some clung fondly to the fabric of ancestral customs that had faded and frayed to a superstitious threadbare thinness. Throughout these many centuries certain individuals rose from within their ranks—not esotericists or those whose names are tied to the Hermetic tradition, but men and women who continued the native traditions, who maintained the connections, marginal shamans many of whom we shall never know. These shepherds of the tribe acted as seed bearers; they had no part in politics, nor did they use their charisma to become popular figureheads. They were the poets, storytellers, folk singers, visionaries, and craftspeople who synthesized the inner vision, whose hidden duty was to translate the native wisdom into something more immediately usable.

These native mystics are represented by, for example, Mother Julian of Norwich (c. 1342–1420), who expressed her insight into the nature of deity through the use of both masculine and feminine imagery and whose concern was for her "even [fellow] Christians" and the immediacy of love's action on humanity (278). In the United States the nonconformist Mother Ann Lee (1736–1784) founded the Shakers, who incorporated into their worship the ecstatic tradition of dance and song (646).

Other walkers between the worlds in the tradition of Kirk's master men are the visionary poets William Blake (1757–1827) and George Russell, or "A. E." (1867–1935), who recorded their connections to the Otherworld in their poetry and other writings (46, 514). While the native nature mystics and poets Coleridge, Wordsworth, and Shelley are better known, Walt Whitman (1819–1892) and Richard Jefferies (1848–1887) explored the pantheistic universe with cosmic insight (644, 268).

The voices of some of the secret people served as embodiments of their dying native traditions. Black Elk (1863–?) spoke of the demise of his people, the Lakota Indians, under the persecution and rule of white culture in America (441), and Peig Sayers (1873–1958), an illiterate Irishwoman who spoke no English, was a font of traditional stories. These two recall the skill of the poet and bard whose native tradition degenerated and then revived, as illustrated in Robert Graves's "The White Goddess." Long after the great Celtic poets had sunk to the level of horny-handed itinerants plying their songs and stories through an impoverished land, the ancient traditional tales and ritual scenarios were remembered and sung by nameless folk singers on both sides of the Atlantic (430, 465).

Similarly, the shamanic skills of healing that long ago fell to the village witch are now being revived in a world that has grown impatient with or skeptical of orthodox healing methods. Stripped of the old healing chants, techniques of balancing the subtle psychic body and its energy fields may be dismissed as witch-doctoring, but many find them effective.

In our world, the craft of creating an object and fixing it by means of wood, clay, or iron—another aspect of the native tradition—is a paradigm of the esotericist's art. The sculptor Eric Gill (1882–1940) reminds us that art originally meant "skill" and that the artist "is the person who actually has the skill to make things . . . to bring into physical existence the things which abide in the mind." (180) In our own generation, however, this holy tradition of working is beginning to be lost as the work of mass manufacturing replaces the handmade article— although there are still those who seek to preserve the old ways. Traditional skills and the reverence of the artist or craftsperson for his or her materials have been remarkably upheld by Nigel Pennick, one of few voices in this age who bring this knowledge to their work and writings (468). Many religious and mystical truths—self-evident and open Mysteries that require no concealment—are transmitted from one generation to the next through the craftsperson. The work of our hands and the intentions of our hearts must be unified if we are to live with truth—a principle that has been absorbed by Paganism, Freemasonry, and Hermeticism. Throughout history the strength of the crafts guilds enabled the traditions to be transmitted in a unified way.

Most often, however, anonymous inspired individuals in each generation were the ones responsible for continuing the connection to the native wisdom, cyclically restating and rediscovering its truth. The work of these people has informed our own century. It is said:

> Every cycle has its prophets—as guiding stars; and they are the burning candles of the Lord to light the spiritual temple on earth, for the time being. When they have done their work, they will pass away; but the candlesticks will remain, and other lights will be placed in them. (646)

The Mother Country

The prevailing interest in what might be called popular occultism—astrology, divination, ghosts, and psychic phenomena—suggests that it is something like the pornography of religion. Writing in the nineteenth century, when magical traditions were referred to as occultism, H. P. Blavatsky commented: "Occultism is not magic, though magic is one of its tools. Occultism is not the acquirement of powers, whether psychic or intellectual, though both are its servants. Neither is occultism the pursuit of happiness, as men understand the word; for the first step is sacrifice, the second, renunciation." (49)

There will be more on the split between religion and magic in part 2, but suffice it to say here that the conventionally religious regard "dabbling in the occult" as dangerous, though they quite happily accept miracles, propitiatory prayer to the saints, the existence of guardian angels, and the sanctity of church precincts. It is interesting to juxtapose this list with the beliefs current among esotericists of many kinds: prayer, the use of magic, the mediation of god forms, the protection of the circle guardians, and the sanctity of ancient temples of both stone and earth. The lists are not so dissimilar. It is often those who seldom or never examine the magical and mystical aspects of their own religious tradition who continue to stress the negative aspects of occultism. From such spiritual bigotry two pictures emerge: The native tradition is exemplified by the witch—significantly, a woman—who, stirring her cauldron, curses all. Her intent is evil and she is depicted either as having a disturbing sexuality or as an ugly hag. The Hermetic tradition fares no better, portrayed as it is by the black magician—significantly, a man—who, safe within his circle and wrapped in his emblematic cloak and hat, invokes demons and commands elemental power. His malicious intent and devious mind threaten the well-being of the world.

It is interesting to note that those who perpetuate these pictures are ignorant of the significance of the complementary nature of the two. While it would be a gross simplification to identify the native tradition with the feminine and the Hermetic tradition with the masculine, there is a symbolic truth to be uncovered here.

We readily recognize the witch as represented by the wise woman or sibyl—someone who personifies the integrated wisdom of the earth and can mediate natural magic and prophetic insight, and we recognize the magician as an alchemist who transmutes perennial wisdom into a way of spiritual evolution. But the prominent negative feminine and masculine images of the hag and the black magician seem related to the fact that the older "feminine" Mysteries of the native tradition have suffered from neglect just as the "masculine" Mysteries of the Hermetic tradition have been overstated.

The introduction to this book mentions that while we are aware of our patrilineal heritage—our exoteric side—we have neglected our matrilineal heritage—the esoteric side of ourselves. The native tradition is the mother tradition into which we are born and whose secret commonwealth we often fail to inherit. The matronym—our mother's surname—is rarely transmitted in our culture today, which instead passes on the patronym, or father's surname, to children. Similarly, the matronym of our mother country has been withheld from us, and to retrieve it we must make a long journey of self-discovery.

How each of us relates to our secret mother country—our esoteric self—is a reflection of how we respond to the Mother herself, the Goddess, who, in the twentieth century, was reevaluated in an attempt to trace the first inward spiral of our spiritual journey. Reacquainting ourselves with and reexamining early modes of worship has produced both some of the most profound and some of the silliest developments in popular consciousness—and the attempts to restore the Divine Feminine to her proper place have been no exception.

It seems extraordinary that for most of the last two thousand years the feminine face of the Divine was banished from the Western world—outlawed, forbidden. In no previous time had this ever happened. Although monotheisms argue that the Supreme Being transcends both male and female, they nevertheless use male pronouns to describe God. Images of the Divine have been predominantly masculine in the West. When the ancient gods were overthrown, all the female divinities went with them. This lost heritage has had an tremendous effect upon our culture. We have been mystically orphaned of the Mother and denied the wisdom that we would have gained from her. When goddesses are dethroned, leaving only the presence of gods, all of society suffers. For close to sixty generations, which is beyond memory's reckoning, most people in the West have forgotten that God and Goddess are the left and right hands of the Divine, which takes its own metaphors and images.

The twentieth century reappraisal of the feminine included the spiritual metaphors of the Divine. While the feminist movement reclaimed the Goddess for women, seeing this as a necessary reclamation of women's power, Pagans and others were exploring what it meant to venerate the Divine Feminine. Some feminist groups argued polemically for the reestablishment of the Golden Age of Matriarchy when the Mother ruled and women were treated suitably. Even within the Craft covens for women alone were established under the cloak of the Dianic Craft (3). On the more popular front, men as well as women were returning joyfully to venerate their ancient Mother and to explore the lost mother country that had been denied them.

The radical wedge of feminism, social change, and spiritual freedom has split with questionable skill old understandings of sexuality and gender and their application to the archetypes of deity (560, 114). Within the field of esotericism and spirituality, however—and indeed throughout this book—there can be no differentiation of intent between the men and the women who walk the Western Way. They are equal walkers between the worlds.

Yet it is true to say that men and women experience work on inner levels differently, as Dion Fortune implies in her enlightening essay "The Worship of Isis":

Isis is the All-woman, and all women are Isis. Osiris is the All-man, and all males are Osiris. Isis is all that is negative, receptive, and latent. Osiris is all that is dynamic and potent. That which is latent in the outer is potent in the inner; and that which is potent in the outer is latent in the inner. . . . This is the law of alternating polarity, which is known to the wise. (158)

But while this circuit of polarity is a fact of our inner workings, there are no hard-and-fast rules. Women are potent on the inner levels, acting as sibyls, seers, bringers of spiritual fertility—though this principle also applies to artists who are male. Men are potent on the outer levels, acting as directors and synthesizers, reflecting inner inspiration and grounding it. We can say generally that women tend to gravitate inward on the spiral path and men tend to gravitate outward; however, once the principle of polarity is understood, these directions can be accommodated in reverse: Thus women can operate as directors of inner work, while men may act as mediums for the inner levels. We shall explore this concept more fully in chapter 9.

There is much confusion around the polarity, and about the gender assigned to the Deity. Ultimately, "male" and "female" are the symbolic masks worn by the Deity for our comfort and understanding. Although the mask of the Divine Feminine has not been exhibited in the West for many centuries, it remains an essential aspect for those who are willing and able to mediate the energies of the Mother. Throughout history there have been women-only and men-only cults, such as those of Bona Dea (26) and Mithras (616), but while there will always be male- and female-oriented Mysteries, none is exclusive.

Sexuality merely determines our gender function as human beings who have the potential to physically reproduce. It is frequently confused with polarity. The sexual circuit is made between a man and a woman. The spiritual polarity circuit is made between outer and inner levels, or between the Otherworld and Middle Earth. When sexual and spiritual circuits are crossed, the result is confusion of intent. The principles of magical polarity can be seen as a form of Western tantra: a purposeful meeting and exchange of energies to bring wisdom to birth in our world.

These definitions play into our understanding and experience of patriarchal religion and matriarchal religion. While feminism has been successful in elevating women from subservient status to equal status in relation to men, and while it has sparked necessary changes in a world in which gender equality is still far from a given, in seeking exclusive rights to the Goddess it is as guilty of spiritual appropriation as are the so-called patriarchal religions.

Women have traditionally held the guardianship of the mother country, acting as the repositories of spiritual wisdom during the dark times, but men too have played their part. Now that the Divine

Feminine has returned to the Western world, it is important that she serve as a healer of the patriarchal trends that have long kept the native wisdom of our mother countries from us.

Paganism has opened the way for both sexes to reexperience the Goddess in a practical sense, but others—such as psychologists M. Esther Harding (227), Sylvia Perera (470), and Helen Luke (341)—have also contributed to our understanding of the Divine Feminine, though we are still a long way from accepting Her completely. We have yet to see the return of a time like the Foretime, when the earth herself was first called Mother.

Time of Regeneration

We are in the midst of a great renaissance of Paganism and shamanism. Modern consciousness has latched onto something old and primeval and with this we have found an understanding of our belonging to the earth. We are discovering the lost mother country, the native wisdom of the secret commonwealth. So how do we apply these ancient principles with intention and authenticity to our own times? Those who walk the Western Way through the native tradition should bear in mind that "the mind of the student must be clearly focused in objective consciousness. Development on top of an atavism is the cause of most of the difficulties that occur in [esoteric] training." (548)

As we have tried to point out, though the soil of the native tradition is fertile for present research and future growth, not all that we dig up from it is useful or appropriate to our times. That something is old doesn't automatically mean it is wise; working with the ancient wisdom of the Foretime requires us to use our common sense. As ideas, groups, and nations have come together, split apart, and regrouped throughout history, some aspects of native tradition have been discarded—and for good reason. Not everything from the Foretime should be regenerated; we must be willing to allow decay and loss, however disorderly the transition may seem. Gradually, the new will grow to blend with the old. What is important is not that the old ways are re-created, but that they are regenerated through modern consciousness.

The images of movement, change, and exile are implicit within the Western Way, as are the literal manifestations of these. In fact, the impulse to seek Otherworld realities is sometimes expressed as a pilgrimage. The Western Way has grown up among peoples who sought new lands during the great migrations of the Foretime. Those migrants whom we call the Celts wandered ever westward across Europe until they reached the farthest western point in the British Isles. In time, however, these invaders were themselves invaded. Their brash entrance into these islands can be contrasted with their sad leaving of them: During the Scottish Clearances and the Irish potato famine of the eighteenth and nineteenth centuries, boatloads of disconsolate people, their spirit broken, bereft of their adopted soil, mourned and lost heart when they sighted their new homeland on the East Coast of America:

> *Thig iad ugainn, carach, seolta,*
> *Gus ar mealladh far ar n-eolas;*
> *Molaidh iad dhuinn Manitoba,*
> *Durthaich fhuar gun ghual, gun mhoine.*

> *They praise Manitoba to us,*
> *They come to us, deceitful, cunning,*
> *In order to entice us from our homes;*
> *A cold country without coal, without peat.* (537)

In time they and those who settled in Australia made new lives, preserving their native tradition and weaving its threads into the new cloth of their adoptive countries. And in settling in new lands, they were partially responsible for the disruption of the native traditions that existed then in America and Australia.

This is just one example of the pattern of migration underlying the development of the Western world, a pattern that continues today as waves of migrant workers and refugees arrive in Europe and America. Unfortunately, though, the deeply rooted tribal consciousness eventually turns to bigotry aimed at those who have newly arrived as it strives to remain in its territorial past. But we must not allow the native tradition to be restated in these terms. We must use enlightened means to make a new, inclusive community. Those in the past have walked the inward spiral of the labyrinth to its center. If we now walk it out from the center, we will release the true ancient wisdom of the native tradition, which can be used in our time as a tool for progress and integration. The insights of the Otherworld can help to facilitate the process of regeneration, for of the two methods of easing new ideas into consciousness—political persuasion and spiritual realization—the latter has the more immediate effect.

In *Future Shock* Alvin Toffler notes:

> If the last 50,000 years of man's existence were to be divided into lifetimes of approximately 62 years each, there have been about 800 such lifetimes. Of these 800, fully 650 were spent in caves. Only during the last 70 lifetimes has it been possible to communicate effectively from one life to another—as writing made it possible to do. Only during the last six lifetimes did masses of men ever see a printed word. (511)

Education has opened the whole world to our generation: "The heritage of any race lies open to another; the best thought of the centuries is available for all; and ancient techniques and modern methods must meet and interchange." (31) Though there are still those who exist on the level of tribal consciousness, many people have developed their individual consciousness—and some seek to take the next step to cosmic consciousness. The complacency that can come with the realization that each of us is an individual is now being challenged on a global scale as communication shrinks the planet. Even more, when we begin to see how the deeds, decisions, and desires of those in one country can grossly distort and affect the lives of those in other countries, and when we witness weather patterns that have been altered due to deforestation and other human practices, we can recognize the relationship of cause and effect. From the late Stone Age, when our ancestors first slashed and burned vegetation in order to grow crops, to the present, we have been learning that we cannot live separately from the earth.

The year 2000 has come and gone, disappointing many prophets of doom who anticipated that the world would end in 1999, and those who insisted that nuclear war would wipe out humanity or that the population explosion would exhaust the world's resources. Yet the gloom and despondency that surrounded these prognostications have not entirely dispersed. As we drift, spiritually rootless, those who believe this lifetime is the only one fear deeply for themselves and their families.

But the fears, changes, and chaotic disorders of our time may not actually denote doomsday scenarios. Another possible scenario arises: Crisis "may be an evolutionary catalyst in the push towards a higher level." (517) We will need the earth wisdom of the native tradition to help ground and manifest all that the tools of the Hermetic tradition can give us. In order to embody our tradition, we need its help as we thread our way out of the labyrinth and assess our present situation. Just as we can trace the arc of the native tradition, starting in the Foretime and extending to just beyond the Renaissance, so can we trace the arc of the Hermetic tradition, starting in the classical period and leading to the present time.

Of course, both traditions extend further in both space and effect than these approximate historical eras—and both can be contacted through the agency of the Otherworld. But more important, these two traditions relate intimately to each other. Each is a harmonic of the other and an echo of a larger cosmic scale. The native tradition is the base chord around which the Hermetic tradition harmonizes. Indigenous peoples worldwide are finding their voice, their note in this base chord, seeking their rights, and, after generations of exclusion, persecution, and genocide, asserting that their own wisdom is best for them.

In this respect we are all indigenous people—the secret people whose enchanted story is sung by the wind.

> The revival of modern Western magic and the renewed interest in "native" cosmologies and shamanism as found among the Amer-Indian cultures, for example, show that a "mythic backlash" has taken place. It has proved to be unsatisfactory, and indeed, possibly pathological, to attempt to repress the vestiges of mythological thought in modern man in the vain hope of eliminating "superstition" with the advance of science. Clearly, we humans require domains of mystery; we need to know where the sacred wisdom of life may be found and how to understand the intuitive, infinite, and profoundly meaningful visionary moments which arise in all of us at different times. (136)

The traditions of the Foretime are available at this time for good reasons. As with the Stone Age village of Skara Brae on the Orkney Islands, revealed by the storm of 1850 to be complete and perfect as the day it was evacuated so many centuries before, we are permitted a rare and unparalleled glimpse into our ancestors' inner life. There is a rising sensibility that our sophistication and civilization may be hollow, that our technology is not the best and only wisdom available, that somewhere along the road to progress we have lost something precious and vitally useful. This sense haunts us.

But, as Dion Fortune writes in *Avalon of the Heart,* the ancient resonances of the native tradition are our stepping-stones on the path of the Western Way, leading us to a stronger connection to each other and the earth as "things come home to our hearts, and we feel the unbroken line of our national life stretching back into the remote past, and know that it will reach into the far future and that we ourselves are a part of it." (159)

Fig. 9. *Pagan Janus (two-faced) figures guard the solitude of Boa Island, County Fermanagh, Ireland.*

PRACTICES

❖ *9. Self-Clarification* ❖

Over the door to the temple of Apollo at Delphi was the inscription GNOTHI SEAUTON, or "Know thyself." This dictum, at the heart of the Mysteries of all nations, should be taken seriously by those who follow the Western Way, for the work of the Mysteries—to bring light to dark places—is carried out by each of us who walk the Way. Of course, if our light is obscured, it cannot shine in the darknes. Yet "knowing" ourselves and clearing these obscurities is no easy task—it is the work of a lifetime and is never finished.

It may be argued that all of the introspection required to walk the Western Way is unhealthy and that the best option is a trip to the psychoanalyst. Yet self-clarification is not equivalent to self-absorption. As any initiate of the Mysteries knows, in order to be of service we have to be aware of both our potentialities and our limitations. Self-clarification also exorcizes our old selves—old scripts and scenarios and worn-out ideas, which calls to mind a famous picture by the pre-Raphaelite painter Dante Gabriel Rossetti entitled *How They Met Themselves*. It depicts a medieval man and woman walking through a wood and encountering their doubles, who glow supernaturally and seem to assert a stronger right to existence. It was probably painted to illustrate the concept in Elizabeth Barrett's poem "Willowwood":

> *And I was made aware of a dumb throng*
> *That stood aloof, one form by every tree.*
> *All mournful forms, for each was I or she.*
> *The shades of those our days that had no tongue.* (377)

If we fail to know ourselves, we may indeed meet old or forgotten aspects of ourselves as we go deeper into esoteric work. But through self-clarification these ghostlike fantasies can be recognized and cleared and the energy we invested in them can be reassimilated, leaving us free to progress unhampered.

Harmonizing all of our outer circumstances, which is the focus of this practice, before attempting inner work is often a prerequisite of the mystery schools today, for imbalances can quickly materialize in magical work, rendering the operation useless. It is important to realize, however, that this practice is concerned only with our present incarnation, not with past lives. It may be that as a bonus this practice will resolve certain past-life problems, but it is not important that you be familiar with these difficulties. Instead, everything you need to know about yourself is near at hand.

A closer look at ourselves—our motives, limitations, and potentialities—reveals our destiny, allowing us to find our way through a self-made maze. As with other practices, comparisons with others are not useful: Some of us may find our way quickly; others may need more time before reaching a turning point.

Remember that though we must conform to the pattern of our present incarnation, our destiny is neither fixed nor predetermined. To some extent we each make our own circumstances, and while self-clarification may highlight or partially explain them, it does not justify them. Further, we cannot simply neglect or off-load whatever responsibilities we have taken on in our everyday lives simply because we suddenly discover a spiritual destiny that does not leave room for them. It may be that we need to follow the path of the hearth fire—establishing a household or raising children—before we can take the initiatic road of the Hermetic tradition, but there is nothing to stop us from creating the temple of the hearth, in the way of the native tradition, and celebrating our rites in our home. Spiritual progress is not a career decision. Wherever, however we live, our spiritual path lies under our feet rather than in the temple, lodge, or circle.

Self-clarification requires that we ask ourselves certain questions. Those listed below are merely guidelines and can easily be adapted or expanded according to your needs. Some of the questions will be difficult to answer honestly. Keep a notebook and pen available to write down your realizations so that there is no escaping difficult issues. You need not show your notes to anyone; indeed, you can destroy them afterward.

Method

Sit in meditation and visualize a door before you. Pass through it and go down the corridor beyond, at the end of which is another door. This opens into a library. No one else is here; you are alone. Although there are countless books on the shelves around you, you are looking for one in particular. It lies before you, on a lectern. On the cover is inscribed "The Book of [your name]." It is the book of your present life, from your birth up until today. (*Note:* It is sometimes helpful to reassess only seven years of your life at one time.) Read what is written in the book, going through it as objectively as possible. Certain episodes will leap out at you, but keep turning the pages to acquire an overall impression of the story's shapes and patterns. After you have looked through the entire book, consider the following questions:

- What experiences have you had? What did they teach you?
- How many of the circumstances that now govern your life have you yourself created?
- What relationships have you had with family, friends, colleagues, and lovers? How have you behaved within them?
- To what degree have those people you've disliked been responsible for revealing aspects of yourself that were obscured?
- What has been the quality of your life in physical, emotional, mental, and spiritual terms?
- What are your potentialities and talents? To what extent have you used them?
- What are your limitations? How can your negative aspects be made positive?
- Are your present circumstances balanced? What parts require help to achieve balance?
- Examine your spiritual life from birth to the present. What spiritual influences have most profoundly affected you?
- Is there a discernible pattern in your spiritual quest?
- What religious affiliations have you had and what has been the quality of your commitment to them?
- If you have never subscribed to any religious or spiritual movement, how and to what are your spiritual faculties committed?
- If you are aware of a destiny, in what way does it relate to your spiritual path? Are they the same thing?

You need not answer all these questions at once; take a few each time you return to this practice and work through them or any other questions that may occur to you As soon as you have realized an answer, or a definitive lack of one, return from the library the way you came to it and write down your findings.

Discovery

This is very hard work and the first sessions may be emotionally exhausting. Once you have been through the book of your life to the present time, you need not keep immersing yourself in the past unless a specific problem warrants it—but pay attention instead to your daily life. A lifetime's habits cannot be broken overnight, but self-awareness will begin the work of enabling your light to shine through. Transforming your limitations will clean your lantern's glass, allowing your soul to shine through more clearly. The central motivating dynamic of your life will enable your progress when the blockages and old imperatives are cleared from your way. All life's experiences, whether good or bad, teach us something: Nothing is wasted. Even major problems can be turned into strengths through this process, allowing you to cooperate with your tendencies rather than work against them.

Make a list of your goals and match them to your potential. We seldom use our potential to its fullest. By maximizing it and working with it, we are creating. Creative spiritual exploration is not about *doing* all the time, but about *being*—listening to the pulse of creation through contemplative reflection.

If you need to move into a new phase, return to the library, look in the book of your life to see what is written on the day just after today, and take what you find there as your meditation. Let it lead you through realization and dream into the new territory that is unfolding to you.

Finally, try to engage in the evening review, your objective observation of the day's activities as they run through your mind backward, like a film in reverse. It is performed by many initiates of the Mysteries, and though it is not really an extension of self-clarification, it is related. You can practice the evening review in bed—and it doesn't matter if you fall asleep before you arrive at the beginning of the day. The purpose of the exercise is to clear your consciousness of the day's activities, leaving it ready for the refreshment of sleep and allowing dreams to be clear of daily accumulations. In the course of the review, apportion no blame and assume no guilt; simply aim at a straight run-through of events in reverse.

Fig. 10. A triple spiral from the interior of New Grange, Ireland

❧ 10. The Retreat ❧

Many of us associate a retreat with a Christian or Buddhist time of chosen physical isolation that is spent largely in prayer and meditation. But any of us, regardless of our religious beliefs or practice, can undertake a retreat as a time away from the world, modifying it to suit our specific needs. Most of us live our daily lives in places that are so tightly packed with people and activity that the experience of being alone is rare; there are few opportunities for moments of introspection and prolonged meditation. A retreat is not an escape from the problems of life but an important breathing space in which those problems may be clarified, a time in which our true potential can be realized. It gives us space and a cessation of time and movement so that we can see things in their real perspective. This "holy hiatus" in the headlong course of life can have lasting effects: Our ability to cope with life improves, the mind is trained, the soul is stilled, and our deep intuitions and insights are free to rise, unfettered.

If you have never followed a particular religious practice, you may not have had the experience of a full-fledged retreat, yet the native tradition gives us plenty of examples: The sweat lodge and *kiva* of the Native American, the solitary vision quest of the shaman, and the tribal descent to the ancestors' burial place are retreats that have been undertaken since the Foretime. The Hermetic retreat of Abra Melin urges a six-month preparation and withdrawal in order to contact the holy guardian angel. Some retreats in history have required the creation of a particular place for physical isolation. For example, the cell of the medieval anchorite constituted a more permanent retreat, as did the cave of the hermit.

Method

Obviously, considerations of time, location, and cost enter into any preparation for a retreat. Generally, the longer the retreat, the more preparation you will need. Try a retreat of one to three days at first. Where is the best place? If you are, say, an experienced camper and have your own transportation, you can take off when you please and head for the ideal: an isolated, known sacred site, preferably one that is little used. *Note:* If you go anywhere alone, especially where there are mountains, bogs, abandoned mines or caves, and a common occurrence of inclement weather or fog, inform someone of your whereabouts ahead of time so that you can be found in an emergency. If you keep your equipment to a minimum, dress appropriately for conditions, and avoid extremes of heat and cold, you have the beginnings of an interesting retreat.

But what if roughing it in the great outdoors is not an option for practical or personal reasons? Surprisingly, both Christian and Buddhist retreat centers are very sympathetic to individuals who desire quiet time away from the world. It's usually required that you choose a time when a center's organized retreats are not in progress. Beyond this, as long as you observe the common code of courtesy and do nothing that is strictly contrary to the tenets of the center, it's possible to have a rewarding experience. Some centers have hutlike lodgings that can be used by pilgrims who are on their own. The advantages of a retreat center or monastery over any hotel or camping area include the guarantee of a quiet and contemplative atmosphere (although, unfortunately, many more people are discovering monastic holidays and some places may be more noisy than you would expect) and the presence of experienced explorers of the spiritual realms, whose attitude toward guests stems from their belief that every visitor is sent by God. Such people will often be willing to talk to genuine seekers of the spirit but will not press themselves upon you.

While the ideal retreat consists of removing yourself completely from everyday life, leaving home may not be easy or possible due to commitments, age, or handicap. Yet carrying out a retreat at home is extremely difficult: Life's problems are all too present there and the distracting stimuli of television, radio, computers, and books are either temptingly within reach or inescapable. If it is your only opportunity, the home retreat is best accomplished in a day or, if you can manage the time, a long weekend. Because telephones are perhaps the worst disturbance, do whatever you can ahead of time to divert calls from friends and family or colleagues. Some friends may regard your actions as downright antisocial; however, you will find that others will be sufficiently intrigued to try a retreat for themselves.

Once you have decided where your retreat will be held and have made your preparations, you must decide what you will do during your time away. We are so capable of—and used to—filling our day with activity that the retreat can become a trap at first as we attempt to pack every minute with soul-searching meditation and strenuous inner exertion. But the state of contemplation is one of tranquillity rather than activity. One way you might start is by attempting practice 9,

Self-Clarification, as a way of defining your goals and how the retreat can be used as a springboard to them.

Remember that most of all, you are attempting to get closely in touch with yourself and your spiritual allies and guides. To this end, you might start by getting used to the feeling of being alone: You may wish to wrap yourself in a blanket or a long coat, covering your head to shut out all distractions. Sit and breathe quietly and evenly, releasing all the tension from your body. Set aside mental distractions and nagging worries. This is your special time to which you are entitled; spending it in this way is neither selfish nor wasteful.

If you think you may reach the end of your resources to start the process, take with you a thought-provoking book that might help to spark some meditation points and a notebook in which you can record your thoughts and realizations, which may have the makings of the beginning of a spiritual journal that could even continue after the retreat is over. You might also try some handwork, such as knitting, that is manually absorbing but frees your thoughts. In this vein, Russian Orthodox monks make prayer beads while they meditate and Cistercian monks hoe vegetables; shamans sing over their drums and wise women whirl their spindles. All these actions are rhythmic, allowing the body its motion and the soul its freedom to engage in other matters.

There is no reason to be still and silent during your retreat. You can sing or chant, walk or dance through a labyrinth traced on the earth, or make a small, natural shrine out of stones or wood. How you focus is entirely up to you. You may wish to take the Otherworld journey of practice 8, The Two Trees, or attempt other practices outlined in this book. Make this time work for you.

One important question often comes up regarding a retreat: Should I fast? The answer involves common sense: Fasting is not a requirement for a successful, enriching retreat. Depending on the duration of your retreat, you might fast only if you have previously attempted it and know how your body is likely to react and if you ensure that you have sufficient water and other fluids. Certainly reducing your intake so that the retreat doesn't become a cordon bleu holiday is reasonable. Stick to simple foods: eggs, cheese, bread, soup, fruit, and fresh vegetables, with springwater or fruit juice to drink. If you are camping, you may need some hot food, but if your retreat is taking place at home, you likely wouldn't suffer from a simple, mostly uncooked diet. Retreat centers inevitably serve quite spartan fare.

Discovery

This practice focuses on the individual retreat, but a well-organized group retreat with an experienced leader who can supply the right kind of impetus for self-discovery and elicit a commitment to self-discipline from all participants can provide necessary support for those who are uncertain of themselves in a solitary condition or those who find the energy of others enriching to their own meditative practice.

Whatever the shape of your retreat, you will emerge refreshed and grounded. Deprogramming and decompressing from the retreat may take a few days. It is good to allow at least one day off after any intense spiritual activity. If it seems that your retreat has been less than successful, don't despair. In ways that you may not yet realize it has given you useful information, perhaps revealing to you which areas of your life need adjustment or rethinking.

If we take away our home environment, our favorite food and television programs, our personal indulgences, and the company of other human beings, we are reduced to ourselves. If we have the sense of being incomplete without these outside stimuli, then we are not in touch with our real selves. Being able to draw a cloak of silence around ourselves and enter deeply into stillness is a nearly lost art today, but if we can return to the stillness of our meditations, which always exists in the spaces between activities, then we will breathe the atmosphere and touch the same reality as that of our ancestors of the Foretime.

The emblem of the alchemist's Great Work—creating the philosopher's stone.
Its inscription reads, "Visit the interior of the earth, by subtle adjustment
discover the hidden stone."

PART TWO

The Hermetic Tradition

Hear with the understanding of the heart.
—THOMAS VAUGHAN, *ANIMA MAGICA ABSONDITA*

*The soul of each single one of us is sent, that the
universe may be complete.*
—PLOTINUS, *ENNEADS* IV, 8, 1

Fig. 11. *The figure of the Aion, a guardian of the thresholds, also known as Agathodaimon, or "the good guiding spirit"*

The Outward Spiral

*T*he Roman cult of Mithras is associated with the figure of Aion, a lion-headed god entwined by a serpent. Aion represents the boundless time that holds sway over the ages and the cyclic divisions of the year. In his hands he carries the keys of the solstices: The silver one opens the Gate of Cancer, the Way of the Ancestors, the door leading beyond the processes of birth and death; and the golden one opens the Gate of Capricorn, the Way of the Gods, through which the gods descend to earth (186).

The Way of the Ancestors and the Way of the Gods, which represent laws as eternal and unchanging as the universe itself, are alternative representations of the native tradition and the Hermetic tradition, the two paths in the Western Way: The native tradition seeks guidance from our ancestors, who have been elevated to the status of gods, while the Hermetic tradition looks to the stars and the angelic presences that inhabit them to be the mediators between mankind and God.

As we shall see, these are different but complementary approaches to the same end: a fuller understanding of our place in the scheme of things. Both have helped to preserve an ancient wisdom that would otherwise have been lost to the world. In Herman Hesse's novel *The Glass Bead Game* a group of esoteric philosophers known as the League of Journeyers to the East are said to have "contributed new insights into the nature of our culture and the possibility of its continuance, not so much by analytical and scholarly work, as by their capacity, based on ancient spiritual exercises, for mystical identification with remote ages and cultural conditions." (243) The same can be said of the explorers of the Western Way, those magicians and Hermeticists who have helped to preserve and transmit the ancient Mysteries to our own times. The magus continues the work of the native shaman and expands our knowledge of the universe through his use of the same kind of "ancient spiritual exercise"' as the philosophers of Hesse's novel.

The path of the esoteric tradition has veered sharply through many centuries in order to preserve its teachings. Sometimes it has been paved and other times it has appeared as no more than a dirt track kept open by the tread of a few solitary walkers. It has never been a common highway, yet it has rerouted itself time and again in order to accommodate all kinds of travelers. It has explored new and different traditions so that "however its continuity may be broken by opposing systems, it will make its appearance at different periods of time, as long as the sun itself shall illumine the world." (589)

In the introduction to part 1 we described the path of the native tradition as the inward spiral of a labyrinth—the way that leads into the heart of ancestral earth wisdom. The Hermetic tradition, we will discover, is the outward spiral of the same labyrinth—a path of evolving consciousness that is informed by the inner resources of our ancestral roots. Neither tradition is "better" than the other, but instead each informs and teaches the other as together the two traditions form the Western Way.

Between these two complementary opposites we can measure and balance our esoteric experience. As we have seen, the native tradition has embodied a move from a tribal or collective consciousness toward an appreciation of individual, self-aware consciousness. The Hermetic tradition takes individual consciousness on the journey toward cosmic consciousness, or the macrocosmic augmenting of our first, collective awareness. Such an evolution is the work of many millennia and can be judged only from where we stand now. We have by no means always moved progressively. Both traditions have a tendency to pull out of true: The native tradition, as we noted in part 1, has a tendency to atavistic reversion, while the Hermetic tradition tends to pull in the direction of speculative projection and the purposely obscure. To remain in balance, it is necessary for us to walk the path in the precious present moment—to be aware of dreams, visions, and realizations, but also to be pragmatically grounded in the way life reveals itself through daily experience. As soon as we move out of this place of balance, the now that is ever becoming, we risk falling into either nostalgia or vain speculation.

The tribe, forged from people, ruler, and shaman, was the unit of the native tradition. Within it shared ideas and concepts took the place of religion, and the ties that held it together were those of blood—shared genetic heritage. But "when blood became mixed by exogamy (marriage out of the tribal unit) . . . close connections with his ancestors was [sic] severed and man began to live his own personal life." (568)

This severing of a direct link with the ancestral realms and the introduction of new blood into the tribal unit enabled the transmission of new messages into human consciousness, allowing it to develop away from a purely tribal heritage. The collective consciousness of the tribe was open to new influences. In place of a succession of shamans, a "philosophic clan moved across the face of Europe under such names as 'the Illuminati.' "(36) A new relationship was established, not with the ancestors, but with teachers upon inner planes. These otherworldly beings include disincarnate ancestors of great wisdom as well as non-human spirits who are understood to guide and shepherd human development. The new kinship began to be one of brother and sister initiates—a subtle transmutation of the old tribal relationships based on blood.

The fellowship of esotericists is a mystical one, creating a spiritual rather than ancestral bond. The role of the esotericist in this age (see chapters 6 and 8) may be likened to the Judaic tradition of the Justified Ones, who sustain the world by their hidden lives, or to the company of Grail hermits, who, while living quietly in the woods and deserts, advise those knights who quest for the Grail.

The aggressive secrecy surrounding the Western Way certainly has not ameliorated the fear and distrust of the shaman and magician throughout the ages. While periods of persecution throughout history have been responsible for this secrecy and thus our distrust, the fact that we have become estranged from esoteric knowledge has contributed to our current misunderstanding: "What is natural in psyche has in our culture become unique, occult, and mysterious." (489) A great part of our misunderstanding is the fear that the esotericist is dealing with forbidden things—terrible powers that could prove destructive.

The myth of the Fall of Atlantis represents to the esotericist what the Fall from Eden symbolizes to the Jew or Christian: a precocious striving for knowledge that upsets the natural order. According to tradition, Atlantis fell—submerged in a mighty cataclysm—due to an abuse of priestly power that disrupted the delicate balance of the environment.

In Eden, the Fall was brought about by disobedience to God's commandment not to eat of the Tree of the Knowledge of Good and Evil. It does not matter whether we can geographically locate Atlantis or Eden in time and space; they remain as mythic paradigms of what has been lost, states that have been withdrawn from us, golden ages that cannot return. Our times resonate strongly with the Atlantis/Eden experiment at the mercy of our technology. Our knowledge of its uses can heal or hurt depending on how we harness it. The danger of human hubris confronts us once again.

Yet despite that Eden is lost and Atlantis destroyed, these places haunt our consciousness as states of primal perfection. Atlantis reminds us of potentialities that are lost or lie dormant within us. And we remember that before the apple was taken from the tree, Eden was a place of joy and innocence.

Since the time of Plato, the mystery schools have looked to Atlantis as the source of their knowledge. It seems as though the seeds of that lost land have been scattered throughout the world, blown by the winds and carried by the tides. Rationalists have sought to find the Lost Continent, and researchers of more or less scholarly repute have tried to assemble the fragments of languages, potsherds, and ethnographical data to account for its disappearance.

But whatever the impetus for our fascination with that ancient place, we must be wary of seeking to inhabit a new Golden Age. As some who have tried know, we can never achieve a community of perfection—yet we do not wish to live with the futility of despair. The truth is that we are neither saviors of the world nor victims of the gods, but intermediaries who can synthesize the wisdom of both the earth and the stars. This ability is illustrated by the figure of the Aion, who holds the keys that enable us to correct the imbalances of our age: We stand between the ancestors and the gods as human beings who can walk between the worlds.

Another way of grasping this concept is through an understanding of the relationship of microcosm and macrocosm, which is the key to the Hermetic tradition and is at the core of mystery teachings of all traditions. The macrocosm represents the eternal reality of light, the realm of God. The microcosm is a reflection or fragmentation of the light, the realm of humanity in creation, the Body of Light scattered throughout the universe. Each created thing bears a spark of the divine light. While some forget their original condition, others remember and become

walkers between the worlds who make the reassembling of the Body of
Light their overriding aim. Yet the Body of Light, like that of Humpty
Dumpty, is so fragmented that it seems the pieces could never be reassembled. Between inertia and the multiplicity of ways to achieve this end, the
task looks impossible. For some, the realization that their individual
divine spark is trapped in flesh brings about a denial of the body itself.

There are some, though, who seek to reassemble the Body of Light
by religious or esoteric means. In each generation there are a number of
people who dedicate themselves to this task. These Justified Ones are
not necessarily in touch with one another, but their work has a cumulative effect because the inhabitants of spiritual reality perceive them as
one family of Light. The Hermetic tradition reflects this same goal: to
rectify and unite the microcosmic light with the macrocosmic light, to
discover the Hidden Stone, the Holy Grail, to forge the seeds of light
into a cube of true gold. This is the Great Work and the aim of esoteric
philosophy.

Esotericism has been accused of being an escape from the world. As
the philosopher Frithjof Schuon has observed:

> All esotericism appears to be tinged with heresy from the point of
> view of the corresponding exotericism, but this obviously does not
> disqualify it if it is intrinsically orthodox, and thus in conformity
> with truth as such and with the traditional symbolism to which it
> pertains; it is true that the most authentic esotericism can inciden-
> tally depart from this framework and refer to foreign symbolisms,
> but it cannot be syncretistic in its very substance. (524)

Hermetic esotericism is concerned with just such traditional symbolism and the truth of its wisdom. Hermeticism is in the peculiar position of guarding the mystical traditions of those religions and systems
that have become exoteric or which have fallen out of history as living
systems themselves. Exotericism and esotericism need each other.
Without its mystical tradition, an exoteric system is like a rose without
its perfume. Without the structures of exotericism, esotericism is an
image without a temple. If high, mystical knowing does not percolate
through to everyday life, it will be forever separate from it—a tempta-
tion to spiritual pride and elitism.

The main problem confronting any newcomer to the esoteric is
motivation. Few people are raised in an environment informed by a

172 THE HERMETIC TRADITION

mystical tradition and even fewer have any experience of a living spiritual tradition at all. The exoteric world views the esoteric as evil, pertaining to the devil, morally corrupt, and sexually depraved. It is all very well for the experienced esotericist to deny these projections—which is what they are—but for those venturing along this path for the first time, there is the underlying suspicion of being involved in something deviant or hostile to spiritual progress. Certainly, without an experienced guide at our side, some of this may be true; what was once familiar territory is now virtually uncharted and attitudes and knowledge that were once widely held are now unknown to most of us. In chapters 8 and 9 we discuss ways to find a teacher or inner guide.

But even with guidance, how is the beginner on the Hermetic path of the Western Way to steer a course through such an unfamiliar landscape? Using common sense and sensitive intuition is necessary, as is resonating with the wisdom of the tradition. Those who seek to walk the Way alone, without the guidance of their tradition, without the sustenance of spiritual bread, are more likely to stray from their path.

Each of us is a microcosm in which matter and spirit are mixed to form totally individual expressions of humanity. During incarnation we all meet certain very necessary initiations of a mundane kind: We struggle from one stage to another in our lives, learning the lessons of childhood, adolescence, and adulthood. Depending upon our experience with each of these initiations, we will formulate a personal philosophy of living. Eventually, once we arrive at an optimum point of experience and maturity, we may decide to try the esoteric way. But how do we know that this is "white" and not "black" magic—the right-hand path or the left-hand path?

Alice Bailey's *Treatise on White Magic* says: "The left-hand path . . . is the path of progress for substance or matter. If our path does not lead us to an evolution of consciousness, to a kindling of spirit within matter, then we are indeed walking the left-hand path which diverges from the Western Way in its intent." (34)

As a rule, the Hermeticist does not talk about *good* and *evil* because these terms are subjective and misleading: One person's evil is another's good. We must see things instead in terms of balanced polarities. We are not saying that good and evil do not manifest in life—we know very well that they do—but we must not think of them in terms of absolute realities. Still, their dualism is hard to escape in our common speech or mental processes. We shall be seeing how the ancients polarized two eternally opposed causes of good and evil. God and the devil, angel and demon are still polarized images in our consciousness, though we must resist such ready definitions of opposites.

This is not to ignore the very real horror of evil as we all experience it. *Evil* remains a name for something unbalanced, something whose origins rest in expediency, selfishness, ignorance, or neglect. Our souls can perceive the evil or unbalanced forces around us much like our noses can detect a bad odor. Evil appears deceptively smooth and charming, often in the form of what we most wish for. But in seeking to acquire it, we often pay with our own integrity. It can lead us from the work of meshing the microcosmic and macrocosmic worlds into the "deepening of the plane." (189) In short, we sell our pearl of great price for ready cash and may even prostitute our immortal soul.

If you wish to read more about this issue—for goodness knows it is not easy to speak about or understand—an excellent source is *The Cosmic Doctrine,* by Dion Fortune (160), which has this to say: "[E]vil is simply that which is moving in the opposite direction to evolution. [It] is that which . . . tends to revert to the Unmanifest. Evil can be viewed, if this is helpful, as the principle of inertia which binds 'the good.' Good can be seen as the principle of creative movement," which resists inertia. We arrive at the expressions *negative* and *positive* in order to enable ourselves to grasp these principles in a more helpful, less relative way. The way of Chaos, as an expression of the negative pole, can be cleansing and effective, just as the way of creativity as an expression of the positive pole can represent an imbalanced fertility. Which of these can be said to be good or evil?

So what does the Hermetic way offer as its contribution to the balanced way of evolution? We all have to face situations and decide whether to grasp the nettle or to flee, like the Fool of the Tarot or the young man in the Gospel who left his garment behind him—leaving everything, if necessary, in order to live and fight another day. All disciplines have their martyrs and their survivors. Those who follow the Western Way are not the elect; they do not offer a dogmatic package to salvation. They are merely coworkers, mediators between microcosm and macrocosm who believe in their tradition as a means of spiritual progression. This essential work is not the sole province of esotericists, but is the work of all religious traditions, arts and crafts, and skills. The mystic, poet, artist—every member of the secret commonwealth (see chapter 5)—contributes to this work.

The safest method of traveling the Hermetic path is by means of a spiritual tradition—whether an orthodox religion or an alternative expression.

> For it is the height of evil not to know God: but to be capable of knowing God, and to wish and hope to know him, is the road which leads straight to the Good; and it is an easy road to travel. Everywhere God will come to meet you, everywhere he will appear to you, at places and times at which you look not for it, in your waking hours and in your sleep, when you are journeying by water and by land, in the night-time and in the day-time, when you are speaking and when you are silent: for there is nothing which is not God. And do you say 'God is invisible'? Speak not so. Who is more manifest than God? (533)

This truth, which comes from a Hermetic—rather than Christian—text, is universally applicable for any who walk the path.

In part 1 we spoke of three different regions of the Otherworld known to the native tradition: the Underworld, Middle Earth, and the Upperworld. Within the Hermetic tradition, the Otherworld, frequently referred to as the inner planes, is often seen as representing the macro-cosmic level of reality. Today, those who are interested in magic and the Hermetic tradition have an increasing tendency to perceive spiritual reality as having a psychological source in the unconscious and the Otherworld as a construct originating in the imagination of human consciousness. This perception is both untrue and misleading. By all means, create your own metaphors for these realms, but do not mistake their origins or confuse them with the workings of your own psyche.

As you read through part 2, there are several instances of usage and pieces of information to bear in mind. Please note that the word *God* appears in the text to signify the intelligence at the source of reality—neither male nor female but pure spirit—unless otherwise stated. We have used the *the God* and *the Goddess* to signify the principles of the Divine Masculine and the Divine Feminine that are operational within mythological or other systems. Within the Hermetic tradition, the Emerald Tablet of Hermes Trismegistos is the Rosetta Stone, which interprets many mysteries. As a symbol it is balanced by the Rose of Aphrodite, signifying the esoteric wisdom of the Divine Feminine—a badge that identifies the fellow pathwalker.

We begin our journey in the temenos of the mystery schools, where we see how native tradition flows into Hermetic tradition and how both traditions have been preserved and fostered from ancient times to today. In chapter 7 we consider the spiritual traditions and their seeming divergence from the mystery schools. In chapter 8 we see how the role of the magician is a continuation of both shaman and priest. In chapter 9 we consider the cosmologies and symbol systems that have informed the divergent Hermetic traditions and give a list of inner guardians or contacts with whom you can work in a practical way. Chapter 10 sees the goal of the Great Work through the eyes of the alchemist, and in the Epilogue, Tomorrow's Tradition, we attempt to take the next step upon the Western Way.

To those who have read part 1 and feel that the native tradition is indeed their way, we would say this: There are many treasures worth seeking within the Hermetic way. Neither path is an end in itself and we do not leave behind the loved, familiar landscapes of home or the earthy wisdom of the ancestors by progressing on the evolutionary way to cosmic consciousness. Dion Fortune had it right when she wrote:

> Do not let us forget that there is our own native esotericism hidden in the superconscious mind of the race, and that we have our own holy places at our very doors which have been used for initiations from time immemorial. Potent alike for the native contacts of the Celts, the work of the Hermeticist, and the mystical experience of the Church of the Holy Grail. (161)

Part 2 differs from part 1 in that we refer to a variety of traditions rather than just one. As you work out for yourself a system of study and practice, please be sure that you do not mix traditions. Certain traditons—such as the kabbalah—may seem to work well with others, but each has its own wisdom to be best appreciated in its own context.

Notes on the Practices in Part 2

Once again, the practices at the end of each chapter—original exercises based upon Hermetic sources—allow you to experience firsthand the realities presented here. Although the Hermetic path has been seen as syncretic, full of pied meanings and tangled imagery and involving complex systems of correspondences, we hope to reveal the unified simplicity at its heart without throwing its Mysteries to the four winds.

Because the material in part 2 is more intellectually demanding than that of part 1 (the native tradition is really most often felt as a gut response or a yearning in the heart), it is particularly important that the exercises be applied practically. Theoretical or armchair esotericism saps all vitality from the Hermetic path of the Western tradition.

Please refer to Notes on the Practices in This Book (page 15) for helpful information on performing the exercises that follow. Remember to set yourself a reasonable regimen for entering your own spiritual landscape, mapping it out over a period of months. Contact your guardian and listen to any instructions or teachings that he or she communicates to you and meditate upon a particular mythology or symbology. A kabbalistic text gives this advice about meditation:

> Make yourself right. Meditate in a special place, where your voice cannot be heard by others. Cleanse your heart and soul of all other thoughts in the world. Imagine that at this time, your soul is separating itself from your body, and that you are leaving the physical world behind you, so that you enter the Future World, which is the source of all life distributed to the living. (286)

If you are looking for a complete magical system here, you will be disappointed. There are many books that deal with the classical methods of ritual magic. If this is where your interest lies, you might want to consult the works of Gareth Knight, William Gray, R. J. Stewart, or Melita Denning and Osborne Phillips, which are listed in the bibliography. We do, however, include an initiatory exercise, practice 15, The Foursquare Citadel, which gives the practitioner a magic circle, Hermetic chamber, or tower of art to work from and offers a firsthand initiation into the power of the elements.

Many of the following practices can be adapted within the limits stated to create the basis of further work. Follow your own path according to your specific preference and requirements. The strength of the Western Way lies in the diversity of its practice and the unity of its aims. As for the native tradition, a list of training centers and established mystery schools for the Hermetic tradition is included at the end of the book.

It is worth stating again that the prerequisites for all meditation and inner work are intent, preparation, conscientious practice and performance, and service. The indication of your willingness to serve can take many forms—perhaps as a short formula or ritual gesture during which the gifts of realization that you have received are mediated with understanding and intention to the world. This formal act is the prayer of the Hermeticist and even if you have not begun to meditate or work formally, you can share in this meditation. At midday, every day—when the sun is at its zenith, regardless of what clocks designate as noon—people from many different traditions all over the world elevate their thoughts to the spiritual sun. By doing so they are tuning in to their spiritual source and sharing a brief communion with all others whose aim is the reassembly of the Body of Light, the redemption of the world—whatever their metaphor may be for the Great Work. To share this moment every day you need only shut your eyes and silently affirm, in your own words, your dedication to the work and your willingness to serve. If you have received an inner gift or realization, offer this in mediation at midday so that others may tune in to it.

This brief meditation is one step toward the union of microcosm and macrocosm and is part of a commitment that Hermeticists call "the unreserved dedication," an unbloody offering of ourselves and our resources to the service of God—however that term is understood. Of course, we initiates cannot offer the unreserved dedication until we actually have something to offer. We must first serve an apprenticeship of patient learning and willing arduous practice. The work of creation is the continual mediation of life itself. Our contacts on the inner planes are the servants of the mysteries, gatekeepers who allow initiates to pass through and experience inner worlds. When initiates are properly trained, they in turn stand at the nexus of the worlds as potential helpers and gatekeepers who can teach the mediation of inner energy to the initiates who come after them.

Those who are drawn to the Hermetic tradition only to wear gaudy robes and wield ritual implements will find that the mere possession of these may inflate the ego but do nothing to increase prowess in ceremonial magic unless wielded with intent. Implements, incense, and robes are props to remind the magician of the sacred nature of the Great Work, and though they are helpful in any magical practice, they are not essential.

Clean garments are all that the beginner requires and more often a bedroom, garden shed, attic, or living room suffices for a ceremonial place. The use of the great outdoors is something that the Hermetic tradition could borrow from the native tradition. While Hermeticists have traditionally met indoors in secret chambers and hidden temples, a secluded outdoor working space can be quite as effective. Ultimately, however, in a crowded world, only the space inside our mind seems solely private.

As you did in part 1, remember to keep a written record of your work—even if your impressions seem trivial, for they actually may be important realizations. Such a record is also useful in revealing, over the years, a pattern to your inner work.

6
Schools of Mystery

There is every reason to believe that the so-called secret societies of the ancient world were branches of the one philosophical tree which, with its roots in heaven and its branches on the earth, is like the spirit of Man—an invisibly but ever-present cause of the objectified vehicle that gave it expression.
—MANLY P. HALL, *SECRET TEACHINGS OF ALL AGES*

Happy is he who passed through the mysteries: he knows the origin and the end of life.
—PINDAR

Flashes of Fire

*T*he mystery schools, ancient and modern, show the way, possessing the maps and compasses necessary to explore the realms of creation. Whoever seeks initiation into the temples and lodges of the Western Way is offered training in the use and mastery of these tools. No one is cast adrift in an open boat to sail uncharted seas or sent forth on a highway that has not already been walked by others. The Mysteries are the spiritual life of the people, and to discover them is to read the story of a divine spark still burning in the temple of the human spirit.

Once there was no purely native or Hermetic tradition, only a universal response by the Firstborn to the earth lore and star magic of their shamans. Later, as the primal impulse of the Foretime split into separate cults, these two approaches, which we may think of as chthonic (earthly) and stellar, grew farther apart, until the beginnings of the Hermetic tradition were seeded in Egypt and the Hellenic world, while in Europe the native traditions remained more or less grounded in the magic earth.

We have to be wary of assuming, however, that because much of the later Hermetic philosophy originated in Greece and Egypt, these areas possessed no native tradition, or that the development of religion and magic in the West was so primitive and slow that it required cross-fertilization with other sources to realize more subtle realms of experience. The earth-based traditions and the Hermetic Mysteries are inextricably linked in the evolution of human consciousness.

Certainly, when Alexander of Macedon died in 323 B.C.E., there was already a high degree of interrelation within the Mysteries. Alexander's vast empire extended from the Straits of Gibraltar to the Indus Valley and from Germany to the Russian Steppe, the Sahara, and the Indian Ocean. Over this huge area, which included Persia, Egypt, and Mesopotamia, the Greek mystery religions were being formed, some on already existing foundations and others from a combination of several cultural sources. As F. C. Grant points out in his excellent survey of the period, "It is important to realize that only very rarely, if ever, did an ancient cult come to an end, supplanted by the dominant cult of the conquerors. Instead the old cults lived on, some of them extremely primitive, others more advanced." (191)

Some were changed, either for better or for worse, by the effect of the philosophical bent of the Greek mind, others as a "result of that mysterious inner source of change and development that affects all our civilizations . . ." (191) Professor Grant is a historian rather than an esotericist, but he points to the relationship between traditions that helped formulate the Mysteries. The more closely we look at this time of fusion, the less it is possible to categorically state that any specific geographic or historic point of origin was responsible for the evolution of the Mysteries. They were all, as Manly Hall suggests, "branches of one philosophical tree." (226) As figure 12 shows, a complex web of interaction does exist, linking schools that are far apart in both time and space. Rather than a literal, historical succession, it seems that all schools drew upon a common source of wisdom that was contactable and available through spiritual practice. None of these schools was superior to or more eminent than another. Initiates have a way of finding and recognizing their spiritual kin, and we know from classical

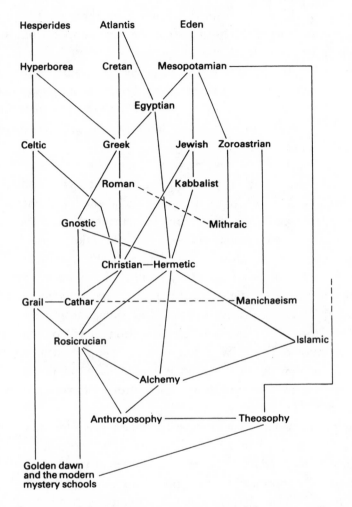

Fig. 12. This "tree of the Mysteries" traces some of the major influences on the Western esoteric tradition.

accounts that initiates offered hospitality to those visitors from other traditions.

It has often been said that the Egyptian Mysteries are the true foundation upon which the Western Hermetic traditions are built. This is due in part to an early identification of the Egyptian god Thoth, the scribe and guardian of the Mysteries, with Hermes Trismegistos, the supposed founder of Western occult practice. Thus in the Hermetic text known as *Kore Kosmou,* we find Hermes addressing his "son" Asclepios in the following words: "Art thou not aware, O Asclepios, that Egypt is the image of heaven, or rather, that it is the projection below of the order of things above? If the truth must be told, this land is indeed the temple of the world." (314)

There is certainly evidence of the extreme antiquity of the Egyptian Mysteries. Persistent traditions relate the Sphinx to a period long before the foundation of religion in Egypt, and the fact that the four beasts that make up the Sphinx appear in later esoteric practice is an indication of this (252).

Other traces of Egyptian mystery teaching are to be found in the Western tradition, however, including the red and white pillars before the temple of Osiris at Memphis, which echo the black and white pillars of justice and mercy in kabbalistic teaching; and the symbolic regalia of the god-king pharaohs—scepter and ark, sword and mace—recalling both Grail traditions (see chapter 5) and the four suits of the Tarot. Other aspects of Tarot symbolism have been attributed to Egyptian influence or origin, but there is little hard evidence for this (see chapter 4). It is also possible to see in the conical headdress supposedly worn by Hermes Trismegistos a recollection of the double crown of Upper and Lower Egypt. While all of this adds up to nothing more than a systematic borrowing from Egyptian beliefs and practices, it has somehow become crystallized into the notion of Egypt as originator of the greatest Western mystery teachings.

Egypt indeed had many mysteries, none more important than those of Isis. Her name is said to mean "throne," "wisdom," or "savior," though she possessed many other titles testifying to the universality of her cult. Above the entrance to her temple at Sais appeared the words: "I, Isis, am all that has been, that is or shall be: no mortal man has ever seen me unveiled." The Roman author Lucius Apuleius, in a famous passage from his novel *The Golden Ass* (14), describes her as crowned with the moon and clad in a robe of stars (see fig. 19, page 287). In Hermetic lore she became identified as the daughter of Hermes, standing for the innermost secret of the Mysteries. Many have sought to obtain a glimpse through her veil, but only she may choose to show herself. Like the Mysteries themselves, she hides from all but the most steadfast seeker.

The deeper Mysteries of Isis, and of her consort Osiris, revolve around his death at the hands of his brother Set, who cuts Osiris's body into fourteen parts and scatters them throughout the world. Isis undertakes a terrible journey, suffering great hardship, to find the broken body of her lord and to reassemble it. She finds all the parts except for the phallus, which was thrown into the Nile and consumed by a fish. But such is the creative power of Isis that she is able to conceive by means of an artificial phallus and bears the child Horus, who avenges his father by killing Set.

This is an archetypal mystery story, introducing themes found later in the teachings of the Hellenic schools and in the work of modern esoteric orders. It prefigures the death and rising of many gods and illustrates the power of the creative principle. It also establishes Isis as queen of heaven, more powerful in the eyes of many of her followers than the great god Ra himself, represented on earth by the pharaoh.

According to one theory, the period over which the Egyptian pantheon ruled corresponds to the entire history of the world, so the sorrows of Isis, in which she mourns the death of Osiris in a way similar to Mary's mourning of the death of Christ, relate to the agonies of our own time. The dawning of the New Age is sometimes seen as heralding the birth of Horus, who will come as a savior and introduce a reign of peace and plenty.

R. A. Schwaller de Lubicz, the great student of Egyptian esotericism, described the magnum opus of the Egyptian Mysteries as "the reconciliation of Set and Horus." Since this great rapprochement has yet to occur in serial time, we may see it as a metaphor of the time span of the gods (527). The reconciliation of opposing forces, the reassembling of scattered lore or fragmented power, and the emergence of a divine principle to bring about the redemption of mankind are recurrent themes in the great mystery cults of the West. Out of these recurrent motifs comes the notion of a divine spark in man, a fragment of godhead buried in each of us.

In Egypt this motif was personified by the pharaoh, the son of the god on earth, whose task it was to perform the rites that would one day restore the world to the perfection of the First Time *(tep zepi),* a lost Golden Age that existed "before anger, or noise, or conflict, or disorder made their appearance." (140) There was no distinction between king and priest, religious and secular office in Egypt. It was to the "King in man," the spark of inner fire, that the people addressed themselves in their worship of the pharaoh. He, the king, was a manifestation of higher orders of creation—what de Lubicz calls *anthropocosmos,* or cosmic man. In the complex structure of the Egyptian Mysteries, every part of the temple, as well as the regalia of the god-king, pointed toward the fulfillment of a godlike state through the enactment of the

Mysteries. Colors, statues, reliefs, and obelisks were all indicators of the stages of an ongoing process toward perfection. Like the steps in the alchemical Great Work or the architecture of the medieval cathedrals or, indeed, the standing stones and circles discussed in part 1, these were concrete externalizations of the highest Mysteries.

In the many histories of the ancient world, only one figure is described as being of greater importance than Hermes. This is the Persian mage Zoroaster, who may actually have lived around 1000 B.C.E. or even earlier, but who clearly did not predate the foundation of the Egyptian Mysteries, which served as the basis of his own system. It is from the Persian Mysteries, of which Zoroaster is the chief author, that we derive the dualistic specter that has haunted esoteric philosophy and teaching ever since. In the Zoroastrian pantheon these opposing forces, Ormuzd and Ahriman, derive ultimately from Ahura Mazda, the divine principle. Known as the Holy Immortals, or Amesha Spentas (*spenta* means "bounteous," or "the effulgence of God's goodness"), they correspond to the levels of creation, foreshadowing the teaching of later mystery schools such as those of Orpheus and Mithras.

Against the Spentas are arrayed the Devas, the companions of the Evil One who rule over the earth. They are comparable to the kabbalistic *qliphoth*. In truth, Persian dualism is confused by a Zoroastrian heresy called Zurvanism, which is often mistaken for mainstream Zoroastrianism. In Zoroastrianism proper, Ahura Mazda is alone the supreme god; his Spentas are not on the same footing. Zurvanism, however, makes Ahura Mazda into a lesser creator, or demiurge, hence the cosmic struggle of good against evil that takes place in the world of matter. In Zoroastrian teaching a savior, or *saoshyant,* will be born who will combat evil and bring the struggle to an end once and for all, betokening the Frasokereti, the making perfect at the end of time (see chapters 7 and 9).

In this we already see both an echo of the Egyptian Mysteries and a prefiguring of the later Gnostic position. This inheritance of dualistic thinking continues to dog our steps. Occasionally, however, there have been moments in which the seemingly endless struggle is balanced by the appearance of a third figure—the Messiah, which, as one commentator has already said, becomes a requirement of all dualistic thinking sooner or later (191).

In Mithraism, which descended from the Persian Mysteries,

Mithras stands as a mediator between light and dark with the battle for the soul being fought out in the territory of the flesh. Mithras, entering there, keeps all in balance, prefiguring Christ, with whom he shares a startling number of other similarities. Mithras is born in a cave on December 25, watched over by shepherds, and at the end of his earthly life he holds a last supper with his elect followers before departing mysteriously for heaven. According to some sources he is supposed to have suffered crucifixion and death and to have risen again three days later. Finally, like Christ, he is to come again as a judge at the end of time and lead his followers to heaven (616). Mithraic initiates lived their lives as mediators of their lord's wisdom, mirroring his life and struggle against the darkness. Both the magician (see chapter 3) and the follower of Christ (see chapter 7) operate in this same way.

Joscelyn Godwin, in his authoritative work on the mystery religions, suggests that Mithraism is a clairvoyant prefiguring of Christianity, which seems more than clear in the following extract from a Persian Mithraic text. Mithras states: "He who will not eat of my body and drink of my blood, so that he will be made one with me and I with him, the same shall not know salvation." (185) Beyond this, the similarities are only superficial. Christianity has certainly never been as tolerant of other beliefs as Mithraism, nor has it guarded its Mysteries half so well. On the other hand, it has survived while Mithraism has not, and to this day little is known of the Mithraic Mysteries. Still, the theme is there: the penetration of the physical world by the Divine, macrocosm entering microcosm, God sending forth an emissary into the world. And certainly Mithraism, which was taken up by the armies of Rome and through them spread to most parts of the world, left its mark on the native traditions wherever it went.

The Mithraic Mysteries succeeded those of Zoroaster, but also followed those of Dionysus, through which the core of Hellenic mystery teaching found its way into the Western Way. Indeed, we can discern two branches of consciousness within the classical Mysteries: Dionysian and Apollonian. The Mysteries of Dionysus, those of the sacrificed king, pertain to the Underworld, the chthonic and ecstatic cult of maenads and bacchantes. The Apollonian Mysteries, on the other hand, relate to reason, to the heavens, and to order, in direct contradiction to the ecstatic Mysteries of Dionysus. Orpheus, whose Mysteries grew out of both cults, combines both facets. His lyre and gift of music come from Apollo, yet he ends like Dionysus, torn apart by Thracian bacchantes. He embodies the shamanic practices of the native tradition overlapping the magical rites of the mystery school.

In the Mysteries of Dionysus we again meet the theme of the divine spark trapped in matter. In this case the divinity is literally torn apart, cooked, and then and eaten by Titans. Zeus, the demiurge, sees this and destroys the Titans, creating mankind from their fragmented substance. Thus elements of both Titanic and Dionysian force are present within man, though the Titanic element holds sway, accounting for the warring nature of mankind. Only when total harmony and balance exist is Dionysus reborn and the perfection of all things brought about. In cosmological terms, the Titans are represented by the twelve signs of the zodiac that rule over our lives; Dionysus is the sun, warming us and causing the fruition of matter.

Dionysus belongs with those gods who descend to the Underworld in search of either enlightenment or some lost aspect of themselves. Psyche's quest for Cupid, Ishtar's search for Tammuz, Isis's hunt for the scattered members of Osiris, and Orpheus's search for Euridice are all synonymous with the initiate's search for the absolute, what is interpreted by the Mysteries as the fragment of divinity within us. Through ritual we follow the god or goddess, enacting the journey.

At Eleusis, where the Mysteries of Demeter were celebrated every five years, the candidates of the lesser Mysteries underwent a symbolic journey, reenacting Demeter's quest in Hades for Persephone, her lost child, with the initiate playing the role of Demeter. The journey was that of the darkened soul: The candidate passed through a door into total darkness. If he survived the experiences he encountered, he passed through a second door into brilliant light, which symbolized rebirth into the heavenly sphere. Here he met the gods, experiencing Demeter's journey as his own recovery of lost enlightenment.

In the Eleusian Mysteries, the birth of the soul into matter is seen as death. It is only by participation in the Mysteries that the initiate can rise to a timeless reality where he is utterly free and alive. The soul sleeps in the body most of the time, awakening only when it has been transformed by ritual and the use of an initiatory drink. To die without this experience is to sleep forever or to wander homeless in the caverns of Hades.

In the broadest sense, all such quests and descents represent the theme of the spirit embodied in matter. The farther Ishtar or Demeter descends in her search, the greater her suffering. Similarly, the farther we humans descend into matter, the more we suffer exile from the blessed realms. The fact that Psyche, Ishtar, Persephone, and Orpheus are able to return from the Underworld is a symbol of hope, implying that humanity can realize the gift of the Divine and assimilate it into the human condition.

The further the Mysteries remove themselves from the reality of earth, however, the more speculative and transcendent they become and the more the embodiment of spirit in matter is seen in terms of the spiritual spark becoming trapped in the prison of the flesh, from which it must be released.

It is in the Orphic Mysteries above all that we first come to terms with this perilous descent into darkness and the reemergence into primal light. The suffering of Orpheus, who loses Euridice through fear, the first pitfall of all mystery knowledge, and who is then dismembered by the Maenads, can be seen as a paradigm of the suffering and rebirth of the sleeping soul. As a descendant of Dionysus, Orpheus is the intellectual image of a demigod raised to deity by his sufferings in the Underworld—perfect symbol for all who follow the path of the Mysteries.

The movement from the cult of Dionysus to Orphism marks a shift from a native response toward a more Hermetic philosophy and mysticism that included belief in the transmigration of souls, reincarnation, and final assumption into godhead. In the Orphic Mysteries, when the first real moment of stillness comes into being, the Dionysian frenzy ends and peace reigns. The strains of Orpheus's lyre tame more than the beasts; they also soothe the Titanic element in humans.

It may be said that the Orphites were "the first real Christians" (185)—in some senses more Christian than Jesus' own followers. For this reason, perhaps, Christianity borrowed much from Orphism through the neo-Pythagorean schools of the first century, among whose initiates were Plutarch and Paul of Tarsus. There is considerable borrowing of Orphic matter in the Pauline Epistles.

The Orphic Mysteries (or rather, the theology built upon them) were complex in the extreme. A full account can be found in G. R. S. Mead's *Orpheus*. (409) Here, it must suffice to say that each of the energies ruling creation was tabulated in Triads, Dodecans, and Monads. Descending from the ineffable One, the Godhead, were a number of lesser powers, demigods, and deities who were each related to one another both within and separate from their individual triads. The overall rate of communication between these correspondences was so swift and total that the mind cannot comprehend it. Only through the attainment of a super-sensible state of awareness—through initiation—could humans attain real understanding.

Orphic cosmology also suggested that each star or planetary sphere contained aspects of all the deities—a lunar Ceres, a saturnine Apollo, a mercurial Hera, and so on. And, of course, there were planetary aspects present within each of the deities, so Dionysus might be modified by lunar, solar, and saturnine declensions. The gods themselves formed a constantly shifting matrix of planetary influence, which means that an initiate who invoked a lunar deity was at the same time in touch with all the gods and thus all the planetary influences of the heavens.

This complex organization kept the cosmos turning and ensured that, however intricate Orphic theology and cosmology became, the most important aspect could be grasped through direct experience. Orphism taught that mankind and the gods are related at the most subtle and sensitive level, where an overlapping of human consciousness and the awareness of the Divine becomes the focus for revelation. The belief "Everything that lives is holy" becomes a reality in the interaction of the divine and the mundane.

The hierarchy of the Orphic creation was supremely complex, but the gods were like a ladder, a system of related possibilities whose potential was seeded within the whole of creation. We are all related, says Orphism, not only to other humans, but also to the earth and water, sky and stone. This relationship was not understood in the modern scientific sense of a universe of the Divine.

The true meaning of the mystery teaching is that the divine spark, the godlike potential of humanity, lies in that part of us that is always seeking a reunion, a reassembly of separated parts into the whole from which they were created: a return to a state of union. The torn body of the divine, scattered through creation, must be restored.

> Man then is of twofold nature, the Titanic and the Dionysiac, the earthly and the divine. The aim of the Orphic life is by purification, asceticism and ritual to purge away the Titanic part of us and prepare ourselves to become fully divine. The body . . . is a tomb from which the soul of the Orphic initiate will finally be released to find the true life. (633)

Though it may sometimes take as many as thousand-year cycles before the Orphite at last flees the weary wheel of incarnation, each lifetime is spent in realizing the spark of the Divine.

The Orphic school was itself made up of many doctrines. Orpheus is credited with the dissemination of the Mysteries, with passing on rather than inventing much that became the basis of subsequent Graeco-Roman theosophy. Pythagoras followed many of the Orphic teachings and made Orpheus the central deity of his own esoteric system, establishing a canon of Orphic hymns that influenced esotericists as far apart in time and persuasion as Pico della Mirandola (127), Athanasius Kircher (183), and Thomas Taylor, the Platonist (589). This is not surprising when we consider that "the Orphic method aimed at revealing divine things by means of symbols . . . a method common to all writers of divine lore." (484) In later times Orpheus was widely recognized for the symbolism of his seven-stringed lyre and the perfect harmonies he was believed to have produced from it. Combined with Pythagorean knowledge, the Orphic Mysteries became central to the Renaissance arts of music and masque and to the doctrine of the Harmonies and Signatures set forth by writers such as Jacob Boehme (1575–1624) and Marcilio Ficino (1453–1499). Orpheus was recognized as a son of Apollo and Calliope, the Muse of harmony and rhythm, while Euridice was seen as a representative of humanity slain by the serpent of knowledge (a borrowing from later Christian sources), who imprisoned her in the Underworld of ignorance, from which only Orpheus could free her. In this understanding the rending of Orpheus becomes an image of the warring factions of knowledge that are nominally pacified by his music. The seven strings of his lyre are the seven keys of the spectrum, or of universal knowledge. (201)

We can see how this wealth of symbolism must have delighted the minds of the Renaissance philosopher-magicians, who sought to reintroduce the Mysteries into the world and, like Orpheus, harmonize them into a single system. That they failed to do so was not for lack of effort, as we shall see in chapter 8. They came as near as anyone could to achieving a synthesis of mystery school teaching, magic, and philosophy— a goal still sought by many today, though with a good deal less understanding of the common points of balance among the disciplines.

Between the birth of the Orphic Mysteries and their partial revival in the Renaissance, there is a long gap in both time and understanding. In part this was bridged by the figure of the magician, whose role will

Fig. 13. A medieval image of Hermes Trismegistos holding an alchemical text

be discussed more fully in chapter 8, and that of the alchemist, whose work we shall investigate in chapter 10. The magician, in particular, is related to the earlier mystery schools; the alchemist draws upon a far wider range of sources, including Arabic metaphysics and Christian mysticism. The single force uniting all these elements is the body of teaching attributed to Hermes Trismegistos, "Thrice Greatest Hermes," whose doctrines stand at the very heart of the Western Way.

The Hermetic Reality

Hermes saw the totality of things, understood what he had seen, and had the power to reveal it to others. He wrote down all he knew, hiding away most of what he wrote, keeping silent rather than speaking out so that every generation that came into the world had to seek out this knowledge. (533)

This strikes the keynote of Hermeticism: The human soul comes into matter without knowledge and each generation must search for the hidden mysterious truths seeded throughout the world in order to gain freedom. What is more, the Mysteries are not calcified or frozen in time. They change and grow with the transformations that occur in humankind. In seeking the interior spark of the Divine, initiates are forever driven: "[A] desire for the truth, especially about the gods, is in reality a yearning for the Deity. For the study and search [for these things] is a reception, as it were, of things sacred." (484)

This is a summation of the Hermetic quest reiterated throughout the vast spectrum of wisdom that we know as the true *Corpus Hermeticum*. These writings are really only a gathering of fragments attributed to Thoth Tahuti (later called Hermes), though few of them are of genuine Egyptian origin. They have been copied, recopied, edited, altered, and in part destroyed by a succession of Hermetic scholars and teachers down the ages. As Iamblichus noted, the earliest philosophers and mystics used to ascribe their own writings to Hermes, god of wisdom and learning, as though he had written them personally (262)! This has given rise to much confusion over the origins of the *Corpus*. To conflate confusion, Hermes often appears as a character in the texts, making it even more difficult to discover actual sources for the material. Though Hermes hid much of his writing, enough still remains to be uncovered and correctly attributed to make it no simple matter to write with authority about the existing *Corpus*.

It is safe to say, however, that it was in the melting pot of Alexandrian mysticism and philosophy during the first three centuries after Christ that the original Egyptian Hermetic writings became crossfertilized with Judaic and Greek teachings of the Gnostics. The influence of the *Corpus* on Gnosticism was considerable, and it is probably this more than anything that helped preserve the Hermetic tradition, though it cast it permanently into a pseudo-Christian mode—so much so that in the sixteenth century the humanist philosopher Francesco Patrizi petitioned Pope Gregory XIV to allow Hermes to supplant Aristotle as the arbiter of learning in the universities, believing he would resonate more harmoniously with Christian doctrine (189).

In Gnostic literature, Thoth became Hermes Trismegistos and Maat, his wife, was identified with the figure of Sophia, or divine wisdom. The three grades of initiation recognized by the early Hermeticists—Mortals (probationers), Intelligences (vision seekers), and Sons of Light (perfected ones)—were renamed Hyle, Psyche, and Pneuma (see chapter 7). Hermes became tutor to Isis and Osiris and was known as one of the sacred *ogdoad* (eightfold) of the Gnostic cosmology—four pairs of male and female *syzygies* (divine partners or consorts; see chapter 9, page 344) whose task it was to maintain balance in the cosmos. According to G. R. S. Mead, this is the oldest form of the Gnostic structure of deity, and within it Hermes has the supreme task of keeping order among the rest.

The title Trismegistos, or "thrice greatest," has had several different meanings attributed to it. One of the most interesting is found in the writings of the monk Syncellus. He claimed to be quoting from the writings of Menetho, whose works, though lost, were probably the earliest gathering of Hermetic lore (533). According to Syncellus, Menetho refers to certain monuments of the Seriadic country, which contained the original teachings of the first Hermes. These were later translated and set down in writing by the second Hermes ("sometime after the Flood"). From this it is possible to posit the existence of a third figure, also called Hermes, who again worked on the texts, perhaps rendering them into a kind of system. All of this indicates three stages of transmission—the "thrice greatest" refers to the third Hermes, to whom we attribute the whole lore and writings of the original Hermeticists.

So what is the *Corpus Hermeticum?* Basically it is a series of exchanges supposedly between master and pupil or between Hermes Trismegistos and his "sons" (disciples) of various names. They are often repetitive and cover the same ground in varying degrees of complexity. The first and perhaps the best known text is the *Poimandres,* a description of the Creation cast in the form of a dream. In it the unnamed adept falls asleep and is visited by Poimandres (translated loosely as "mind of the sovereignty"), who explains to him all that he wishes to know concerning "the things that are, [how to] understand their nature, and [how to] get knowledge of God" (533): "When he had thus spoken, forthwith all things changed in aspect before me, and were opened out in a moment. And I beheld a boundless view: all was changed into light, a mild and joyous light; and I marvelled when I saw it . . .”

Following is a description of the Creation, a mingling of light and dark from which comes forth “a holy Word . . . and methought this Word was the voice of the Light.” When the seeker desires to understand what he has seen, Poimandres tells him: “That light . . . is I, even Mind, the first God . . . and the Word which came forth from the Light is the son of God.”

When the dreamer asks how this may be, he is told: “Learn my meaning . . . by looking at what you yourself have in you; for in you too, the word is son, and the mind is father of the word. They are not separate one from the other; for life is the union of word and mind.” (533)

Again and again this message is affirmed: There is a god within us that gives life to the body and inspiration to all that we do—events in the sphere of incarnation reflect those in the heavenly sphere. It is this emphasis on unity rather than disharmony that defines the Hermetic Mysteries—unity of God with man, of higher with lower, of divine with mundane, of all things. It finds its clearest expression in the Emerald Tablet of Hermes, with its famous injunction that has been so often quoted and so little understood by occultists throughout the ages: “as above, so below.”

Various legends exist concerning the origin of the Emerald or Smagdarine Tablet. According to one source, it was found by Apollonius of Tyana (see chapter 8), who entered a hidden cave and took the tablet from between the clasped hands of the corpse of Hermes himself. Another version recounts how it was Alexander the Great who found the tomb and carried off the tablet to Alexandria—an interesting explanation for the transmission of the Hermetic Mysteries from their possible place of origin to the city from which their truths became widely disseminated (333). In reality, for a long time the text of the Emerald Tablet was known only in Latin versions dating from the time of the philosopher Albertus Magnus (1193–1280 C.E.), who was believed to have written the material himself. Subsequently, Arabic texts were discovered that dated the Tablet to the time of the alchemist Gebir (722–815 C.E.), or to an even earlier time so that the traditional ascription of its composition to Apollonius may in fact be closer to the truth than any of these theories. Whatever we choose to believe, there is no getting away from the fact that the Emerald Tablet is one of the most profound and important documents to have come down to us. It has been said more than once that it contains the sum of all knowledge—for those able to understand it.

The Tablet outlines a doctrine of signatures and correspondences that reflect the mind of the Creator. The Greek word from which we derive *cosmos* means "order": We live in an ordered creation through which we are able to move at will, yet always find a point of recognition. This is because the cosmos is the product of a single act of generation that has set a signature upon everything. In the finite world to which we attempt to bind ourselves, this is scarcely recognized by anyone, yet the youngest mystery school initiate would have known it, no matter how many different gods he worshipped.

The Smagdarine Tablet describes just such an ordered cosmos: It tells the story of Creation, including its history and its goal, in terms of such blinding simplicity that much like othe,r equally simple statements (such as "Love thy neighbor as thyself") it has been subject to frequent misinterpretation. Our own suggestions as to its meaning will be discussed in chapter 8. There you will find the text of the Emerald Tablet, at the end of the chapter, where it forms an exercise in controlled meditation and where you may study it free of any commentary.

It is said that initiation is always a one-on-one experience: The seeker stands alone (however supported by his or her brethren) before whatever principle he or she seeks to know. In the Western Way, as we have tried to show, all knowledge and experience thus gained is part of a single initiation we must all undergo. It was for this reason that the Temple of Thoth was called the House of the Net, meaning an enclosing snare of matter. To escape this, "captives" (initiates) must learn the parts of the net—its poles, ropes, weights, and so forth—in order to turn it to their own use, as a means of catching the food of the spirit. An ancient prayer in G. R. S. Mead's *Vision of Aridaeus* reads: "Hail, ye net inverters, fishers and catchers of the spirit which alone nourishes! By refining your higher selves, ye have produced that which produced you." (408) Again we find the familiar theme: Discover yourselves and you discover God. The imagery here echoes that of Christ in Mark 1:17—"I will make you fishers of men," which can be read as meaning that those who follow the way will find themselves and in themselves find God.

This is why Hermetic teaching emphasizes the place of humans in the cosmos. We are viewed as central in that we touch the boundaries of creation at every level and because we possess within ourselves the encoded Mysteries of matter, spirit, and mind. Plato recognized this in *Timaeus* (480), which he is believed to have taken from Egyptian sources. Here he defines the cosmos as a living creature, formed in the same way as the most perfect synthesis of creation—the human cosmic being familiar to us from the Egyptian anthropocosmos, or Adam Kadmon, Adam of Light, who, according to the Kabbalah, mirrors the macrocosm. Proclus, in his commentaries on the *Timaeus* (104), states that this being can be equated with the Orphic Man of Light, who is threefold and contains the essence of all creation. This threefold division of matter into Phanes (shining), Erikepaois (power, male), and Metis (wisdom, female) represents a profound understanding of the breakdown of matter into its component parts, which, when reassembled, make up the perfection that is the closest we can get to understanding the nature of God.

It is on this doctrine of unity that the foundation of Hermeticism rests. Ever since Zoroaster, we have grown used to dualism in Western philosophy, but in the Orphic and Hermetic schools the emphasis was on balance, polarity, and the coming together of elements into a unique whole. This is why the gnostic Hermes is represented as being the uniting principle in the system of the *ogdoad* (eightfold). As one ancient text has it: "One is the All . . . and if the All did not contain the All, the All would be nothing." (35) Once again we hear the echo of the divine interaction between God (the One) and creation (matter, the All). It is not just incidental that Hermes' symbol is a staff entwined with twin serpents of wisdom and understanding, illustrating the same principle as that in the Kabbalah, where the central pillar holds those of left and right in balance.

The Mysteries were always intended to be understood in three ways: with the spirit, with the mind, and with the senses, a triple understanding that has continued to be recognized in Western esoteric practice ever since. In this way sacred words uttered in temple or lodge echo through three worlds—the divine, the intellectual, and the physical— and are brought together in a union that causes them to vibrate together harmoniously. The universe (or God) is always willing to respond to a harmonious note emitted by those in tune with the infinite Word of creation. To find that note within ourselves is the most important action of those of us seeking the mysteries. It is initiation that leads toward this harmonious note. Study and self-observation, discipline and obedience, self-knowledge: All of these are aimed first at realizing the divine harmonic within ourselves and then at tuning this to include the whole of creation of which we are part.

The elements of creation may well be divided and scattered, as the myths of the Titans and the rending of gods such as Dionysius and Osiris suggest, but what has been divided can be joined again. In the story of Isis and Osiris, even the absence of the phallus did not prevent the creation of the divine child, Horus, the uniting principle that ushered in a new age of peace and harmony.

In this sense the passions of Christ, of Baldur, of Tammuz, and of all the other savior gods can be seen as a wholly natural process in which matter seeks out its component parts and reunites, conforming with the original design of the cosmos. It is no surprise, then, to find stories in which God sends forth into matter his beloved son—the nearest aspect of himself—to seek out those lost ones.

Christ, Hermes, and all of the other shepherd gods have come to gather their flocks, but they cannot do so unaided. We must be willing to cooperate, to harmonize with them as we do whenever we celebrate the Mysteries. Thus the glorious *anamnesis,* or ritual remembrance, of the Christian Eucharist, the love feast of the Mystery's Agathadaimon, are aimed at giving us a glimpse of the peace and tranquillity outside the walls of our chaotic, fractured universe. It can be ours—if we wish it to be.

The Hermetic reality is devoted to the establishment of a divine unity within the mundane sphere, which in turn raises that sphere to divine heights. As above, so below, always. At the moment of Creation, God imprints everything with a divine signature, the DNA of the cosmos, making every flower a flower, every human being a human being, every beast a beast. And this signature contains the very essence of the Creator, the message to all that is brought into being, like to like, very like to very like, the One and the All contained in each other. As a seventeenth-century Hermeticist put it:

> The Sun and the Moon I see above me influence me neither for good nor bad, but the Sun and Moon and Planets [with] which God's providence has adorned the heaven in me, which also is the seat of the Almighty, these have the power to rule and reform me according to their course ordained by God. (153)

Let us examine the practice behind the theology—methods by which we can attain such a realization.

The Language of Desire

The mystery schools are containers for certain concepts and images designed to assist in the building of inner worlds where the perfection of humanity and the full potential of all material things can take place. A fully functioning and active mystery school is a powerhouse generating energies from which both the individual seeker and the great teachers of the age can draw strength and sustenance. Those of us who seek the Mysteries, however, must be aware that "[t]he highest of our initiations here below is only the dream of that true vision and initiation; and the discourses [on the Mysteries] have been carefully devised to awaken the memory of the sublime things above or else are of no purpose." (410) In other words, the "sublime things" must be reflected by those who attempt to realize them; they must be remembered by the initiate so that he or she can embody the divine truth in him- or herself (169).

Entrance to the Mysteries depends upon first a degree of maturity. In Egypt it was said that before we can know the spiritual Isis we must know her terrestrial aspect. This means that a thorough grounding in knowledge of earthly and mortal existence was necessary before the Mysteries were opened to the initiate. This is no less true today: No serious students should begin seeking before they have "put their house in order," learning to cope with the stresses and strains of the everyday world. If you cannot survive the daily grind of living, you will certainly find it difficult to sustain the rigors of a magical working. Once you have mastered both aspects of being, however, they will gradually overlap: Your normal life will become permeated with magical understanding, and your magical life with the fruits of human wisdom. In the end, both will be transformed.

As it states in the Wisdom of Solomon 6:17, "The beginning of wisdom is the most sincere desire for instruction, and concern for instruction is love of wisdom. . . . For she is a reflection of eternal light, a spotless mirror of the working of God, and an image of his goodness." Desire is a beginning, but once we, the initiates, make contact with the invisible hierarchy, it is up to us to keep alive the flame of our intention and to learn to be a reflection of "the working of God, and an image of his goodness . . ." Without that initial spark of desire, however, there can be no progress, no swift or easy journey. Years of study, discipline, and concentration lie before would-be seekers. We must come to terms with our innermost longings, fears, and hopes before we can even begin to reach that state of consciousness in which we may walk with gods and converse with angels.

An initiation, by its very nature, is a form of inner pressure designed to "shock" initiates into a sense of their inner capability. In almost every instance we find that the Mysteries contain the dramatic reconstruction of a primary myth, with the would-be initiate taking either the central role or the part of an onlooker, but always engaging directly in the events. At Eleusis human procreation and birth were shown to be the first steps on an initiatory journey, a preparation for the soul's passage through life and the voyage into the Underworld. The small death of initiation prepared the way for greater life and the greater death. The little Kore who descends into Hades is not the same as the Persephone who returns to her mother, Demeter, for she has been married to Pluto. Similarly, the initiates survive their ordeals but will never be the same again. Finally, the soul is freed to return to its origin. As Plato knew, this world is but a reflection of the Elysian fields. In its mirror, we see ourselves—but transformed.

Nevertheless, initiation is not a ceremony or set of rituals that automatically ensures enlightenment. Initiation ceremonies are often merely a formal, witnessed acknowledgment that the candidate's attraction to the sacred has been met with answering desire. The changes brought by initiation into the lesser Mysteries mark the deeper exploration of the candidate. In this transition period, knowledge is gained by inspirational and instinctive means, as initiate and deity enter into a deeper relationship. If initiation into the lesser Mysteries constitutes the engagement period, then initiation into the greater Mysteries marks the marriage, when initiates fully dedicate their lives to the sacred path, formally acknowledging the Divine Being through whom they have been brought to knowledge. Though the path is by no means an easy one, certain common practices are as much a part of contemporary training as they were in the great classical schools.

Apart from preliminary suitability, good health, a sense of integrity, dedication, and devotion, the candidate must resign him- or herself to patient effort during the seemingly tedious period of technical training. Whatever the teacher requires must be met, in equal measure, by the student. The goal is not success but the honest effort at attainment. Nor is speed important—sometimes what takes one student six months another may accomplish in two or three years. A seemingly brilliant student may sprint ahead in the early stages of training and then lose interest because he is unable to plod through the donkeywork, while a seemingly dull and overly conscientious pupil might take longer to assimilate training but achieve a higher level of understanding.

Basic to early training is a thorough acquaintance with and mastery of the elemental qualities within us. Fire, water, earth, and air make up the foursquare basis of magical competence. Without a complete understanding of the elements we have within us, we students will be like the Sorcerer's Apprentice (who could not control the element of water in either a spiritual or a physical capacity). In *Magical Ritual Methods* (199) W. G. Gray gives many excellent exercises for familiarizing ourselves with our elemental strengths and shortcomings. Familiarity with the elemental kings and kingdoms is often scorned and neglected as too basic for the Hermetic student, but like the skills of breathing and relaxation, it is essential knowledge for the esotericist (see practice 15, The Foursquare Citadel).

Once the initial training is over, one of the primary requirements of a traditional magical school is to charge the candidate with making a set of ritual implements. These working tools are the mainstay of the magician—the extension of the personality and the elemental symbols of his or her craft. The Wand, Sword, Chalice, and Pentacle or Patten signify the elements of air, fire, water, and earth, respectively. Initiates are expected if not to work the metals themselves, at least to work upon the naked blade until it resembles the sword of their will. Likewise, they must cut the wood and fashion the wand, engrave or cut the pentacle, and paint or scribe the sigils on the cup or chalice. A practical mastery of the elements is basic at this point.

As we shall see, the Gnostics and Mandeans left instructions for their initiates as to how they should leave the earthly sphere and progress through the spheres, or levels, of the Archons, the rulers of the planets. The next step in seeking the Mysteries is similarly a familiarity with planetary powers and influences. Initiates may acquire this in a variety of ways, becoming familiar with the correspondences devised in the Orphic schools, but the method most likely to be used in our own time is the investigation of the planetary attributions on the kabbalistic Tree of Life, which is a living glyph of the universe. The Tree of Life becomes the spiritual template of the student who learns to balance his or her life by reference to its ten mighty emanations in meditation and daily actions. Each sphere, or Sephira, on the Tree has its ruling planet whose qualities and powers must be mastered and balanced within the self—for just as the loving charity of Tiphareth (the Sephira of harmony) can easily degenerate into selfishness, so the dynamic strength of Geburah (the Sephira of severity) can turn into destructive violence if there is no balance. Candidates for higher initiations will be expected to progress through these Sephiroth one by one as stages along the way, and to balance the positive and negative qualities within themselves. (See fig. 26, table 1, page 350, and chapter 7.)

Gradually initiates refine many levels of the self, attuning them to the inner—a task that is ongoing and lifelong. We never completely root out the basal urgings of our lower nature, though we can keep them under control. Even adepts experience periods of trial and all the problems of human life, from the trivial to the earth-shattering. From those who receive, more is required, goes the occult adage.

The responsibility of the adept, the experienced walker between the worlds, is not just to those students and coworkers in the outer world, but also to the beings of the inner plane, who rely upon their mastery of the outer world as well as their aptitude in mediating the power and influences of the inner plane to everyday life. We shall discuss this important aspect of training more fully in chapter 8, which deals with the magician and his work.

The first demand of the mystery schools is "Know thyself." The lesser Mysteries are spent in readying for this knowledge. The greater Mysteries come only when this basis is established, when we initiates can stand alone, in command of our inner fortress. Only then is all made ready for the descent of the holy guardian angel or the inner master or the divinity who is the one initiator. Once preparation is complete and we clearly perceive the levels of the self, we are ready for identification with the god forms or archetypes of our particular school.

Identification with a god form demands a great deal of objectivity and cannot be attempted in the early stages of training. The initiate is like a dancer or actor who may spend years perfecting the body or the voice before finally stepping upon the stage before a live audience. When the initiate assumes the god form, there can be no confusion between theory and practice, no running to the wings to consult a book or a teacher on a point of technique. The initiate's identification with the god form must be a total communication so the energies of the archetype can be mediated successfully. It is easy to spot actors who are not really acting: Their eyes lack conviction, as though they are telling a lie; they do not carry through with their movements; their voices veer from the sense of the script; and they do not seem to truly interact with the other actors on stage. As a result, the whole performance of the play suffers. An initiate's mediation can suffer in this same way, and the audience—in this instance, those in the outer world, for whose benefit a ritual is performed—does not receive the fruits of the meditation.

The first kind of identification required of an initiate comes when he or she is asked to serve as the officer of a quarter, mediating an elemental quality to the lodge or circle. The circle or working area is seen as a division of matter into elements, and those most at home in one quarter with one element will feel drawn to that area. An ability to work from any quarter is important and should be cultivated; it will anyway follow naturally if the inner elements have been properly balanced. Serving as the officer of a quarter is no easy task, for the qualities of the elemental kings must be present and operative within him or her. The initiate becomes a doorway or channel through which the quarter guardians (who may be either god forms or angels) can come. This requires concentration and alertness. It is work of a privileged kind and reveals to the initiate the priestly qualities inherent in his or her craft. A very good breakdown of this traditional kind of work will be found in Gareth Knight's *The Rose Cross and the Goddess* (310) and in W. B. Gray's *Inner Traditions of Magic* (197). R. J. Stewart's *Living Magical Arts* (571) also discusses this work.

After this first service, the initiate may be asked to participate in ritual dramas enacting the stories of the gods employed by his or her school. Here the initiate represents the Mighty Ones themselves, just as the shaman embodies the spirit in a shamanic séance or as initiates represented the gods in the ancient mystery schools. This is an awesome function that is assigned only to those who are ready and prepared. While there are dangers of overidentification or egocentric appropriation inherent in this role, they may be avoided by one of two procedures followed before the rite proceeds.

First, the initiate visualizes as a mask the archetype he or she will assume. Then, before the ritual, just as in the Greek mystery dramas, the initiate silently contemplates the mask, holding a dialogue with it, establishing it as a separate entity from him- or herself. The symbolism surrounding the archetype can be rehearsed objectively and the stories and correspondences of this figure can be compared to those of other pantheons and traditions. Finally, the intiate "puts on" the mask just before "performing" the rite. The second method takes this a step further, though it may not be suitable in all cases or for certain kinds of individuals. The initiate visualizes the enshrined mask and offers it flowers and incense. With the archetype in question becoming, for a time, one of the "masks of God," the initiate says prayers, invoking the qualities required in the rite. Certainly, the moment in which the mask is assumed becomes an awesome one for the initiate, but there is no danger of overidentification.

At the end of the ritual, the initiate performs the same procedure in reverse, relinquishing the mask and returning it to the shrine, or visualizing it facing away from him or her, returning to the inner plane. It is important to note that the initiate does not assume this type of identification for self-gratification—for the inner pressure and resulting exhaustion resulting from such rites are enormous. Dion Fortune speaks wisely when she says that the work of a blacksmith is lighter than that of the ritualist, who assumes pressures and strains on not only the physical body, but the subtle body as well.

At the conclusion of a ritual, it is important that the energy that has built up is mediated properly, not left to slew around in a vacuum. The initiate who has embodied a deity may find that some of the divine energy remains or that some minor depletion of energy has occurred. There is nothing abnormal in this: Particularly important pieces of work require more energy than others, and reenergizing afterward will take correspondingly longer. The larger the working group, however, the less this effect will occur—in a large group the energies are shared and the demands on each individual are less significant. Some nourishment and a good night's sleep usually suffice to replenish those who are extremely exhausted after a ritual. In cases where an initiate suffers extreme exhaustion following a rite, a good night's sleep and an intake of nourishment will normally suffice to replenish him or her. Practice 19, The Shepherd of Stars, can also be helpful. More often than not, however, ritualists are energized as a result of their work.

Unfortunately, modern mystery schools tend not to train the body as they train the psyche. A good ritualist should have a supple torso and good posture and carriage, and be able to operate without falling over his or her feet. Physical clumsiness is often the result of mental unpreparedness or lack of concentration. The demands of ritual upon the body are immense, and if the initiate receives insufficient training to keep his or her physical instrument in good working condition, the magical work ultimately will suffer. Sports and dance are obviously helpful here, but they cannot cater to the peculiar requirements of the esotericist, who has to consider all of his or her bodies! Surprisingly, the mature body is better equipped than the younger body for the strains of ritual, and while the aged body depletes quicker than both of these, it has greater staying power (477).

The rewards of working within a mystery school can be great, provided you do not expect them to be material. While esoteric work may have therapeutic or beneficial effects, despite what many in our modern world may believe, it is not pursued for this purpose. Service is its basis. The trials, tests, initiations, and rituals must lead to the desire for humanity to align with its infinite potential.

Within each individual is the possibility of becoming, microcosmically, Adam Kadmon, Adam of Light. The final outcome of this will be the uniting of all humanity in one being—the Body of Light, which Poimandres speaks of as the source of the Word. For this reason many modern schools describe themselves variously as servants or societies of light. To be a servant of the light is to be, as the initiates of the original schools were, dedicated to the freeing of the divine spark.

Unfortunately, this quest has been warped by the theme of "light without darkness" so predominant in New Age thought, which is often intolerant of darkness because it is associated with evil.

Sometimes the search for the divine spark leads to an ecstatic response, and historically the ultimate experience of the Divine has been sought through both asceticism and an ecstatic sexuality. But if, as the Dionysian Mysteries suggest, we are made up in part of the stuff of the Titans, it is not surprising that our response to the infinite arises as much from a sexual as a religious basis. Because the archetypal presences invoked within the Mysteries may be symbolized by the basic elements of life itself—the sperm and ovum—it is important not to confuse the nature of the union. The ecstatic sexual union between human beings can be expressed on an another level as the divine union of the god or goddess with his or her beloved devotee. This concept lies behind the ritual union of the ancient Mysteries when a priest or priestess embodied the deity and lay with one or more of the faithful. Several classical authors who traveled in the Middle East, where their own Mysteries had assumed more ascetic forms devoid of the earlier, earthy celebrations of the native tradition, remarked with distaste upon the abuses of temple prostitution.

In earlier times, the identification of the priest or priestess with the deity enabled the people or their ruler to have congress with the divine guardian of the tribe. The classical Mysteries still incorporated this union within their celebrations, yet within the Mysteries of Eleusis, for example, the hierophant drank a draft that specifically inhibited his sexual function. He was always chosen from an Eleusian family and was himself married in the normal way—not, as with many of the Eastern cults, castrated in the service of the Goddess (636, 615).

Sexuality within ritual is thus a constant reminder of earlier resonances. It should never intervene in the flow of energies in any operation, thereby allowing the work to become earthbound. The esoteric Judaic and kabbalistic practice of husband and wife uniting in order to mirror the union of God and the Shekinah comes nearer to an understanding of how sexuality can be made to express the deepest religious impulse upon earth (383). The abuse of this in magic occurs when the levels are confused. On the ecstatic or tribal level of consciousness, sexuality is an honest expression of religious fervor translated into human terms.

All mystery schools and orders exist to train the mind and the heart, or the intellect and the soul, until they are working together in a unified way. Although the emphasis in this book is on the practical, it should not be considered in any way a substitute for proper training or belonging to an order or contacted magical group. There is an increasing tendency today toward solitary working or distance learning. If you work alone, by either choice or circumstance, this book is aimed at giving you a grasp of the essential requirements of the would-be initiate. However, if the opportunity to work with a group comes your way, do not pass it up—providing, of course, that it appears to be properly organized and offers suitable training for your needs and aptitudes.

Choosing a school can be a difficult process—there are so many and their approaches are often bewilderingly different. Some feel very formal and old-fashioned, as if they were founded in another century—as many of them were. Instinct and inner awareness alone can tell you when you have found one that is right for you—though, of course, this does not necessarily mean that you will feel right to its members. If all goes well, however, and you are accepted as a candidate, it will be the beginning of a satisfying and rewarding association. These pages are desined to give you some idea of what to expect. To give you the fullest picture, though, we must follow the thread of the Mysteries to the present.

Guardians of Tradition

Just as the medieval and Renaissance Mysteries can be traced to a Hermetic impulse, so the schools and fraternities of our own time owe their origin primarily to what may be termed the Rosicrucian impulse. Yet, by one of those paradoxes that seem to govern the Western Way, there is no evidence that either the Rosicrucian Brotherhood or its founder, Christian Rosenkreutz, ever really existed. Nevertheless, let us examine the myth.

The first that anyone in the outside world knew of the Rosicrucians was in 1614, when a curious document entitled *Fama Fraternitatis of the Meritorious Order of the Rose Cross* (8) appeared in Germany and was widely circulated. It purported to be a description of the life of Christian Rosenkreutz, philosopher, mystic, and magician who had lived to the age of 106 and whose body was then concealed in a secret tomb that was not discovered for another 120 years.

This means that Rosenkreutz lived at the end of the fourteenth or the beginning of the fifteenth century, though there are no records from that time—or indeed any time—that relate to his actual existence. The description of the finding of the vault containing his uncorrupted remains is written in highly symbolic language that reads like an initiatory text. From it we can gather that to follow the steps leading to the discovery of the body, to encounter the vault itself, and to meditate upon the remains can be a richly rewarding experience.

In the *Fama*, the opening of the vault is cast as an event of far-reaching significance: "for like as our door was after so many years wonderfully discovered, also there shall be opened a door to Europe which already doth begin to appear, and with great desire is expected of many." (8) Judging by the reaction across Europe to the *Fama* and to the manifestos that followed it, the desire and expectation must have been considerable. From all of this a new hope was seeded that had nothing to do with the effects of the Renaissance; medieval attitudes still held some sway, and enlightenment battled uneasily with a mysticism that retained the blinders of dogma and superstition.

The authorship of the first Rosicrucian manifesto has been traced speculatively to the University of Tübingen and more precisely to Johann Valentin von Andrae. But beyond the voice of human authors we can detect in the *Fama* the beginning of a powerful new stream of inner teaching. (332) No one knew the whereabouts of the Rosicrucian

Brotherhood, but this did not stop those who read and understood the true value of the manifestos from trying to make physical contact with it. The fact that there were writings that told of a brotherhood of adepts who could be contacted through "proper channels" was enough to prompt many to advertise in news sheets for more information. Even the philosopher René Descartes went to Germany to seek out the brotherhood and, not surprisingly perhaps, found nothing. Yet on his return to Paris in 1623, so many rumors were circulating that he was forced to show himself publicly in order to prove that he had not become invisible—that he was not a Rosicrucian (655).

When enthusiasts who sent inquiries for more information to nonexistent addresses received no replies, they were driven to publish their own books and pamphlets in order to see whether their ideas resonated harmonically with other would-be Rosicrucians. Thus the original manifestos spawned a succession of imitators and commentaries, constellating their writers into the formation of a mystery school whose doctrines were set out for all who could understand them—an odd reversal of the classical schools, which hid their teachings from all but their initiates.

This is a prime example of the way a mystery school receives its impulse to form and has certainly been a much repeated method since the age of the Rosicrucians. This does not mean that the written doctrines of mystery schools created in this way are clear statements of intent or belief. The language they use is allusive and full of symbolism that likely prevented all but those "in the know" from understanding what was being said—for this is how the Mysteries guard themselves from idle curiosity.

Initially we may see von Andrae and his fellow philosophers at Tübingen reacting against the climate of the times, which is why the writer of the *Fama*, who had long since admitted its composition and denied its importance as a document, included in his will the words: "Though I now leave the Fraternity itself, I shall never leave the true Christian Fraternity, which, beneath the Cross, smells of the Rose, and is quite apart from the filth of this century." (352)

At its heart the Rosicrucian impulse was a combination of esoteric Christianity and the kind of straight mystery school teaching that had been kept alive in the work of the magician and the alchemist. That it transcended both points of origin is an indication of the power of the inner impulse that brought it into being: The symbols of the Rose and the Cross combined to make the first real synthesis of magical and mystical teachings since the original Hermetic impulse.

The idea of an invisible college of adepts is not as rare as we may think, as we shall see in chapter 9. Rosicrucianism survived because it had no visible foundation, no headquarters, no officers, no dogmas, and no rules of membership. The effect of this on the European world of the seventeenth century was deep and lasting. It paved the way for the French esoteric revival of the next century, which was thus able to draw upon both native and Hermetic traditions at a deep level. This was aided in part by the operations of another body of initiates—the Freemasons; though we cannot say for sure that Rosicrucianism and Freemasonry were formally connected, Freemasonry did become an important vessel of Rosicrucian survival.

Freemasonry itself grew out of the crafts guilds and friendly burial societies of the pre-Reformation. The master of his "mystery" or craft profession was a powerful man, and together the crafts guilds exerted considerable pressure on society. We can see a similar phenomenon today where an ostensibly esoteric movement wields a high degree of political influence. Masonry's origins, like those of Rosicrucianism, were built retrospectively. But while the supposed life of Christian Rosenkreutz, like the building of Jerusalem's temple and the murder of Hiram, is thematically important, to claim these resonances as historically traceable is to confuse myth with ordinary reality.

If Rosicrucianism was, as many have suggested, the Germanic Protestant impulse, then Freemasonry was a British esoteric one. Their fusion was not entirely surprising. The Protestant ethic had left sad lacunae in the life of medieval fraternities, whose esoteric pursuits had probably been no more than an occasional mass celebrated by the guild's priest or the usual kind of initiatory highjinks practiced upon freshmen at college or apprentices in crafts today. After the Reformation, the guilds and some of their customs remained, but their ritual life was severely curtailed. Freemasonry may well have been formed by masters of their crafts upon the principles of the crafts guilds as an "inner circle." From there it spread to learned gentlemen of leisure, whose antiquarian and classical background would have given them ample scope for the creation of rationalizing legends to accompany these new "mystery schools." The mystery story of Freemasonry made God the architect of the macrocosm and Christ, his apprentice, a carpenter in that microcosm we inhabit. The idea of coinherence was thus carried forward into a new era of esoteric belief.

There is something fundamentally Protestant in the conception of the Divine Architect—something that is also akin to the more puritan lines of certain Judaic traditions as well as those of Mithraism, which Freemasonry echoes. Freemasonry today has followed a course similar to that of Mithraism, which rose through a tangle of syncretic cults to become a unifying principle within the Roman Empire. Military and chivalric orders were certainly continued within Freemasonry, as were the ideas of monarchic restoration and ritual chivalry. Further, the unfolding translation of kabbalistic texts enabled Freemasonry to assimilate a certain amount of Judaic esotericism.

The theologian and apologist Philo of Alexandria once asked of the pagan mystery schools: "Why, O initiates, if these things are good and profitable, do you shut yourselves up in deepest darkness and render service to three or four individuals alone, when you can render it to all by presenting these advantages in the public market?" (475) In our own time perhaps this question is being answered to some extent by schools such as Freemasonry. Reliance on authority or tradition is fading today. The gradual dismantling of the awesome temple scaffolding, the secrecy devolving upon initiates in times of ignorance and persecution, and the solitude of the seeker are largely behind us now. Instead of temples, we have the concert or lecture hall and the spontaneous gathering of seekers. Instead of robed occultists, we experience the free dissemination of hidden wisdom—which nonetheless remains intact. Instead of isolation, we are part of the growing network of those sensitive to cosmic purpose.

There have always been guardians of the mystery traditions, however elusive they may have seemed. Teachers have always been on hand to impart the eternal truths. In the last two centuries, with the gradual relaxing of the laws governing the open dissemination of esoteric beliefs, many schools have come forward, each one claiming the right to train and initiate its followers into the divine Mysteries of creation. Some have proved false, having nothing of value to offer. Others have grown, flourished, and then faded with the passing of their founders. But some have passed on their knowledge to those who came after.

In the late nineteenth century, when certain members of the notable occult organization the Theosophical Society began to tire of the emphasis given to Eastern Mysteries, they looked elsewhere, finding within the newly translated Egyptian papyri and the wealth of classical writings a fund of Western wisdom to be explored in a practical way. Enthusiastic explorers rather than scholars, they delved deeply into the neglected heritage of the past and came up with a whole system of magical and theurgic Mysteries.

Thus the Hermetic Order of the Golden Dawn was born. It admitted to its ranks Freemasons, poets, clergymen, and thinkers and outlasted many of its own offspring to become, in the next few generations, the most prestigious organization of its kind since the Renaissance. Most modern esoteric schools trace their descent from the Golden Dawn, and through it, knowingly or not, make contact with both the Rosicrucian impulse and the great classical and preclassical foundations.

Behind the often overly elaborate nature of the Golden Dawn rituals lie a multitude of sense experiences that are unattainable to those who, rather than understand, merely follow meaning. The incantatory power of these rituals goes far beyond the sum of their parts. It does not matter whether we can distinguish Chaldean, Egyptian, Graeco-Roman, and Gnostic elements within them; in reading the "knowledge papers" of the order, edited in a single compendium by Israel Regardie (504, 506), we can readily see that here is a valid system of esoteric working that has not been exceeded by any other modern-day school.

In the early nineteenth century Theosophy, which indirectly gave birth to the Golden Dawn, had already begun to awaken aspects of Western esotericism that had long lain dormant. Its contact with the East brought in a language and symbolism that helped define those areas of the Western Way that had remained indistinct since the Renaissance or had been relegated to the crypt of Christian mysticism. The leader of the theosophical movement, Madame Blavatsky, achieved the reputation of a typical shaman from her travels to the East and her meetings with hidden masters. She bluffed her way through areas of ignorance, contacted the light of the perennial wisdom in ways that now seem haphazard, and believed beyond all else that whatever was true must come from outside her own consciousness. Yet her two monumental studies of esoteric tradition, *The Secret Doctrine* (48) and *The Veil of Isis,* appeared at the right time to bring a revitalizing influence to the Western Way.

The schools that followed Theosophy were founded by those trained in Blavatsky's school and thus have been, to some extent, continuations of her work. Anthroposophy, which is still a thriving movement, resulted from Rudolf Steiner's break with Theosophy, which he found too overtly Eastern for his taste. A recent commentator called Anthroposophy a "demythologised Theosophy" (143) because it rejects the magical in favor of education, the arts, and holistic living. Steiner emphasized Western elements and in his autobiography describes Anthroposophy as "a path of knowledge, leading from the spiritual in man to the spiritual in the universe." (564) He saw the universe as living and hierarchical, very much in line with the teachings of the classical schools. He was also convinced that the ancient mystery knowledge was communicated in picture dreams—"pictures which revealed the spirit-world." (564) In his view imagination was a door of communication between the worlds—he consciously encouraged entrance to the ancient Mysteries through the spiritual contact engendered when the senses are stimulated by art. His exercises, designed to liberate thought from the body, also recalled traditional techniques.

Interestingly, Steiner also developed three forms of higher knowledge: imagination (a higher seeing of the spiritual world); inspiration (a higher hearing of the spiritual world, through which is revealed its creative forces and its creative order); and intuition (the stage at which an intuitive penetration into the sphere of spiritual beings becomes possible). This kind of structure recalls the grading practiced by some descendants of the Golden Dawn.

The Golden Dawn itself worked a system of grades based on the kabbalistic Tree of Life, starting with Zelator, or Malkuth, and rising to Ipsissimus, or Kether (308). This is still used by many magical schools today, which practice certain initiatory ceremonies connected with each grade. Incidentally, while many initiates may be disappointed to find that their teacher is not an Ipsissimus, it's important to know that a claim of this grade should be questioned. The grades themselves are symbolic of the initiate's efforts to attain proficiency, much like the degrees of bachelor, master, and doctor are in the academic world. Of course, just as doctors of philosophy do not know everything, nor do those who have had high grades conferred upon them by their schools. There is, remember, no end to knowledge.

Beyond grades, the division of the Mysteries into Greater and Lesser is another form of structuring practiced by contemporary mystery schools. A period of probation precedes both the Lesser and the Greater Mysteries. The Lesser Mysteries teach initiates of the "outer court" of the temple, where the images and symbols of the order are embodied in a mythical framework. In the Greater Mysteries this earlier work is subsumed in the personality of the initiate—it becomes a living reality that cannot be questioned. For this work, the initiate enters the "inner court' of the Temple and finds him- or herself in an empty room. Here no deity is enshrined, no great teaching is written, and there is no symbol to distract or enter the consciousness. The only presence is the emptiness of the cosmos, which is, of course, far from empty. Initiation into the Greater Mysteries is indeed a confrontation with the self and with the summation of the presence of the Divine within everything (see the Epilogue, Tomorrow's Tradition). There, macrocosm and micro-cosm join and are reflected. Even so, there cannot yet be sublime merging with the divine principle; the initiate must return to the outer world again and continue to act as a mirror of the macrocosm.

Many such *psychotechnologies,* to borrow a term from Marilyn Ferguson (150), are practiced today by hundreds of modern mystery schools in the Western world. All attempt to mediate the inner Mysteries of life in some way. We have lost much in the way of methodologies, but tentative experiments are reviving them—in part analeptically—to an efficient standard. It is obviously not possible to discuss even one tenth of the schools offering training today. There is no hard-and-fast rule about joining such groups. Common sense and clear sight will guide you in your first steps and after that your inner guides should be in a position to take over.

The Rudolf Steiner school combines elements of Christian esotericism with Rosicrucian, Hermetic, and native Mysteries. If you prefer to seek kabbalistic training, the Servants of the Light organization offers a thorough and effective way into the Mysteries of the Tree of Life and the symbolism of the Grail (15). The Alice Bailey school is strongly theosophical in origin, subscribing to belief in masters and hierarchical cosmology. It supports an evolutional development through mundane as well as esoteric means. The vast literature underpinning this group, dictated by Master D. K. to Alice Bailey, is read by many outside the school, where it has contributed widely to the spread of Aquarian and cosmic consciousness. The Rosicrucian Fellowship and the Ancient Mystical Order Rosae Crucia (AMORC) are rival schools following the teachings of Christian Rosenkreutz. The former was founded by Max Heindal in 1906. Active in Theosophy, he was contacted by a Rosicrucian master and took instruction. Some of the school's teachings include world evolution and reincarnation and its contacts are inner helpers and masters. AMORC was founded in 1915 by H. Spencer-Lewis and is based on

Freemasonry with a developed philosophy and practice. It declines the titles of religion and cult. The Builders of the Adytum (BOTA), founded by Paul Foster Case after he was expelled from the Golden Dawn for publishing its secrets in his Tarot publications, is probably the most Hermetic of the contemporary schools. BOTA was founded in 1920 through inner contact and still uses the Tarot and the Kabbalah as its main implements.

Another interesting school that has released its teaching papers is the Aurum Solis, or Order of the Sacred Word. Since its reconstitution in 1971, it has operated as a private magical group and not a school. It was founded in 1897 by Charles Kingold and George Stanton, two occultists who were in touch with the Kabbalah as well as Greek and early magical systems. The Magical Philosophy (129), which comprises these teachings, is, like the Golden Dawn collection, a complete magical system that can be studied and worked by the esotericist who does not belong to any group.

Magical groups are still being created today, usually when one adept is contacted by the inner plane and receives the go-ahead to organize a preliminary meeting with those close to him or her. These may be short-term organizations, lasting only as long as it takes to fulfill their function as determined by inner contact. Training schools, however, which can be used as a foundation for more important work, are likely to have more longevity.

Self-training is a difficult route to take. Without a teacher or training school behind you, the work is uphill and cannot be matched appropriately to your development. Clearly, following medieval magical systems is not practical. If you do choose to self-train, clarifying your intent; taking clear, easy, and logical steps; preparing carefully; and practicing self-discipline can go a long way. The groundwork of self-training is not acquired through book learning, although that may be a good place to start for inspiration.

You may ask if it is necessary to have an outer-realm magical teacher. In fact, nothing can replace the guidance of an experienced fellow worker, but finding one willing to take on students is another matter. Most people proceed without one in the earliest stages of training, keeping their eyes open, reading, studying, and correlating their life's experiences with the strong inner impulse, which leads them deeper into the Mysteries. Some students join groups unadvisedly and regret it, leaving with their illusions shattered. Others work alone for what seems a lifetime and then suddenly find doors opening for them. There is no rule or set timing for finding a teacher, but once you do find one, do not expect your task to be easier from then on. A teacher will demand regular work and certain results and if you, the student, do not measure up to your teacher's expectations, you will be considered someone who is unworthy of the teachings.

There is certainly no shortage of schools, some better, some worse, but as the theologian Don Cupitt expressed it, "[T]he truth now is no longer in fixed positions—it is in the quest." The modern quest for knowledge, whether within the mystery schools or elsewhere, takes many forms. For many the Mysteries are now best taught in open court, in small groups or seminars where the Mysteries are discussed and practically engaged by gatherings of interested people. We can testify to the remarkably powerful and effective nature of this kind of work, where seemingly random combinations of peers are brought together by the inner plane to do some specific piece of work, after which they separate, sometimes for long periods of time. Magical training groups whose members gather to meet and learn from each other usually form around at least one competent esotericist. Regular meetings through the seasons create a rapport within the group and contribute to a group mind, which often attracts an inner teacher who will focus the work and study.

Many more opportunities exist that combine lectures with practical applications of magic techniques. It has been said that the time of the mystery schools is over, and while this may not necessarily be true, the old closed orders of adepts are growing fewer in number. As we have tried to show, however, the solitary worker or the small dedicated band of workers can be just as effective as a fully fledged school—especially once inner contact is established.

One of the ways into a study format is presented by myth. All myth, legend, and poetry derives from the Mysteries in some sense—after all, these are the potential sparks that can ignite a sense of the wonders of creation and the purpose of life. Almost any of the countless themes, characters, or fragments of tales, whether from ancient Greek, Egyptian, or Welsh sources, can be quarried for exploration individually or with a group. Once you begin to work with the matter of the Mysteries you will find the experience something like controlling a team of eager, high-stepping horses. Feel the reins in your hands and the pull of their heads at the bit. Your chariot will carry you far, across land

and sea, to both in inner and outer realms. The Mysteries are not something locked away in dusty tomes on a library shelf—they are here and
now, living lines of contact that allow our entrance into a wholly different dimension.

> The object of the Hermetic search is that life which is capable of
> being transmitted to a specific being in order to lead that being to
> its own perfection . . . this available "life-essence" is called the
> King, cosmic man; but it must be recognized that attaining the aim
> of the Hermetic opus is not an end; it is the beginning of the light
> that illuminates reality . . . the true King, is the living being who
> has reached the stage of immortal and conscious return to the
> source of the Soul that animates him. (528)

This "return to the source" is the objective that animates all magical work, fueling Orphite and Hermeticist, Gnostic and Cathar alike.
As we shall see in the next chapter, it is present in esoteric Christianity
as well as in the Hermetic schools. Divine knowing is all important if
we are to find our way farther than the first few steps on the road we
have elected to travel.

PRACTICES

❖ 11. The Labyrinth of the Gods ❖

In his discussion of the Mysteries, the Roman historian Ammianus
Marcellinus gives an interesting account of "certain underground gal-
leries and passages full of windings which, it is said, the adepts in the
ancient rites (knowing that the Flood was coming, and fearing that the
memory of the sacred ceremonies would be obliterated) constructed. . . ."
These, he says, contained buildings "which were mined out with great
labour. And levelling the walls, they engraved on them numerous kinds
of birds and animals . . . which they called hieroglyphic characters."
(252)

This may well be a distant memory of a visit to one of the great pyramids of Egypt, on whose walls were cartouches relating the history of
its onetime occupant—or it may be a fleeting reference to the great

labyrinth at Mareotis, mentioned by Herodotus and other ancient historians. Whatever the truth, it conjures up a fascinating image of a vast and secret labyrinth, containing on its walls the knowledge and history of the Egyptian Mysteries—perhaps even of an earlier Atlantean mystery center.

The purpose of this practice is to enter such a place in order to encounter the living god forms who will be our guides and instructors in this particular area of the Western Mysteries. As we saw in part 1, the gods are many things: They await the moment when we are sufficiently in tune with ourselves to recognize that we are living vessels of the ancient wisdom to be filled with as much as we are able to hold. In this exercise we will make our first contact with some of the powers that we will be working with in times to come. In this instance we shall come under the guidance of Hermes, who will conduct us on the first steps of the Hermetic way.

Much of the imagery here comes from Egyptian sources, but this should not be seen as the only way into the Hermetic tradition. There are many other doorways that are just as valid. As with other practices in this book, you should make no attempt to embark on this inner journey until you feel sure the time is right. Once you feel ready, you should begin, as always, by sitting comfortably in an upright chair, relaxing, and breathing to a regular rhythm.

Fig. 14. The ankh, Egyptian symbol of life, gave its shape to the keys that unlocked temple doors.

Method

You are standing at night on softly yielding ground. At first it is quite dark, but as you grow accustomed to the place, the moon comes out from behind a cloud and by its radiance you perceive that you are standing on fine white desert sand. It surrounds you, stretching away to the horizon on all sides in softly sculptured waves. Ahead you see several vast shapes rooted in the desert and rising toward a sky filled with stars. They are strangely familiar, and as your eyes grow accustomed to the subtle light you recognize their shape. You are in Egypt and before you rise the Pyramids of Giza.

Filled with awe, you walk toward these vast and towering monuments that gleam softly silver in the light of the moon. As you draw near, you see that they are not quite as you may have seen them pictured, crumbling and aged by time and weather, but are instead smooth and sharp-edged and faced with white marble upon which you dimly discern hieroglyphs in seemingly endless rows. The whole pyramid before you is covered with writing, but though you may long to pause and examine what is written there, you are drawn onward toward a dark entrance opening in front of you. At first you hesitate, for the way ahead is very black and there is no light to show what lies within. Ancient fears of the dark and of becoming lost beneath the great weight of stone stir within you and you feel reluctant to proceed farther.

Then, as you stand uncertainly before the dark entrance, a figure detaches itself from the shadows and comes toward you. You recognize him from his shaven head and white kilt as an Egyptian priest. He holds out his left hand, in which he carries the symbol of his office, an ankh, the ancient Egyptian symbol of life. You see that he is welcoming you, and you reach out and take the proffered sign in your own hand. It feels warm and smooth to the touch, and as soon as you have hold of it, it begins to glow brightly.

The priest now stands aside and indicates that you should proceed through the doorway. You find that your earlier fears left you once you touched the ankh and that you are eager to discover what lies within. You enter through the narrow stone portal, and as you pass farther into the heart of the pyramid the ankh glows more brightly, illuminating your path.

With the symbol of life in your hand, you go forward unafraid. The passageway is narrow and twists often to the right or left, doubling back upon itself more than once until you have lost all sense of direction. Time also seems without meaning here. Is it only a few moments since you entered or have hours passed? You walk on, holding the glowing ankh before you, until at last you feel a draft of cool air on your face and you emerge into a larger, open space.

You are now standing in a long, narrow hall, its roof upheld by an avenue of pillars. Those on the right are painted red and those on the left are black. As you walk forward between them, you see that the walls of the hall are painted with brightly colored figures. Some are in Egyptian dress, but others seem clad in costumes of other lands and times. Though they are only painted scenes, they seem almost to move with a life of their own. You do not feel moved to stop and look at them in detail, but much that you glimpse there may return to you later, either in sleep or in meditation.

Your feet are drawn onward toward the end of the hall, where you see a door flanked by two great red-and-black pillars carved with symbols and hieroglyphs. As you approach, the door opens and a figure comes forth and stands waiting for you, arms folded on his breast. He is manly, tall and powerful, but from his shoulders rises the head of a jackal, its ears pricked and its eyes gleaming in the light.

You recognize the figure of Anubis, guardian of the Mysteries of Egypt and keeper of the threshold of the gods. You stand before him, waiting to hear what he will say. He may ask you your name or he may wish to know your reason for coming to this place. Think carefully and take time before you answer. You may not lie or speak falsely before Anubis, for he can read the heart as you might read a book. Allow yourself to pause as you gather your thoughts.

Satisfied with your answer, Anubis stands aside, welcoming you to the place of the Mysteries, then he bids you to enter through the door by which he arrived. Before you do so, Anubis softly speaks the sacred password that will admit you to what lies beyond. Thus prepared, but still not without some trepidation, for it is a great step you now take, you move forward and find yourself walking down a short corridor connecting the door through which you came with another one a little way ahead. You pause for a moment at this next door to collect your thoughts and to weigh your intention, for beyond it lies the chamber of the inner Mysteries and you must be certain of your reason for coming before you enter. If you do not feel ready, you may turn back at this point and retrace your steps without fear or shame. Many have come this far and have turned away. If you decide to do so, you may return at another time.

If you decide to go on, you step forward and open the door before you. Walking through, you find yourself in a small, many-sided room. As you hold up the ankh before you, you see by its light that the walls are faced with mirrors of bronze, which, as you advance slowly toward the center of the room, give back a thousand images of yourself. But not all the images are the same. As your vision grows accustomed to the strangeness of the place, you see that there are many different aspects of yourself reflected back from the walls. You may see yourself at different stages in your life up to this moment (but never beyond—the future is not for you to read) and perhaps also of other lives. But you must be careful how you interpret the images you see, for it is easy to become dazzled by a particular form or image. If you feel drawn toward one or another, you may look more closely, but always hold the ankh symbol in front of you as your sign of life and intention.

After encountering the pictures, you look toward the center of the room. There you see a circular platform with steps leading up to it. Upon it stands a mighty figure holding a book and writing implements. You recognize Thoth, the scribe of the gods, keeper of the sacred Mysteries, and teacher of wisdom, known by some as Hermes Trismegistos, founder of the Hermetic Mysteries.

As you approach, he demands by what right you come there and you respond with the word or phrase given you by Anubis. Thoth then asks your intentions in seeking the Mysteries and whether you are drawn to any one aspect. Answer this as truthfully as possible, but do not be afraid to say that you do not know. Thoth records your name and response in his great book and bids you step up to the platform at his side.

As you do so, the walls of the chamber begin to turn slowly, gradually speeding up until they are a blur. Only the platform and the wise head of Thoth, shaped like the sacred Ibis, remain unchanging. As you stand at his side you realize that this is the center from which all the mystery teachings are spun. All are contained in the great book that lies beneath Thoth's hand.

Now in the blur of the circling walls, images form, flicker for a moment, and then disappear. You see the faces of those who worked with you on the inner planes and others who are strangers to you. Try to notice and to remember as much as you can, for these things and people may well become important to you later on. (Pause.)

At last the spinning slows and stops. The walls of the chamber in which you stand no longer show pictures but are instead lined with mirrors. You see yourself again in the mirrors and realize that you are alone. There may be subtle changes now in the way you behold them, for Thoth has entered your name in the Book of the Mysteries and you are a part of them from now onward.

Slowly you descend from the platform and depart from the chamber the same way you came. In the outer chamber Anubis awaits you, and as you pass before him he places upon your brow a plain circle of silver or gold. You understand that this is a token of the Mysteries that you have now entered. The circle is plain because your journey has only just begun, but in time it may bear symbols or letters acquired by you on your way.

Taking leave of the jackal-headed god, you return to the open air, finding no difficulty in retracing your path through the labyrinth. At the entrance, return the symbol of the ankh to the priestly guardian and go by the way you came, slowly allowing the scene to fade from your consciousness, to be replaced by the surroundings in which you began your journey.

Discovery

Whenever you begin an inner journey or take part in some magical activity, you should imagine the circle of silver or gold given to you by Anubis; it will be your sign to others that you have passed through the labyrinth of the gods and returned.

❧ *12. Building the Body of Light* ❧

This ritual, one of great potential power, is designed to awaken a sense of the cosmic dimension of the Hermetic path. We make no bones about including here what is in effect an advanced technique. Those who are ready to undertake work at this level will find themselves drawn to it, but those who are not should still be able to perform the working and obtain from it a sense of balance and potential. Note that it should not be performed over and over once you have experienced its totality. When you make your midday salutation (see Introduction to

Part 2, page 167), you may focus on your experience with this practice in order to refresh your Body of Light.

Method

Begin quietly, seated or standing in a place free of interruption, center yourself, and then begin to stretch farther and farther upward with your soul until your physical body is far below and a new self, hazy and without substance as yet, stands with head and shoulders in the heavens. Allow your soul to fill this larger self. Slowly reach forward with your senses, feeling them newly cleansed, like windows that have been wiped clean of the grime of centuries. Look around you and be aware of the vastness of the heavens, of the mighty beings who guard the cosmos, of those who have responsibility for our own solar system—or each planet that whirls around the star that is our own Sun. Take time to hold this new reality and fear nothing. You are, as is each of us, an immortal soul whose right it is to travel the uttermost reaches of the universe under the protection of the Holy Ones who helped in its formation. Listen and you may hear their voices raised in the music of the spheres.

Now stretch forth your hands and find before you in the uttermost blackness and singing darkness of space a shape that your senses tell you is a vast bowl or crater. You cannot perceive this with your sight; you can only feel its outlines beneath your hands. As you touch it, you feel with your fingertips certain scenes and images that are depicted upon it. But it is not yet for you to see such things and there is another purpose for you now.

Look now into the depths of the bowl, which is perfect blackness and impenetrable darkness. Far below, as though you were looking into the uttermost depths of the cosmos, a tiny gleam of light begins to form, impossibly far away and bright. It shines like a jewel and, as you look, it begins to grow gradually larger. Stretch your hand down into the bowl and take the glowing thing. It may look like a living flame (which cannot burn you) or like a jewel of surpassing brightness. As you hold it in your hand, its light begins to spread through your insubstantial form, filling you with a sense of peace and joyousness.

Look around you now and see that surrounding you in the vastness of space are other figures that were invisible to you before but are now revealed in a glory of light. They greet you in many different tongues that you have no difficulty understanding. You come to know that you are now like them, that you share a common radiance that is within you and yet fills the corners of the universe.

Gradually begin to draw your soul back down into your body far below. Keep the light within you, for it is a spark of that divine fire from which the cosmos was formed and which has always been a part of you.

Become aware of your surroundings once more, feeling the ground under your feet and, if you are seated, the chair beneath you. Close the circle of power by performing your chosen closing ritual.

Discovery

You are now part of the Body of Light that surrounds and dwells within all of creation. Wherever you go, you will take it with you, and you will always be able to recognize it within others. You will also always be able to converse with the myriad souls who inhabit the vastness of space and who have welcomed you among them as a brother or sister.

Reaffirm the light within you by performing a brief ritual of attunement at least once daily.

7

The Divine Knowing

In their religion they are so unev'n,
That each man goes his own by-way to Heav'n.
Tenacious of mistakes to that degree,
That ev'ry man pursues it sep'rately,
And fancies none can find the way but he,
So shy of one another they are grown
As if they strove to get to Heav'n alone.
—DANIEL DEFOE, THE TRUE-BORN ENGLISHMAN

Wisdom reaches mightily from one end of the earth to the
other, and she orders all things well. For she is an initiate
in the knowledge of God, and an associate in his works.
—WISDOM VIII, 1 AND 4

The Gifts of Wisdom

*G*nostic, illuminatus, Hermeticist, magus, mystic—what a glorious muddle the Western Way must appear to the outsider! The diverse nature of the Western tradition has made it difficult to accept for those who prefer their concepts in tidy packages. Yet Dr. Dee's medium, Edward Kelly, reminds us that what we see as a fragmented set of disciplines is indeed derivative of those great mystery schools we have been considering:

This Art found its way into Persia, Egypt and Chaldea. The Hebrews called it the Cabbala, the Persians Magia, and the Egyptians Sophia and it was taught in the schools together with

Theology: it was known to Moses, Solomon, and the Magi who came to Christ from the East. (209)

Kelly is appealing to a common tradition across a breadth of disciplines, specifically relating his argument to alchemy and to the completion of the Great Work. But the Great Work can be achieved through many disciplines: through the science of alchemy, through the art of magic, and through the philosophy and devotion of the mystic. It is because the disciplines of the Western Way have been fragmented that there has been so much dispute as to which provides the correct way to proceed. Science, magic, and religion seem to be eternally estranged, yet each of these disciplines corresponds to a cosmic law that must be obeyed: Science observes the law of nature; magic, the law of correspondences; and religion, the law of God. In truth, these laws are not irreconcilable, yet science and religion have passed beyond the point where they were complementary and the esotericist is now regarded as a godless creature by religion and as a crank by science.

In order to appreciate all sides of this problem, we shall be examining the science of alchemy and the art of magic later; here we will scrutinize the philosophy of religion, the spiritual science. But first of all, let us examine the Western Way from the standpoint of the perennial wisdom.

The term *sophia perennis,* or "perennial wisdom," was first coined by the German philosopher Gottfried Leibnitz (1646–1716), who understood that different religious traditions were not only valid in themselves, but could also inform each other. The syncretism of the classical mystery schools comprehended something of this understanding, as does the modern Ecumenical movement today, but the Western esoteric tradition is left out of the mix because few class it as a valid tradition at all.

The problem confronting us today is that most religious traditions have become empty structures—exoteric walls with empty esoteric space within them. The Western Way, however, suffers from the opposite problem: It is made up of a rich store of esoteric wisdom that has been discarded by religious traditions, yet it has few accessible structures in which to house this treasure. So how is the ancient wisdom preserved and transmitted?

A tradition begins to die when it becomes theoretical. This is the danger not just within the Western Way but also in religious traditions the world over. Once they begin to be studied for their own sake rather than being applied directly to everyday life, they lose their impetus to transmit wisdom. More than ever we need skillful mediators who know how to blend traditional wisdom for our own time. The professional defenders of tradition—once the poet and shaman, now the academic and priest—often fail to preserve the essential quality of tradition: They have lost their ability to communicate its wonder and wisdom; they have lost the magic. Where, then, are the visionaries who can show us the divine truths? We seem to have reached a plateau period when the old metaphors have been overhauled and found wanting, yet new metaphors are not easy to find. All things change and evolve—as they should, but when a tradition is confined within narrow, rigid forms, it cannot easily reach those for whom it is intended. As religion takes a nosedive into fundamentalism and whatever is "popular," as churches cleanse their liturgy of mystery, many alternatives come into being at the request of those who want to see their own visions and dream their own dreams.

So is the Western Way some new kind of religion? It includes the whole spectrum of paths, from the overtly esoteric to the inherently mystical, and comprises its own branches and disciplines, each of which, in turn, has its own traditions, devotions, and practices. Some find that while religions bind the spirit with the discipline of form and obedient conformity, following a well-trodden esoteric path leads to a freedom in which the spirit can soar.

We encourage you to find a tradition that appeals most to you and to inhabit it for a while before you make up your mind as to your own path (72). Seeking the inner kingdom outside a traditional system, without either spiritual allies or earthly mentors, may leave you vulnerable. A true tradition will preserve mystical and symbolic teaching in a safe manner while giving transformative realization of the inner kingdom. The need to explore inner worlds and realize our oneness with the whole universe, seen and unseen, does not decrease with succeeding generations. Instead it appears to be on the increase as traditional systems sell themselves short by offering quick and unsatisfying answers to those who hungrily ask questions and long for participation in the Mysteries.

The impulse of the Hermetic path of the Western Way derives from this predicament: the need to evolve and the need to preserve. It has produced the natural philosopher, the amateur theologian, and the ritualist to counterbalance the stasis of many religious traditions. It has encouraged the skillful adapter, the cunning preserver, and the quiet rec-onciler. Few of these men and women have left the tradition into which they were born; indeed, the most successful among them made their way within it and even despite it. Mystics and saints such as Clement of Alexandria, Vladimir Soloviev, Nahman of Bratislav, Saint Hildegard of Bingen, and Blessed John Ruysbrock were not renegades determined to show up their traditions, but rather explorers and revealers of the orthodox mystical way for others. They were not afraid to retain the esoteric riches of their tradition, often in the face of exoteric disapproval.

This division of mystical and mundane, esoteric and exoteric has become pronounced in our own day. Many followers of the Western Way would put the blame squarely upon the advent and promulgation of Christianity in the West, which is seen by them as the disturber and destroyer of native tradition. This view has blinded many to a true appreciation of the treasures of Western wisdom that seeded within Christianity and grew to maturity there. After all, Hermeticism grew up within the Christian era—most of its proponents were Christian not due to fear of persecution, but because that was their means of religious expression. Later in this chapter we will consider more closely why the Church became suspicious of its own mystical tradition, but the reason, at its root, was due to a division between the way of faith and the way of knowledge, or gnosis.

Neither faith nor knowledge on its own can gain us entry into the inner kingdom; we need, primarily, the gift of wisdom to guide us and to bind together faith and knowledge harmoniously.

> *The Lord himself created wisdom:*
> *he saw her and apportioned her,*
> *he poured her out upon all his works.*
> *She dwells with all flesh according to his gift,*
> *and he supplied her to those who love him.* (Sirach 1: 9–10)

Those who yearn after the eternal and wish to know for themselves the inner kingdom of the soul's spiritual treasury speak the language of wisdom, which transcends the limitations of human speech. It is the common tongue of mystics and esotericists everywhere, and of followers of the Western Way—whether of the native or the Hermetic tradition—and the Eastern Way. All of these know that they journey in the company of sophia perennis.

Any practicing member of a religious discipline is free to enter deeper into the Mysteries of his or her tradition at any time. It is a matter of involvement, of identification with and dedication to its inner wisdom. We have all met sincere religious people who go through the motions prescribed by convention, yet never touch their tradition's inmost heart—they travel by faith alone, in blind hope. But if they ever were to contact this inner heart through prayer or meditative awareness, they would become knowers as well as believers—confirmed within their adherence to the tradition.

On the other hand, there are those who steer solely by knowedge, who spurn the way of faith. Some esotericists see themselves as the Children of Light, the race of the new Aeon—but they are not the inheritors of the inner kingdom. Instead they have succumbed to the sin of spiritual pride, much like those fundamentalists who see themselves as the Elect of God. The true initiates of gnosis are those who become teachers and nourishers of wisdom wherever it struggles to be made manifest, who encourage the growth of inner potential in others rather than boast of their own spiritual achievements.

The companion on the way to the inner kingdom is wisdom—the law of knowledge and the mother of faith. She keeps knowledge within safe boundaries and distributes it to all Gnostics, and she guides faith, encouraging it to grasp the true nature of eternal things. A firm wisdom contact is essential in esoteric work, especially for those outside a living tradition. (See practice 13, The Temple of Inner Wisdom.)

In today's world, childhood faith is threatened, traditional metaphors no longer work, power is syphoned from spiritual to political ends, and fundamentalism reduces mystery to literalism. The deep magic of the inner story has been spoiled. In response to this fragmentation, a kind of vocational consciousness arises from the peoples of the world—and this response is not nationalist, but global. People from all backgrounds, all kinds of religious expressions, both traditional and nontraditional, perceive the dangers threatening our world. Often their response is humanist or ecological rather than spiritual, sometimes it is steered by faith and sometimes by knowledge—regardless, it is motivated by the earthy ancestral wisdom that is the birthright and gift of every human being who loves creation. Together with them, the mystics and esotericists, through sophia perennis, strive to mediate the healing of the inner world and the outer world. Awareness of the danger and responsibility for finding a way out of danger brings humility enough to the children of wisdom, whether they steer by means of faith or of knowledge.

The sophia perennis is not a religion or an end in itself, but a bond between different traditions. It can easily sink to an intellectual appreciation of comparative religion or a collection of New Age aphorisms where one tradition can easily be substituted for another. It is important to remember that each of the many traditions that make up the Western Way has its essential character, but wisdom is eternally true, through all of the changes that traditions may undergo. Those who have never considered the Western mystery tradition in the light of religion may find it helpful to see it as an esoteric philosophy along these lines.

Perhaps we may start by admitting that we are wounded: "The metaphysician [is a] wounded man. A wounded man is not an agnostic—he just has different questions arising out of his wound." (415) Like the shaman, the wounded healer is one who knows that the true cause of pain is loss of inner reality—the inner kingdom. This realization fired the Gnostics to go upon their own voyage of discovery, just as it later inspired those who went on a quest for the Grail and the healing of the Wasteland. There are many ways of achieving the Great Work.

The Fruits of Gnosis

"The life of the Gnostics is, in my view, no other than works and words which correspond to the tradition of the Lord," wrote Clement of Alexandria (512). This early Christian theologian was a lone voice rising from a sea of discontent and disapproval of the Gnostic experiment. Since Gnosticism, the Western world has never been the same. Its suppression left the Christian tradition poorer, although fragments of its teachings are still to be found in the Hermetic tradition. Gnosticism still rises periodically to haunt orthodox religion, but it stirs painful memories and provokes bigoted reactions. What was Gnosticism that it still has power to awaken hopes and fears? First of all, it is important not to confuse *gnosis* (which simply means "knowledge") with Gnosticism. It is possible, for instance, to say that Saint Teresa of Avila was gnostic, but not that she was a Gnostic. Gnosis as divine knowing is the birthright of all spiritual traditions and does not imply any connection with historical Gnosticism.

Gnosticism can be seen as a synthesis of the mystery schools that preceded it. It is "perhaps the first religion, at least in the West, which is wholly non-tribal and centred upon the discovery of infinity within the [individual] psyche," (143) and that makes it a vitally important link in the development of the Western Way. It is not without reason that many revival mystery schools in the modern age have claimed the Gnostics as their spiritual predecessors. Perhaps these schools have warmed to its teachings because Gnosticism did not attempt to explain "the sacramental rituals . . . as mere magic performed in memory of [historical] events, but as the externalisation of internal psychic alchemy," and because it regarded "the Bible not as history but as mythology of the most sublime and valuable kind." (143) As we shall discover, the Gnostic thread runs through the whole Hermetic tradition.

What we know of Gnosticism today emerges from an incredibly complex welter of traditions: In its melting pot it is possible to find Persian, Egyptian, Hellenic, Platonic, Christian, and Jewish elements. These fused at the nexus of Mediterrarian culture—Alexandria—where a great proliferation of traditions and teachings could be found. Although the great Alexandrian Library was burned in 391 C.E. and its remaining wisdom was subsequently destroyed in the early seventh century under Muslim occupation, the accumulated teachings within its scrolls had already escaped into the living traditions that made their home in Egypt.

The chief features of Gnosticism were inherited from Zoroastrian sources as well as from the many baptizing sects such as those of the Essenes, both of which were functioning before the onset of Christianity. The seeds of Gnosticism took root in the garden of Christianity and flourished there in a riot of color and spectacular abandon, in contrast to the more sober seedlings of the early Christian church. Gnosticism already had behind it the conceptual apparatus of the Mysteries, while Christianity was still finding its feet. Christian Gnosticism expanded from the middle of the first century C.E. and had its demise during the sixth century, although its influence continued after this period. The only true descendant of classical Gnosticism operative today is the Mandean sect in Iraq, which preserves the ritual purity of the early baptizing sects. This sect, however, is non-Christian, nearer in type to the Zoroastrian tradition than to the neo-Judaic. Many doubt whether its primitive traditions will outlast this century (512).

As Gnosticism developed, it rejected the Jewish basis of Christianity, though retained figures from Jewish scripture—Seth, Melchizedek, Adam, and Eve—as forerunners of its traditions. Of course, the rewriting of received texts is not merely a Gnostic phenomenon; it occurs today in many New Age groups and Christian-based cults that strive to purge mainstream Christianity while retaining some of its elements. This rescripting centers mostly upon the figure of Christ himself—new tales about him are spun and new sayings and commandments are attributed to him, though in reality these often emanate from the cult's leader rather than from divine sources. It is natural that all religions should seek to promote their antecedents, and Gnosticism was no exception.

If Gnosticism has had bad press, it is because it has been known mainly through its detractors. Its surviving texts were so fragmentary that a full picture of Gnostic belief could not be gleaned until the discovery of the Nag Hammadi library in 1945 and the Qumran texts in 1947, which have enabled scholars to begin piecing together an understanding of the religion. These Gnostic codices, like the contents of a time machine, have survived miraculously to land in our own century. The extraordinary story of their discovery may be read in John Dart's *The Laughing Savior* (117). Prior to their availability we could turn for information only to the invectives penned by Church fathers. The almost universal hatred of Gnosticism by the orthodox wing of the Church ensured the infamy of the Gnostics for all time. Their championship by Clement of Alexandria brought him little reward: This balanced theologian who was ahead of his time in seeing the truth within other traditions, especially within Platonism, was demoted from sainthood by Pope Clement VIII in the sixteenth century.

The Egyptian alchemist Zosimus wrote about a race of wisdom lovers who live forever at the inner door (410). This image applied neatly to the Gnostics, whose existence was regulated by communications that came from behind the inner door. The Gnostics were knowers—possessors of an inner wisdom and inheritors of the mystery schools. They envisaged humanity as a set of divine sparks trapped in matter. The true God was unknown and hidden—he alone was the origin of the light. Creation was the work of a false god, the demiurge. Every Gnostic lived in the hope of rejoining the true God in the fullness of the Pleroma (heaven). Belief in a demiurge—a false creator who must be destroyed—as well as in the true and unknowable God is persuasively explored in Philip Pullman's brilliant trilogy of novels, *His Dark Materials* (493), which incorporates many Gnostic elements. Gnostics believed that a return to Pleroma was possible, but that the way was fraught with difficulty because the divine spark within each individual lived in the forgetfulness of the flesh. It was necessary to combat the king of the world (the demiurge) by whatever means possible. He could be denied by practicing asceticism, which denies the currency of creation, or licentiousness, which scorns the created order. Some Gnostic sects were so extreme in their practices that they doubtless earned the censure heaped upon them. Not all sects, however, used these means. Interestingly, similar accusations have been leveled against modern practitioners of the Western Way, but there has been little evidence to support these claims. The fact is that unscrupulous individuals have long used the cover of esoteric ritual to front their sexual practices, none of which has any bearing on the practice of dedicated initiates. Ultimately, we must bear in mind that though there were common elements within the Gnostic sects, there were also many variations, which makes it impossible to generalize. Unfortunately, we have space to present only the barest outline of Gnostic belief and practice as they highlight elements within the Western Way. See *Sophia, Goddess of Wisdom* (383) for a wider view of Gnosticism.

The complex apparatus of Gnostic practice was designed to stimulate the divine spark within so that it would be prepared for its release from the flesh and the hazardous journey of the soul through the kingdoms of the archons, the servants of the demiurge, who ruled every sphere between earth and that of the Pleroma itself. This journey through the spheres is dealt with in more detail in chapter 9, where we will also unfold something of Gnostic cosmology.

The descent of the soul into flesh and its eventual return to heaven is epitomized in the metaphorical Song of the Pearl, from the apocryphal Acts of Thomas (13), in which a prince (the messiah) journeys from his home in the East (the Pleroma) into Egypt (the earth) in order to "bring back thence the one pearl which is there . . . girt about by the devouring serpent." In order to achieve this, the prince puts on the garments of Egypt (the flesh) in exchange for his own glorious robe (the divine nature). He forgets who he is, where he came from, and the purpose of his quest. A secret scroll is sent to him by means of an eagle, bidding him awake and remember that he is the son of kings.

He wins the pearl (the divine spark), strips off his filthy garments, and takes the way of return, guided by the secret scroll (the hidden gnosis). As he returns, the jewels and robes that he removed at various stages of his journey (just as Ishtar had to remove her garments at each of the gates of hell) are restored to him. "But suddenly, I saw the garment made like unto me as it had been in a mirror . . . and I knew and saw myself through it." He remembers everything and, fully equipped as a royal prince, is brought before "the brightness of the Father."

The parallels between this and the parable of the prodigal son (Luke 15:11–32) are not accidental. There are also resonances with the story of Joseph (Genesis 37–45): On behalf of his brothers, who have forgotten their divine spark, he undergoes captivity and imprisonment in Egypt and a subsequent change in fortunes. Christ himself is figured in this Gnostic parable, which recalls his flight into Egypt, obscure childhood, and subsequent return to his Father with the "pearl"—the fruits of Redemption. Robert Southwell, the sixteenth-century Jesuit poet, recalls this theme in his poem "On the Nativity of Christ":

> *Despise him not for lying there:*
> *First what he is enquire.*
> *An orient pearl is often found*
> *In depth of dirty mire.* (551)

This is a theme we will be returning to when we examine the inner resonances relating to alchemy and the quest for the Grail (chapter 10). Here this mystery story of the prince and the pearl gives not only a sense of the Gnostic mind, but also one of the timeless themes that appear again and again through the centuries.

Why am I born? What is my purpose? How does evil originate? These were the philosophical questions that absorbed the Gnostic and were the forerunners of the kind of scientific enquiry that dictated the shape of the Renaissance and brought about yet another clash between believers and those inclined to resurrect Gnostic ideas. The Gnostic prefigures the alchemist in his ability to believe in the possibility of transformation and to use the images and archetypes close at hand to attain this state. The imaginative resources of the Gnostic creation dramas are astounding in their conceptual scope.

Central to the return of the divine spark of the soul were the dual themes of anthropos and sophia, both of which represent that continual focus of the Western Way: the interpenetration of the microcosm by the macrocosm. The *anthropos* is the Adam of Light, otherwise known as Adam Kadmon in Kabbalah. He is the first man, the mirror of the macrocosm, but the demiurge and his archons deceive him into forgetting his heritage. Together with the spirit of Sophia (wisdom), whose

232 THE HERMETIC TRADITION

daughter he partners (the Eve of Paradise), he is lost in matter. Adam's body is the body of the world, his soul the totality of souls. The sufferings of Sophia, the exiled wisdom of the true God, were analogous to the sufferings of the created world. Her ultimate union with Christ—her Savior and that of the whole world—was the expected portion of Valentinian Gnostics, who conceived of the union of Christ with Sophia as the signal for the *apocatastasis,* or the restoration of all things. Adam and Eve and Christ and Sophia were seen as types of syzygy (partners or consorts) whose reconciliation was important for the balancing of creation. This theme is also of critical importance within the Western Way, as we shall see in chapters 9 and 10.

It is evident that Gnosticism fostered many levels of dualism, which was merely a reflection of the contemporary concern with the fallen nature of humanity, but which also polarized an eternally warring good and evil. These concerns, prevalent in early Christianity, were also deeply ingrained in classical belief. Saviors, redeemers, and messiahs of both genders could be found in almost every mystery school and religion at this time. They were the symbols of hope and release from the vagaries of inexorable Fate, which was the obsession and scourge of the classical world. The fusion of elements from belief systems as disparate as Platonic, Orphic, Zoroastrian, and Christian made Gnostic dualism particularly confusing, especially from our modern standpoint, which is comparatively naive in its conceptualization of good and evil. The stoic purity of Orphism, the endless battles of Zurvanist gods and demons, and the semitic dualities of male and female all appear in Gnosticism in different forms. The Gnostics, it seemed, enjoyed making their pieces of the cosmic jigsaw puzzle fit.

Having established their own idiosyncratic gospels and rich cosmology, they were free to relate to them. They considered themselves to be "the kingless race" or, conversely, "the king's children," the offspring of the true hidden God. The Neoplatonist Plotinus (third century C.E.) was shocked that they should class themselves with the divine, "brothers and sisters of those above!" (481) Yet the Gnostics believed they had the assurance from the mouth of Christ, no less, who, in conversation with the apostle Andrew, states: "Know ye not . . . that ye and all angels and all archangels and the gods . . . are out of one and the same paste and the same matter and the same substance, and that ye all are out of the same mixture." (435)

This spiritual elitism arose from the way in which Gnosticism divided humanity. There was the *hylic,* or fleshly man; the *psychic,* or partially enlightened man (usually understood as one who was nominally Christian); and the *pneumatic,* or spiritual man, who was fully gnostic (one who had heard and was conversant in the secret revelations of Christ and his disciples). This concept of division is described in *The Origin of the World* (435) as the three Adams. The Gnostics believed their enlightenment was predestined—an element that appeared in the form of Calvinism in a later century. The pneumatics were variously called the Elect or the Perfected. As representatives of the new Aeon, the Gnostics built upon early Christian beliefs to create a system whose catholicity and impact were immense. But the promotion of knowledge over faith was too unbalanced. Having envisaged a fallen Sophia (wisdom), their gnosis was correspondingly less applicable to daily life. The idea that the Gnostics strove to follow was: "The beginning of Perfection is the Gnosis of Man, but the Gnosis of God is perfected Perfection." (410)

Apart from Marcion and possibly Valentinus, there was no attempt to codify the complexities and varieties of expression within Gnosticism itself. Marcion (?–160 C.E.) was the only one who tried to fashion a Gnostic church based on the Christian model from the loosely based circles into which Gnosticism was organized. There were, however, fundamental differences of organization between Gnosticism and Christianity. Gnosticism appealed to the intellectual and cultured section of society, while Christianity appealed to a universal need and even accepted slaves, unlike the mysteries schools, which accepted only free men and women. Following the ancient model, the Gnostic priesthood was both male and female, whereas Christianity maintained a male priesthood. Gnosticism was suppressed for a variety of reasons: Its lack of well-distributed literature, its elitism, its reluctance to proselytize, and its uncodified nature were a few contributory factors. Crucially, Gnosticism did not offer to the empires of Rome and Byzantium the opportunity for Imperial cohesion that orthodox Christianity did. Its suppression was swiftly carried out, though not finally effective: Gnostic traces could not be completely rooted out of orthodox Christianity.

Many of Saint Paul's letters to the churches in Asia Minor and Greece attempted to address the unruly effects of Gnosticism upon his proselytes: "Avoid the godless chatter and contradictions of what is falsely called knowledge, for by professing it some have missed the mark as regards the faith." (1 Tim. 6:20) This is what lies at the heart of the dichotomy between Gnosticism and Christianity, which has had, ever since, a love-hate relationship with its own esoteric tradition. The effect of Gnosticism was to widen the gap between knowledge and faith to the extent that Saint Ignatius of Antioch could write:

> It is better if a man knows nothing and does not perceive a single cause of things created but abides in faith in God and in love, rather than that, puffed up by such knowledge, he falls away from the love that makes man alive, and rather than that he falls into godlessness through the subtleties of his questioning and hair-splitting. (512)

The way of gnosis is indeed fraught with such dangers, but its dismissal was a prelude to the Church's continual distrust of its own saints and mystics. The Gnostic experiment may have been unbalanced, but then so was the reaction against it.

Christ's words "Let your light so shine before men, that they may see your good works" and "I come not to abolish [the law and the prophets] but to fulfill them" (Matthew 5:16–17) were to become the lost Christian legacy. The challenge of Gnosticism reappeared to haunt orthodoxy again and again in the form of many heresies, and the words of the Gnostic Christ still echoed: "I am the actual call which causes a call to resound in each one, and thus they recognize [me] through [knowledge], since a seed [of light] is in [them]." (512)

The battle for divine knowledge has led to many experiments that orthodoxy has termed heretical. These experiments focalize some of the key elements that still polarize orthodoxy and esotericism today and which often erupt within the extremes of orthodox religion itself: believing versus knowing, asceticism versus luxury, spiritual purity versus heterodoxy, fallen and imperfect universe versus a potentially perfect universe.

Heresy is a word deriving from the Greek for "choice." It is usually applied by orthodoxy to designate those who have chosen to deviate from the straight and narrow way of obedience. We must be careful to distinguish esotericism from outright heresy in considering the Western Way, for they are not synonymous. Esotericism honors the mystical traditions and respects the way in which they are wound with exoteric belief, whereas heresy is reactive, a break from the core tradition in the interest of exploring the extremes.

One area in which these extremes make it difficult to distinguish among orthodoxy, esotericism, and heresy is dualism. Within esoteric tradition, dualism can set up dichotomies that esrange the seeker from a holistic perspective. Historically, some spiritual movements drew heavily upon the dualism that permeated both Gnosticism and mainstream Christianity.

Good and evil, light and dark, man and woman, spirit and matter— these are the dualities that guardians of spiritual traditions everywhere understand as essential to bring balance to the universe. However, when one half of any one of these dualities is invested with more importance than the other, belief in these dualities becomes belief in dualism and heresy is the result.

Gnosticism created myths that focus upon the fruits of gnosis, which, like the apple in the garden of Eden, bring knowledge of good and evil. The primary concern of Gnosticism was the union of the dualities into a paradisal unity, a re-membering of the Body of Light. Gnostics rejected the original sin of orthodox Christianity, preferring to focus instead on how eating the fruit of our experience leads to the opening of our inner eyes. It was only by Adam and Eve's theft of knowledge that humanity could pave the path to the reunion of the universe (373).

Gnosticism was merely one contender for the control of Christianity during the early days of the Church, when doctrinal matters were still being codified. It failed at about the same time as the barbarian hordes swept across Europe, eclipsing the continent's rich classical heritage. The Byzantine Empire maintained certain ancient traditions; Church and state joined forces to strengthen each other against the onslaughts of armed insurrection and spiritual darkness. It was no time for personal revelation. While Christianity struggled to make its impact upon Europe, using the vehicle of native traditional practices and customs as a teaching aid, the Gnostic vision was borne eastward and westward by Manichaeism and Catharism, respectively.

Manichaeism is not a direct derivative of Gnosticism so much as a parallel development. Its founder, Mani (216–276 C.E.), was born in Seleucia of mixed Persian and Gnostic-Baptist background. At the age of twelve he had a vision in which his heavenly companion assured him of help and protection. Further revelations led him to regard himself as "the Paraclete of the Christians, as the Messianic son of Zarathustra, and as the Maitreya Buddha" (512)—no small claim! He shared the Gnostic belief in imprisoned particles of light that must be released by spiritual means. Humans were light-bearers who must be active in the combat with darkness—a Mithraic concept as well as a Christian one.

All apostles of light, Manichaens believed, saw their culmination in Mani: Noah, Seth, Enoch, Buddha, Zoroaster, and Christ. Extreme asceticism marked Mani's followers: Their practice was typified by vegetarianism, abstinence from wine and sexual intercourse, and a general avoidance of harm to all potential vessels of light, whether human, animal, or plant.

The success of Manichaeism was due to Mani's determination that his teachings be written down and widely circulated. His church spread rapidly, despite persecution, especially in the East. Mani was martyred by being flayed alive and his disciples were banished from Persia. While a few came West, Manichaeism continue to develop, mainly in the East, where it held its own against the Nestonan church and Buddhism. It became particularly strong in central Asia, in Turfan in Chinese Turkestan, where its members proselytized and enjoyed a tolerant hearing until they were suppressed in the wake of the Mongolian invasion. Manichaen scriptures found in Turfan early in the twentieth century are still being investigated (512).

The legacy of Manichaeism in the West seems small, probably due to the intervention of Islam, which effectively drove a wedge between West and East. Yet Mani's prophecy, "[M]y hope will go into the West and will also go into the East," came true. Elements of Manichaen dualism can still be discerned within Christianity due to the theology of Saint Augustine, who, despite his refutation of his early adherence to Manichaeism, nevertheless introduced a flavor of dualism into his writings.

While Manichaeism trekked eastward, another remnant of Gnosticism went westward through Bulgaria and Italy into France and Spain, where it became known as Catharism (316). It is perhaps significant that the journeys of both of these Gnostic descendants came to an abrupt and bloody end during the thirteenth century, almost as though the influence of Gnosticism had run its course for that era. But where Manichaeism developed and flourished apart from other Christian rivals, Catharism was as much a product of Christian reactionism as a continuation of Gnostic principles.

The roots of dualistic belief, such as Catharism, are very deep and difficult to eradicate:

> Dualism carried with it . . . the need for revelation, and the need for redemption. If man cannot, while living in the body, truly find god, the God must make himself known. And if the life of the body

drags down the aspiring soul to its level and weakens its powers of flight, then the body and its activities never achieve their destined end without some infusion of divine power from outside, from above. (191)

Within historical perspectives of the Western mystery tradition, the Cathars are often promoted as martyrs to a shared esoteric principle. But though their destruction and persecution at the hands of the Inquisition has aroused much sympathy, the full rigor of the Cathar way of life and their spiritual stance would find little favor almost anywhere today. The way of the Cathar is not the way of the Hermeticist. Though its appeal to a certain purity of living might be attractive, Catharism teeters upon the brink of a dualism of hopelessness wherein matter is utterly dissolved. We shall return to this point in chapter 10.

For both Manichaens and Cathars, flesh and matter generally were creations of the evil demiurge. An ultimate dualism—an eternal polarization of evil and good—stood at the core of their belief systems. The agents of the light had somehow been imprisoned and uniformed in the colors of darkness. It is perhaps difficult for us to appreciate this doctrine, living as we do at the beginning of the the third millennium, mostly ignorant of the spiritual perspectives that underlie our culture, but it is essential to understand and avoid the pitfalls of dualism now as it was then. Dualism flourishes wherever mind or spirit or both are seen as distinct and separate from matter, leading an individual to neglect earthly duties and responsibilities in favor of the striving for unattainable spiritual perfection. Fundamentalist religions of all kinds frequently harbor strong dualistic elements that deliver the saved to heaven and everyone else to Hell, regardless of their good deeds. Dualism is more likely to denounce rather than befriend those of other viewpoints, preferring to see its own adherents as "the chosen" and all others as "the damned."

Dualism was a recurrent problem within Christianity. The Incarnation and the Redemption were concepts that were often misunderstood, and without their balance heresy flourished. The earth and its creations were not cause for joy to a medieval peasant plowing his feudal lord's fields, nor to his wife burdened with "boon work" and many children. For these people, respite came only on feast days and at death. The Cathars found the Creation a cause of sorrow because it imprisoned the divine spark. Food, sexuality, and enjoyment of the world's goods were either rejected or subjected to a deep antimonianism that compartmentalized the body and spirit so that they could have no inter-action. Cathars wanted release from this condition; they yearned for a spiritual condition with all the zeal of the Orphite. Spiritual purity could have nothing to do with the body, and for this reason, the Cathars said that Christ only seemed to be born of a woman and only seemed to die on the cross. In this same vein, the sacraments, which exalt matter as the gateway to spiritual grace, were totally rejected.

Because the Church traded in matter, the Cathars viewed orthodox Christianity as the agent of the demiurge. It is interesting to speculate just what caused the development of Catharism within Provence, where courtly love flourished, where troubadours sang ballads of forthright love, and where the lush cultural climate was a product of the bounti-ful south. Perhaps "the Cathar notion of body-soul division and the need to ascend through a cycle of purification to a dimension of non-material light had some affinities with the more idealist side of courtly love." (334)

Like the Gnostics and the Manichaens, the Cathars had three ranks of adherents: hearers, believers, and the Perfects. "There was thus in effect the same division as among the Catholics between the Religious or Monks and other Believers." (334) The Perfects reached their exalted position by renouncing evil, living continently, and abstaining from flesh meats and the fruits of sexuality. They alone could reconcile sin-ners by means of a ritual called the *consolamentum*—a sacramental method of purification. Its effect was considered final and was possibly not repeatable: If a Perfect fell into sin after having received the conso-lamentum—whether by eating meat or committing murder (both equally reprehensible acts)—all those who had received purification at his hands were rendered likewise sinful. In other words, a chain of evil had been released. Vigilance and a high degree of integrity were key fea-tures of Catharism. Often the consolamentum was not received until death, when all sin was remitted. Women were admissible to ranks of the Perfect; widows kept Cathar communities, educating children and practicing the Cathar way of life. It was a form of ideal Christianity, but dualist to the heart.

The Cathars' plain life, simple food, laying on of hands, celibacy, and adherence to the Gospel of Saint John make them seem to be mod-els of the faith. Yet these very characteristics are what focused the Church's attention on them—such cases had occurred in Europe before. The Church and the French king launched the Albigensian Crusade

(1208–1218) against the Cathars, though its causes and success were due as much to dynastic and geographical as religious reasons (316). By 1242 Catharism had retired to the fortress of Montségur in the Pyrenees, and after a yearlong siege, its inhabitants were burned and dispossessed of their lands. By the end of the fourteenth century, Catharism was all but dead. The works of the English doctor Arthur Guirdham, however, who has claimed Cathar incarnations, have repopularized the movement somewhat. Today there are various Gnostic churches in America, as well as a neo-Cathar movement, known as the Lectorium Rosicrucianum, in Holland.

We have followed the threads of Gnosticism into heresy, but the trail does not stop there. Gnosis—esoteric knowledge gently led by wisdom—reveals itself within the mystical essence of Christianity. Though the impulse of the Western Way has been considered heretical by the exoteric Church, it resonates strongly with esoteric Christianity.

Aslan Is Not a Safe Lion

In *The Lion, the Witch and the Wardrobe*, C. S. Lewis presents Aslan—a lion, king of the beasts, and son of the Emperor Over the Seas—as a Christ figure. Some of the characters in the story expect him to be a tame, domesticated lion, an anthropomorphic, storybook beast, but they are told, "Aslan is not a safe lion." We expect to see Christ in the same guise—as a safe, tame, familiar god—but the reality is quite different. It is telling that many adults who read Lewis's story as a child and only now realize the nature of his allegory have said, "Jesus was a bearded man in the Bible, someone I couldn't relate to—but I could have died for Aslan."

This shows how much we have lost touch with the story of Christianity. The dynamic Christ of the Resurrection, the one who flogs the money-changers in the temple, the one who blasts the fig tree for its barrenness, who will come to bring fire and the sword, is at odds with the downtrodden man of sorrows in the mode of Attis and Adonis, the savior god who lies dead in his mother's lap—the one who has become gentle Jesus, meek and mild. Christ is not safe. He is the Anointed One whose tongue is a sword (Revelation 1:16)—the Logos or Word of God. We must not see him as a comfortable icon.

Commenting on the implicit dualism in Western religion, Dion Fortune says: "The great weakness of Christianity lies in the fact that it ignores rhythm. It balances God with Devil instead of Vishnu with Shiva," (164) which are the preserving and destructive aspects of Brahma. More challengingly, Jim Garrison says: "God as experienced has been shown to possess light and dark dimensions and to be as savage and terrible as God is merciful and forgiving." (177) What are we—especially those of us to whom Christianity seems to be the deadest of dead ends—to make of this?

More words have been written and more blood has been spilled over the founder of Christianity and his intentions than many can bear to contemplate. Christ has become the figurehead and puppet of both saints and sinners, and the measure of his doctrines a tawdry mockery of the Gospel. After nearly two thousand years of substitutes, it is time to see the reality.

Here we shall be looking at the esoteric, not the exoteric, side of Christianity—we will consider the Church as a preserver of tradition and as a living mystery school. In part 1 we saw that Christianity played a large part in the transmission of the native tradition, for it was the Church that upheld the customs of ancestral importance and national cohesion. It likewise rescued the Hermetic tradition from oblivion. While it "designed to obliterate and extinguish the memory of heathen antiquity and authors . . . contrariwise it was the Christian Church which . . . did preserve in the sacred lap and bosom thereof the precious relics even of heathen learning which otherwise had been extinguished as if no such thing had ever been." (27)

People today are in a unique position in that those who join a spiritual tradition rarely have any spiritual baggage to bring with them. It wasn't always this way:

> Greeks, and Syrians and Egyptians . . . came to the Church loaded with packs of their own, crammed with metaphysics and mystical experience, with cosmic lore and traditions . . . nor did they dream of dropping all this on the threshold of the Church and forgetting all about it. . . . On the contrary they prized these things as heirlooms, as their dowry. (190)

The validation of spiritual life does not come from some projected set of dogmas, but from inner experience resonating with a tradition. In our times outsiders come to gaze on the exterior architecture of tradition, yet few see the vision in the sanctuary.

The Church has always taught a mystery: that Christ is both fully human and fully divine. This is usually translated into Christ the man or Christ the god—rarely both together. But the implications of the Incarnation and the Redemption are of overwhelming importance to the Hermeticist if he or she is engaged in the Great Work. Neither of these concepts appears to command universal respect, even among those who are nominally Christian, though the Incarnation and the Redemption are the two pillars between which the Christian cosmos is balanced. The central point of balance is the Crucifixion and the Harrowing of Hell: "[T]his central event is the meeting of many power lines: whatever their provenance before this event in time, whatever their divergence after it—all lines [of tradition] lead through the mystery of the Resurrection." (380) In order for us—Christians and non-Christians alike—to fully appreciate the mystical content of these concepts, we must dispel the ideological smoke screens that cloud them.

As a result of popular theosophical understanding, Christ is often now seen as one among many saviors of East and West. Or he is seen as yet another of the dying and rising vegetation gods of the mystery schools. The reality is much more complex: The Hellenic notion of the Logos, the Jewish idea of the Messiah, and the mystery schools' own saviors are combined in the figure of Christ (149). The Eastern Orthodox doctrine of *theosis* (literally, "deification") may give us a key to understanding this: "God became man that man might become God," said Saint Athanasius in his *De Incarnatione*. Though this is not one of the concepts that the Church publicizes, it stands out uniquely in the Mysteries of Christianity as the key not only to Christ's actions but to Christian belief as well (353). Whether or not we are believers, it is clear that the Incarnation caused a change in direction, for it represented not just the birth of a tradition, but also the opportunity for consciousness to evolve; it acted as a necessary bridge between the dualism of the classical world and the cosmic hope of the Mysteries.

Saviors in many guises had come before, but none made the impact of Christ. "What is this mystery that touches me? I received the divine image and did not keep it. He received my flesh to save the image and grant immortality to the flesh." (337) This promise, which has been obscured and remains to be rediscovered, is unique within Christianity, a religion that is, despite all appearances, a visibly present, though invisibly operative, mystery school. The Hermetic tradition draws heavily upon the archetypal myths of classical, Christian, and native

Fig. 15. The Resurrection, alchemical symbol of the Great Work

Mysteries until each has become part of the other so that they can rarely be distinguished.

The occult enclosure of Hermeticism has been a self-protective measure as much as a means of preserving the Mysteries from the profane. The Christian Mysteries, on the other hand, are open, though inherently hidden. They remain, yet their traditional wisdom and liturgical symbolism have all but disappeared through oversimplification. The *disciplina arcani,* the Christian mystery guardians, once kept non-initiates from observing the higher mysteries of the consecration of the host by erecting the medieval rood screen, which prevented the common faithful from becoming too familiar with the sacramental operation.

Now, however, anyone can see the Great Work taking place quite openly.

The Great Work is carried out daily on altars in nearly every country of the world as the *prima materia* of the sacred elements—the bread and wine—are miraculously changed into the body and blood of Christ. How many alchemists achieve the same and show it publicly? (See chapter 10.) The relevance of the transubstantiation of the bread and wine into the body and blood of Christ was not lost upon alchemists in later times who used the Eucharistic symbolism as an emblem for their own work. The transmutation of the mundane into the divine, the central sacrament in which the Incarnation and Redemption are enacted, was archetypally representative of the Great Work. Those who received the sacrament were enabled, mysteriously, to become members of the mystical Body of Christ.

The Hermeticist who is aware of the indwelling divine spark and of the attempt he or she must make to kindle it and take the evolutionary journey into the heart of the macrocosm has only to consider the implications of Christ's Incarnation—a journey into the heart of the microcosm in order to bring divine fire to the indwelling spark. The amazingly universal application of this action is not just for those who can produce a certificate of baptism, but rather applies to all. It is the skillful use of this story of the divine spark—whether we use the Christian model or some other—that brings us out of "the vale of tears" and into the inner kingdom: "Not that one should give up, neglect or forget [one's] inner life for a moment, but [one] must learn to work in it, with it and out of it, so that the unity of [one's] soul may break out into [one's] activities and . . . activities shall lead . . . back to that unity." (438)

The Resurrection is just as significant, for it breaks through and overturns the tides of time. As with all Mysteries, the Christian ones happen outside of time. All that happens within time is subject to the laws of both time and nature, which is why the imperfect face of the Church reveals not the tranquillity of the inner kingdom but the battered makeshift within the world (317). The Redemption reconciles the two trees of Eden: the Tree of Life and the Tree of the Knowledge of Good and Evil. The dualism of matter and spirit is reconciled by the realization that all created things have within them the potential of resurrection, of transubstantiation, of the completion of the Great Work itself.

Such are the possibilities of esoteric Christianity—but, many will demand, where is it practiced? While there have been many specifically occult Christian spin-offs from the time of the Gnostics right up to the liberal Catholic Church with its Theosophist tenets, we will not find this full mystical kernel anywhere except within the traditional folds of the Catholic and Eastern Orthodox churches, which have hosted and preserved their spiritual traditions with rigorous care.

The mystical way of tradition has had to work hard to survive the battle between faith and knowledge that began in the time of Gnosticism. We have only to look at the very beginning of Christianity to see how pitiful and unnecessary this battle has been. Two sets of visitants come to the manger in Bethlehem: the shepherds and the kings. The shepherds, impelled by angelic messengers, accept the proclamation of the newborn messiah with uncritical enthusiasm—with faith. The kings, by means of their gnosis, follow a star that is the certainty of their faith until they too reach their destination. It is perhaps of note that the shepherds go straight to the manger, while the kings waste time calling upon Herod to offer unwanted congratulations. (See chapter 8.)

"The faith of uneducated men is not the less philosophically correct, nor less acceptable to God, because it does not happen to be conceived in precise statements. . . . The ears of the common people are holier than are the hearts of the priests," wrote Cardinal Newman (446). While faith and knowledge are not exclusive, as we have seen, the Church does not have the apparatus for coping with the mystic who has progressed beyond blind faith into certain knowing, which is the gnosis of spiritual illumination.

We have seen how the Gnostic and Manichaen movements catered to the disparate needs of their followers. Modern Christianity, however, seems saddled with a system in which only the minimum belief of the faithful and the highly inflected way of the monk and nun can be accommodated. We need what Jacob Needleman calls "intermediate Christianity" (438). The mystical traditions are too circumscribed by experts to be richly and readily available to all; they are not widely taught as a matter of course and those who do stumble upon the esoteric side of Christianity (usually by accident) are without the guidance or assurance of experts in the field, or else are so frightened that they mistake their findings for heresy. As for those psychically gifted or esoterically involved believers, they find themselves out on a limb:

For centuries the tradition has been to distrust the psychically sensitive people as representing the pagan religions from which the

Christian faith has liberated the countries into which it has perco-
lated. . . . But in Europe, the Church has driven the psychic into
the underworld. It never disappeared; but it was always threatened, so that it allied itself with pagan rather than with Christian
ideas. (472)

The infancy of the Church is passed, yet the Church seems unwilling
to push forward to new growth and adulthood. Those within it who
seek spiritual maturity find themselves held down in spiritual adolescence. It is little wonder that a mass exodus of Christians is occurring in
the direction of other religions or spiritual systems that bother to teach
the techniques of prayer and meditation and which not only treasure but
also are willing to transmit to others the traditions they have inherited.

This neglect by the Church of its inner life has led many to speculate
as to whether a spiritual renaissance is due. The world now has many
spiritual pilgrims and fewer guardians of tradition. If such a renaissance
is abroad, then it is more likely to arise from the laity rather than from
the clergy, who seem hell-bent on a program of steady demythologization,
liturgical impoverishment, and theological inertia—the new chastity,
poverty, and obedience of the modern age. Few Hermeticists and non-
Christians foresee any continuing hope within Christianity as a church-
administered religion. The steady devaluation "in the price of what it is
to be a Christian" had so accelerated in the philosopher Kierkegaard's
day that he wrote, "[A]t last it became such an absurdly low price that
soon the opposite effect was produced, that men hardly wanted to have
anything to do with Christianity." (300) Some would see the demise of
Christianity as poetic justice in the sense that it has been directly or indirectly the undertaker and executioner of many other traditions.

If the esoteric Christian mysteries are guarded anywhere, it is by the
unheralded mystic who lives, like a hidden hermit, within his or her
tradition. We return once again to our concept of "marginal shamans"
who inform the traditional values of the secret commonwealth. For
every mystic whose realizations are written down, there are probably
hundreds whose silent practice is unknown. Mysticism is still tarred
with the brush of Gnosticism and heresy. From past records it would
seem that the mystic, like the shamefully neglected poet, is immediately
lauded upon his or her death after a lifetime of being hounded from pillar to post. The incarceration of Saint John of the Cross and the inquisition of Saint Teresa of Avila are extreme instances of this practice.

Stigmatics and wonder workers, far from reveling in the reputation enjoyed by pre-Revolutionary Orthodox hermits, have been relegated to obscure monasteries. It's understandable to feel that a real live Saint Francis would upset the Church as much now as he did in thirteenth-century Umbria.

The mystical way is a trackless path on which the pilgrim seeks to encounter God face-to-face, believing utterly in the promise "I will give you the treasures of darkness and the secret places." (Isaiah 45:7) Finding our own inner way is by no means dependent upon how others have traveled, but the journey is considerably shorter if we spend it in the company of others who are traveling. The great mystics of the Church have long acted as pilgrims' companions—from medieval mystics such as Julian of Norwich (278), the anonymous author of *The Cloud of Unknowing* (604), Thomas à Kempis (291), and Saint Catherine of Siena (83) to the mystics of our own day, such as Thomas Merton (415), Caryll Houselander (254), and Ida Gorres (190). The restoration and preservation of the Christian tradition has been the concern of many mystics and spiritual writers in the past century. Two remarkable women from disparate backgrounds have contributed much to our understanding: Rosemary Haughton (234) and Lois Lang-Sims (317). Both are aware of the Christian Mysteries and the "lost" esoteric side of their faith. Their books rise from a babel of theological dispute and fundamentalist cant. It is perhaps significant that they are both women within a tradition that, though it has boasted "there is neither Jew nor Greek, there is neither slave nor free, there is neither male nor female" (Galatians 3:28), has held tenaciously to the very sexual disqualifications that Saint Paul's words were meant to abolish.

When Teilhard de Chardin, writing in the middle of this century, said, "[T]here is the general question of the feminine, and so far it has been left unsolved or imperfectly expressed by the Christian theory of sanctity," (122) he was hardly underestimating his own tradition's failing in this regard. Though Christ's ministry can be seen as bounded by the feminine poles of Mary the Virgin, his mother, who accomplished his Incarnation by her willingness to serve God, and Mary Magdalene, who discovered the empty sepulchre on the morning of the Resurrection, the Church has been slow to meditate on this. Much feminist theology has tried to rectify this state of affairs, but has often succeeded only in setting matters on their head, substituting female for male symbology and promoting the ordination of women over more crucial issues (383). Our esoteric understanding is disrupted when we see a willing acceptance of a symbol for liturgical purposes (e.g., the representation of and anthems to the Blessed Virgin and Lady Mary) but an exclusion of her daughters. Mystics have been particularly drawn to the Virgin Mary: "Mary is a dimension of Jesus, a dimension which he expressed when he said, 'My yoke is easy and my burden light;' it is advantageous to address oneself to this dimension in order to reach totality." (524)

Fig. 16. Lady Mary and her son in the Ship of Faith,
which is piloted by Wisdom

The Logos and his mother, as the manifest incarnations of God's love, who share in the lot of humanity, are the balances of the spiritual totality. Jung was right to acclaim the doctrine of the Assumption of the Virgin into heaven as supremely important for our time, for through it the dualism of male and female stands some chance of being flushed out of Christianity. The spirit—symbolized frequently by Christ—is important, but so is the body, which Christ could take on only with the help of Mary. If the body or soul of a man (i.e., Jesus) had been assumed heaven, then it was right and fitting that the body and soul of a woman should be so assumed, says the dogma. "From this earth, over which we tread as pilgrims, comforted by our faith in future resurrection, we look to you . . . O Sweet Virgin Mary." (431) It is interesting to note that though the Protestant churches after the Reformation forsook devotion to or mention of Mary, Hermeticists and alchemists never abandoned her. Entrenched within the Protestant enclaves of Rosicrucianism, in the writings of Boehme, Vaughan, and others, Our Lady's memory is alive. We shall look further at the Divine Feminine in chapter 10, where we consider the identifications of the Goddess, the World Soul, and the sophianic lady herself, Our Lady Wisdom (383).

The Hermeticist may often find him- or herself at odds with the exoteric or dogmatic nature of the Church, but seldom with its esoteric mysteries. "What the microcosmic heart does not tell, the macrocosmic heart—the Logos—tells us in a symbolic and partial language." (524) Christ's parables reveal two levels of understanding: On one level they are story, on another they are keys to the inner kingdom. Jesus speaks about himself in a symbolic way, urging his hearers to squeeze the last drop of meaning out of his parables. His telling is aimed to provoke response from among those listeners who have the native wisdom to use the story practically. While he was an enemy of theoretical knowledge, especially when it was imposed upon people who live by simple faith (Matthew 23), he also encouraged the faith that leads to better knowledge (John 10). More abundant life, not less, was his saying. Whatever salvific story we live by, first we must believe in it and trust it to show us its treasures. Awareness of the macrocosm, of the inner kingdom, lies within the Gospels.

Mystical revelation is not a forbidden, exotic thing; it is merely the skillful understanding and use of spiritual symbolism. In part 1 we spoke about the ways in which we can read the landscape, the ancestral stones of our native tradition. The same holds true for the Hermetic tradition:

The Gothic cathedrals were known as the Bible of the people—their architectural mysteries embodied the esoteric story of Christ. To visit one of these today is to step within a forest of stone pillars in whose nemetons and groves are the depictions of saints, angels, prophets, the yearly round of the seasons, and the secret tokens of Christ and Lady Mary. At Chartres we can enter the labyrinth, which symbolically represents not only the pilgrimage to Jerusalem, but also a return to the heart's home, the inner kingdom that is reached by means of life itself (647, 108, 2). The labyrinth is also our reminder of the inward and outward spirals of the Western Way. It even seems that in this cathedral-forest we might glimpse the white hart, the emblem of spiritual search and the quarry of the Grail quest (495) or, from an earlier time, the quarry of Pwyll from the *Mabinogion* or Arawn's wild hunt.

Thus the quest begun under the native tradition continues without break into the Hermetic tradition. From the Gundestrup Cauldron, with its depiction of Cernunnos as Guardian of the Sacrificial Hunt, to the words of Saint John of the Cross—"for the wounded hart appears on the hill" (269)—seems a long step, but it is not difficult to reconcile these interrelated images. From within the temenos of a medieval cathedral it is easier to make such an important connection. The stones there were hewn and erected when spiritual chivalry was abroad—a quest that included the laity, lady, knight, lord, and peasant. The virile epics of spiritual chivalry, exemplified by the Grail legends, combined the Christian mythos with the vigor of native storytelling. Love, both earthly and spiritual, was present in all its complexity: From the Templars, those monks on horseback, and their urge to protect pilgrims to the otherworldly Courts of Love where Celtic paradise and medieval simplicity combined, everyone wanted to be part of the story.

Saint Francis of Assisi, his head stuffed with such stories, had attempted to be a chivalrous knight before he rode out in defense of Lady Poverty in nothing more than a tattered habit, owning nothing more than a handful of ideals—yet he never lost sight of his love for spiritual chivalry and the quest. He founded two orders, one for monks and one for nuns, but so overwhelmingly eloquent was this troubadour of the Lord that his storytelling almost emptied the villages of Italy, so he founded an order for laypeople that they might not be left out of the story.

The tribal stories did not retreat but instead were reworked and incorporated into the story of the White Hart, or Christ himself. And while this and the story of the finding of the spark of light that is a central part of the Hermetic tradition are challenged by new metaphors, they still have the power to draw in listeners.

Over time the thirst for knowledge became powerful as well, often engulfing what the Church saw as the more important concerns of spiritual quest. Before long the earlier splintering of religion from shamanism was to be unhappily mirrored once more between religion and science during the Reformation and Counter-Reformation. Faith and knowledge joined battle again with the help of new combatants—tradition against the word, laws of God against laws of nature. Radical experimentation in the area of physics and metaphysics resulted in an almost total schism within religion. Scientists and magicians were hard put to reconcile their activities with their beliefs.

The most important aspect of any quest is its resulting exploration of consciousness. However far we go in spiritual quest, we always find within ourselves what we are seeking. The prime concern of the mystic, scientist, and magician remained the exploration of our internal workings, the microcosm. And although each sought at different levels of experience, each quest was valid. It is, after all, our God-given task to reconcile and harmonize the spiritual and the material. As the Jewish Hasidim expressed it, man is called "to advance from rung to rung until, through him, everything is united." It is through us, then, as microcosms that the world is summed up; as mediators, we are the ones through whom the world is offered back to God (635).

This realization is shared by Christianity, Judaism, and Hermeticism, which are mysteriously joined, as are all the traditions of the West, by a wonderful ladder of light. We have spoken earlier of the tribe and of the tradition of wandering. Within the Jewish spiritual tradition, these two come together.

The Shattered Vessels

God arranged the order of creation so that all things are bound to each other. The direction of events in the lower world depends on entities above them, as our sages teach: "There is no blade of grass in the world below that does not have an angel over it striking it and telling it to grow." (288)

So wrote the Jewish mystical leader the Hai Gaon (939–1038 C.E.). Resonances of this pronouncement can also be found in the Hermetic

Emerald Tablet. It is a statement about the interrelatedness of the worlds that Kabbalism, above all other systems, has understood and given to the world. The development of the Kabbalah within Judaism is extraordinary because of its amazing success and acceptance not only as a mystical tradition within Judaism itself, but also as an esoteric system that non-Jews have adopted.

The Kabbalah provides an instance of a mystical tradition arising organically from its exoteric shell while remaining totally integrated within it. It evolved from the oral teachings of the prophets, took on mystical elements and techniques during the Babylonian exile and the Diaspora, and from there developed in significantly localized ways. The exoteric laws of Judaism, rather than fighting against its development, have welded it more strongly, keeping the esoteric secrets in the hands of adepts who were also religious leaders.

Two factors above all determine the hardiness of Judaism: tribal cohesion, as exemplified in the family unit, and the adaptability of a nomadic people, which is what the Jews have been forced to be until this century. The minutiae of Judaic law are often represented as a tiresome burden by non-Jews, but for those within the fold of Judaism, they are opportunities for contact with God: the touching of the sacred text of the Shema ("Hear O Israel,"—Deut. 6:4.) in the *mezuzah* on leaving and entering a house; the wearing of the *tallith* and *tefillin*, the prayer shawl and phylacteries; the dietary laws and seasonal celebrations; the divine rest of the Sabbath—these are the interactions of the faithful people with God (607). Judaism's mystics are not monks and nuns but married people, living in the world, who understand the necessity of reconciling the lives of the body and the spirit.

No one can date the inception of the Kabbalah. It remained an oral teaching for centuries, with the first texts appearing in early medieval Spain. The cross-fertilizations affecting the Mediterranean during the early Christian era are also apparent within the cosmological speculation and formulations of the Kabbalah. Because worship at the Temple in Jerusalem was disrupted first of all in 586 B.C.E., when the Solomonic Temple was destroyed, and then in 70 C.E., when the rebuilt Second Temple was burned during the Roman occupation, certain religious obligations and duties could not be fulfilled. Moreover, with the dwelling place (the Ruach HaKadosh) of God's spirit (the Shekinah) destroyed, the Shekinah had nowhere to abide but in the souls of the faithful. This is central to an understanding of Judaism's obsession with the preservation of tradition. No matter where the chosen people lived, there also went the Shekinah to share their exile invisibly. When the tribes followed Moses through the desert, they were led by a pillar of cloud by day and a pillar of fire by night—the mystical appearance of the Shekinah that dwelled between the cherubim upon the curtained Ark of the Covenant. In the new exile of the Diaspora, each member of the congregation bore the added duty of retaining for the indwelling spirit a secret tabernacle that could be wrought only by an upright life and constant study of the traditions. From such intense study was born the mystical system of the Kabbalah.

The Kabbalah itself is like a microchip in which is encoded the whole of Jewish mystical tradition. Because of its unique compression, it is a system that the Hermetic tradition has borrowed to codify its own complex symbology. But we should not forget that, first and foremost, the Kabbalah is a Jewish spiritual expression, not a Gentile magical system. It is made of many levels of mystical experience and has had many commentators. We do not have space to list them all, though a number are included in the bibliography (287, 288, 248, 266, 145, 218–221, 572).

What is evident is that the techniques employed by Kabbalists included prayer, fasting, and the repetition of the holy names of God—the usual religious devices—alongside what we may consider to be more esoteric techniques such as meditation, rhythmic breathing, chanting, the adoption of certain postures in order to perceive the divine vision, and many means of visualization. These techniques have been carefully guarded from the uninitiated because, used without guidance, they not only can be physically dangerous, but also can mislead the practitioner into realms where the shells of creation are inhabited by demons.

One of the main sources of the Kabbalah is the *Zohar,* or Book of Splendor, attributed to Moses of Leon (1250–1305 C.E.), but which doubtless dates before this in oral tradition. Together with the *Sepher Yetzirah* (Book of Creation), it gives us the basis for all subsequent kabbalistic study, establishing a sephirotic system upon the Tree of Life—the Otz Chaim—and the means of undertaking the series of spiritual ascents known as *merkabah,* or ascents in the chariot. The Sephiroth are the ten essences or "sapphires" of God's emanations. They have tended to become useful filing cabinets within Gentile use of the Kabbalah, but their original meaning is the jewel-like light through which the different qualities of God's glory are manifested. The merkabah, or chariot, is the vehicle by which the mystic contemplates the heavenly halls of God. This form of mysticism derives from the vision of Ezekiel, whose account of the wheeled chariot and the living creatures surrounding it became the object of much meditative study and was considered to be the highest in the canon of Jewish mysticism (266).

When we gaze upon the diagram that represents the Otz Chaim (fig. 17), we must remember that it is only a diagram. The roots of the Tree of Life penetrate to every part of the universe, while its fruits can nourish the spirit, enabling us to experience the embodied presence of the Divine in every place.

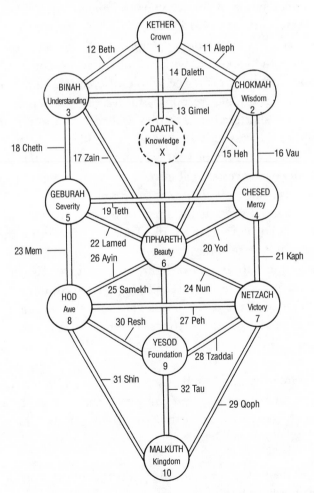

Fig. 17. The Tree of Life showing the ten Sephiroth and the hidden Sephira of Daath

Some Kabbalists followed their own intense meditations, notably Abraham Abulafia (1240–1292 C.E.), whose permutations of the Hebrew alphabet brought him fiery visions (1). His techniques were considered to be very dangerous. It is possible that there was some link between him and the Christian esotericist Ramon Lull; their systems were very similar (see chapter 8). The Spanish school of the Kabbalah did not continue long after the expulsion of the Jews from Spain in 1492. Exiled again, some returned home to found a center for kabbalistic studies in Palestine, at Safed, where Joseph Karo (1488–1575 C.E.), Moses Cordevero (1522–1570 C.E.), and others had the opportunity to codify the disparate disciplines that had sprung up during the Diaspora. At this center the course of the Kabbalah changed, maturing through the work of Isaac Luria (1534–1572 C.E.)

Luria's system was exceedingly complex: He developed the notion of the ten Sephiroth as existing within four universes concurrently. In order that God might permeate the whole of creation and that everything might have its godlike response, the vessels (or Sephiroth) that held his light were shattered so that they spilled into a lower universe. This shattering of the vessels is analogous to the idea of the fragmentation and scattering of the divine spark. From their primal but unrelated origin, fragments of the vessels fell into successively lower universes, or levels of existence, until the light was so fragmented that imbalances began to appear. Luria preached the rectification of the light in a state called the Universe of Rectification, the Tikkun (28). Within the many levels and sephirotic vessels, the fragmented light could be reassembled as archetypes—miniature bodies of light, which, at the Tikkun, would constitute an integrated whole. This complex system combines not only the Hermetic theory of the divine sparks becoming united into a Body of Light, but also the union and reconciliation of the syzygies (see chapter 9, page 344), a feature of Gnosticism that also preoccupied alchemists.

The final state toward which mystic, alchemist, and Kabbalist work may seem to be an exalted one that cannot be hastened or anticipated in any way. Truly, these are cosmic matters, yet as Chaim Vital (1543–1620 C.E.), Luria's chief disciple, wrote:

> In his ascent the mystic is irradiated by the light of the tree and in
> his descent the light finds a medium through which to flow back
> into the daily world. . . . In the descent a magic is worked and all

the pretended way of ascent (through imaginative meditation) is rendered "greater than reality." (209)

The meditative techniques through which the secrets of the Tree of Life might be understood became the means by which the Kabbalist made the ascent and descent—thus the higher universes and lights of the Sephiroth might be experienced with the help of the imagination. This experience was not for individual retention, however, but to hasten the return of the Shekinah and her people out of exile.

Luria's teachings spread throughout the Jewish world, particularly into Russia and eastern Europe, where they influenced the Hasid movement. The Hasidim ("the devout") were subject to frequent persecution, but in them the living Kabbalah took root. They brought it firmly back from the mystical flights of Spanish medieval fantasy into the realms of everyday life. Most famous of the Hasidim was the Baal Shem Tov (1698–1760 C.E.), who founded a tradition of kabbalistic wonder working. The sufferings of the people were so great at that time that it is no wonder that the Hasidic masters were looked upon as magicians and saviors. It is interesting to note that this same ability to work wonders was a feature of the Russian Orthodox wandering hermits, the *startsi*. Their continual repetition of the Jesus Prayer, "Lord Jesus Christ, Son of God, have mercy on me, a sinner," was in many ways similar to the recitation and permutation of the Holy Names of God performed by Kabbalists. Perhaps Kabbalism and remnants of northern European shamanism touched at this point? Without doubt, the complex systems of the Kabbalah were brought to the people by means of a storytelling tradition that had its roots in the native tradition. The great Rabbi Nahman of Bratislav (1772–1810 C.E.), who taught entirely by story, communicated the Tikkun, the creation dramas, and the qualities of the Sephiroth in the format of simple folk stories (436).

As Aryeh Kaplan remarks, "[T]he closer one gets to the present, the less dangerous and more universal the methods of kabbalistic meditation become." (288) The Hasid dances and sings in ecstatic oneness with God, the Lurianic Kabbalist performs the mystic unifications that bring together in divine embrace male and female aspects of God, the Spanish Kabbalist sits enthroned within the radiance of the Holy Names. These days few aspire to return to the beginnings of the Kabbalah, to attempt the last ascent in the chariot of fire to the Seventh Holy Hall, where God himself sits in glory.

Cabals still meet today, drawn from Orthodox or observant Jews, not Gentiles. Their work is part of the Western Way's rich heritage, presenting its face to the inner world in order that the light of the divine countenance might shine more clearly upon the outer world. Their task is not unlike that of mystics from other traditions:

> A man is born into this world with only a tiny spark of goodness in him. The spark is God, it is the soul; the rest is ugliness and evil, a shell. The spark must be guarded like a treasure, it must be nurtured, it must be fanned into flame. It must learn to seek out the other sparks, it must dominate the shell. (491)

Many Jewish Kabbalists cannot comprehend Gentile or even Christian Kabbalism, as it often called (see chapter 8). For them, the Kabbalah is the ultimate expression of their religion, not, as it is for Western occultists, merely a technique. In the next chapter we will look more closely at the ways in which the Kabbalah has passed from spiritual tradition into psycho-spiritual technique. Occultism, it seems, has done for the Kabbalah what psychology has done for religion. One person's mythology is another's religion, after all. Those of us who have not had direct, firsthand experience with a living spiritual tradition will likely never understand or even recognize the images, symbols, and states involved in the practice of the Kabbalah. Those Hermeticists who employ kabbalistic techniques should have more than a passing acquaintance with the tradition from which it arose. The books of Z'ev ben Shimon Halevi (see bibliography) offer a firm background in this area and provide a system of training in authentic kabbalistic method.

This Hebrew children's prayer has been used in other, esoteric contexts:

> In the name of the Lord God of Israel, may Michael, the protection of God, be at my right hand; and Gabriel, the power of God, at my left; before me Uriel, the light of God; behind me Raphael, the healing of God; and above my head Shekinah El, the presence of God. (21)

PRACTICE

❧ *13. The Temple of Inner Wisdom* ❧

This practice is designed to establish a temple of inner wisdom, a common meeting place where those of disparate religious traditions, or from no specific religious tradition, may meet. If "religious loyalty is nothing else than the sincerity of our human relations with God, on the basis of the means which he puts at our disposal" (524), then we must find and use the most skillful means. Although an accident of birth determines our cultural background, and though we may find our own tradition only after having come to maturity, there exists a companionship of the sophia perennis in which we all partake.

The temple of inner wisdom is circular. Around it are set many antechambers that give access to the central area. You will enter through one of these. The inner temple is approached through the antechamber representing your own tradition. This will be furnished according to the appropriate symbology and correspondences of that tradition. It should be a place where you feel at home.

If you have no tradition, consider the many paths that have led you to where you stand today. These paths may not necessarily be traditions in themselves, but rather fragments or derivatives of one. Perhaps you have used a meditation technique that has been helpful, or read a book whose philosophy resonates with yours so that you have adopted it. You may have explored a symbol system such as the Tarot or Tree of Life; you may have used techniques derived from Eastern religions, such as yoga and I Ching. If you wish, you may visualize these antechambers around the temple's center, but make sure you are at home in one of them; do not attempt to work from a tradition that alienates you. Before entering the temple, make sure you comprehend the tradition you have chosen on more than a surface level. Each of these chambers will have a guardian—a master or mistress of that tradition—who is at liberty to admit you to the temple. Listen to his or her advice.

If you are still traveling toward wisdom (and when do any of us finally possess it?) or if you are totally bewildered by the multiplicity of traditions available to you, do not hesitate to enter the antechamber of the amethyst sanctuary. This is a bare, holy room in which hangs an ornate silver lamp with an eternal flame burning in an amethyst-colored glass. Anyone may enter this place and will be hospitably welcomed. Its only furnishing is a chair where you may meditate on the Eternal Flame. If you truly wish to enter the temple of inner wisdom, you must bring something of your spiritual experience with you. A guardian will come to you from within the temenos to talk with you and instruct you. He or she will invite you to enter the temple from the amethyst sanctuary only when you are fully prepared, and not before.

Method

There are as many antechambers to the temple as there are traditions in the world. To prepare to enter the temple from your chosen room, sit in meditation and build the antechamber about you, evoking its essential qualities using the tools of the senses. You should, in effect, be inhabiting your tradition before you are allowed to draw aside the curtain that separates you from the temple's heart. The chamber's guardian—who can appear as a religious leader, prophet, mystic, or established guide along that path—will indicate whether you are fully prepared.

You draw aside the curtain. The circular hall is of vast proportions. Around it, supporting a golden central dome, are seven pillars. There are no symbols of any tradition here—these all remain in the antechambers, for they are the outer semblances of an inner tradition. The sanctuary of the mysteries is an empty room representing the imageless truth of wisdom.

In the center of the temple is a round table on which is a dish of bread and salt and a cup of red wine. All who enter must partake of this meal to have a place here. This bread and salt of hospitality and the wine of fellowship are served by Sophia herself. She may appear as a beautiful crowned queen of mysterious aspect or in some other guise. It is possible that the meal will be served by invisible hands, that you will see no figure at all. Yet the presence of Sophia pervades this temple, making it the meeting place of all who are engaged in the search for her gifts.

You may come here to meditate and to meet with those from other traditions. This temple is a place of convocation—those who come here have been called together in common quest, and they come from many different paths. You may meet those from other times and places. Because all of you have eaten the bread and drunk the wine, there is concord among all who come here. You may ask questions about a tradition's aspects that are troubling to you or that you do not understand. Because you represent your tradition in the temple of inner wisdom, do not be surprised if others ask you questions.

Discovery

This practice may grow in importance to you over the years; its effect is a cumulative one. The temple can be used as a place of tranquillity and refreshment. Just as you may meet other pathwalkers here, you may meet guardians, saints, and mystics of many traditions. You may even sit at the round table of fellowship and take in the counsel of Sophia.

Do not feel that you have come here on a second-class ticket if you are entering by way of the amethyst sanctuary or if you are not readily invited into the temple's center. You will enter when you are ready. Love and desire open the doors in this place. You will not enter through duty or a sense of obligation. The temple is by no means for those who have reached the end of their search for wisdom. Sophia leads us by winding roads and though you have entered by way of one tradition in the past, you may find that door temporarily closed to you if your road should lead you away from it. Be patient; another door will open in time. Meanwhile, the amethyst sanctuary is always open to those who thirst and hunger after wisdom and her gifts.

8

The Magus and
His Magic

The Return of the Shaman

Three magicians were attendant at the birth of Christ. As the Gospel of Matthew tells it: "Now when Jesus was born in Bethlehem of Judea in the days of Herod the King, behold, wise men from the East came to Jerusalem, saying, 'Where is he who has been born King of the Jews? For we have seen his star in the East, and have come to worship him.'" (Matthew 2:1–2)

The New Testament Greek calls them "sages" but tradition has called them magi almost from the start. Early Christian iconography depicts them visiting the infant Jesus in a cave, their Phrygian caps identifying them as Persian or possibly as Mithraic priests. As we saw in chapter 6, there are at times startling similarities between the lives of Christ and Mithras, so it seems appropriate that the servants of one sacrificed god should come to the nativity of another.

260

Who were these first visitors to the incarnate God who recognized his kingly and divine character in a way that the Jewish people themselves did not? We may presume little about them save that they came from the East, that they were perhaps Zoroastrian, Mazdian, or Mithraic priests, and that they followed the courses of the stars. Traditionally, their names were Balthazar, Melchior, and Caspar. Balthazar was of the white race of Shem and brought the gold of incarnation; Melchior, of the black race of Ham, brought the frankincense of crucifixion; Caspar, of the yellow race of Japheth, brought the myrrh of embalming and resurrection. Each stood for a race and an art and each was an aspect of ancient wisdom coming to pay homage to its newest manifestation. They are there at the beginning of Christianity but are accorded no place in its subsequent development. Yet "they saw the child with Mary his mother," presumably identifying them with statues of Isis and Horus, Cybele and Attis, and other such prefiguring archetypes, and presented with the living icon of mother and child, they fell on their knees and worshipped:

> The children of the Chaldeans saw the Virgin holding in her hands
> Him who with His hands fashioned mankind. Though He has
> taken the form of a servant, yet they knew Him as their Master. In
> haste they knelt before Him with their gifts and cried out to the
> Blessed Virgin; Hail, Mother of the Star that never sets. (322)

Who, then, were these men who acknowledged Christ as their master before the start of his earthly ministry? They have been described as men who were "able to understand god" and who knew "how to minister to the divinity." (484) Both of these descriptions could be applied without alteration to a shaman. The magi are priests, close enough to the gods to recognize a new avatar and to wish to act as intermediaries between divinity and mankind. They are the precursors of the magician, or perhaps we should say his ancestors, and they bear within them the seeds of his craft.

Although there is a great distance in time between the shaman and the magician, there is almost no essential difference in their respective functions. Both stand as mediators of an inner impulse to the outer world: the shaman as a public figure, the center of his tribe's relationship to the gods; the magician as a private figure working often in obscurity without official sanction, but continuing to mediate cosmic forces to his fellow men. No longer the priest of the tribe, he is constrained to a position of isolation; he lives a hidden life that touches the lives of those in the street only tangentially. He is "neither a saint, nor a saviour, nor a prophet, nor a seer. He is a shaman-in-civilization." (143)

The magician operates in a manner wholly different from that of his precursor, the shaman: Where one had a direct line to the god or gods of his tribe, the other works with different techniques and contacts, yet is always seeking to break through into the inner realm itself, to speak directly to God, as his ancestors had once been able to do. Thus his magic is the practical extension of a philosophical or mystical underpinning, and without that foundation it would not exist. To look at the magician without taking into account his dream of unity with deity, however partial or superficial, is to mistake his whole purpose.

We make the same mistake if we look at magic or ritual simply as an exercise in seeking power, like examining the body of a new car without bothering to look at the engine. Magic and ritual are microcosmic expressions of the macrocosm, our tiny torch of desire lifted to the fire of the stars. We plug into the universe through the enactment of ritual beginning, as we saw for the native tradition, with the propitiation of the elements and a desire to enter the womb of the world

Fig. 18. The magician works cooperatively with the elements
water, earth, air, and fire.

mother. The Hermetic approach as adopted by the magician is more
intellectually motivated, celestial rather than chthonic. The astrological
calculations of the "star-led wizards" of Milton's "Ode on the Morning
of Christ's Nativity" are a far cry from the instinctive actions of the
tribal shaman—yet they are motivated by the same needs and desires.
Only the methods have changed with the movement from tribal consciousness to individual consciousness.

There is no such thing as an archetypal magician in any age. To
speak of his role with any certainty, we are forced to generalize. If we
look at some of the major figures who are magi or wizards, we will see
why they are classified in this way. We may also begin to notice certain
points in common among them. For example, Apollonius of Tyana
flourished in the first century C.E. and was considered by some to be a
god rather than a man. He was said to have been begotten by Proteus,
god of the winds and patron of shapeshifters—very appropriate for the
father of a magician—and to have possessed miraculous powers that
enabled him, among other things, to prophesy accurately the death of
the Roman emperor Domitian. He traveled extensively, performing
feats that defied rational explanation, and vanished mysteriously after
a long life during which he frequently escaped death at the hands of the
angry priesthoods of various cults with which he conflicted. He is also
said to have visited Hades in order to ask the god of the Underworld
what was the purest philosophy then available to humankind. He
emerged five days later with a bound copy of the precepts of
Pythagoras, whom he followed from that point on, observing a five-
year vow of silence until his initiation was complete. Many of his contemporaries compared him with Christ and found him superior, while
others regarded him as a figure of evil (37). His *Letters,* which are all
that remain of his once voluminous writings, are full of sound advice
and mystical perception. To one neophyte he wrote: "Listen well to me,
my son, and I will reveal to you the mystery of wisdom, a mystery unin-
telligible, unknown and hidden for many, concerning the seasons and the
times, the hours of day and of night, concerning their denomination and
their influence and concerning the true wisdom hidden therein." (528)

He goes on to cite four books of his own, "more precious than
golden jewelry and stones of great value the fourth of which, noblest of
all, contains powerful and terrible signs . . . that teach the first elements
of the visible things created by God, so that he who reads this book may,
if he chooses, be successful in realizing such wonders." (528) He speaks

of methods of "tying" and "untying" the elements through the pronouncement of the secret names of God—a method of magical practice that, interestingly, is like that of the kabbalistic magicians of a later age.

Here, then, is a magician who is able to exercise control over the different aspects of nature and who has evolved or acquired a system that he can use to relate magical activity to any hour, day, month, or year. And all of this, he claims, was taught him by God—an important point that we shall return to shortly.

Meanwhile, let us look at another magician, who is somewhat more notorious than Apollonius: Simon the Magician, or as he is better known, Simon Magus (first century C.E.). Unlike Apollonius, whose claims he out-vaunts, Simon has come down to us as a picture of the failed magician. His famous contest with Saint Peter, in which he offered to take to the air like a bird to prove that Christianity was a false religion, ended in a plunge to the unyielding earth. Yet during his life Simon attracted a large following and showed himself to be by no means bereft of wisdom.

Having learned magic in Egypt, he became the leader of a Gnostic cult after a spectacular magical battle with its former leader (67). His followers elevated him to the status of godhead, yet when his miracles were bettered by those of the disciple Philip, he renounced his former beliefs for a time and was baptized a Christian. Later, however, he reneged on his conversion when he unsuccessfully tried to purchase the power of the Holy Spirit with money. After this he became a deadly enemy of all Christians, contesting the miracles of the disciples at every turn until his fatal contest with Peter. His innate Gnosticism can be recognized in the following passage from his writings:

I say what I say, and I write what I write. And the writing is this. In the universal Aeons there are two schools, without beginning or end, springing from one root, which is the power of invisible, inapprehensible silence. Of those shoots one is manifest above all, which is the Great Power, the Universal Mind ordering all things, male, and the other [is manifested] from below, the Great Thought, female, producing all things. Hence pairing with each other they unite and manifest the Middle Distance, incomprehensible Air, without beginning or end. In this is the Father who sustains all things, and nourishes those things which have a beginning and an end. (226)

We can see here the basis for a whole esoteric philosophy, a structure of the cosmos that spans from before time to beyond it. Invisible, inapprehensible silence is the very stuff from which all things are generated: One feels that modern philosophers like Wittgenstein and Nietzsche would have approved of the nakedness of this idea.

But does it add to our conception of the magician? Simon Magus has come down to us as, at best, a victim of spiritual pride and at worst a monster of depravity and a servant of evil—and the magician has been colored by this ever since. Yet in his writings (or the writings of whoever penned the words attributed to him) are the seeds of a philosophical vision that still informs the work of the magician. Simon's "universal mind," placed side by side with the "I am Mind" of Poimandres, parallels the conception of the evolution of consciousness presented in part 1 (see chapter 1) and shows the magician becoming aware of the primal light.

By comparison, the magicians of the Middle Ages seem positively backward in both their spiritual and their philosophical motivations. This may be due to the influence of medieval scholasticism, which could be described as the intellectual arm of the Church in Europe because it governed the physical extent of knowledge—in the form of books, manuscripts, and documents—under its scrutiny and pressed upon them a wholly Christian view. In this world the magician had no place, although it is ironic that the conventional stereotype of the magus as a celestially cloaked individual conjuring demons from a safe distance actually originates from this time. We must consider that these demons were, in reality, daemons, spiritual helpers who were esoterically akin to angels and who communicated the wisdom of higher worlds.

Psychologically speaking, magicians who resorted to such methods of conjuring were actually recognizing and integrating those aspects of their inner selves that communed with an Otherworld reality. To view the helpful daemon as a demon was to tussle with those inner aspects of the self that were as yet unbalanced or unintegrated. Bad individual aspects were demonic; good aspects were polarized as angelic.

During the medieval era there existed a far greater degree of curiosity about the regions uncharted by Christianity than is generally understood. Alchemy flourished—admittedly, under difficult conditions, as we shall see—and scientific investigation was a powerful force to be reckoned with, despite being curtailed severely by Rome. Actually, we cannot really talk about science in terms of the Middle Ages, when "natural philosophy" existed as an early form of scientific investigation. The Franciscan Roger Bacon (c. 1214–c. 1292 C.E.), whom many consider the archetypal magician of the age, was in reality a protoscientist, although he by no means excluded magic from his studies, believing it to contain at least "some truth. Yet in regard those very truths are enveloped with a number of deceits, as it's not very easy to judge betwixt the truth and the falsehood." (67)

Bacon certainly studied magic from the grimoires that were then available and wrote a treatise called *The Mirror of Alchemy,* which contains much that is still valuable (67) Indeed, it seems he took to heart the words attributed to Saint Jerome by another medieval writer, Gerald of Wales: "You will find many things quite incredible and beyond the bounds of probability which are true for all that. Nature never exceeds the limits set by God who created it." (181) In his own cautious way Bacon was more of a magician than many of his notorious contemporaries. He (like the poet Virgil) had the doubtful honor of being called a worker of marvels after his death, was said to have had a magic mirror that enabled him to see what was happening anywhere in the world, and was said to have constructed a "Brazen Head" that would faithfully answer any question put to it. In all probability, given Bacon's farsighted genius, this was more likely to have been the world's first computer than a magical implement. There has always been a practical, inquisitive side to magic, which Bacon's lively mind represents as well as any.

The most famous magician of all time—Merlin—is perhaps as much a product of the Middle Ages as any of the figures we have been examining. In the light of his extraordinary qualities and legendary status, it is not surprising that he is found to embody the whole range of roles through which the magician has passed. Beginning life as a shamanistic figure living in the wilds with animals for company and prophesying the life and destiny of kings, Merlin develops rapidly through a succession of metamorphoses into the mage and wonder worker of the Arthurian cycle. Cloaked in mystery, appearing and disappearing at will, moving in and out of the stories of Arthur and his knights in a completely unpredictable manner, he becomes the possessor of ever-greater powers. He can assume any shape at will and call forth whole pageants of imaginary beings from the air and dismiss them with consummate ease. He is, in fact, the preeminent power in the land during Arthur's reign, credited with orchestrating the mysteries of the

Grail and the various quests undertaken by the Round Table knights (599).

He is first and foremost, in the consciousness of many, a literary figure, though he in fact stands for a great deal more. Merlin is one of the great masters who guide the steps of those traveling the Western Way. To quote the words of a modern magician, Gareth Knight, "The importance of Merlin is his role as a way-shower to a new phase, or epoch, of conscious evolution." (311) More than this, he represents a humanized, Western form of the ancient gods of learning and civilization such as the Greek Hermes and the Egyptian Thoth. In addition, he is akin to those who, like Melchizadek in the Old Testament, are "without father or mother, without descent." (311)

To find Merlin compared with Hermes or Thoth should not surprise us, but what is interesting is that it demonstrates his dual nature as a master of both native and Hermetic traditions. As we have said, he is more a god than a human being and, as such, represents the magician on a higher arc of evolution—he is almost a summation of all that the worker with magic seeks to become.

If Merlin resonates with the inner world, then Dr. John Dee must be considered something like his manifestation in the outer world. Dee is probably the single most influential aspect of the magician ever to have lived and is a worthy successor to the Arthurian mage. Though his abilities have often been called into question, his influence has continued to be felt right up to the present time.

Born in 1527, Dee rose from comparative obscurity to a position of power as adviser and court astrologer to Elizabeth I. Considered to have been the foremost mathematician of his day, he traveled widely and left an abundance of writings, diaries, and notebooks that testify to his largeness of spirit, depth of occult understanding, and qualities of perception. Born while Henry VIII was still on the throne, he lived on into the age of James I, through five reigns and five changes of religious allegiance in that troubled age. He finally died in 1608, all but forgotten by the world that he had subtly influenced for so long. During his long life he synthesized much that has come to be accepted as an integral part of the Hermetic tradition: Neoplatonism, Pythagorianism, the Kabbalah, and alchemical and Hermetic materials were shaped to fit his intricate system of correspondences, which are clearly indicated by his lengthy lists of angelic beings. His influence on Sir Philip Sidney and his circle, which Shakespeare refers to as the

School of Night, was considerable. In addition, the cult of the Virgin Queen that came to be attached to Elizabeth may well have come through him.

In 1598 Dee visited Heinrich Khunrath in Germany, where he may have had a part in planting the seeds of Rosicrucianism (657). Certainly his *Monas Hieroglyphica* (126) seems to have formed a basis for the *Consideratis Brevis* and the *Confessio Fraternitatis,* while the figure of the sleeping Venus in *The Chymical Wedding* (313) reflects the way in which Elizabeth was regarded by her courtiers through Dee's influence.

Dee is a prime example of the magician in the political arena, transmitting inner impulses to the outer world, which is always, as we have said, the foremost task of the magus. But though he still moved in a twilight world of mystery and wonder, his work had begun to assume cosmic dimensions. He no longer worked solely with elementals or demons, but was said to converse with spiritual entities of a higher order. Within the confines of his circle Dee, like his fellow countryman Owen Glyndwr, could call up spirits from the vast deep, but they were spirits of another order now, and the reasons for calling them had changed as well.

It is almost impossible to categorize the magician in any satisfactory way: As a character he eludes us with continual changes of shape and action, so a modern-day magus would find it hard to model himself on any single archetype. Fortunately for those who follow the way of the magus today, they do not have to. Their training, like that of any other initiate, comes most often from within, where they will likely find themselves in direct contact with one of the great magicians of the past, who appears in his inner plane guise. It is still possible to be overshadowed by the spiritual form of Dee or of Michael Scott or of Roger Bacon or of Giordano Bruno, each with his own wisdom to teach and his own rich store of knowledge to impart.

Though the guise of the magician may have changed through the long ages since he first stepped upon the stage in the skin robe and antlered headdress of the shaman, his aims have remained the same. For all that their approach and techniques may have changed, contemporary magicians like Gareth Knight (304, 307) and W. G. Gray (197, 201) follow the same path as Apollonius or Merlin or Dee. Each still uses symbol-laden ritual and visual techniques to focus his inner-guided intention to a point where it becomes actualized. Like the alchemist striving to be born into the inner realms (see chapter 10), the magician of any time seeks to bring the inner impulse to the outer world. As Gareth Knight has written, "[T]he function of the advanced initiate is to act as a pioneer in the march of human evolution . . ." (168)

That he shares his role with the mystic, the saint, and the philosopher accounts for the difficulty in assigning the magician to any single category. Like the "shaman-in-civilization" at the beginning of this chapter, his function has become fragmented, held together only by the esoteric philosophy that underlies so much of the Western Way. To understand why this is so, we must look more closely at that philosophical underpinning and how it has helped shape the magical life.

Expanding the Universe

The great traditionalist philosopher René Guénon first pointed out in his book *Crisis of the Modern World* (212) that with the dawn of philosophy in the Hellenic world there came about a division between exoteric and esoteric in the Mysteries. The exoteric came to denote a radically realistic view of nature, argued from a purely logical point of view, while the esoteric suggested an inner spirituality that was wholly transcendent. For philosophy to survive as an abstract discipline, it became necessary to concentrate on the exoteric to the exclusion of everything else—and this the first philosophers did, creating in virtually a decade a wholly different way of looking at the universe.

Of course this was not the end of the Mysteries, but it did cause a shift away from their open celebration toward a protective secrecy that has cloaked the magician and his magical activities ever since. It was secrecy different from that of the mystery schools; although the Mysteries were kept secret by their initiates, they were still accessible to all. Those who followed the road of the magician, however, had to move in a twilight world in order to survive. This resulted in a curious dichotomy: Despite the reputation of the Greek philosophers as antimystical and determined to follow a course of pure intellectualism, many continued to be openly devoted servants of the gods at the same time as they were seeking to dispute them. Plato was a mystery school initiate who was attacked several times for revealing secret doctrines in public debate. Indeed, the Platonic writings may be read in part as mystery teaching due to their author's continued activity as an inner planes teacher and initiator.

Plato was in fact a disciple of Pythagoras. Although best known as a philosopher, Pythagoras was himself initiated into several schools in Egypt, Greece, and Babylon, where he undoubtedly picked up the basis for his numerical theories, as well as a cosmic attitude toward matters of the spirit. He was recognized in his own lifetime as an avatar of Apollo—probably the Hyperborean aspect of the god if we are to credit the significance of his meeting with the Hyperborean priest Abaris (see chapter 4). He untypically initiated Abaris into his doctrines without the customary probation of five years of silence and obedience—in all likelihood because he recognized the similarity between his own beliefs and those of the druids, of whom Abaris was probably an initiate. Certainly there have been frequent claims ever since that the Pythagorean system influenced or reflected the druidic.

Pythagoras's followers lived lives of strenuous abnegation, being both vegetarian and nomadic. Their master was virtually outcast from normal society because of these tendencies, which were abhorrent to the Greeks. It is interesting to note that the eremitical traditions within Christianity can probably be traced from Pythagorean inspiration. Certainly the Essenes followed the Pythagorean mode in their lifestyle, which included common goods, sun worship, and numerology. They in turn influenced the development of the Desert Fathers in Egypt and Syria, elements of which could still be found in modern Ethiopia until recently.

But Pythagoras would not permit his disciples to speak about his doctrines, and those who broke their vow of secrecy were publicly mourned as though dead. Because of this rule of secrecy, many garbled notions have been attributed to the movement and much of the core of Pythagoras's teachings remains unknown. But elements of what little we do know became incorporated into Platonism. Plato drew upon the teachings of his master and reworked their mystical aspects into a more general philosophy that influenced both Porphory (589) and Plotinus (481), which makes it difficult to know whether these two ought to be classed as Neo-Pythagoreans or Neoplatonists.

Pythagorean beliefs continued to be practiced from the sixth century B.C.E. to the sixth century C.E., when the Eastern emperor Julian closed the Platonic Academy in Athens. After this the Pythagoreans exiled themselves to Persia, where they found a welcome and the recognition of many of their own doctrines in those of the East. By this time Pythagoras's teachings had deeply influenced the direction of both philosophy and magic and had helped to preserve the Mysteries far beyond the point at which they might otherwise have perished.

When the great Renaissance philosopher and magician Marsilio Ficino compiled a line of descent for the masters, he put both Pythagoras and Plato firmly among them:

> The first was Zoroaster, the chief of the Magi; the second Hermes Trismegistus, the head of the Egyptian Priesthood; Orpheus suceeded Hermes; Aglaopharnus was initiated into the sacred mysteries of Orpheus; Pythagoras was initiated into the theology of Aglaophamus and Plato by Pythagoras. Plato summed up the whole of their wisdom in his letters. (410)

This was written with hindsight, of course, but there is little reason to quarrel with the list, and it clearly shows the inheritance of the Western magician.

Platonism effectively stood things on their heads. Instead of following the direction of the mystery schools, which believed the spirit was prisoner of the body, it made everything in this world a shadowy copy of an original that existed somewhere else, in a spiritual realm far removed from our own world. Thus, while outwardly dealing with philosophical structures, the Platonic schools really fostered an esoteric system of thought that had its roots in mystery school teaching. Thus in Plato's *Myth of Er* (479), as in Cicero's *Dream of Scipio* (133) later on, the seeds of the Greater Mysteries were preserved. When Christianity was in the process of formulating its own doctrines, "it denounced Platonism even as it confessed doctrines that it could not have formulated . . . without the illumination of Plato, thus speaking the language of Zion but with the unmistakable accents of the Academy." (466)

Plotinus, Plato's chief disciple, forged even more solid links with the magical teachings of the mystery schools: "The primary purpose of his teaching was to lead men (those few who were capable of it) back to awareness of and eventual union with the source from which they and all things came—the 'One or Good, which in giving them being gave also the impulse to return.'" (608)

Thus Plotinus came to see matter as a principle of evil because it was an absolute limit, the utter negativity and deficiency of being marking the end of the descent from the good through successive levels of reality. Yet he found the material universe good and beautiful as a living structure of forms and the best possible work of the Soul—unlike the Gnostic view of matter, which he detested—and he sought to perceive the true nature of the puzzling world around him. Because of this, Plotinus's system of Neoplatonism connects with both magic and science as well as philosophy and relates all three to their most ancient roots. Born of humanity's striving to know about its origins, it parallels Christian theology closely enough to be acceptable to later generations of thinkers as well as those following the inner way.

As we have seen in chapter 6, finding the origins of Hermeticism is difficult. Certainly we can look to Egypt for much of the material, and perhaps catch glimpses of Chaldea beyond. Or, as a recent commentator suggests, we can believe that the whole tradition is a cultural projection of the Ptolomaic dynasty (35)! But in reality, the nearest we can come to the beginning of the Hermetic impulse—and through it, to the origin of magic—is the period when Christianity was establishing itself in the Roman world both politically and sacerdotally. Here, in the fertile soil of the Graeco-Roman synthesis, the inheritor of Platonic wisdom and Pythagorean understanding, there came into being not only what we now think of as the Hermetic Mysteries, but also Gnosticism and alchemy.

The climate of the times being largely unwelcoming for such things, the Hermetic Mysteries went "underground." Some teachings were later honored and studied by Islamic scholars, who became, in some cases, the only readers and guardians of certain Greek manuscripts from Ptolemaic Egypt and Asia Minor—texts that became lost and were unknown in the West until the sack of Byzantium in the fifteenth century. Centuries later this cross-fertilization would bring Hermeticism full circle in the shape of the medieval Mysteries of alchemy, the Grail, and natural magic. In this space of time Hermeticism gathered not only the philosophies of Plato and Plotinus, but also the esoteric teachings of the Sufis, combining a vast hodgepodge of East-West Mysteries made up of diverse mystical lore, magical systems, and esoteric philosophy.

When Hermeticism returned to Europe, the reaction was at first one of shocked surprise, which turned fast to hatred at what was seen as a foreign invasion. Those who sought to oppress the Hermetic revival never realized that what they saw advancing toward them was an old and familiar figure who had left their part of the world long ago and now returned, wearing new clothes.

Throughout this time magic was continually being redefined: in religious terms, as science, and as philosophy. Each person who took up the fragments of the magic-oriented past impressed his or her own tradition upon it so that during the period between the demise of pagan belief and the early Renaissance, magic developed from a religious discipline to a philosophy—and today it continues to share both approaches. The figure of the magician, as we have seen, changed with his medium, mutating through several guises until he arrived at what we consider a magician today, which bears little or no relation to its origins. Despite the fact that it was the age when all magical activity earned the ultimate penalty for those found practicing it, it is the medieval image of a magician that remains most firmly fixed in our consciousness. We readily envision a strange figure wearing a robe of stars (a leftover from the Persian magi), a pointed hat, and thick lenses (symbols of his protoscientific attitude). Yet it is figures like Roger Bacon who typify the medieval magician as he really was: scholar, cleric, seeker, probably in the minor orders of the Church (which was the only way he could obtain the books he needed). Such magicians are the real inheritors of the classical tradition and the philosophies of Pythagoras and the Platonists.

Surprisingly, however, the medieval magus likely understood very little of the original material related to the Mysteries; there were few in the West who knew of the existence of these texts and even fewer who could read them. Yet the hidden words of Hermes did survive: Fragments continued to filter through until, at the height of the Renaissance, the trickle became a flood. How this came about is a fascinating story in itself, though one we can only touch upon here.

That we still have the legacy of these works is actually due to the scholarship and devotion of one man, Michael Psellus (1018–c. 1078 C.E.), who collected and codified many of the Hermetic texts as well as those of Plato, Plotinus, and others. As it was, the *Corpus Hermeticum* was not translated until 1463, when the great Renaissance philosopher and natural magician Marsilio Ficino worked on a huge collection of manuscripts at the behest of his patron, Cosimo di Medici. Significantly, Ficino was required to translate the *Corpus* before the works of Plato because it was believed that the Hermetic texts originated in Egypt, which was then considered of far greater interest than classical and neoclassical Greece.

With the publication of the *Corpus Hermeticum,* the Western world was once more in touch with the Mysteries, however tentatively, for the Renaissance Hermeticist had only texts, not living traditions, upon which to base his revival. Using translations of pied manuscripts and tattered classical references, he had to grope painfully toward an understanding of what had once been clearly comprehended and practiced by the mystery initiate. It was work of unimaginable difficulty, yet the Renaissance Hermeticist was equal to the task in enthusiasm if not in full comprehension of its complexity.

The form of Hermetic gnosticism propounded by Ficino and his contemporaries actually dates from Hellenic Egypt and not, as was once believed, from the time of the pharaohs. But this misunderstanding happily enabled a kind of reconciliation between post-Christian and pre-Christian lore, giving the Renaissance thinkers an excuse to delve deeper. Thus a mistake in chronology permitted a new blossoming of magic and provided the foundation for the French magical revival of the eighteenth century. In the late eighteenth and early nineteenth centuries, once again mistakenly, the literature of the earliest times was related to biblical sources.

With both scholarly hindsight and good translations in hand it is easy to condemn the medieval magician and the Renaissance investigator, with their ragbag of Judaic and Babylonian spells and secondhand grimoires purloined from wandering Arab astrologers. But we must not forget the length of time and the cultural lacunae that lay between them and the richly syncretic mysteries of classical Alexandria. In some ways the Renaissance Italy of Ficino and Pico della Mirandola resembled more the spirit of Alexandria or the Greek academy than the deeply dyed ignorance prevailing in the cloisters of Europe.

In late-medieval Europe the endgame of native spirituality and magic was being played out with pieces of dynastic greed and clerical exactitude. Just as in the Chessboard Castle of Chrétien de Troyes's *Conte du Graal* (95), fantastic pieces were moving seemingly of their own volition across a landscape whose interior focus was forever shifting away from the shining turrets and splendid pavilions to a new Hermetic vision. The medieval blindfold of ignorant acceptance was off and other rose-colored glasses of Renaissance knowledge were donned in its place (256).

The Renaissance produced many factors that brought about the death of the spiritual life of the Middle Ages. As Guénon has rightly pointed out (212), the adoption of neoclassicism fostered only those parts of the Hellenic and Egyptian Mysteries that had already been externalized sufficiently to make them acceptable—and as a result, less pure. The loss was immeasurable and it meant that the Hermetic systems were from the start founded on insecure ground. They had lost touch with their original spark, and every step they took from that point on brought about a narrowing, an exclusion of more and more of their old power. Even Renaissance adepts such as Ficino, Bruno, Dee, and Francis Bacon succeeded only partially in reconstructing the sources of their own speculations and in disseminating some of their realizations in their own blend of Hermeticism. Perhaps they were too cautious, but nonetheless their efforts became the foundation of modern Western esotericism, just as Hermeticism became, through them, a part of the Renaissance and a product of medieval and pre-medieval magic and religion.

Pagan, Christian, and Hermetic leftovers bobbed in the same melting pot. It was possible to re-create in the images of the classical gods those archetypes that had long been outlawed except as educational paradigms. Ficino, who was a Christian priest as well as a natural magician, wrote and sang hymns to Apollo; Bruno couched his philosophical speculations about the origin of the cosmos in dialogues between Jupiter and Mercury (61). In art, classical subjects began to replace the ubiquitous Christian nativities and depositions from the cross and new passions and new nativities were depicted—the flaying of Marsyas and Botticelli's foam-born Aphrodite. Primavera, decked in the garb of long-awaited spring, stepped from Attic to Tuscan forests. The scent of classical heritage hung in the air everywhere.

In this atmosphere the Mysteries were secularized. The great thinkers and natural magicians were first and foremost Christian; other options were scarcely open to them. Yet here were the old traditions: of Greece, Egypt, Persia—their beliefs could not easily be discounted. And so there slowly began to emerge a new system based on the ancient Mysteries but viewed as taking place within the framework of God's law. To be sure, these were still seen as heretical at the time—but those who practiced them found a comfortable balance. To them the deities were spirits of the air, angelic beings created, like humanity, to serve God and creation. Thus, while they became Christianized to a degree, they lost none of their energy; they escaped being reduced to the fundamental levels of, for example, the "mythology" of Christianity today. They kept their potency, but under a new guise.

Into this world stepped the figure of the magician, escaped from his hawthorn tower, like Merlin, after a sleep of centuries. To the magician the riches of this newly translated heritage were as intoxicating as wine. Hermetic texts, kabbalistic translations, scientific experimentation—all of these spoke of the possibility of new interiors. Utopia, the City of the Sun, New Atlantis—discussion of these visions of a perfect world, perfect reflections of macrocosm in microcosm, ran from the urgent pens of Thomas More, Campanilla, and Francis Bacon.

The Renaissance magician must often have wondered how close to perdition his kind had been during the previous centuries, when all esoteric pursuits earned their inevitable stigma. The magician had lived in his esoteric hutch, a tame shaman chained in the king's cellars, a coiner of gold pieces, a demonic mascot against divine disfavor who sometimes pandered to the superstitious needs of the people and other times sailed among the stars with gods and angels at his side. But now he was released. The gift of literacy offered by the great medieval universities was no longer solely in the hands of clerical academics. Had Roger Bacon still been living, he might have thrown off his clerical habit and joined the throngs of alchemists and proto-scientists who loved not only God's Mysteries, but nature's as well.

The Hermetic revival shook the world from its sleep. Europe's gain was Byzantium's loss. The capture of Constantinople by the Turks in 1453 saw the dispersal of the Eastern Empire's wealth and learning— yet this disaster enabled the Hermetic texts to make their way to Europe. Further, while the *Corpus Hermeticum* had its effect on the esoteric revival, the expulsion of the Jews from Spain in 1492 made another tradition available to the West: The Kabbalah has altered the face of Western esotericism and has been central to the practice of ritual magic since the Renaissance, providing a fresh angelology, a language of exact macrocosmic correspondence, and a ritual framework that has become the norm.

As we have seen, Spain was the cradle of the European Kabbalah and fostered the great Kabbalists such as Abraham Abulafia and Moses of Leon. It is often thought that the Kabbalah was unknown among Gentiles until the Renaissance, but there is clear evidence that the Catalan philosopher Ramon Lull (c. 1232–1316 C.E.) was aware of its teachings to some degree. Lull was born one year before the publication of the *Zohar*, the major source for the Spanish Kabbalah, and was a contemporary of Abulafia, whose permutations of the Hebrew alphabet Lull in some measure imitates within his own system. The Ars Raymundi, as it was known to later esotericists, was a system of astral science based on the Aristotelian elemental categories. It also combined the divine epithets as they appear on the Tree of Life, for they could be applied to all aspects of life, from the mineral kingdom to the angelic hierarchies and beyond. Lull's aim was to provide a system that would harmonize all religions. He himself learned Arabic and saw his system as part of a missionary effort to convert Jews and Muslims to Christianity. He was eventually martyred in northern Africa.

Lull's influence was considerable: Giovanni Pico della Mirandola (1463–1494 C.E.), who moved in the circle of the Medici court at the height of the Hermetic revival, recognized Lullism as a proto-kabbalistic system. Pico had some knowledge of Hebrew and prior to the Jewish expulsion from Spain was able to obtain kabbalistic manuscripts, which he then translated and used as the foundation for his *Conclusions,* a vehicle, he hoped, to confirm the Christian religion by means of Hebrew wisdom. Other esoteric sources that contributed to his *Conclusions* included Platonic and Neoplatonic texts, Orphic hymns, and Chaldean oracles. Pico's philosophy is in many ways a restatement of Lull, but instead of turning to Muslims and Jews to prove the truth of Christianity, he went to Rome in order to show how Christianity is a natural successor to Judaic gnosis. In 1487 he was forced to make a formal apology for his conclusions as a result of the furor that broke out over them (657). In his apology Pico divided the Kabbalah into two parts: the *ars combinandi,* or the method of per-muting Hebrew letters, and "a way of capturing the powers of superior things" (meaning the powers of angels and spirits). These were undoubtedly magical rather than theological distinctions. It is Pico who was responsible for assigning planetary ascriptions to each of the Sephiroth, which lead the aspirant from the mineral and elemental kingdoms to the planetary, angelic, and divine realms that form the four worlds of the Jewish Kabbalah.

In imitation of Lull's ambition to combine and reconcile divided faiths, he was the first to make the link inexorably welding the Kabbalah to Christianity: He sought to prove that by the addition of one letter, the Tetragrammaton, the Most Holy Name of God—which is always left unpronounced by pious Jews and is always substituted by a euphemism such as Adonai, Lord—could be turned into the name of Jesus. The Tetragammaton is composed of four letters: Yod, He, Vav, and He, or Yahweh. By the addition of a finial Shin, YHVH becomes YHSHVH, or Yeheshuah—Jesus. Such questionable Christian interpretation may seem insignificant in our day, but this conclusion was to have a widespread effect throughout Europe.

Along with the synthesis of texts and systems, the Jewish expulsion from Spain resulted in the resettlement of Jews throughout Europe, which meant that wonderful meetings of minds could take place. kabbalistic manuscripts were discussed and translated, and in 1494 Johannes Reuchlin (1455–1522 C.E.), a scholar of the German Renaissance, published his *De Verbo Mirifico*. Following Pico's ideas, Reuchlin gives us a Platonic dialogue in which a Jew, a Greek, and a Christian discuss the kabbalistic "proof" of Jesus as the Messiah. Other books followed this: The Franciscan Francesco Giorgi (1466–1540 C.E.), working from Venice, fully synthesized the Kabbalah with Christianity, adding Neoplatonic and Hermetic elements for good measure as part of an esoteric Christian system (657). Finally, Henry Cornelius Agrippa (1486–1535) brought the Kabbalah into the form in which it is best known today—as a magical system. His *De Occulta Philosophia* (1533) presents a universe divided into three worlds: the elemental, the celestial, and the intellectual. This division naturally leads into a discussion of natural magic, celestial magic (following Ficino's model), and ceremonial magic, which aims to influence the angelic world by means of kabbalistic magic.

Thus a Judaic mystical system became in one stroke the basis of both a Christian gnosis and a magical system. The Kabbalah remains the lingua franca of Western esotericism, although one that inevitably has its detractors. With this evolution of the Gentile Kabbalah, Lull's vision of a reconciled and harmonized microcosm is partially fulfilled. It is ironic that Christianity, having rejected its own esoteric tradition, should have taken over and developed the esoteric system of Judaism, which provided the roots of Christianity! And though the fathers of the Jewish Kabbalah might quail at the thought of a Christian Kabbalah, it provides yet another example of the subtle spread of esoteric concepts whose Mysteries live to seed new traditions with old wisdom. The words of Isaac Luria still hold for those who study the Kabbalah in any form: "[F]or every handsbreadth [of the mysteries] I reveal, I will hide a mile. With great difficulty, I will open the gates of holiness, making an opening like the eye of a needle, and let him who is worthy pass through it to enter the innermost chamber." (287)

The esoteric way is still a narrow one. Those who find their way easy and their passage unobstructed are likely traveling away from, not toward, the Mysteries. There are no ethical standards approved by occult examining boards. Those who dismiss the whole esoteric world as evil and misguided are fearful because of this very lack. Yet the esotericist should not be complacent on this score. If you have no teacher and no tradition behind you, how can you be sure that your work is truly aligned with the will of God, however you understand this term? As we have seen, the mystery and training schools that still exist often have extremely rigid standards; students must either adhere to them or leave. Still, many charlatans exist in the esoteric community.

While there is no Hippocratic Oath for esotericists, there is a tacit agreement upon standards among genuine practitioners of the magical arts. This may appear to outsiders as a kind of "honor among thieves" arrangement, but these unwritten standards are nevertheless based upon the law of the land and have a level of integrity that would be applauded by many professional boards who oversee public standards. The ultimate authority is the contract between the initiate and the inner contact of the school to which the initiate belongs. Service to the universe is the only real mortar in the divine contract—those who seek to serve themselves with their magic use the blood and power of others to seal theirs, and in this way they create a prison of the universe. In our own times not only magicians have gone down this route to black magic. All those who divert the commonwealth for private profit, whether it be in politics, business, or religion, have taken the first steps along the road to black magic.

The Divine Chariot

Magic in the West has had a long and sometimes ignoble history. This is due partly to the development of Western Christianity, which has excluded many practices fundamental to all religions. Religion formalizes disparate beliefs into an authorized set of practices and chooses which to set aside as unauthorized. Christianity has retained prayer, for instance, but excluded magic. Perhaps may it be said, then, that prayer is formalized magic?

In his role as mediator, the magician embodies the answer to this question by becoming a coworker in the progressive state of the cosmos, which should never be thought of as static or complete. Through ritual the inner motivation of prayer becomes externalized as the magician becomes the representative of both humanity and the orders of creation, while his magic becomes a visualized prayer technique. When magic works, we can presume that dedication and commitment to the world's good have borne fruit. But magic is not foolproof or the answer to every ill or want, as might think some who rush in to practice it without knowledge or understanding. It will not work on request any more than a prayer for a million dollars or miraculous healing necessarily works for a Christian, nor will it turn the tide of events any more than lighting a candle will stop a massive power outage.

Magicians, like believers, are not saints and they do not have superhuman resources; they fail as all other human beings fail. Yet while an "ordinary" mortal is allowed—even expected—to fail now and then, it seems a magician is not. If either the ritual that helps manifest an answer fails or the mediation falls short of its purpose, the consequences are serious. And if the failure is due to the magician's personal imbalance or pride, he or she will suffer.

In fact, it is an occult truism that if the magic performed is not in accordance with God's will, the work will rebound on the sender—some say threefold. This scenario might be similar to praying for a thousand dollars and then receiving it in the form of an insurance payment after a seriously debilitating accident. We should always be careful what we wish for; if our motivation is strong enough, we will surely get it.

Though the ethics of magic are not clearly drawn anywhere, like other social understandings and rule-of-thumb moralities, magic has its own rules that must be discovered by each individual through experience. One basic principle of operation is that no one is harmed, that nothing is unbalanced or distorted by the activity of the magician—an understanding that is based upon the laws of cause and effect.

No magician could progress very far in his search for knowledge without coming to the point at which he realizes, at least tacitly, the unity of all things, and that realization nurtures compassion. Even the use of an effigy is a tacit recognition that the copy is connected intimately to the original regardless of the vastness of time and space (617). The signature recognizable in everything makes all matter interactive, in turn promoting the understanding that whatever we do has repercussions for the rest of creation (617). Compassion must inform the magician's work or it will be for nothing. As Saint Paul says: "If I speak in the tongues of men and angels, but have not love, I am a noisy gong or a clanging cymbal. And if I have prophetic powers, and understand all mysteries and all knowledge, and if I have all faith, so as to move mountains, but have not love, I am nothing." (Corinthians 1:13)

Magic is not an exact science. The effects of working magically are subjective, as they are for any art—clay can be molded into many shapes, and words can be rearranged to alter the writer's original intention. Even so, magic, like the science of engineering, can be used to build bridges and convey loads that would seem to be impossible in terms of physical laws. The magician is himself a bridge between upper and lower realms. When he stands within the circle of the lodge or temple, he steps outside time to become a mote of dust in the light emanating from God—a mote that nevertheless has a causal effect far beyond the magician's normal, human ability. Here, ritual becomes an enactment or symbolic form of inner reality. However the symbolism is transmitted, the magician forms a direct link with the inner realms. We may see how this happens in the following example: When a sudden rush of purgative power from the inner world is experienced in the outer world, each person may detect this and interpret it differently.

- A magician perceives this inner movement as a necessary purgation that will have its effect on the outer world. In cooperation with God's will, he creates a ritual to help direct the energy. His life will be made intolerable until this action is performed.
- A seer or medium receives the power and imagizes it. A purgation of this type will often appear to the seer with disturbing clarity.
- A mystic perceives God's will, the forces of creation working to fulfill a divine purpose. He says prayers for harmony within the universe and seeks a greater unity with the will of God.
- A poet picks up the energy and transforms it into verse; an artist captures it on canvas or in a bronze cast; composers introduce new harmonies into their instrumentation; all artists seek to trace the energy to its source.
- Within countries and social groups the response is less cohesive; if the force is purgative, then civil unrest may occur or wars or disturbances may break out until the inner force loses its cyclonic energy. People may instinctively register in ordinary outer ways the force that is communicating itself. Peace movements may be strengthened and criminal activity may increase; police vigilance will be prominent.

This is, of course, only a projected paradigm. The inner forces can and do manifest in many other ways, and those who feel their effect receive and interpret it differently according to personal differences and to the strength and origin of the forces. When inner forces of this kind are at work, all we can do is cooperate, help them pass, and perhaps even feel their beneficent qualities.

But the forces of the universe are not always creative; they may also be destructive. We can remember that in order to bring regeneration, structures often have to be torn down. Purgation is a mighty and terrible thing, but it is not evil in itself. Inner activity is more often exerienced as a creative force that will contribute a fresh impulse and vitality, which can only be helpful to all. Those who look for the will of God in such cases need not passively resign themselves to doing nothing, but rather can take up their appointed tasks as they best can: "For each of those who is allotted a place in the divine order finds his perfection in being uplifted, according to his capacity, towards the divine likeness; and what is still more divine, he becomes, as the Scriptures say, a fellow-worker with God and shows forth the Divine Activity revealed as far as possible in himself." (130) In pursuing our tasks we are doing what all followers of the Western Way must do: We are putting aside our interests to become workers in the great force of creation. It is a theme we should be familiar with by now—the divine spark sees its identity within the greater whole, the mystic seeks union with God.

The magician, then, places himself as close to the heart of creation as he can in order to work from and with it. He seeks to realize his potential within the framework of matter, becoming a priest in order to carry forward the work of the inner realms, the will of God. To be a magician is to be artificer, artist, and priest in one. It is a noble calling.

If the foregoing picture seems too attractive, however, let it also be said that the life of a magician is not easy. William G. Gray once remarked that there are no handouts in magic, only earnings collected when they fall due. This is as true today as it ever was, and is one of the first things we ought to remember before embarking on any esoteric work. It was the first precept of the magicians of the past and their lives were full or empty, beneficial or harmful to the degree that they either accepted or denied it.

Magicians, like everyone else, have ordinary lives, jobs, and families. While they may be aware of other laws operative within the ordinary life, they seldom or never engage in the kind of role-playing games

described in occult pulp fiction. Moreover, certain adepts who special-
ize in the kind of psychic first-aid work described by Dion Fortune in
her Doctor Taverner stories (168) seem to bear out this fantastic image
of the magician, but in reality there are few who regularly engage in this
kind of practice. It is work for a responsible specialist who deals with
the genuine disorders brought about through psychic imbalance and is
best left to those who are experienced on multiple levels of reality, who
are big enough to take the knocks, so to speak, that inevitably occur.
Magicians who work with the spiritual cause of illness and imbalance
are today's true successors to the shamans of the Foretime (381).

While on the subject of psychic attack, we should note that the student is rarely aware of or troubled by such a phenomenon. Those
responsible for sending out negative energies would hardly be bothered
with a mere minnow when their intended catch is more likely to be a
salmon. The worst a neophyte is likely to encounter are his or her own
imbalances and their equilibration. To mitigate this possibility, we
should always observe certain commonsense measures in esoteric work.
We have mentioned these before, but they bear repeating:

- Seal off your aura.
- Place clear boundaries around your psychic activities through the
  use of opening and closing signs at the beginning and end of your
  practice.
- Maintain clear motivation on whatever level you operate.
- Use your clan totem as a shield.

Murray Hope's excellent book on psychic self-defense (253) gives many
practical means of coping with life in this seemingly unmapped area,
and Dion Fortune's *Psychic Self-Defense* is the standard in the field.

The magical life is lived through the seasonal rituals that govern the
tides of the year: The spring tide begins at the spring equinox and gov-
erns the growth and inception of new projects or ideas; the summer
tide, which runs from the summer solstice, is concerned with consoli-
dation and active working; the autumn tide of harvest begins at the
autumn equinox, when projects are brought into fruition or maturity;
and the winter tide of dissolution begins at the winter solstice and clears
out stale ideas and projects.

It also relates to the monthly cycle of the moon, the weekly progression of the days, and the hourly microcosm of the day from dawn

to noon and twilight to midnight. These minor cycles are superimposed with the planetary and zodiacal patterns and all are recognized by the magician, who makes them a part of his inner and outer life (309). He also takes into account periods of cosmic time and the greater pattern of the eons—as in the Piscean and Aquarian ages, which meet and change the flow of activity during our own lifetimes. Of course, it is by no means easy to correlate all these factors—hence the need for stringent training before the magician practices. Even the adept will find it difficult at times to adjust to these many combinations, yet all ritual magic is at its basis a method of relating higher to lower, celestial to chthonic, and divine to temporal. The complex systems of interrelated powers taught by the mystery schools, the detailed tables of correspondences to be found in the grimoires of the Middle Ages and the Renaissance, and the techniques of kabbalistic training all aim at these same targets.

Thus the work of the magician is organized around great cyclic events that occur outside of space and time, those recurring patterns that are the balancing act of the cosmos. They constellate in his magical year just as they feature in the dreams of the sensitive, and are reflected mundanely in the outer world. The magician may formulate these events into rituals in which the seasons and elements and the positions of the stars become an expression in the outer world of an inner reality, a sacramental encounter between the desires of humanity and the power and might of God.

We must be careful, however, of seeing the powers of creation as merely symbolic tools that we can work with but which have no ultimate reality. It is possible to evolve a theory of archetypes every bit as complex as anything to be found in the *Corpus Hermeticum,* but this would be useless unless it was informed with practical application and realization. A grimoire is of no help to someone who fails to understand its correspondences as keys to a larger reality. The literal-minded cannot work without the reach of metaphor, nor can the total rationalist get his mind out of the way sufficiently to receive intuitive perceptions. The would-be magician must learn to draw down the elemental powers into his own sphere of working, just as he must elevate his human understanding to the point at which he can appreciate the mysteries of creation and the presence of the divine principle within it.

Magic is essentially the higher understanding of nature, a true vision of the universe as it whirls and roars around us. From ritual to Renaissance to the modern occult revival, this has been the heart and center of magical work. The work of practitioners from the tribal shaman to the present-day magus has arisen out of a fundamental belief in an ordered cosmos—that we are not simply born into the world for the sole purpose of providing amusement for some distant god or gods or nourishment for the soil, or for pursuing blind animal existence. Rather, we are to become part of the universal process of becoming: "You must understand that this is the first path to felicity . . . the theurgic gift . . . is called indeed the gate to the Demiurge of Wholes. . . . It possesses a power of purifying the soul and . . . produces a union with the gods . . . givers of every good." (262)

Magic as a branch of Hermeticism does not seem to concern itself with saving the soul. To the outsider it seems merely a way, a technique, a methodology. But to participate in magic is to become part of the fabric of creation as a coworker, to be purged and purified and made whole, to do the will of God in our own life. It means living close to the wind, ready at all times to veer where it wishes to take us. The qualifications of the kind of magical work we have discussed here should be written large over the temple door of all those who think they are ready to follow the life of the magician. These words might read: "A sense of ritual, a sense of humor, and common sense." With these you cannot go wrong.

In any lodge, brethren should meet in harmony and depart in peace and silence, but this is not always the case. While it is not often understood, the magical life imposes subtle pressures that can turn reasonable and pleasant people into aggressive and nitpicking individuals. Under stress, human nature will out, and ritual work is highly pressured in part because ritual exteriorizes inner forces that can in turn magnify personal problems. It is the duty of the magister of the lodge to ensure that this is understood. Some ritual work can be quite disturbing, even to the experienced magician. If the quarter officers are mediating their roles properly, the risk of emotional upset among those participating is substantially reduced. Minor irritations with fellow ritualists can grow from molehills into mountains very quickly, especially when the ritual has exaggerated any personal imbalance. Emotional reactions are usually harmless and quick to pass if everyone remains objective about them and sees them as concomitant with the ritual.

In a magical order, each candidate is scrutinized for his or her intentions and present mode of life. The imbalanced, the discontented, the egomaniacal, the depressed, the unhealthy, and the uncommitted are all excluded for their own good. In magic only the best is good enough—anything less than total commitment is a waste of energy and time.

All of this may read strangely to those who consider magic as only black. Surely all this talk of world service (34) and dedication is merely a smokescreen covering some ultimately evil intention. Despite what the papers say, this is not so, as we have tried to show. Yet there exist unbalanced individuals in magic just as in all other walks of life. Such people are usually bad news and some of them have unfortunately left their mark on the practice of magic. We must bear in mind:

> Theurgy, or high magic, is the raising of consciousness to the appreciation of the powers and forces behind the external world in a pious intention of developing spiritual awareness and subsequently helping to bring to birth the divine plan of a restored earth. Thaumaturgy, or low magic . . . is the production of wonders by the use of little known powers of the mind. (305)

The effort of the magician was summed up long ago by the Roman historian Dio Chrysostom when he wrote, "[T]he magi . . . hold that the universe is steadily being drawn along a single road by a charioteer who is gifted with the greatest skill and power." (410) The magician does not seek to become the charioteer, only to prevent the chariot from running away with him and those who journey at his side. The magician does not usually begin his work under the age of thirty, for the twenties are a time when the mundane life—education, family, and so forth—is being established. The primary responsibility at this time is to the family life—the path of the hearth fire. When children are grown or sufficiently fledged, those of us who are called to the magical life can begin in earnest.

Such strictures of age do not normally apply within the native tradition because its ways can very easily be upheld and studied within the family unit. After all, they derive from tribal consciousness. The Hermetic tradition imposes more rigorous standards on its adherents because the candidate must follow the way of involution until he or she stands at the initiatory gates of life and starts the way of return on the evolutionary path (310).

However strict its requirements, magic is returning on all fronts in our own time. It is not always purely Hermetic or native in its approach, but is instead a mixture of old and new. The return of the magician is also the return of the shaman and "shamanism is being reinvented in the West precisely because it is needed." (229) Its techniques as well as those of the Hermetically trained magus point the way to the inner worlds, and it is from there that the long climb begins to the highest expression of both traditions: the mysteries and techniques of alchemy.

Fig. 19. Isis as described in Lucius Apuleius's The Golden Ass, *from Athanasius Kircher's* Oedipus Aegyptiacus, *c. 1652*

PRACTICES

14. The Hermetic Way

The two texts that follow illuminate much that we have discussed in earlier chapters and act as a preparation for the exercises and techniques that come after them. We suggest that they be read with attention over a period of two weeks, taking sections or sentences from each in turn and meditating upon them. Write down whatever realization comes to you. This should enable you to build up your own commentary on the Emerald Tablet and the extract from the *Corpus Hermeticum*. At the end of this period you might wish to pursue a longer meditation (generally periods of twenty to thirty minutes are sufficient), incorporating material from both texts and from your own notes. This should be seen as the beginning of a prolonged study and extended working with the Hermetic texts in general, which may become the framework for a lifetime's activity as well as deepen your awareness of the Mysteries addressed in the remainder of this book. Please note that writing is not the only means of recording your realizations. Consider drawing or sculpting them, or dancing or singing them. You may find *The Emerald Tablet,* by D. W. Hauck, a useful guide to this text.

The Emerald Tablet of Hermes Trismegistos

1. In truth certainly and without doubt, whatever is below is like that which is above, and whatever is above is like that which is below, to accomplish the miracles of one thing.
2. Just as all things proceed from one alone by meditation on one alone, so also they are born from this one thing by adaptation.
3. Its father is the sun and its mother is the moon. The wind has born it in its body. Its nurse is the earth.
4. It is the father of every miraculous work in the whole world.
5. Its power is perfect if it is converted into earth.
6. Separate the earth from the fire and the subtle from the gross, softly and with great prudence.
7. It rises from earth to heaven and comes down again from heaven to earth, and thus acquires the power of the realities

below. In this way you will acquire the glory of the whole world, and all darkness will leave you.

8. This is the power of all powers, for it conquers everything subtle and penetrates everything solid.
9. Thus the little world is created according to the prototype of the great world.
10. From this and in this way, marvellous applications are made.
11. For this reason I am called Hermes Trismegistos, for I possess the three parts of wisdom of the whole world.
12. Perfect is what I have said of the work of the sun.

The Teaching of Hermes

If then you do not make yourself equal to God, you cannot apprehend God; for like is known by like. Leap clear of all that is corporeal, and make yourself grow to a like expanse with that greatness which is beyond all measure; rise up above all time, and become eternal; then you will apprehend God. Think that for you too nothing is impossible; deem that you too are immortal, and that you are able to grasp all things in your thought, to know every craft and every science; find yourself home in the haunts of every living creature; make yourself higher than all heights, and lower than all depths; bring together in yourself all opposites of quality, heat and cold, dryness and fluidity; think that you are everywhere at once, on land, at sea, in heaven; think that you are not yet begotten, that you are in the womb, that you are young, that you are old, that you have died, that you are in the world beyond the grave. Grasp in your thought all this at once, all times and places, all substances and qualities and magnitudes together; then you can apprehend God. But if you shut up your soul in your body, and abase yourself, and say, "I know nothing, I can do nothing, I am afraid of earth and sea, I cannot mount to heaven; I do not know what I was, nor what I shall be"; then, what have you to do with God? Your thought can grasp nothing beautiful and good, if you cleave to the body, and are evil. For it is the height of evil not to know God. But to be capable of knowing God, and to wish and hope to know him, is the road which leads straight to the good; and it is an easy road to travel.

—*Corpus Hermeticum*, XI, II (533)

❧ 15. The Foursquare Citadel ❧

The following practice is worked in five parts and is a complete initiatory system suitable for readers of any tradition. There is a built-in failsafe in that the foursquare citadel can be built only from your personal meditation: No one else can help you work this exercise, nor will you find the answers in any books. Because it is based on a thorough knowledge of the elements, you will succeed only if you meditate sufficiently upon each element. In the fifth and final part, you will be able to construct the foursquare citadel that will forever be your own personal temenos from which you may meditate or work. This practice is ideal, then, for those who have no working area in their home, for it establishes an inner chamber of art.

Work each part successfully before going on to the next. You may need several sessions for each part. On no account attempt to work the whole exercise in one go. At the beginning of the practice, state your intention in these or your own words:

I seek the citadel with no foundations that lies within myself.

Then add for each quarter:

I seek the power of the East [or South/West/North], the seed of power that lies within.

If you have difficulty realizing the elemental qualities, *Magical Ritual Methods,* by William Gray (199) and *The Practice of Ritual Magic,* by Gareth Knight (309), give excellent pointers on how you may come to experience them.

For those who are practicing this meditation in the southern hemisphere, please visualize the elements appropriately: Your South will correspond to the North in this meditation. If you need to adjust the Eastern and Western quarters in accordance with the continental landmass on which you live, please do so. If your wettest wind blows from the East, then substitute West for East in this meditation.

Method

1. Sit in meditation with your chair in the middle of the floor, if you have space. Visualize a circle around you. If you have a Tarot deck, you

might place the four Aces around you at the quarters—if the circle were a clock, at the 12, 3, 6, and 9. Place the Ace of Swords in the East, the Ace of Wands in the South, the Ace of Cups in the West, and the Ace of Pentacles in the North. Face East and visualize the following scene around you. The circle expands until it becomes the utmost limit of the earth, from horizon to horizon; the edges of the world tilt away into infinity. You stand at the center of the world and at the four quarters stand four figures of mighty power. They are fixed at the farthest point of four blue paths that begin where you are standing, which is where they have their crossroads. Each of the quarters is a different color: The Eastern one is white, like crystal; the Southern one is a transparent red; the Western one is as green as an emerald; and the Northern one is of opaque blackness. Each power holds back the elemental forces from rushing into the center of the circled world. Turn to face each power and sense the nature of the elemental energy that is being controlled.

In order to build your foursquare citadel, you will have to enter into relationship with each element by means of an initiatory meditation. Face East and meditate upon the power of Air, which is white as crystal. Consider the elemental quality of air from every level of your understanding. The whole Eastern quarter of the circled world is flooded with white light as you meditate and as the power of the Eastern One builds. The ground becomes white as well so that the path disappears. You must journey along the invisible path toward the Eastern edge of the world and bring back the gift of the Eastern power. You travel blind across the whitened world. The snow is deep and cold, but you must move on without stopping. Despite your uncertainty, tune in to the Eastern power and feel it magnetically calling you. A white hare crosses your track and you understand that you are to follow it deeper into the snowscape. Wherever the hare runs, there a path opens up and the ground is easy to travel. Elsewhere the ground is covered by deep drifts, so you continue to follow the path.

Suddenly the hare stops, turns, and asks you: "Where do you journey and what do you seek?"

You reply, "I seek the citadel with no foundations that lies within the East."

It then asks, "What are the powers of the Eastern One?"

You answer in your own words, drawing upon your own meditative realizations. If the hare is satisfied with your answer, you may proceed. If it is not, then it will vanish and you must return to your starting place at the center of the circled world. You may not continue, for the path ends, the winds blow, and the snow deepens. If your answer is satisfactory, the hare will leap forward into the middle of the whiteness ahead, drawing you behind it until you stand at your journey's end. Before you is the archon of the East, arrayed as a mighty power in the mantle of the snows. (*Note:* The archons of the quarters may appear as male or female. The archons of the elements are the elemental rulers. Some readers will recognize Enochian undertones in this initiatory system. To those who can read the clues, a very interesting game of Enochian chess can be played in a three-dimensional meditation. See Regardie (504) and Casaubon (81) for more information on the archons.) In his right hand is a sword of adamant and on his head burns a crystalline crown. His force and presence are overwhelmingly strong. Pay your respects to him and accept whatever gift he gives you as a token of your regency of the power of Air. The gift will be an object that you can easily hold in your hand. Only you know what it is. Take the first thing that you see, however inappropriate your rational mind considers it; first impressions are generally correct. This is the first gift that you will use to build your foursquare citadel. Take your leave of the archon of the East, giving thanks.

Swift as thought you return to the center of the circled world down the path that is now visible to you and easy to travel. Stand at the center and face East once more, seeing the path before you and the archon, with his crown of white crystal, standing at the farthest Eastern point of the world. Raise your gift in salutation and thanks, and set it down in the Eastern quarter of the circle.

As you work each quarter (see steps 2–4 below), lay each gift in its corresponding place until you have worked all four. It is effective to draw on a sheet of paper the mandala of the circled world with colored quarters, placing each gift upon it, or, if you have a sacred working area, to make a symbolic representation of each gift in the appropriate quarter of your room. Remember that these are your personal symbols and are not for others to see; they are the keys that unlock your foursquare citadel, so keep them safe.

2. Now face South and establish the path to the farthest South of the circled world. At the end of it stands the mighty power of the South, to whom you must journey. Meditate this time upon the power of Fire, which is a transparent red, like a ruby. As the power builds, the whole

Southern quarter is flooded with light, obliterating the path before you. Once again, proceed by instinct across the landscape that opens before you. The earth is red sand through which you trudge under the heat of an invisible sun. The sand is hot and hard on your feet, your throat and mouth are filled with its grittiness. Feel the power and orient yourself once more. Before you appears a sand lizard that is the same color as the ground. Follow it and your path will be easier. Wherever it goes, you can walk safely.

It turns and asks you, "Where do you journey and what do you seek?"

You reply, "I seek the citadel with no foundations that lies within the South."

It asks: "What are the powers of the Southern One?"

You answer in your own words. If the lizard is unsatisfied with your reply, you must return to the center and travel this way another time. If your answer is satisfactory, the lizard will dart swiftly forward, taking you with it until you stand before the mighty archon of the South. He is arrayed as a mighty power in a mantle of red, glittering sand. In his right hand is a spear of adamant and on his head burns a crown of ruby. His force and presence are overwhelming. Pay your respects to him and accept the gift that can be seen and known only by you as a token of your regency over the powers of Fire. This is the second gift that you will use to build your foursquare citadel. You take your leave and, swift as thought, you return to the center of the circled world down the path that opens before you. Stand at the center, facing South, and raise your gift in thanks to the archon fixed at the point farthest South on the path. Salute him and set down your gift in the Southern quarter.

3. Now face West and establish the path to the Westernmost quarter of the circled world. At the end of it stands the mighty power of Water, which is a transparent green, like an emerald. Meditate upon the power of Water. As the power builds, the whole Western quarter is flooded with green light, obliterating the path before you. Again, proceed by instinct across the landscape that opens before you. Everything around you is green and damp. A jungle of plant life surrounds you, the ground beneath your feet is moist and swampy, and the air is hot and clammy. The way is difficult and winding, but you continue to seek the Westernmost point. As you struggle to break through the tangle of

thick, green growth around you while avoiding the swampy patches, a water snake slithers across your path. Follow it and the way is instantly easier.

It turns and asks you, "Where do you journey and what do you seek?"

You reply, "I seek the citadel with no foundations that lies within the West."

It then asks, "What are the powers of the Western One?"

Once again, you answer in your own words. If your answer is unsatisfactory, the snake will vanish and you must return to the center of the circled world to attempt this journey at another time. If your answer is satisfactory, the snake glides forward swiftly, drawing you with it, until you stand before the archon of the West. He is arrayed as a mighty power, wearing a mantle of glimmering greenery. His force and presence are overwhelmingly strong. Pay your respects to him and accept whatever gift he gives that can be seen and known only by you as a token of your regency over the powers of Water. This is the third gift that you will use to build your foursquare citadel. You take your leave and return, swift as thought, along the path that is now open for you, to the center of the circled world. Stand at the center facing West and salute the archon of the West, raising your gift in thanks. Then set it down in the Western quarter.

4. Now face North and establish the path to the Northernmost quarter of the circled world. At the end of it stands the mighty power of Earth, which is as black as obsidian. Meditate upon the powers of earth. As the power builds, the path before you is obliterated and flooded with blackness. Again, proceed instinctively through the landscape around you. This time there is barely light to see by, forcing you to proceed mainly by touch. The ground beneath your feet is alternately as hard as rock and as shifting as sand; the loose earth has the consistency of gunpowder. Your way is hindered by the shifting ground and the darkness, but continue to feel your way to true North. The air is cold and the wind is dry. You hear a scrabbling sound on the ground nearby and a small furry creature brushes your feet. It is a mole with eyes that see in the night.

It asks you, "Where do you journey and what do you seek?"

You reply, "I seek the citadel with no foundations that lies within the North."

It then asks, "What are the powers of the Northern One?"

As before, you answer in your own words. If your answer is unsatisfactory, the mole will disappear and you must return to the center and travel this another time. If it is satisfactory, the mole will scramble into the darkness, drawing you with it until you stand before the archon of the North. He is arrayed as a mighty power in a mantle of glittering blackness outlined by silver light. In his right hand is a book of adamant and on his head glints a crown of black diamonds. His force and presence are overwhelmingly strong. Pay your respects to him and accept whatever gift he gives that can be seen and known only by you as a token of your regency over the powers of Earth. This is the final gift that you will use to build your foursquare citadel. Take your leave and return, swift as thought, to the center of the circled world along the path that is now open and lit before you. Stand at the center facing North and salute the archon, raising your gift in thanks, and then place it in the Northern quarter.

5. It may have taken you many sessions and months of meditation to reach this point, but you have persevered. This last portion of the working may also take longer than one session. You will now proceed to build your foursquare citadel.

In meditation set your four gifts in their appropriate quarters around your feet where you stand at the center of the circled world. Slowly circle, regarding each of the paths in turn: East, South, West, North. All paths lead to your feet. The gifts at your feet are your instruments—these and no other—that you will use to build your foursquare citadel.

Meditate upon their meanings, which are applicable only to you and your own theory of correspondences. Here there are no right answers. If you have trouble realizing their meanings, then look along the path of the quarter from which they came and ask questions of the creature and guide of that quarter until you are clear. When each gift is activated by your understanding, power will rise from it in a clockwise, spiraling movement from the ground upward.

The walls of your citadel rise around you. Do not be afraid that you will be trapped inside, for each side has a door. Altogether, the tower has five levels with a connecting spiral staircase up the center of the structure. In each level there are four windows that look out on each of the quarters. Beginning at the ground, the rooms on each level correspond to first Earth, then Water, then Fire, and finally Air. There is one more room on the topmost level as well.

This is your foursquare citadel, where you can observe the motions of the inner world. Go to the topmost level and look out over each quarter in turn. As you circle the horizon you can see that in each quarter where the archon stood there is a tower. These are the watchtowers of the circled world, and each is in communication with your own citadel. You may come to this topmost level when you wish to communicate with the four watchtowers and their guardians, the archons.

Now look over the land through which you traveled so laboriously as you sought the initiations of the elements. In the East the snow is beginning to melt. The thaw of early spring breaks over the land and the ground is covered with young plants and green shoots. Only the Eastern tower is still white. In the South the endless, sandy desert gives way to a land where the summer's heat is tempered by lakes and rivers and where trees give shelter from the noonday sun. Only the Southern tower is still red. To the West the rain forests and swampy terrain are tempered by the gentle coolness of autumn. There are red and brown leaves upon the trees, contrasting with the green. Only the Western tower is fully green. To the North the black rocks and barren soil give way to fallow wakefulness and winter. There are evergreens growing and though the earth looks bleak, it harbors the hope of spring. The light is the clear brightness of the North. Only the Northern tower remains deepest black.

Discovery

There is much work that you can effect in your citadel. In the rooms of Earth, Water, Fire, and Air you can work rituals and meditations that suit these elements, furnishing each room according to your preference but observing the conventions of the element to which it corresponds. From these rooms you can also balance the elements. For example, you may look out of one of the windows of the room of Earth toward the quarter for the power of Air, which results in the combination Air of Earth. The other combinations possible from this room are Fire of Earth, Water of Earth, and Earth of Earth. Each combination affords months of meditative activity.

In meditations from your citadel you would normally work with the guides or creatures of the quarters rather than with the archons of the elements themselves. The creatures are messengers and intermediaries and are easier to work with than the raw powers themselves. However, if you find it difficult to work with animal forms, you may request each of the beasts to transform into a human shape. Working with the archons themselves is best accomplished by means of the symbols of adamant. These are:

East: Sword of Adamant
South: Spear of Adamant
West: Cup of Adamant
North: Book or Tablet of Adamant

Adamant is a legendary substance of great durability—you may visualize each symbol as made of a diamondlike stone in the appropriate quarter color. The topmost level of the citadel can then become the Chamber of Adamant, where each of the symbols can be displayed on the corresponding wall of its quarter. To acquire the symbols, work a ritual appropriate to the quarter and request of the archons, by means of their messengers, the symbols you require. For this you may adapt the structure of the working for obtaining your four gifts. Each of the

Fig. 20. The four-gated heavenly city

original symbols remains with the archon; you are given an authorized copy that is the same in all respects. Of course, the archons and their servants are at liberty to refuse you until you are worthy of obtaining the symbols, for they are powerful tools that should be considered archetypes of any actual weapon or object that you may make in the future.

To enter and leave the citadel, envision each of your four gifts. To build it again, set down your gifts and meditate on their qualities until you feel the tower rising around you in a clockwise spiral. To dismantle it, go to the lowest level and dissolve it in a counterclockwise spiral until you are left with only your gifts. Of course, no one else can have access to your citadel because no one has gifts just like yours. Your gifts are your keys and can be personalized symbols of the elements that you may meditate upon whenever you need the help of a particular elemental energy.

Always carefully close each meditation session—and beware of any imbalances that may arise from working with elemental energies. Remember to use practice 9, Self-Clarification, when necessary.

9
Through the Inner Door

Understand that you are a second world in miniature,
and the sun and moon are within you, as are the stars.
—ORIGEN, *HOMILIAE LEVITICIUM*

All have their keys, and set ascents: but man
Though he knows these, and hath more of his own,
Sleeps at the ladder's foot.
—HENRY VAUGHAN, *THE TEMPEST*

The Language of Correspondence and Symbol

*I*f the Otherworld of the native tradition is the earthly paradise, then the major otherworldly resonance of the Hermetic tradition is a celestial model. In this chapter you will find no dogmatic presentations of the cosmos—only many maps drawn from different perspectives. All initiates proceed according to their own lights. The macrocosm, like the microcosm, is an evolving entity, not a static phenomenon (160), so we should not try to confine it with restricting definitions. These maps of reality, then, are not locations in the universe but rather working metaphors of a world model.

The medieval world inherited the Hellenic cosmos consisting of the earth, the seven planets, the fixed stars, and the zodiac extending in spherical progression, beyond which lay the Empyrean. Through these spheres filtered the power of God by means of the angelic hierarchies as defined by Dionysius the Areopagite. This understanding of the cosmos is now lost to us: Science has shown us that the moon is a dead piece of rock, that the planets do not behave as Ptolemy believed, and that the earth is not the center of the universe any more than it is the center of our solar system. Those who travel externally to these heavenly bodies will find only empty planets. The real cosmic universe is an interior one. Here we will look at how and why the celestial world model has faded from scientific importance, yet remained central to Hermeticism.

Up until the Renaissance, humanity believed itself to be not at the top of a Darwinian evolutionary ladder, but at the bottom of a vast celestial hierarchy and cosmology—which resulted in a very proper humility. However, the revision of the Ptolemaic world model in favor of the Copernican system during the Renaissance resulted in a radical disassociation with the macrocosm, producing an existentialist or, as the medievals would say, a melancholic state of consciousness within humanity. The accepted universal model was overthrown, the religious

Fig. 21. The Hierarchy of Creation: the four worlds of creatures, man, angels, and God

housings of that model were torn loose, and a state of uncertainty prevailed. This broken connection with the macrocosm has been partially remedied in our own time with a realization, once again, of the interdependence of human and animal, tree and river, rock and star. Even so, the lack of a cohesive world model that embraces both scientific and metaphysical understanding is reflected all around us in a fearful attitude, masked by mockery, toward the metaphysical or to the spiritual in general. Those who mock have grown up in an era where many religious or metaphysical world models have been rejected or overturned. Without a universal model that embraces both the scientific and the spiritual, we are left with a vacuum.

C. S. Lewis suggests that "you must go out on a starry night and walk about for half an hour trying to see the sky in terms of the old cosmology." (331) Within that system the sky was closer than our science now knows it to be and the moon was thought to represent an unpassable boundary, the sublunary realm in which nature alone held sway. Beyond this realm the stars, rotating in their fixed courses, were represented by a treasury of corresponding imagery.

The Ptolemaic system of cosmology—which said that the earth was the center of the universe—has remained the metaphysical inner world model of the macrocosm among Hermeticists. This is not to say that they reject the Copernican and post-Copernican heliocentric cosmology. Adam McLean points to the Hermetic work of Robert Fludd, (1574–1637 C.E.), who valued the importance of the Ptolemaic system for its underpinning of the Hermetic concept of inner space, yet was also scientifically aware of the Copernican system (358). His work *Utriusque Cosmi Historia* (The History of Both Worlds, 1617–1621) was a defense of the old world model, which he retained because he understood that the Copernican system, once established in the Hermetic realm of thought, "would give rise to a non-spiritual picture of the Cosmos." (356) He saw that in essence, our sense of cosmic unity was on the line.

The Ptolemaic cosmology viewed the world in its relationship to humanity: It was a system of steps on the ladder of the cosmos that reflected and related the microcosm and the macrocosm. Fludd's book (155) presents us with this old cosmology not in terms of astronomical understanding, but as a valid spiritual philosophy for the Hermeticist. He follows the emanatory movement of spirit into matter in much the same way that Kabbalists attended to the prismation of God's glory through the broken sephirotic vessels. McLean points out that Fludd's system of spiritual evolution was established three centuries before Steiner and Blavatsky presented their theories deriving from Eastern sources. The emblems that illustrate his work are still the clearest expressions of this cosmic understanding—in fact, we can find great reward in meditating upon their principles (186); they are the Western mandalas of the inner spaces, emblems of the soul.

Another contributor to the medieval world model was Plato's *Timaeus* (480). This alone of Plato's works was known to the medieval world through a Latin translation by Chalcidius. As a result, Plato was known not so much as the founder of a philosophy but as, "next to Moses, the great monotheistic cosmogonist, the philosopher of creation." (330) *Timaeus* presents a benevolent demiurge—unlike the Gnostic demiurge, who enslaves the spirit in matter. The celestial hierarchies of such cosmologies and their inhabitants are very much the concern of the Hermeticist, who often unknowingly uses their archetypes in his or her work.

Dionysius the Areopagite (c. 500 C.E.), the mystical theologian, supplied both the Christian and the esoteric corpus with the authoritative work on angels in his *Mystical Theology and the Celestial Hierarchies* (132). This book deals with the interrelation of the divine intelligences, each of which, according to its sphere, receives power from the order of beings above and passes it to the order below. This lyrical study stresses that only by poetic and symbolic means—and not mundane language—can such high Mysteries be understood. Dionysius's angels originated perhaps from the Iranian *spentas* (see chapter 6) or from Babylonian guardians. From there they filtered through Judaism into Christian teaching.

As we have seen, the divine intelligences who govern the celestial hierarchies have not always been seen as beneficent beings. The Gnostics held that the rulers, or archons, of each successive level of their complex cosmology were the servants of the evil demiurge. Each archon governed one of the planetary spheres. The Gnostics believed that after death they would have to encounter and overcome these dread instruments of Fate and that in order to reach the point of no further incarnation, humans would have to make a number of interior journeys through the spheres of the archons, which was a notion also held by the Orphites. Certain of the Elect (the pneumatics), such as Enoch (51), Baruch, and Ezra, were believed to have reached this goal. To aid themselves in reaching it, the Gnostics made and used a series of psalms and invocations so that after death each might overcome the power of the archons. The Gnostic Mandaen sect had the largest body of literature on this subject, including detailed instructions on how to render up the body to the elements and the vices assigned to each of the planetary archons who ruled each specific zone. These form, in effect, a Gnostic Book of the Dead, like those of both Egypt and Tibet. The Gnostic Naasene psalm says, "[A]ll the worlds shall I journey through, all the mysteries unlock." (629, 512)

We have only to consider Dante's *Divine Comedy* (116) as a similar Book of the Dead to see how widely held and practically understood these complex worldviews were. Dante travels through "all the worlds," through many levels in Hell, Purgatory, and Heaven, to gain his initiatory experience. Of course, as the *Divine Comedy* illustrates,

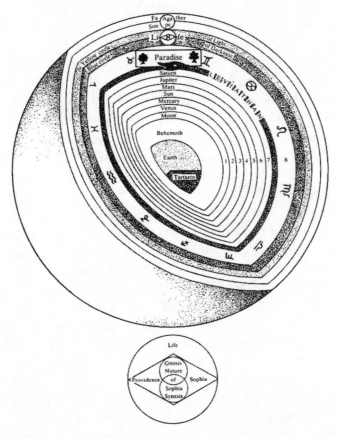

Fig. 22. *The Gnostic cosmology reveals the eight zones encompassing the earth. The detail at the bottom of the figure is an enlargement of the Circle of Zoe, or Life, the region where Sophia, Mistress of the Ogdoad, is enthroned.*

there are guardians along the way to guide us through these worlds, which we shall be considering more closely later in this chapter. Enoch (51) is also a traveler through the worlds—in his instance, through the halls of heaven, the realms of earth, and the Hebraic Underworld, Sheol, accompanied by visions of apocalyptic terror. The Kabbalist who explores the linking worlds of the Tree of Life is another such traveler. The initiate can follow the path of the great ones who, at each gate linking the Four Worlds of the Tree, prayed appropriately by reciting the unifications through which the light of God was restored (288).

For all the relevance of these old cosmologies, however, the esoteric world is not without cosmologies written in our own time. Blavatsky presented an Eastern-influenced world model that has subtly penetrated many levels of consciousness. Rudolf Steiner, rejecting Blavatsky's Theosophical outline, envisioned an Anthroposophist cosmology that is positively Gnostic in its complexity and detail (563). Many followers of the Western Way favor Dion Fortune's received text, *The Cosmic Doctrine* (160). Indeed, there is no lack of world models to use for experimentation and exploration.

All of these conceptions of the celestial are attempts to comprehend the macrocosm and to order it according to human understanding. In the works of Plato and Pythagoras we see a similar attempt to order the inner world model, but this time by means of music. In *The Myth of Er* (479) we meet the Spindle of Necessity, which stands for the cosmic system of stars and planets rotating around the axis of the universe (see fig. 23). On each whorl of the Spindle sits a Siren singing a single note. Pythagoras's cosmic ship of music (189) embodies a similar theme: It sails through the heavens emitting *rhoizimata,* or rushing sounds. These examples of the Music of the Spheres give us an insight into the cosmic order that is far more than mere planetary correspondence.

If we skillfully strike the seven-stringed lyre of our beings, we resonate with the Music of the Spheres so that microcosm and macrocosm sound in harmony: "Were it not for the orders of music hidden we should be claimed by the preponderant void." (189) The seven strings of the lyre corresponded to and gave order to the seven planets known to the classical world. A hypothetical eighth sphere was thought to correspond to the octave, and thus the scale of creation was closed. Robert Fludd invented an instrument that could express this very theory: The monochord's strings could be divided and subdivided, much like a musical abacus, in order to produce intervals or fractions of the origi-

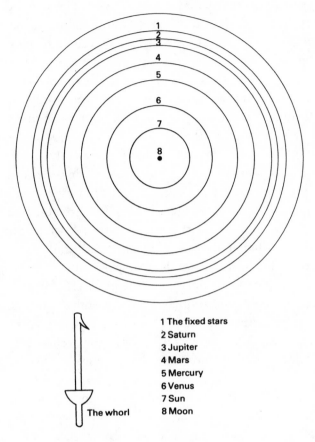

1 The fixed stars
2 Saturn
3 Jupiter
4 Mars
5 Mercury
6 Venus
7 Sun
8 Moon

The whorl

Fig. 23. The Spindle of Ananke, or Necessity, from Plato's Myth of Er, *reveals the Music of the Spheres.*

nal note (186). Thus the original note sounded at the Creation could be "refracted"—which calls to mind the Sephiroth on the Tree of Life.

John Dryden wrote in his poem "A Song for St. Cecilia's Day":

> *From harmony, from heavenly harmony*
> *This universal frame began:*
> *From harmony to harmony*
> *Through all the compass the notes it ran,*
> *The diapason closing full in man.*

Music, then, deals with the note and its correspondence to planetary archetypes. "There is another music of the soul and of the spheres which gives to actual music that is sung by voices and played on instruments its reason for existence." (310) Combinations of notes such as major and minor thirds can be heard as syzygies (divine partners) in harmony, while discordant intervals sound like the warring and irreconcilable archons. The Music of the Spheres is merely one more illustration of music's aural light, pouring inspiration through the prism of the ear, informing us of archetypal natures, of Platonic forms. From the aulos and lyre celebrating the Mysteries of Apollo to the hymns to Orpheus sung by Ficino, music has long been one of the Hermetic arts. Ficino sang his hymns in a talismanic way, suiting the musical mode, with the apposite robes, incense mixtures, planetary symbols, and so forth, to the deity he aimed to evoke (426). Even the birth of opera can be seen as a development of the Renaissance preoccupation with the correspondences that link gods, planets, ritual, and music. Masques enabled monarchs, attired as gods, to participate in mystery dramas. Indeed, modern stagings of operas are the nearest many of us can come to experiencing the Mysteries that were once staged in the amphitheaters of Greece: In them archetypal forms are presented by means of light, music, color, and highly choreographed movement. In appreciating it, we come to understand what Plotinus meant when he wrote:

> We are like a company of singing dancers who may turn their gait outward and away notwithstanding they have the choirmaster for centre; but when they are turned towards him then they sing true and are truly centred upon him. Even so we encircle the Supreme always; but our eyes are not at all times fixed upon the centre. Yet in the vision thereof lie our attainment and our repose and the end of all discord: God in his dancers and God the true centre of the dance. (482)

Music, then, much like the correspondences associated with Hermeticism, is a symbol of interior states of being. Symbolism is the language of the inner kingdom and its laws are those of the Emerald Tablet. Though the exoteric world is no longer literate in the language of symbol, the vestigial traces of planetary correspondences remain in our fascination with astrology and divination. Yet these half-understood sciences are but two strands in the fabric of correspondences and signatures. In a world so closely linked by television, radio, and telephone through the physical means of satellites, we should be prepared to consider the communication network of the inner world, which is linked, in an incredibly sensitive manner, by means of symbolism. "The lower must symbolise the higher, but the opposite is impossible," writes the philosopher René Guénon (213).

From the standpoint of a material world, however, it is hard to realize this fully. The archetypal forms of the macrocosm are no longer potent realities from which the formation of our own microcosm stems. Instead they are remnants of a rejected world model, archaic ghosts echoing in windy streets. If the Hermeticist clings somewhat superstitiously to the resonant correspondences of ancient worlds, it is in order to have some equipment by which to steer. But just as we have refreshed the once-faded archetypes of the native tradition, so must the Hermetic tradition revise its symbologies and estimate their value.

In part 1 we spoke about the Celtic poet's riddling dialogues and boasting pronouncements in which were hidden the mystery teachings of the tribe. Such teachings have been hidden not only in language, but also in number, color, music, sign, symbol, smell, dress, and god form. These correspondences, like the sum of the notes upon the Spindle of Necessity, are harmonized by the aid of one faculty: the gift of the Muse Mnemosyne—memory. The oral traditions of earlier times were upheld under the Hermetic dispensation by means of memory systems. Memory is part and parcel of the law of correspondences, provoking a "Pavlovian" response to the macrocosmic transmission. Analogous signs, symbols, and mnemonics encapsulate certain meanings. Memory is indeed the nervous system of Adam Kadmon, Adam of Light, connecting microcosm with macrocosm.

"Individual souls," said the Neoplatonist Henry More, echoing Plotinus, "proceed from the universal soul; hence that ability to reason, remember and initiate action." Frances Yates, in her exhaustive work on the Theater of Memory, has shown that memory systems were obsessively employed from earliest classical times right up until the Renaissance and beyond as a feature of basic education. After widespread literacy prevailed, such systems became the preserve of Hermeticists (656). The Theater of Memory was an imaginative device whereby sets of facts were associated with locations. A person could, for example, "store" the titles of the Bible's books by associating them visually with the rooms of his house. It was a clumsy system, but it gives an insight into the methods of imaginative visualization employed by Renaissance Hermeticists. These rather cumbersome methods of memorizing were the stock in trade of actors and orators in the ancient world, but for the magician today memorization is a much livelier business that is less dependent upon the scaffolding of immense learning.

The emblematic conceits of alchemical and Rosicrucian books were pictorial initiations using images to trigger inner remembrance. All mediums and psychics who are in touch with the inner world use the screen of their inner senses to receive impressions in this way. But not everyone has the skill to pick up these transmissions. Those who can are the prophets of our age. This is—or should be—the real stuff of divination. The scryer sees not what will be, but rather a hologram of past, present, and future resonances that form a totality that could never be manifested in one particular time scale.

In modern terms, the state of the diviner is nearer to Einstein's theory of relativity: where it can be realized that "matter and energy actually are the same, only in different forms . . . that a tremendous amount of energy exists in a very small amount of matter." (487) For the diviner, time is suspended while the molecules of matter reveal the vast extent of their energy. Such work needs the dedicated exactitude of only the most patient esotericist. Memory of the inner world requires a trance of concentration that can be triggered by the use of suitable correspondences. The prophet Elisha required music to restore his psychic faculties: " 'Let the harper be brought,' said the prophet. And while the harper played behold the hand of the God was upon Elisha." (II Kings 3:15)

An important method for recognizing and organizing inner-world information was the doctrine of signatures, an innate mode of identification in which one part of creation acted as a diagnostic agent or even a healing agent for another part. The greatest of its exponents was Paracelsus, the Hermetic physician, alchemist, and philosopher. To him everything appearing in nature was a sign of an inner reality: "[Y]ou can discern man's immortal part of his visible, innate, characteristic signs, and you can know him even by his appearance; for the outer reveals the inner." (228) Paracelsus not only preached but also practiced this doctrine in his work of healing. Jacob Boehme's doctrines were structured within a complex cosmology, as we have discussed, and his theories underlie not only Steiner's work but also that of Blavatsky. Along with including many Gnostic features such as Sophia and the androgynous Adam, Boehme strove to realize the macrocosmic signatures within the human microcosm.

Hermetic correspondences have been rendered unwieldy due to the accumulation of symbolism. It is axiomatic to cite Venus's day as Friday, her metal as copper, her perfume as rose, and her color as emerald, for instance—yet the list might be prolonged indefinitely and different practitioners might argue over it for eternity. The planetary and other significances of archetypes extend from Sumerian practice down to Ficino's day with great consistency. Add to this the imagery that Christian Kabbalists have heaped on the Tree of Life, which stands like an over-burdened Christmas tree in some textbooks on kabbalistic practice, and finish with Aleister Crowley's book of correspondences, *777*, and you have an ill-assorted relish tray from which to choose (110).

Symbol systems are the memory of a tradition and require a minimum of application if we are to learn the language. The ritual use of some god names is now deemed questionable on the grounds that if the operator does not know the meaning, nature, and therefore the correspondence of the name pronounced, he or she cannot ensure results. The Chaldean Oracles advise: "Change nothing in the barbarous names of evocation, for they are titles of divine things energized by the devotion of multitudes, and their power is ineffable." (660) At the other extreme we must also beware of ascribing modern meanings to ancient metaphors or of considering Hermetic wisdom separate from its contemporary context and the light of present-day understanding. The use of Hermetic and other symbolism by certain psychological schools may lead to a degradation of the traditions represented by these images and archetypes. In addition, it is a dangerous practice in that it involves the nonintegrated use of powerful inner energies.

The current semantic gap in psychic matters is often bridged by the use of psychological language—again, a misleading and inexact terminology when applied to metaphysics. Conversely, the language of spiritual disciplines has been applied by modern physics to those physical phenomena that cannot be scientifically encapsulated—but here there is a venerable tradition in that the medieval and classical proto-scientists, who were often also philosophers, metaphysicians, or physicians, used a common spiritual semantic for describing phenomena in either world. Ultimately, we must make our own correspondences and our own metaphors and models—and if, for convenience's sake, we seize upon earlier esoteric models, we must be aware that these are metaphors, not the thing itself.

It is always important to bear in mind that there are levels of meaning in symbolism. Because we may not perceive all of them at the same time, we should always be prepared to explore deeply before discarding an image. We should beware, however, of allowing the symbol to usurp the inner reality. For example, in the Middle Ages it was a convention to symbolize God the father as a hoary, bearded patriarch. Eventually this symbolism took over so that now God is almost totally identified with this image in most people's minds. The reality, however, is that God is neither father nor mother, male nor female, but pure spirit. Levels of meaning are easily muddled by those used to thinking literally rather than metaphysically—which is why we need the poet, the lucid mystic, and the pragmatic esotericist, who can all operate objectively in the worlds of symbolism and interpret them to the metaphysically confused.

Yet it remains that correspondences are the essence of the magical art and no hard-and-fast rules can be applied. The individual practitioner must make his or her own lists—too often Crowley's book 777 is referred to by students in search of a quick way into a magical system (110). We say, create your own correspondences and then experiment cautiously with their working possibilities. If they don't work, change them.

How do you go about selecting a list of correspondences? This, of course, will be dictated by the spiritual system or mythology with which you are working. The normal seven-planet system is a useful coat hanger on which to drape your magical garments. The normal ascriptions of the Greek and Roman pantheon need not necessarily be employed; any set of archetypes drawn from either native or Hermetic sources can be used. You might use Celtic, American Indian, Egyptian, Platonic, Christian, or kabbalistic archetypes and their correspondences. It is sensible to work with the god forms, spirits, and contacts of your own land and culture, yet many people learn their magic through foreign symbols. The only criterion is that you personally should seek, select, and work with these symbols. We give the following list merely to show a few examples.

USEFUL SYMBOLS AND CORRESPONDENCES

Planets	Angels	Saints	Egyptian Gods
Sun	Metatron	Saint John the Baptist	Re
Moon	Gabriel	Saint Joseph	Khonsu
Mars	Michael	Saint Barbara	Sekmet
Mercury	Raphael	Saint Christopher	Thoth
Jupiter	Tzadkiel	Saint Gregory	Ptah
Venus	Haniel	Saint Mary Magdalene	Isis
Saturn	Uriel	Saint Jerome	Osiris

If the planetary system does not appeal to you, then use another symbol system, such as the Tarot or the Kabbalah. Figure 26 on page 350–351 gives further suggestions on working with correspondences in the Tree of Life. None of these schemes can be pursued, however, without the help of the inhabitants of the inner realms. Plotinus says:

> Even the Celestials, the Daimones, are not on their unreasoning side immune; there is nothing against ascribing acts of memory and experiences of sense to them, in supposing them to accept the traction of methods laid up in the natural order, and to give hearing to petitioners: this is especially true of those of them that are closest to this sphere, and in the degree of their concern about it. (481)

These "Celestials" are those very lordly ones we encountered in part 1 who stand midway between our world and the spiritual realms. It is important to know who they are and how they function upon the inner world. We can know these only through the great scriptures and writings of mystical traditions and through the subjective experience of those who have journeyed to meet them in these worlds. Before we set foot through the inner door ourselves, let us meet some of the beings who will guide our way.

Hidden Masters, Secret Sibyls

In part 1 we spoke extensively about the inhabitants of the Otherworld. These are based on the ancestral wisdom of tribal progenitors, though the archetypes they represent are merely localized expressions of principles that transcend native experience. The Hermetic tradition, as might be expected, has its own inner beings, some of which have been transposed directly from the native tradition with little or no change, while others have originated solely in the Hermetic reality. Some, such as Elijah, appear from the ranks of the ancestors or, in the case of Osiris and Isis, from the realms of the gods. Some arise from hero sagas and other literary sources. The tribe sees its ancestors, the shaman sees greater beings, and the Hermeticist sees the inhabitants of the inner realm, who may appear either in local dress or in the guise of different cultural traditions. It is important that we establish two vitally important principles at this point: (1) The inner inhabitants, which we can call spiritual contacts, have many means of appearing to our consciousness and (2) although they are coworkers on the spiritual plane, they are not God.

Many people may wonder exactly where contacts come from, whether they actually exist, and what their purposes might be. Hidden masters from lost continents, otherworldly visitants—it does not matter whether they have ever really existed or where they have come from. What matters is that people have always behaved as though these contacts were real. Despite appearances, we are not deluding ourselves in this suspension of belief. If the expression "believing or acting as though . . ." offends anyone's reality, then consider the use of x in algebraic equations. If our knowledge of the inner world is sketchy, we are reduced to relying on this x in order to proceed with our research. We take a lot on trust, but we always refer to our known experience in these matters. And this is something that everyone can do. Perfect belief is not possible until spiritual contracts have proved their worth, in much the same way that we cannot count a new acquaintance as a friend until we have entered into the contract of trusting friendship. The human psyche is a plastic substance, allowing itself to be molded, wrapping itself willingly around a desired image. Telesmatic forms, built in meditation, are supplied by our imaginations to house the force of contacts. The fact that these telesmatic forms are drawn from our personal cultural context does not invalidate the existence of contacts. There are more kinds of existence than merely the physical. Our contacts—even if we are unaware of them— show the way and act as companions on our way to inner understanding.

Any of the differences in practice that have existed within the Western Way are due perhaps to the multiplicity of forms and images used in its practices. The teeming variety of hierarchical entities, angels, saints, prophets, masters, and ancestral sages who are "transmitted" to different esoteric practitioners makes it difficult to generalize about the inner world. So often a medium is contacted by or contacts one entity and then bases a world message on the results without "testing the spirits to see if they be of God." The result is a worthless stream of loquacious aphorisms. Discrimination is vital.

On the inner plane, every level of disincarnate entity may be encountered, from atavistic demons to archangels, which is why it is necessary to work through approved channels and with tested contacts. The spiritual contacts with whom we work must be the ones who stand nearest to us in love—they are interested in us just as we are interested in them. The work of our spiritual contacts is not to mislead or endanger us, but to put us on those paths where we can best learn what they have to show us. Failure to develop ourselves with discipline, love, and service is often the reason why certain high-powered contacts are hard to maintain.

Within the context of spiritual contacts, there appears the concept of the hidden master. In modern esotericism the term *hidden master* first appears within the German order known as the Golden and Rosy Cross Brotherhood, which was operational in the eighteenth century. This had a line of "secret chiefs"—a term that would be bandied about a good deal in both Theosophy and the Golden Dawn. But the masters were never clearly defined, even into our own time. Madame Blavatsky's statements about her Tibetan masters seemed to add some clarity, yet these were only expressions of deeper archetypes. Each age pictures the masters differently, each individual clothes these archetypal forces in such a way that Dr. Dee, Merlin, and scores of reverend gentlemen appear to fit the bill. Personality cults of the masters are misleading and unnecessary, as we can understand if we refer to Dion Fortune's *The Cosmic Doctrine* (160): "The Masters as you picture them are all 'imagination.' Note well that I did not say that the Masters were imagination . . . [they are contacted] through your imagination, and although your mental picture is not real or actual, the results of it are real and actual." This book, together with Gareth Knight's essay "The Work of the Inner Plane Adept" (168), cuts through the "informed superstition" that surrounds these figures.

So what exactly are the masters? "Human beings like yourselves, but older. They are not Gods, nor Angels, nor Elementals but are those individuals who have achieved and completed the same task as you have set yourselves." (160) The masters are those adepts who are not incarnate, but who mediate from the inner world those energies that mesh the earth's microcosm and macrocosm. To many it seems that these guardians of tradition, whether incarnate or not, are disproportionately male. There seems to be a superabundance of masters, yet many wonder where the mistresses of tradition can be found.

Why is it that women do not manifest themselves as masters and adepti on the inner planes, or indeed the outer? We find that powerful female contacts are found more commonly within the native tradition because it honoured the divine feminine and representatives of wisdom in feminine forms. Most of the writings about female adepti and inner contacts are of relatively recent date and are the inevitable product of a long neglect of the feminine. However, in the future this trend will change. Even now there are certain adepti in female bodies who have definite inner plane missions and who are genuine adepts. (161)

This text, emanating from the master who stands behind the Society of Inner Light, is frustratingly elusive on the subject. We know that female adepts have existed in all times; we also know well why their work has not been extolled. The period during which the Hermetic tradition has come into being has also been the period in which women have been excluded from the realms of study by virtue of their sex alone. The monopoly of male dominance is now passing and the influence of female initiates is again rising. From the late nineteenth century onward this influence has gathered momentum. It should be pointed out that many women have been preeminent in the rebirth of the Mysteries in the modern era: Madam Blavatsky, Annie Besant, Florence Farr, Alice Bailey, Dion Fortune, and others have all been instrumental in the reformation of the Mysteries for our time (207).

Mystery schools and esoteric movements have been quick to claim as past masters of their orders those who have been famous for their cultural and philosophical achievements: Socrates, Francis Bacon, and Hypatia, for instance. But though the mystical hierarchies of ancient streams of wisdom establish an inner chain of initiates, this does not necessarily imply an apostolic succession of famous incarnate initiates. As we indicated in part 1, knowledge is not necessarily handed down from person to person through the generations, but is often fragmented, hidden, and rediscovered in other ways. Julius Sperber, a German Rosicrucian, writes that the wisdom of Christian Rosenkreutz was an inheritance from Adam, who retained some knowledge of Paradise after the Fall. Apparently this knowledge had passed into many traditions, including Zoroastrianism, Chaldean, Persian, Egyptian, and kabbalistic streams, had been fulfilled in Christ, and ultimately had passed to the Christian theurgists of the Renaissance and to Sperber's own tradition (353). Of course, many mystery schools speak of their tradition in much the same way. More important to consider is our own spiritual lineage (see practice 18, Honoring Our Spiritual Lineage).

If the lineage of the masters and the multiplicity of forms, images, and correspondences employed within the native and Hermetic traditions point up anything, it is that language and symbolism, which are based in material expression, fumble at explaining metaphysical concepts and inner dimensions. The language of the inner world is that spoken by the prophets and sibyls: Elijah, Isaiah, Saint Hildegard of Bingen (244), Joachim de Fiore (351), Saint John the Divine, to name a few. These all speak with the fiery tongue of revelation from a place outside of time, and they each breathe apocalypse and new hope. Like poetry, prophecy is eclectic: Certain images are programmed to trigger in the heart of the initiate a response that remains enigmatic to those who would only be fearful if they understood the inner language. The masters speak in this manner but, as we shall see, only according to the individual understanding and capacity of the pupil.

In the Western Way, there is a tradition that the prophet and sibyl sustain a joint guardianship: They are the Hermetic equivalent of the native tradition's shaman and shamanka and are roles that can be found on both inner and outer planes. Theirs are the voices of the Underworld and of the Stars. If the initiate makes contact with this ancient partnership, he or she is privileged to be a part of its work of weaving the worlds.

In many ways, the archetype of the sibyl comes from deeper or earlier levels of cognizance than that of the prophet. But, though we can polarize sibyl and prophet by associating sibyl with the native tradition and prophet with the Hermetic tradition, we must remember that we are speaking in symbols. The prophets are nearer to our own consciousness and cultural conditioning and are therefore familiar to us. The sibyls exist in a phase of consciousness that is outside modern understanding, although it is beginning to resonate once again. The Muses of classical mythology, the mountain mothers and cailleachs of native tradition, and the sisterhoods of sibyls and priestesses of ancient times are all contained within the sibylline tradition. They come from such deep levels that they often appear as a collective entity rather than as individual entities (384). The Muses also act as a corrective to the over-masculinization of the Western Way.

Sibyls usually work chthonically from the earth in antiphonal exchange with the prophets, who work from the heavens. The sibyl receives and synthesizes the impulse mediated by the prophets and the prophet receives and synthesizes the impulse of the sibyls. Thus each informs the other and is incomplete without the other. The gender of magical polarities is used powerfully as well as symbolically in this paradigm:

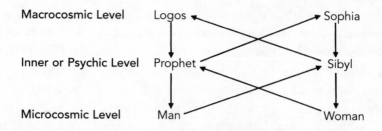

Fig. 24. *On every level of being there is a natural balance between the polarities of masculine and feminine.*

Just as there can be a relationship between man and woman, so there can be a relationship between man and sibyl or woman and prophet. Each male or female operator stands directly under both the inner-level archetype and the macrocosmic archetype with whom he or she may establish a relationship. We have used the terms Logos and Sophia to indicate the Divine Masculine and Divine Feminine principles, but God and Goddess can be substituted, as could any other suitable images. This system of relationships is supraphysical but of great importance to an understanding of magical working. The inner level on which prophet and sibyl stand is the creative and inspirational one. Thus various schools of thought have typified this function variously as *anima* and *animus,* daimon and Muse, or, negatively speaking, incubus and succubus. To find and interrelate with their source of inner wisdom is of paramount importance to walkers between the worlds. Although no specific exercise for this is suggested here, you are certainly invited to meditate upon this interrelationship. If any symbols are required for meditation, the cards of the High Priestess and the Hierophant from the Tarot bring awareness of the sibyl and prophet polarity.

The song of sibyls and prophets interweaves microcosmic and macrocosmic levels. They are the just men and women made perfect who hear our despair and pain, who understand our dedication to the Great Work, and who inspire us secretly within our souls. We might think of them as a celestial and chthonic system of communication that can put us in touch with any part of the cosmos—past, present, or future. Any contact we have with them is tenuous and cannot be sustained for long periods. Like the Mighty Ones in part 1, sibyls and prophets are impersonal, yet their hearts are set on the will of God. A greater understanding of their role might well help revise the rather outdated concept of the master in Western esotericism.

Certain adepts already perform the role of sibyl or prophet while they are still incarnate among us. These, like the saints, live in obscurity, rarely teaching openly. They are known after their death through the work of their disciples. Such adepts are the real hidden ones who perform the work of mediation on behalf of the microcosm. Some are guardians of the ancestral land, others sing the song of Paradise. These marginal shamans are indeed the Just Ones, a quorum of which is traditionally believed to sustain the world from destruction. Their work synthesizes "whatsoever things are good, acceptable and perfect." (Romans 12:2)

Beyond masters and mistresses, prophets and sibyls, there are other guardians, teachers, and contacts who wait for us beyond the inner door. The very concept of an inner communicator is comprehended within the word *maggid,* or "inner teacher," (221) who accompanied the kabbalistic adept. This could be a past master or an expositor of the Kabbalah such as Isaac Luria or Abraham Abulafia or one of the prophets, perhaps Abraham or Elijah. We shall be going on to speak more about such teachers, but let us consider that guide who is nearest to us and with whom we established a rapport in practice 7, Contacting the Guardian: our inner guardian, our angel.

We are told that "[w]hen a person keeps a commandment, he earns an Advocate [angel]." (287) This idea of a heavenly other or guardian angel has become rather thinly strained in its passage from Jewish tradition to Christian tradition. In fact, the Church seems to have become embarassed about its heavenly hierarchies and rarely alludes to the positive work of angels despite Dionysius the Areopagite's codifications of inner inhabitants. The popular view of angels is not much better, and even that great angelologist Dr. Dee himself was not immune to the narrow view of his own age when he was confronted by an angel in female shape. This meeting, recorded in Merrick Casaubon's *A True and Faithful Relation of What Passed for Many Years Between Dr. John Dee and Some Spirits* (81) and occurring through the mediumship of Edward Kelly, was Dee's first encounter with a spirit. He asks, rather indignantly, how she can appear thus. She replies, "Angels (I say) of themselves neither are man nor woman; therefore they do take forms not according to any proportion in imagination, but according to the discreet and appliable will both of [God] and of the thing wherein they are Administrators."

Both Jacob Boehme and Emanuel Swedenborg enjoyed angelic conversations similar to Dee's. Inspirational writers of all kinds attest to angelic assistance, and one of the aims of the medieval magician was to cultivate the knowledge and conversation of his holy guardian angel.

Angels, unlike masters, are not, nor have they ever been, human. They are an order apart. There are angels not only of individuals, but of countries as well. They are the watchers and intelligences of God. G. Davidson's *A Dictionary of Angels* (118) and Peter Lamborn Wilson's *Angels* (653) are recommended for those who wish to read further.

Making Contact

After looking at the many manifestations of those in the inner realm, you might well ask how we are to make contact. Where and how are the sibyls and masters to be found? This is a question that has been asked since the Rosicrucian manifestos first made their impact upon early-seventeenth-century Europe (see chapter 1). The answer is quite simple and involves our clear perception of levels. Theophilus Schweighardt writes in "The Mirror of Wisdom" (531): " . . . according to the announcement of the brethren although the incorporated gathering of all Rosicrucians does not take place in one particular place, nevertheless a true-hearted, devout and upright man can easily and without great trouble come to speak with one of the brethren."

He proceeds to give clues as to the location of the brethren and advises readers to turn "towards the sunrise, noon and evening and finally towards midnight" if they wish to seek the College of Rosicrucian adepts. This reads like a mystery instruction that tells the seeker to look within, not without. The keys of the foursquare watchtower of the day are precisely noted. More openly he says, "Thou seest that the Collegium hangs in the air, where God wills, he can direct it. It is moveable and immovable, constant and inconstant . . . and thou must undergo . . . examination." In this he is telling us that the college of masters is contactable through the common means at our disposal: meditation, prayer, a good life—the very "boring" commonplaces that hide the Mysteries so effectively that few realize their value. Ultimately, he promises us that those seekers whose inner sight and senses are roused will find a master: "I assure thee that a brother will appear in person to thee. It seems wonderfully incredible, but . . . I assure thee, thou shalt find the Art and Collegium, and thus is the only way, for else there is no avail to seek the place, for it is not and yet it is." (531)

Beginners in the Mysteries are often driven to their wits end by this sort of calm assurance that when they are ready, a master will appear. What does this mean? What are the proper channels for approaching him or her? So many great promises seem to be made by mystery orders that we may do well to look closely at the kind of answers one school gives:

> If a man sets out to look for the Path he evinces a desire. That desire is noted by those who watch on the Inner Places and he will be "assigned to a class" according to his temperament. After he has gone a certain way under that tuition he will be put in the care of what is called a "guide" . . . [who] will try to impress the teaching he wishes to convey on the soul óf his pupil by telepathy, and the pupil must try to catch what is "said." Later the pupil will be put into touch with one of the Lesser Masters and be one of a number of pupils for whom that Master is responsible. A guide has only one pupil at a time, but a Master has many. As the pupil advances further he will be passed to Masters of higher grade. His problem will always be to catch what his Master says. (160)

This neat hierarchical system coincides with that of both the theosophical and the Alice Bailey schools. It is in fact from *The Cosmic Doctrine,* by Dion Fortune, the founder of the Society of the Inner Light. In reality, the workings of the system are not always so neat and tidy and progression is not ensured. There is, in effect, no merit system of an earthly kind. This longing for grades and titles of progression is very much an obsession of a past era, although not entirely for those students who want some earthly token or certificate of their divine reward. Some esotericists do indeed form lasting attachments with their inner teachers and progress as Fortune's text describes, but most attend different seminars in the "college of the masters and mistresses of tradition" and learn a balanced curriculum, specializing later on in their experience.

Gaining a contact is something that occurs consciously only later in a student's training. It is not something a student will either be aware of or feel the need for—at the outset it is enough to learn the basics. Yet even in the early stages of training, students should be alert for the contacts that perhaps have already laid their foundations.

The choice of a magical name can very often reveal our secret affiliations with the inner world. Members of the Golden Dawn took Latin tags as their names, often using the acrostic formed from it. W. B. Yeats, for example, took Deus Est Demon Inversus (God Is the Devil Reversed), or DEDI ("dedicated"). Dion Fortune (Violet Firth) took as her own name a contraction of Deo Non Fortuna (God Not Luck). Not all initiates choose names or affiliations in this way. Very often the candidate places him- or herself under the patronage of a past traveler of the Western Way, which may be a case of an overshadowing inner plane teacher or it may be a case of soul-likeness.

Soul-likeness is sometimes misunderstood as reincarnational memory, but as one modern occultist has remarked, "Yes, I remember some incarnations, but are they mine?" This is a valid question to bear in mind: Those who are sensitive to the workings of the inner world have at their disposal a great deal of information. Just because your psyche has keyed into the Egyptian Book of the Dead does not necessarily mean you were a priest or priestess of Maat in a past incarnation. Soul-likeness is that immediate recognition between the worlds that we sometimes experience with people and places in our everyday life. It is possible that both genetic and inner memory are at play here. We instinctively recognize our spiritual kindred and the signature of our spiritual lineage. In the cycles of occurence it is inevitable that there should be an overlay of worlds when that allows us to see down a corridor of time. If you have an experience like this, view it as an opportunity to use wisely and do not discuss it publicly.

Isaac Luria, the Kabbalist of Safed, "could look at a person and tell him how he was connected to the Supernal Man, and how he was related to Adam." (288) Not all of us are so discerning, and even those in the position of teacher would be chary of finding such relationships for their students. Correspondences of this kind can be fraught with danger. When you are operating between the worlds, never confuse yourself with any inner role or entity and always seal off one operation from another. Weak personalities may easily be engulfed by stronger ones. Those esoteric students who take divine names as their magical names should always remember to assume their own street names again when removing their robes!

A true inner teacher will not seek to dominate a relationship with a student; indeed, he or she will strengthen the weak aspects of the student's personality as well as develop the strong, nurturing aspects of the student's essential self without imposing an exclusive imprint. Of course, great teachers do leave their mark upon good students—we have only to listen to some of the most accomplished musicians of our time to hear the unmistakable technique and discipline learned in the master class of a past virtuoso of their instrument. Learning from our contacts is quite similar.

Many new students will ask, "How will I know when I've made a contact?" or, fearfully, "How do I know that my inner teacher is reliable?' The answer to the first question is that we all make spiritual contacts throughout our lives. When our hearts go out to distant friends or when our imaginations are engaged in a gripping book, we are using the same facility that we use in inner realm workings to contact something that is not present.

It is unlikely that you acquire and maintain one without a good deal of basic training, usually of the kind found in a formal mystery school. If you follow a particular tradition, an inner teacher will be standing ready on the periphery of that tradition to help those students who seek the esoteric depths. As to the inner teacher's reliability, Isaac Luria's standards are good ones to measure by: "It must certainly speak the truth, motivate one to do good deeds, and not err in a single prediction." (288) We judge by results or by our intuitive rightness in this matter. Our own wishes and those of our contacts are easily confused, unfortunately, and it is often difficult to tell when we are labeling the inner teacher as unreliable simply to smooth our own way. Inner maturity is a complex thing for anyone to learn; the inner teacher will not spare your feelings when it comes to showing up your imbalances. The best course in these circumstances is to be humble and take advice.

But as much as service to the inner world can be difficult, it can also have benefits. Service to to the will of God, as mystics would term it, is rendered with love, which leads to a reciprocating love that more than balances our efforts. This does not mean that money and all good things will necessarily shower upon you, but that spiritual gifts are given to the coworkers of God.

As we have said before, the pressures of inner work are immense. Esotericists have jobs like other people, and have to cope with children, bills, and difficult circumstances. Life is tough sometimes and only the very resilient or impervious survive the everyday pace. There is no ideal Hermetic existence in a country retreat where dedicated disciples do your living for you while you meditate in blissful quiet. You must manage the brief solitude of your study and meditation period so as to provide a daily refreshment of your spirit. Only in this way can you emerge from your study to face your daily life. The increasing "impatience" of the inner world to bring through certain teachings may sometimes be hard on sensitives who undertake to mediate these into the outer world. Yet this mediatory work is of such importance that many make the sacrifice of time and effort to ensure its proper grounding. At this point we can see that the work of prayer and mediation is very much the same and that each has a reciprocal function.

Mediating the impulse of the inner realm is a matter of timing and rhythm. The esotericist must be familiar with his or her own rhythms and align his or her personal pattern with the macrocosmic one. All esoteric work is done according to prevailing inner currents, tides, and influences. These are measured by means of moon phases, astronomical alignment and conjunction, and the flow of seasonal tides. Time and time again, synchronistic events prove that rhythm is of the essence in the inner world, especially when it is aligned with purpose, pattern, and power. Certain inner alignments come around once in a millennium, much like alignments in the stars, whereby the resonance of one historical time scale is available to us centuries later. As we have described, this is happening now with the rediscovery of the native tradition. Certain aspects of the Hermetic tradition, on the other hand, are not "in phase" at this time.

The resonances of the inner world are mediated to us via the hidden masters and secret sibyls—but this does not mean we are merely passive receivers. After an apprenticeship serving the inner realm, the student is given the means to become a journeyman. Esoteric books often speak of this process as the foundation of a magical personality, which sounds grandiose but amounts to simply having assumed suitable traveling clothes for work in the inner world. This magical personality is acquired through a long process involving a deep knowledge of the self, an integration of our imbalances, and a strengthening of our potentialities until the working image of the self—the Body of Light—can be constructed. This is not an exalted self-image but a vehicle of the higher self, the merkabah or chariot by which we make the ascents. The magical personality is an identification with the holy guardian angel, the Otherworld guide. This stage is accomplished when the student has served his or her apprenticeship in the Great Work and pays homage to no one under God, but is prepared to get on with the work of his or her destiny as a trusted cooperator of the inner realm. Eventually, the student becomes a teacher.

It is often asked how, at the practical level, we go about this process of integration: by faithful practice of daily meditation, continual awareness of the tides of our own life, observation of the shifting pattern of inner and outer tides, dedication to the Great Work, and working harmoniously with our contacts. Adepthood is the adulthood of the inner realm—the inner maturity to work among the many levels of life effectively and responsibly without inflicting our imbalances on others. To be adept means to be skilled, to be master of our craft. An adept is no more than this.

We should remember, however, that there is no such thing as final enlightenment. The cyclic nature of human life renders us all subject to forgetfulness as well as to awareness. We spend our lives striving to establish the ever-shifting parallels by which the inner realm can be perceived and mediated, yet once the magical identification of self with teacher occurs, things can never again be the same. The subtle process of integration and deeper comprehension of both inner and outer events does not make the adept into Superman. In fact, the farther the adept travels into and cooperates with the inner kingdom, the less noteworthy he or she becomes in outer matters. The adage of the magician is: "To know, to will, to dare, and to be silent." In such a perfect balance of elemental attributes, the magician needs no robe in daily life.

It may be that you have already started your apprenticeship in the college of masters, that you have a set of working contacts and that you travel often through the inner door. In the next two sections, those who have not begun their exploration may find a few indicators of how they might start. There are many ways into the Hermetic landscape, and many guardians.

Archetypes and Initiators

Marcilio Ficino wrote: "These great ideas [archetypes] are not at all sterile, they multiply their likenesses throughout the universe." (152) Some archetypes that appeal to national consciousness rarely cross their localized frontiers, but, mythologically speaking, many do emigrate from their native traditions because their archetypal energies are universally recognized. Thus Hermes appears locally in almost every culture, though under different names—Merlin and Thoth are well-known resonances, as we have seen.

Before referring to the following list of archetypes that you might contact, it will be helpful to recall the concept of the regeneration of forms (see part 1, chapter 3). It is the task of each generation to make local the forms it intends to contact. There is no point in working with any energy, however it is imaged, if we have no cultural or personal rapport with it, if its form is inappropriate for the time, or if it has been unused for a long period of time. In these instances the form must be regenerated in our imaginations by means of practical work. For instance, we may decide to use a little-known Sumerian deity in our ritual. If, however, the form whose energy we require has been unused for many centuries, then we must regenerate it, working up to the ritual by first meditating on every known aspect of that deity in great detail and then earth the principles behind the outer form by mediating them through ritual. If there are few or unbalanced results from this method, then the form has not been successfully regenerated. This applies in the Hermetic tradition as well as in the native tradition, where we may often encounter extremes of atavistic reversion.

The following list is made up of archetypes that can be contacted, as well as concepts permeating the Hermetic tradition that can be used as symbolic meditation subjects. We have provided only minimal information on each. If you intend to work with any of the figures or concepts mentioned, be sure that you find out as much as possible about them if they are unfamiliar to you. Most of us are woefully ignorant of the stories that inform our culture. Many of these archetypes are now known only through folk stories, mythological cycles, or psychoanalytic commentary, which leaves them at some remove. This objective distancing of ourselves from the living essence of inner life has been the prime cause of the erosion of our spiritual tradition. A religious tradition is, after all, nothing other than a story to live by—and there are as many stories as there are human lives.

If you intend to use any of these or any other archetypes as a basis for ritual work with others, be aware that the archetype whom you know and experience as a guardian may not necessarily appear so to someone else. In any group work with a specific archetype, make sure that everyone present is experienced in mediating that degree of energy.

This leads us to a reminder about respect. The following is good advice:

Angels won't be invoked
Ancient folios are not Yellow Pages. (412)

As we have said before, we must request—not command—the appearance of any energy from the inner realm. This respect must also extend to systems of belief or practice: We must retain the integrity of each of these, which means, simply put, don't mix systems. Celtic and Enochian systems should not mix; nor should Gnostic and native systems. Isis and Demeter should not appear in the same ritual—one is an aspect of the other, but they are from different mythos. True enough, the Gentile Kabbalah has successfully combined both Jewish and Christian aspects and Gnostic and alchemical systems have much in common, but correspondences can be pushed too far.

Finally, use this list imaginatively—add your own examples and work with any that excite you. It may be that one of these archetypes carries the key to your own spiritual heritage. If you find a particular preference for a tradition arising as a result of your experience with one or several of these archetypes, you might well combine this experience with practice 13, The Temple of Inner Wisdom.

Abaris

Master of the Hyperborean mysteries, which are based in northwest Europe, some say in the region of the British Isles, Abaris was a servant of Hyperborean Apollo. He lived without food and traveled on a golden arrow (the symbol of Apollo). He is said to have been initiated into the Pythagorean mysteries. His fragmentary mythos bears a similar ring to that of Bladdud, the legendary founder of the pre-Roman city of Bath, who also had the ability to fly and instituted the temple and worship of the goddess Sulis—later to become Sulis-Minerva—under the Romans. If Bladdud visited Greece, as legend credits, and was initiated into the Mysteries, it is possible that the two myths have become identified with each other. Abaris links the Celtic native tradition with the early Hermetic tradition. The Hyperborean Mysteries, of which he is master, are safer to work with than those of Atlantis.
References: Stewart (576), Chapman (87), Lievegoed (332)

Adam and Eve

These two are our primal parents, the first father and mother. They can be understood mythologically as the progenitors of every man and woman. Sibyl and prophet are their inner resonances, just as Logos and Sophia are their cosmic and ultimate realities. Their Fall and expulsion from the garden, however interpreted, is representative of a loss of the perfect state. Their prayer of return to that state can also be ours:

> O precious Paradise, unsurpassed in beauty, Tabernacle built by God, unending gladness and delight . . . with the sound of the leaves pray to the Maker of all: may He open unto me the gates which I closed by my transgression, and may He count me worthy to partake of the Tree of Life and of the joy which was mine when I dwelt in thee before. (322)

The Orthodox icon of the Descent into Hell shows the glorified Christ extending either hand to Adam and Eve; he stands upon the bridge of the Cross, and the unregenerate ancestral forces, depicted as locks and bolts, are broken asunder. The Fall may also be seen as the means by which human evolution and experience are initiated.
References: W. Graves (196), R. Graves and Patai (195), Every (146), Apocryphal New Testament (13), C. Matthews (380), Stewart (572)

Adam Kadmon/Anthropos

Common to many traditions, the concept of the hidden Adam or macrocosmic man finds its fullest expression in the kabbalistic Adam Kadmon, whose body is seen as a cosmic glyph of the Tree of Life itself: All ten emanations (Sephiroth) of the Tree of Life are superimposed upon Adam Kadmon's Body of Light. The original stature of Adam was that of the cosmos itself, but, as in the Orphite belief in the apportioning of the deity into men by Titans, the Body of Light is scattered. However, Adam Kadmon, made in the image of God, is the universe in its totality. "The body of Adam is the body of the world, and the soul of Adam is the totality of the souls." The concept of Anthropos is a Hermetic resonance of the kabbalistic Adam Kadmon: "but All-Father Mind, being Life and Light, did bring forth Man (Anthropos) co-equal to Himself." Practice 16, The Caduceus of Hermes, provides a method for experiencing this energy. Any extensive work with the Kabbalah will put us directly in touch with this archetype.

References: Halevi (218), Mead (410), Rudolph (512) Drower (134)

Aeon/Aion

The Aeon is seen as the coming age in which a savior figure will arrive to restore all things to their proper order. Just as the Christian looks to the Apocalypse as the restoration of God's kingdom, so many have looked more recently to the Aquarian Age as a fulfillment of their hope. The child of the Aeon is Horus/Harpocrates. Aion, the god of time, was associated with the cult of Kore at Alexandria. His birth was celebrated on the night of January 5, which is now the eve of Epiphany, which strengthens the connections between the Aeon and Aion. Aion was also identified with Mithras as a god of time. A statue from the Mithraeum at Ostia shows him as a lion-headed man with a serpent girdling his body six times; in his hands are a key and scepter. He has wings with symbols of the seasons on his back and a thunderbolt on his breast, and at his feet are the hammer and tongs of Hephaistos (representative of the alchemist), the pine and tongs of Asclepios (representative of the healer), and the caduceus of Hermes (representing the Hermetic tradition). He is often fused with Agathodaimon (186).

References: Guénon (213), Godwin (185), Lindsay (333)

Agathodaimon

His name means "good spirit." Porphyry tells us that the Egyptians represented him as anthropomorphic, with blue-black skin, a girdle around his waist, a scepter in his hand, and a winged crown on his head. He is the first aspect of Hermes Trismegistos, identifiable with the Anthropos, or cosmic man of light, "who has heaven for head, aether for body, earth for feet and for the water round [him] the ocean's depths." He is perhaps also identifiable with Kneph-Kamephis or Lord of the Perfect Black, who teaches Isis the mysteries of alchemy. Agathodaimon is the shepherd and guardian of all initiates who invoke him thus:

> O mayest thou come into my mind and heart for all the length of my life's days, and bring unto accomplishment all things my soul desires . . . come unto me, Good, altogether good . . . thou whom no magic can enchant, no magic can control, who givest me good

health, security, good store, good fame, victory and strength, and cheerful countenance. (185)

References: Denning and Phillips (128), Lindsay (333), Mead (410)

Akashic Records

Although there is no Western name equivalent to this Eastern concept, the akashic records have become part of the Hermetic way. They are like a vast computer chip of the inner realm, whose guardians are the recording gods, Thoth and Hermes. In earlier times, this role was held by Mnemosyne and the Muses, who are the guardians of the Well of Memory from which the initiate drinks (see practice 2, Analeptic Memory). The Hermeticist's task, like that of the shaman, is to tap this memory system of Hermes and retrieve information not currently available by other means.

Angels

These are the inner protectors of humankind and the helpers of God. They are beings who have never been incarnate and therefore cannot attain the perfection of perfected man. They have been common to the Middle Eastern Mysteries from the time of Sumer. The archangels Raphael, Michael, Gabriel, and Uriel are still invoked to protect the ritual temenos of the magician, just as the evangelists Matthew, Mark, Luke, and John are still invoked to guard the beds of sleeping children. The Hebrew version of this protection is given on page 256. All have their origin in the Babylonian invocation: "Shamash [sun god] before me, behind me Sin [moon god], Nergal [Underworld god] at my right, Ninil [earth goddess] at my left." Such invocations are called *lorica* prayers—prayers that act as spiritual breastplates. They are often found in Celtic tradition, one example being the invocation to Saint Patrick's breastplate, by which the one who prays binds to him-or herself the armor of spiritual protection. Dr. Dee and Edward Kelly worked out a complex angelic system. The Kabbalah has its own angels and archangels. Practice 15, The Foursquare Citadel, will give beginners a taste of the archangelic qualities as represented by their elements.

References: Davidson (118), Dionysius the Areopagite (132), *Oxford Dictionary of Nursery Rhymes* (459), Wilson (653)

Anima Mundi

This is the world soul, the planetary angel or mediator. In Plato's *Timaeus* she is described as the animating principle of creation. She can be visualized as an angelic figure or as a caring mother who holds her mantle of mercy around the totality of the globe. Christians may wish to visualize her as Mater Misericordia, Mother of Mercy, sheltering all human souls under her cloak. Her imagery is closely associated with that of the Shekinah and Sophia. Those who are ecologically minded will find that this archetype can be worked in meditation for the healing of the earth on more than a physical level. (See practice 21, Guardians of *Anima Mundi*.)
Reference: Plato (478)

Anubis/Asclepios

The son of Nephthys and Osiris, Anubis is a form of Asclepios, who, as the son of Apollo and Coronis, is the god of healing. In his sanctuaries, or *asclepeia,* at Tricca, Epidaurus, Cos, and Pergamus, a patient would sleep either on the skin of a sacrificed animal or near a statue of the god, and Asclepios (Anubis) would appear in dreams to him or her to offer counsel. Later, the dreams would be interpreted by a hereditary priestly family. This form of temple sleep can still be performed under Asclepios's aegis, either in a consecrated circle or in bed after having invoked the healing power of sleep. Anubis is depicted as a mature bearded man leaning upon a staff or tree trunk around which winds a serpent. His symbols are the pinecone, the cock, and the caduceus of healing. He is sometimes shown accompanied by a child in a hooded cloak known as Telesphoros, "finisher" or "healer." Asclepios heals on all levels.
Reference: Kerényi (297)

Christian Rosenkreutz

Christian Rosenkreutz is the hero of the *Chymical Wedding* and of the Rosicrucian *Manifesto the Fama Fraternitatis,* a text that has great implications for the Hermeticist. He is the initiate who has entered the Hermetic chamber of the Rosicrucian vault for this time and who has made a compendium of ancient wisdom that all who walk the Western Way may use. His life as told in the *Fama* is parallel to that of Christ: He travels in the East and is acclaimed by sages; he returns to contact the wisdom of the West and founds the Fraternity of the Rose Cross.

The members of the brotherhood, who agreed to meet yearly, traveled into many countries, pursuing their various arts. The discovery of the vault or tomb of Rosenkreutz is told in the *Fama*. Rosenkreutz appears either as a venerable man in his guise as master of the Rosicrucian tradition or in the guise of a candidate to the Mysteries: a young man or youth in simple clothes with crossed red bands over his shoulders—a figure reminiscent of the Fool in the Tarot.

References: P. Allen (8), Knight (313, 310), McLean (353), C. Matthews (380)

Cundrie

The Grail messenger in von Eschenbach's *Parzival,* Cundrie is analogous to the figure of Sovereignty and appears as the Loathly Lady of Celtic tradition. She is the personification of the Wasteland, yet is closely associated with the Shekinah and Sophia. In *Parzival* she admonishes King Arthur, saying that his kingship and the fame of the Round Table have been diminished by the behavior of Parzival, who has neglected to ask the Grail question that will heal the Wounded King and the Wasteland. She laments and demands that a champion ride to right this wrong. Ultimately, Parzival succeeds in his quest, but only at her urging. Cundrie later brings news of the redemptive hope of the Grail's achieving to the Templeisen, as von Eschenbach calls his Grail company. She appears to them dressed in a white wimple, covered by a black hood embroidered with golden Turtle Doves—the sign of the Holy Spirit, of the Divine Feminine principle, and of the Grail itself. Her cloak of black can be visualized as having an emerald green silk lining, indicative of the emerald itself—the Grail. Cundrie is of hideous aspect, a woman of disfigured beauty lined by grief. Her beauty is restored when the Grail is achieved—although this is not stated within von Eschenbach's story. She is the guardian of the Grail quest and a fund of wisdom who will accompany the initiate and advise him or her.

References: C. Matthews (383), von Eschenbach (622)

Dante

Dante may act for our age as Virgil acted for him, conducting him through two of the three regions of existence by virtue of his shamanic experience as poet and Underworld commentator. A meditative reading of the *Divine Comedy* will give us many insights into these realms of states of being. Dante's historical appearance—wearing a scholar's gown with tightly buttoned sleeves and black hood—is appropriate for visualizations.

References: Dante (116), Jackson Knight (265)

Daimon

The daimon is the inner entity or guardian who guides our steps or inspires us. Although we have discussed the daimon as pertaining to the inner masculine quality, which Jungians call the animus, here we consider it in its general sense. Much like the angel, the daimon is the psychopomp of the soul and the mouthpiece of the inspiring god. Orpheus may be seen as a type of daimon, as may the Agathodaimon, who, like the Good Shepherd, leads the soul through the tangled paths of the worlds. Plato's daimon is discussed by Plutarch. In Roman myth every man had his genius, a concept similar to the animus. The figure of the daimon is the inner helper of the Hermeticist. The Tibetan concept of the personal inner deity, or *yidam,* is the Eastern equivalent of the daimon. The word *daimon* is often confused with *demon,* which is indeed a diminishment of the archetype by those who make the gods into the demons of succeeding generations. The concept of the medieval magician who conjures demons to do his will is a faint permutation of an adept working in close harmony with the daimon.

References: Saint Augustine (24), C. Matthews (377), Plato (478), Plutarch (485)

Demeter/Cybele/Rhea

The name Demeter means "mother." She mediates the initiatory sacrifice of motherhood to the initiate. Her mythos was intertwined with that of Isis, so there are many resonances between the two. She is the bountiful earth and with Kore and Hecate she forms a powerful triplicity of goddess energy. Her search and mourning over the lost Kore is at the heart of the Eleusian Mysteries, which she instigated during her wandering in exile. She strove to make an immortal out of Triptolemus, the child of her host, but initiated him instead into the mysteries of agriculture, which, in combination with good husbandry, renders fruitful the barren earth. In her sorrowful aspect she appears as the Black Demeter of Phygala and is thus closely associated with the goddesses Cybele and Rhea. Rhea was the Titaness married to Cronos. She and Metis escaped the banishment of the Titans when Zeus, her son, contended with them. Like her Asiatic counterpart, Cybele, and the Celtic Cailleach Beare, she

is a mountain mother, a wielder of Titanic force. Cybele's mythos deals with an earlier resonance of Demeter's sacrificial motherhood, but Cybele herself is much more dynamic. Hecate seems to have taken over the more terrifying aspects of Cybele and Rhea as a goddess of the cross-roads and of wild beasts. Demeter appears with barley sheaves, usually accompanied by Kore and Hecate. Rhea is a massive seated figure of hieratic power. Cybele appears in a chariot drawn by lions. The image of the Empress in the Tarot is an objective form for beginners to use.
References: R. Graves (192), Pausanius (464), Vermaseren (615), Lucian (339)

Demiurge

In Plato the demiurge, or creator, has none of the malefic overtones associated with the Gnostic demiurge, or false god. He is seen as a benign creator in the *Timaeus*. The Christian image of God the Father has been much devalued because of its association with a white-bearded patriarch who has become a tetchy demiurge after the Gnostic model, which is akin to William Blake's Old Nobodaddy, or the Authority in Philip Pullman's trilogy, *His Dark Materials*. But we can initiate a rerouting of this false image by meditation if we consider the statue from Chartres Cathedral showing God lovingly creating Adam from the dust. A reading of Proverbs 8 will provide the image of God creating the world with the help of the Shekinah/Sophia. Here he is described as a "master workman" delighting in creation.

Non-Christian Hermeticists might wish to consider working with the Egyptian form Khnum or Ptah. Khnum created children upon his potter's wheel and was responsible for implanting the seeds in the mothers' bellies. Depicted as a ram-headed god, he was called Father of Fathers and Mother of Mothers. Ptah was the master of gold smelters and goldsmiths. His temple was called the gold smithy and his priest had names like the Great Wielder of the Hammer and He who knows the Secrets of the Goldsmiths. Ptah is the craftsman god who appears as a closely wrapped figure with a tight-fitting cap, carrying a scepter with the *djed*, or sacred tree symbol, on it.

The images of God as Creator have received the fearful projections of many ages and this archetype stands in need of much positive meditation if the true energy of creation is to flow smoothly. The Gnostic demiurge is analogous to Satan or the devil in Christian terminology—a misapplication of symbolism confusing God and God's antagonist.

References: Blake (46), Lurker (342), Plato (480), Pullman (493), Rudolph (512)

Dionysus

As Dionysus Sabazius, he is the breaker-in-pieces, the Western equivalent of Shiva, yet he is himself rent in pieces by the Titans. His devotees were the Maenads, frenzied, inspired women whose rites good citizens took care to avoid. Dionysus has the chaotic power of Cybele and should be invoked cautiously. He may appear in his Underworld aspect as a rather dark man with long hair and beard, wearing richly embroidered robes and enthroned with his consort Ariadne, whom he raised to immortality as his bride. He also appears as the young lord of the hunt, his nakedness casually draped with a panther skin, in his hand a *thrysos,* or pinecone-tipped wand. He is also called the "child of the double door," signifying his joint birth both from the womb of Semele, his mother, and from the thigh of Zeus, his father. This title also denotes the two births of the initiate: the physical and the initiatory.

References: Daniélou (115), R. Graves (192), Otto (455)

Elijah/Enoch/Metatron

Elijah is the great wonder-working prophet of Jewish tradition (I Kings 17 ff). He ascends to heaven in a fiery chariot and passes his succession to his disciple, Elisha, who prays for a double share of his master's spirit. Elijah then enters the seventh hall of God and perceives the divine will. From then on he is a master or prophetic guardian of tradition. He appears in times of danger to comfort and lead the way to justice. As a coworker of God, he helps all who call on his name. With Enoch he guards the seventh level of Paradise. During *seder* (the Jewish Passover supper), Elijah is invited to join the guests at the table: "Elijah opens up for us the realm of mystery and wonder. Let us now open the door for Elijah." He anounces the Messianic promise to creation. He can be envisaged as a prophet in desert dress, venerable and bearded yet not aged. His oracular bird is the raven. His Islamic name, Khidir, means "green one." He is "the psychopomp whose duty is to stand at the crossways of Paradise and guide the pious to their appointed places." He has been identified with the archangel Metatron.

Enoch, who guards the gates of Paradise with Elijah, is called Idris in Islam. His name means "dedicated or initiated." He never tasted death but was taken up to heaven in a fiery chariot. From there he oversees and instructs the world and, like Elijah, is identified with the archangel Metatron. His journey through the regions of the inner and outer worlds is found in the apocryphal Book of Enoch, which has awesome prophecies regarding the end of the world. Enoch is known among the Mandaens as Anosh.

Metatron is the greatest of the archangels. His stature is "equal to the breadth of the whole world"—which was the stature of Adam before the Fall. Clearly, Metatron is identifiable with the Body of Light. He stands at the gate of Kether on the Tree of Life and can be visualized as a shining angelic form with many wings.

References: Bronstein (58), Davidson (118), Book of Enoch (51), Halevi (220)

The Fisher King

The Fisher King is the wounded monarch of the Grail cycle. All but he partake of the Grail mystery—his suffering suspends him between the worlds. He is at once identifiable with the wounded land, the Grail guardian, and Christ. The Corpus Christi carol is sung of him. He usually appears as an ancient, wasted figure lying on a bed. To offer the cup of healing to him is to work for the mending of all riven things. He is the wound in creation, which only the highest form of self-sacrifice can restore. He cannot relinquish his role as Grail guardian until the Grail achiever comes to take his place.

References: J. Matthews (396), C. Matthews (382), Stewart (575)

Four Holy Living Creatures/Elemental Guardians

These mighty correspondences are best understood as guardians of the cosmic year. They equate to the elemental guardians and are applied in many traditions (see the following chart). They appear in Ezekiel's vision and are applied to the Four Evangelists in Christian tradition.

Vision of Ezekiel	Evangelist	Kabbalistic World	Element	Fixed Zodiacal Sign
Human	Saint Matthew	Aziluth	Fire	Aquarius
Lion	Saint Mark	Yetzirah	Water	Leo
Bull	Saint Luke	Assiah	Earth	Taurus
Eagle	Saint John	Briah	Air	Scorpio

References: Halevi (220), Knight (309)

The Grail

This is the vessel of redemption, knowledge, and fulfillment. It is sought everywhere but achieved by few. It is not a physical object, although real cups, chalices, and cauldrons have embodied its virtues as the inner symbol was superimposed over them by means of worship or cult focus. It is a powerful resource for meditation and many pathworkings can be made from the texts having it as their subject. The Grail is important to followers of the Western Way because it unites native and Hermetic traditions in its forms as cauldron and alchemical stone. It represents a passing forward into other realms and gives direct access to the Greater Mysteries.

References: E. Jung and von Franz (285), Knight (311), Malory (364), J. Matthews (396, 399), Matthews and Green (403), *Quest of the Holy Grail* (495), *Perlesvaus* (471), Chrétien de Troyes (95)

Hermaphrodite

The perfected Great Work is symbolized by this figure, sometimes called the Rebus or Androgyne. Rather than viewing it as a blatantly sexual anomaly, the ancients realized the hermaphrodite as the summation of perfection. Practice 19, The Shepherd of Stars, gives a meditative use for this figure. The word is a conflation of Hermes (god) and Aphrodite (goddess), and can be considered the symbol of the yin-yang in the West.

Reference: Fabricius (147)

Hermes

The messenger of the gods, the guardian of travelers, and imparter of wisdom, Hermes invented the lyre and exchanged it for the caduceus of Apollo, which he used to care for the celestial herds. He can be visualized as Roman Mercury, with winged sandals, cap, and caduceus, or as Agathodaimon. He lays his staff upon the eyes of the dead and is sometimes called the whisperer. As chthonic Hermes, he is the keeper of wisdom and ancient knowledge, coming in dreams and meditation to impart his secrets. As Thoth-Tehuti, he is seen as the inventor of the Egyptian system of hieroglyphs and the keeper of the book of initiation. Hermetically he can be seen as he appears on the famous pavement at Siena: a mature figure in heavy robes, wearing a high pointed cap.

References: R. Graves (192), Kerényi (294), Mead (410)

Horus/Harpocrates

Horus is the child of the Aeon, the son of Isis and Osiris from a union effected by Isis after Osiris's death and dismemberment. The symbols of Horus are two eyes—of the moon and the sun. He is also is seen as a hawk-headed man. As a child he appears seated in a lotus with his finger to his lip, signifying silence. He shares the symbolism of both Apollo and Mabon (see chapter 3, page 85).
References: Hope (252), Lurker (342)

Isis

Isis is the divine savior goddess; her power alone brought together the scattered fragments of her brother/husband's body, which was a feat emblematic of the unification of the Body of Light. Her cult spread throughout the Roman world as far as Britain. Like the Virgin Mary, she holds under her cloak all lesser manifestations of the Divine Feminine. She is a particularly relevant archetype for the present age, being a comprehensive manifestation of the Goddess. Her influence continues to the present day: The Fellowship of Isis, a worldwide network of all pathwalkers who acknowledge the Divine Feminine, was founded in Ireland in the 1970s. Isis appears dressed in white robes with rainbowlike translucence, holding an ankh or *systrum* in her hand. The knot on her girdle makes an ankh-shaped loop. A beautiful invocation to Isis and her many aspects can be read in Apuleius. (See fig. 19, page 287.)
References: Apuleius (14), Hope (252), Plutarch (484)

Joseph of Arimathea

Joseph is the Jew who gave Christ burial in his own tomb and provided his shroud. He also collected in two cruets the blood and water from the side of Christ at the Deposition from the Cross—the earliest form of the Christian Grail. After the crucifixion, Joseph was imprisoned for many years and was kept alive only by the Grail, which miraculously nourished him physically and spiritually. He was instructed secretly by Christ during his captivity and afterward fled to Europe with his family to found a line of Grail guardians. He is said to have landed in France or, more usually, in Glastonbury, where he founded the first Christian church in honor of the Virgin Mary. He is the contact for Grail wisdom.
References: de Boron (120), J. Matthews (396), Apocryphal New Testament (13)

The Just Ones/Sibyls/Prophets

The Lamed-Vau, or thirty-six hidden saints, are those for whom the world exists, according to Jewish tradition. They reveal themselves in times of danger and keep our world in balance as mediators between the worlds. Like the angels, the sibyls and prophets can be seen entirely as inner figures, but their role is also a grade of inner working to which those still incarnate may attain. Like the Just Ones, they are the hidden inspirers and sustainers of the earth (266). They can be visulized as a double choir that sings the song of creation antiphonally. Jan van Eyck's painting *The Adoration of the Lamb* may serve as an inspiration for this visualization. Alternatively, we may see sibyls and prophets in a classical Greek mode, as a chorus of women and men who chant the mighty themes of the story while circling in a round dance.
Reference: Schwartz-Bart (530)

The Logos

The Logos is the word of God just as Sophia is the wisdom of God. Gnostics, Platonists, and Christians have all integrated this concept. Chapter 1 of Saint John's Gospel offers much for meditation regarding the Logos. For practical purposes, the Logos can be visualized as Christ the King—crowned, robed in glory, and standing triumphant upon the cross—or as Christ Pantocrator, Lord of the Earth, with an open book. The Logos comes to ransom the soul in order that it may unite with its syzygy: with Sophia in the Gnostic tradition or, in the Christian tradition, with the individual souls of the created faithful in the person of the Virgin Mary. The energy fo the Logos is that of God the Son, who shows the Way. The following chant is his promise:

Send me, O Father!
Seals in my hands, I will descend;
Through Aeons universal will I make a Path;
Through Mysteries all I'll open up a way!
And Forms of Gods will I display;
The secrets of the Holy Paths I will hand on,
And call them Gnosis.

References: Mead (410), Rudolph (512)

Mary the Virgin

The Virgin is also known as Lady Mary. Just as Isis subsumes all earlier goddesses under her aegis, so Mary comprehends all the goddess aspects of the Divine Feminine throughout the world. Eventually, all goddess shrines in all locations where Christianity has penetrated have become remembered as "Our Lady of [name of place]." Mary shows us God as Mother. Although orthodox theology does not consider her a goddess and instead accords her the kind of honors that are shown to angels and saints, Lady Mary is enshrined in the hearts of the faithful with a special love because she shows them the face of their first homely Mother. She can be visualized in either of three aspects that correspond to the three Mysteries of the Rosary: as a young maiden dressed in white with a blue cloak, as the sorrowing mother in black at the foot of the cross, or as the Woman Clothed with the Sun (Revelation 12).
Reference: C. Matthews (383)

Mary Magdalene

One of the female disciples of Jesus, she was first to discover his Resurrection and declare it to the disciples, who were in hiding. The loyalty and special place of Mary Magdalene are so notable that they have passed into folklore—often to the extent of making her Christ's physical consort. She shares the virtues of Sophia and Cundrie and knows Christ's inner teaching, which he entrusts to her (although the other disciples complain that she is only a woman). Her reputation as a reformed prostitute is due to her identification with the penitent woman in Mark 14. She and the Virgin Mary are the female pillars flanking the Incarnation of Christ, just as the two Josephs—Lady Mary's husband and Joseph of Arimathea—are the two male pillars. While the Virgin Mary is depicted wearing blue, Mary Magdelene is often shown in green, a woman of mature beauty with long, unbound hair.
References: Baigent, Lincoln, and Leigh (29), the Bible (45), Rudolph (512), *The Nag Hammadi Library* (435), C. Matthews (383)

Melchizedek

Melchizedek was the priest-king who came to welcome Abraham with gifts of bread and wine after his victory over the kings of Edom. This is seen as a prefiguring of the Eucharist and of the eternal high priesthood of Christ. Hermeticists consider Melchizedek an inner master because he had neither "beginning of days nor end of life." He is regarded to have come from the planet Venus, bringing honey and asbestos, and his motif is woven into the Grail legends. Melchizedek is a strong and high contact who will bring the reader into the presence of eternal things. He can be seen in the statue outside Chartres Cathedral, crowned as a king and bearing a cup that holds a stone or a piece of bread.

References: The Bible (45), J. Matthews (396), Fortune (169)

Merlin

Merlin is the archetypal magus of the Western Way, the genius of Britain, and a guide to many inner realms. He can appear as a white-bearded sage, a beautiful youth, or a savage wild man. His contact can produce high prophetic insight. He is especially important to the Western Way because he stands behind the native Mystery impulse and yet has strong affinities to the Hermetic path. His origins are obscure but his name means "from the sea." He has been identified with an Atlantean master. (See also chapter 3, page 87.)

References: Knight (311), Stewart (573), Stewart and Matthews (578), Tolstoy (598)

Mithras

God of creativity and light and divine child born at the winter solstice, in his mythos Mithras bears a strong resemblance to Christ. As a slain god his symbol is that of the bull, the raven, and Sol Invictus ("the triumphant sun"). His cult was decidedly male-oriented and had a series of initiatory grades: the Crow, the Secret, the Soldier, the Lion, the Persian, the Runner of the Sun, the Father, and the Father of Fathers. Mithras usually appears as a youth dressed in Phrygian cap and short tunic. He is an excellent overseer of esoteric training, upon which his followers set great store.

References: Godwin (185), Cumont (112), Vermaseren (616), Mead (407)

Mnemosyne and the Muses

Zeus lay with Mnemosyne for nine nights, after which she gave birth to the nine Muses, who do the work of the sibyls. She is "memory as the cosmic ground of self-recalling." Her dual role is of memory and forgetfulness (Lethe). These two aspects are combined in practice 2, Analeptic Memory. When the Muses sing, sky, stars, seas, and rivers stand still to listen. They can appear in the shape of a bird or as depicted in the Mantegna Tarot. Their names, patronage, and symbolic representations are given in the following chart. While their energies have been greatly neglected since the Hermetic revival of the Renaissance, no subsequent forms or symbolic representations have appeared to replace them.

Muse	Patronage	Symbols
Clio ("giver of fame")	history	heroic trumpet and waterclock
Euterpe ("giver of joy")	flute playing	flute
Thalia ("festive")	comedy	shepherd's crook and comic mask
Melpomene ("the singer")	tragedy	tragic mask and Hercules' club
Terpsicore ("she who dances")	lyric poetry and dance	cithara
Erato ("awakener of desire")	love poetry	tambourine
Polyhymnia ("she of many hymns")	storytelling and heroic hymns	lyre or portative organ
Urania ("the heavenly")	astronomy	celestial globe and compasses
Calliope ("of the beautiful voice")	epic poetry	stylus and tablets

References: Kerényi (294), McLean (354)

Nephthys

Nephthys is the sister of Isis. Her function, like that of Saint Brigid, is to be the midwife and guardian of the Holy Child. She has the ability to be a revealer of hidden things and appears as the supporter of Isis, her arms protectively raised. Her headdress bears the basket of offering, which is her symbol. She can be seen as an inner guardian of Isis's veiled role as mistress of the Mysteries.

Reference: Hope (252)

Orpheus

Orpheus's early beginnings bear traces of the Thracian shaman. Ovid's *Metamorphoses* gives a romantic story of his descent to Hades to reclaim his wife, Eurydice. Like Hermes and Thoth, he often appears as a spokesman for the gods. His reappearance in medieval times as Sir or

King Orpheo established him in native tradition as a harrower of the Underworld, a visitant to Faeryland. The Orpheus of the Renaissance is the spirit of music incarnate, the master of the Muses. The character of Tamino in Mozart's *The Magic Flute* is based on Orpheus; he winds through the tangled webs of the Queen of Night in order to rescue Pamina. Orpheus is an oracular god, like Bran the Blessed. His dismemberment and beheading make him akin to Osiris and others. Ficino restores Orpheus as a psychopomp, divine intermediary, and celestial musician. He appears very like Apollo, of whom he is a close resonance. Traditionally, he is depicted as singing in the wilderness, surrounded by enthralled beasts, or, as in figure 25, with the Muses.

References: Warden (633), Ovid (456), *Orphic Hymns* (454)

Fig. 25. Orpheus plays his harp within the circle of the nine Muses.

Osiris

The brother and consort of Isis, Osiris is one of many verdant gods who are cut down. His mythos is in Plutarch. His appearance as a green-skinned figure in white wrappings recalls his nature, as does his symbol of the *djed,* or tree, in which, according to some legends, he is imprisoned. Like John Barleycorn, Dionysus, and others, he is the grain of wheat that must fall into the earth in order to bear seed.

References: Budge (62), Hope (252), Plutarch (484)

Persephone

Persephone is the Underworld name of the Kore (maiden). Abducted by Hades, she descends to the Underworld, where she changes her nature rapidly from that of maiden to chthonic hag. While she is under the earth, Demeter mourns and winter reigns. She is the merciful maiden and is hospitable to the initiate who takes the Underworld journey. Her appearance can be that of a spring maiden of hieratic stillness and simplicity or of a heavily robed queen with a glittering black diadem upon her head and her unbraided hair frozen into lines of icy water. Her Underworld aspect should not be shunned, for the initiate must either go the way of the White Cypress to the Well of Memory within Persephone's realm or turn back from the Mysteries.

References: R. Graves (192), Stewart (575), Kerényi (293), Fortune (164, 167)

Prester John

Prester John is the mysterious Christian king of the East and the son of Parzival's half brother, Feirfiz, and Repanse de Schoye. A description of his kingdom and its strange inhabitants (the phoenix and the unicorn) paint it as a type of Paradise. The Grail is sometimes said to be kept there in a great temple. Prester John is considered by some to be the Grail guardian for our own age. Sometimes he appears as a glorious king in rich robes, wearing a triple crown, but more often he is a young man in a plain white robe who has features with a slight Middle Eastern cast. He holds the keys to several inner landscapes, including that of the Eastern Grail and the paradisal home.

References: J. Matthews (396), Silverberg (540)

Prometheus

It was Prometheus who stole fire from heaven in a fennel stalk to give to human beings. He is considered to be the Titan who created humanity and who resisted his race's planned destruction by Zeus. The sufferings of the world were visited upon him because of his championship of the earth's inhabitants: He was chained to a pillar, where a vulture tore out his liver—which grew anew every night—throughout eternity. With the exiled Shekinah of Jewish tradition, he represents the pain of incarnation, but he is ever hopeful of humanity's potential. He is a mighty man and a rugged wielder of the earth's elements. The symbol for nuclear disarmament seems to be his symbol of upheld stalk in reverse. This might well serve as a useful symbol for meditation.
References: Kerényi (294), R. Graves (192)

Psyche

The story of Cupid and Psyche is told in Apuleius and is useful for meditation. Beautiful Psyche is of the soul, which is what her name signifies. She marries the god Cupid but lies with him only in darkness. Her sisters suggest that she has wedded a monster, so, at their bidding, she hides a lamp to later reveal the beautiful sleeping god. She incurs the jealousy of Cupid's mother, Venus, and must perform the well-known impossible tasks. She achieves these with Cupid's help and is made immortal. Her story has been retold by C. S. Lewis in a way that highlights the interrelationship of the goddess's light and dark aspects.
References: Apuleius (14), Lewis (331), Knight (310)

The Saints

Saint Paul calls the saints "a great cloud of witnesses." In the early days of the Church, all Christians were saints, but later the title was reserved for those who merited honor in recognition of their holy and exemplary lives. All elements of humanity are represented by the saints. Many people in the Christian West are given the names of saints who might be their inner world patrons. A great number of energies that were once associated with gods are now represented under the patronage of saints. Their patronage of us can be invoked by prayer and meditation and they can serve as guardians for those who walk the path of the Way. They can be envisaged as facets of a mighty crystal that is the Body of Christ.
Reference: *Oxford Dictionary of Saints* (460)

Seth

As the inheritor of Adam's paradisal experience, Seth has been a figure of redemptive hope to many traditions. His descendants, both earthly and spiritual, partake of the gnosis of life. Among the Mandeans Seth is called Shitil; at his death the soul must outweigh his purity if it is to enter into the kingdom of light. He can be seen as a tall, strong man whose form is almost angelic. His head is intelligent and between his brow is a flame of light representing his inner illumination. He is one of the guardians of gnosis.

References: *The Nag Hammadi Library* (435), Quinn (496), Rudolph (512)

Shekinah

Shekinah is the Jewish figure of wisdom. She "brings the gift of the queen to them that wander with her in exile." (209) She is God as Spirit, the coworker at Creation (Proverbs 8). Shekinah represents the emanatory presence of God among created life and is thus closely associated with both Sophia and Anima Mundi. Her symbolism bears traces of earlier goddess cults. She is the pillar of cloud by day and by night the pillar of fire that accompanied the Ark of the Covenant in the desert. She is the cloud on the sanctuary in the temple of Solomon. It is best to visualize her in these images or as a mighty pair of wings outstretched overhead (see the prayer on page 256). She is also seen as a sorrowful widow who walks the road in exile, much like Isis.

References: Matthews (383), Patai (463)

Sophia

Divine wisdom herself and syzygy (see below) of the Logos, Sophia can be found in many forms throughout the world. She is represented as a winged angelic figure dressed in red and gold, with a diadem on her head and the world at her feet. Practice 13, The Temple of Wisdom, will give a direct contact with her. She "dwells with all flesh," according to the gift of God, and can therefore be the possession and heritage of all living things.

References: *The Nag Hammadi Library* (435), Rudolph (512), the Bible (45), C. Matthews (383)

Syzygies

According to Gnosticism, syzygies are divine partners or consorts. Sophia and the Logos are the prime syzygies, but Solomon and Sheba can be seen as illustrations of this concept as well, representing the union of knowledge and wisdom. William Blake's theory of emanations, which was probably derived from Eastern sources, embodies a Western view of the syzygies Shiva and Shakti. His poem "Jerusalem" reveals a system of deities and their consorts. In alchemy the union of syzygies is illustrated by the image of the *coniunctio* or the *hieros gamos,* the "holy wedding."

References: Blake (46), Rudolph (512)

Zeus

Zeus, who subdued his father, Cronos, by castrating him, seems to have taken on the mantle of the evil demiurge. Yet he is aptly named Pantomorphos—"of many forms." Like the Celtic Math and Gwydion, Zeus is a shapeshifter. His many amours and unions, rather than philandering, are actually to be read as reflections of the divine union with all life. A type of the Norse god Odin, Zeus lies with Mnemosyne for nine nights (while Odin hangs on Yggdrasil for nine days and nights). Both of these gods are initiates of the mystery knowledge. Zeus is married to divine female representations of the three native levels of existence—Persephone (the Underworld), Maia (the earth), and Hera (heaven)—and so has knowledge of the three realms, much like the shamanic Odin, who comprehends the three levels of the World Tree, Yggdrasil. Zeus may appear in any form but his symbol of the thunderbolt suggests his power. He can be visualized as the Emperor card of the Tarot.

References: R. Graves (192), *Kore Kosmou* (314), Kerényi (294)

The Hermetic Landscape

Everyone has an inner landscape. Thomas Vaughan wrote in his *Lumen de Lumine* (614): "[T]he way to this place—and the place itself—[has] been unknown for a long time, and it is hidden from the greatest part of the world. But notwithstanding that it be difficult and laborious to discover this way and place, yet the place should be sought after." If you have already attempted practice 8, The Two Trees, you will have begun to see certain facets of the Otherworld, that inner reality of the native tradition.

The Hermetic tradition has its own landscape, which unlike the rarely depicted Otherworld has frequently made its appearance within the emblematic designs of both magical and alchemical texts. We will remember that in the Otherworld, one of the aspects of the native tradition's inner reality is the island paradise or garden. We can see elements of this aspect in medieval illuminations, which include angels sporting in Paradise and fantastic beasts prancing in the Garden of Earthly Delights as in Bosch's painting. This image of the garden is also present in the Hermetic traditions, and here we can step from one side of reality into the other. This fusion of Otherworlds is achieved by the connecting impulse of Rosicrucian and alchemical imagery, both of which used native symbologies as a basis for their own inner explorations. The result is a compelling mixture of both native and Hermetic traditions. The key image of this mixture keeps its perfume.

> *O no man knows*
> *Through what wild centuries*
> *Roves back the rose.* (626)

The rose is a signature of the tranquil continuity of the esoteric tradition: Wherever it grows, there the tradition flourishes. Esoteric knowledge has been personified as a beautiful veiled maiden who must be sought by the lover of wisdom. This identification has made it possible to address the Virgin as *rosa mystica*. There is no way into the *hortus conclusus* ("enclosed garden") save by love, the desire to find the hidden rose that grows within. That which is spoken *sub rosa* is "under the rose": the knowledge that is transmitted only within the hidden garden itself, the wisdom that is freely given by the beloved to the lover. In alchemy the rose symbolizes this wisdom, and the *rosarium*—the rose garden—symbolizes the Great Work itself. The symbol of the Rosicrucians is the rose cross—the rose of the spirit blooming upon the cross of the elements—also a symbol of the marriage of pagan and Christian streams. Before the rosa mystica became the symbol of the Virgin Mother, it was the Lady Venus's sign (380).

The garden makes its easy transition as an inner landscape for both native and Hermetic traditions not only through the medium of pictorial representation, but also through the works of poets and mystics. From the medieval allegory *Le Romaunt de la Rose,* in which the poet's quest is for the rose itself, to Edmund Spenser's *Faerie Queene,* the otherworldly paradise slowly becomes transformed. Enclosed within the intricate knot gardens of sixteenth- and seventeenth-century Europe, the spiritual journey is enacted by Christian in Bunyan's *Pilgrim's*

Progress and by Christian Rosenkreutz in *The Chymical Wedding* (313). The esotericist makes his or her way through the ceremonial mazes planted to reflect spiritual progress. Trees, arbors, and herbs are arranged to mirror planetary correspondences so that the microcosmic hortus conclusus mirrors the macrocosmic garden of the heavens.

Within the landscape are the hermit's oratory, the alchemist's laboratory, and the astrological tower from which planetary movements are observed and computed. There are lakes, streams, and cunning displays of water fountains from classical water deities and creatures of the deep. Sometimes the overtly Hermetic nature of the garden is apparent, as at Edzell Castle, Angus, Scotland, where a garden of the planets can still be seen (358), or as at the now desolate gardens devised by Salomon De Caus for the elector Palatine at Heidelberg (355).

Beyond the places of habitation, in the wilder and inaccessible regions, stands the Mountain of Initiation—sometimes called Mount Abiegnus or the Invisible Magic Mountain—where the initiate stakes his or her adepthood on pilgrimage and discovery. As in the Kingdom of Prester John, here too the traveler encounters beasts that seem to have leaped from the pages of heraldic and alchemical scrolls: the green lion, the crow, the unicorn, and the phoenix. Here sits the pelican in her piety and there soars the crowned eagle. Each beast symbolizes a secret process to be undergone. The traveler finds the way by means of sigils engraved in the rock. The totemic symbols of the Hermetic tradition are as powerful and elusive as the ancestral totems we sought in part 1.

These are only some of the aspects of the Hermetic landscape waiting to be discovered. Just as books of hours presented biblical scenes with glowing intensity for the active participation of the faithful in the Middle Ages, so do the emblem books of Hermetic allegory reveal a rich mine for our own meditation. *The Western Mandala,* by Adam McLean (359), is a particularly good starting point for the apprentice Hermeticist, but more and more alchemical texts, complete with their illustrations, are being made available. Imaginative work with some of these offers us further opportunities to enter and explore the Hermetic landscape. Your own means of entry may be the black and white pillars of the Tree of Life, which we can visualize as a gateway before us. Just remember that your guide should be someone appropriate to the scene you will be contemplating—Hermes or Christian Rosenkreutz, for instance.

But the emblem books are not the only sources for inspiration. The

Tarot, which we now interpret in the light of modern consciousness, is actually a book of medieval emblems embodying important aspects of the esoteric world model: Death's Grim Reaper; the rota of Fortune's Wheel; the savage, sublunary world of the Moon. The four suits of the Tarot represent the four elements. The origins of the Tarot have been hotly debated in esoteric circles. The argument that they derive from Egyptian sources can be traced to the rediscovery of Egypt that motivated the French esoteric world at the time of Napoleon's Egyptian campaign, during which the Rosetta Stone was found. Some two decades later the stone was deciphered, and this achievement, like the translation of the *Corpus Hermeticum* in the fifteenth century, led to a series of revivalist inventions. In his *History and Practice of Magic* (96) Paul Christian gives a splendid pathworking in which the initiate is asked to imagine initiation within the Great Pyramid, wherein all the images of the Major Trumps are operative. The initiate travels a route, meeting frightful and tempting images along the way that are overcome by means of the Major Trumps. The initiate fails only if he or she cannot comprehend the lesson of each Trump. A similar pathworking can be found in Basil Rakoczi's book *Fortune Telling*. In it the initiate passes through three caverns of initiation (499).

Adam McLean (354) has suggested an alternative source for the development of the European Tarot based on his study of the Mantegna Tarot (c. 1465). These cards—fifty in all—emanate from the School of Ferrara and are based upon the Platonic academies of the mid-fifteenth-century Renaissance. The cards are split into five decades, representing (1) the conditions of life from Beggar to Pope; (2) the nine Muses and Apollo; (3) the seven liberal arts, including philosophy, poetry, and theology; (4) the seven cardinal virtues with the spirits of astronomy, chronology, and cosmology; and (5) the celestial hierarchy of the seven planets together with the eighth sphere, the *primum mobile* and the First Cause. Despite its different title, the symbology of this Tarot is remarkably similar to that of traditional packs. The card representing Mars in the fifth decade, for instance, is identical to the Chariot; Jupiter stands in a mandorla, like the World. Obvious qualities like Justice and Strength are almost identical. The "conditions of life" decade gives us the Fool, the Beggar, and the Magician, who is clearly derived from the card of the Artisan, shown in the Mantegna Tarot with his table and tools of the trade. The Squire and Knight pass into the Minor Trumps as court cards.

Although there are fragmentary Tarot packs that date from before this time and follow the traditional schema, it is interesting to conjecture just what kind of symbolism is common to both. The Mantegna Tarot shows the basic virtues, qualities, cosmologies, abilities, and conditions of human life that were the unwritten norms of medieval life. These images were familiar to all, even the unlettered. Look through your own Tarot pack with new eyes: What kind of symbolism and culture created this book of wisdom, which its numerous archetypes? With the key of the Mantegna Tarot we can unlock many of these Tarot enigmas for our own time. Few modern Tarots have succeeded in replacing the old symbolism with one that is efficient in our age, despite the vast number now available. The mighty archetypes behind the Major Trumps are now commercially mangled by formal latter-day Tarot readers who, in striving to bring the cosmic message to their clients, reduce even the microcosmic message of the Tarot to a handful of glib material applications. But it is possible to enter each card as though it were a picture, explore the scene, and speak with the archetype. In this way the Tarot can become an initiatory system and a way of initiatory training, for its Mysteries bear a great deal of meditation (12, 206, 289, 487). It was the custom of the Golden Dawn that every initiate create his own Tarot. This method of teaching is one that many people have adopted. Some of these Tarots have been published but most are highly personal, and only a handful reach beyond and work upon a macrocosmic level.

The Kabbalah too provides a rich opportunity for initiatory training. To the uninitiated, the Tree of Life appears like an underground map—a two-dimensional set of circles connected by lines. But each of the Sephiroth is a multidimensional place and is as real a destination as New York City or San Francisco. Of course, here we can in no way include the infinite number of possibilities for exploring such a complex glyph as the Tree of Life, but *A Practical Guide to Qabalistic Symbolism,* by Gareth Knight (308), explains where the usual correspondences and inner symbolism may be more readily explored within the Tree of Life. It is indeed a vast field of exploration that has occupied both Hebrew and Gentile Kabbalists for centuries. There is no one method of applying correspondences—you find some of your own, but there are many who have shown the way and provided signposts. The Kabbalah presents a unique method for exploring the Hermetic landscape in that its system is also a way of life for those who can realize its possibilities.

TABLE 1: MAGICAL CORRESPONDENCES ON THE TREE OF LIFE

Number/Name (translation) of Sephira	Planetary Image	Virtue	Vice	Magical Image
1 Kether (crown)	Primum mobile	Attainment of the Great Work	None	An ancient bearded king in profile
2 Chokmah (wisdom)	The zodiac	Devotion	None	A bearded man, a father
3 Binah (understanding)	Saturn	Silence	Avarice	A mature woman, a mother
X Daath (knowledge)	Sirius	Selfless perfection	Spiritual pride	A head with a male and female countenance facing in either direction
4 Chesed (mercy)	Jupiter	Obedience	Bigotry and tyranny	A strong king, crowned and seated on a throne
5 Geburah (severity)	Mars	Courage	Cruelty	A warrior in a chariot
6 Tiphareth (beauty)	Sun	Devotion to the Great Work	Pride	A child, king, or sacrificed god
7 Netzach (victory)	Venus	Unselfishness	Lust	A beautiful naked woman
8 Hod (awe)	Mercury	Truthfulness	Dishonesty	A hermaphrodite
9 Yesod (foundation)	Moon	Independence	Idleness	A beautiful naked man of strength
10 Malkuth (kingdom)	Earth	Discrimination	Inertia	A young woman, crowned, seated on a throne

Tree of Life diagram with Sephiroth and connecting paths:

Sephiroth:
- KETHER Crown 1
- CHOKMAH Wisdom 2
- BINAH Understanding 3
- DAATH Knowledge X
- CHESED Mercy 4
- GEBURAH Severity 5
- TIPHARETH Beauty 6
- NETZACH Victory 7
- HOD Awe 8
- YESOD Foundation 9
- MALKUTH Kingdom 10

Paths:
11 Aleph, 12 Beth, 13 Gimel, 14 Daleth, 15 Heh, 16 Vau, 17 Zain, 18 Cheth, 19 Teth, 20 Yod, 21 Kaph, 22 Lamed, 23 Mem, 24 Nun, 25 Samekh, 26 Ayin, 27 Peh, 28 Tzaddai, 29 Qoph, 30 Resh, 31 Shin, 32 Tau

TABLE 2: TAROT CORRESPONDENCES ON THE PATHS OF THE TREE OF LIFE

Number of Path	Hebrew Letter	Golden Dawn Ascription of Tarot Trumps	W. G. Gray Ascription of Tarot Trumps	Path between Sephiroth
11	Aleph	Fool	Hierophant	Crown–Wisdom
12	Beth	Magician	Hermit	Crown–Understanding
13	Gimel	High Priestess	Star	Crown–Beauty
14	Daleth	Empress	Judgment	Understanding–Wisdom
15	Heh	Star	Emperor	Wisdom–Mercy
16	Vau	Hierophant	Temperance	Wisdom–Beauty
17	Zain	Lovers	Death	Understanding–Severity
18	Cheth	Chariot	Hanged Man	Understanding–Beauty
19	Teth	Justice	Justice	Mercy–Severity
20	Yod	Hermit	Strength	Mercy–Beauty
21	Kaph	Wheel of Fortune	Empress	Mercy–Victory
22	Lamed	Strength	Tower	Severity–Beauty
23	Mem	Hanged Man	Devil	Severity–Awe
24	Nun	Death	Lovers	Beauty–Victory
25	Samekh	Temperance	Chariot	Beauty–Awe
26	Ayin	Devil	Sun	Beauty–Foundation
27	Peh	Tower	Wheel of Fortune	Victory–Awe
28	Tzaddai	Emperor	High Priestess	Victory–Foundation
29	Qoph	Moon	World	Victory–Kingdom
30	Resh	Sun	Magician	Awe–Foundation
31	Shin	Judgment	Fool	Awe–Kingdom
32	Tau	World	Moon	Foundation–Kingdom

Fig. 26. Figure and tables refer to the magical correspondences associated with the Sephiroth and the paths on the Tree of Life.

The Tree of Life is a depiction of the Man of Light, Adam Kadmon, in whom the ten prime attributes of God are manifest (218). These may also be seen as the emanations for the many archetypes that are used in magical workings (see fig. 26, pages 350–51). The middle pillar of the Tree is the spine of Adam Kadmon, upon which we find the Western equivalent of the chakras. The side pillars of Mercy and Severity, the white and black pillars, are the right and left sides of Adam Kadmon. The totality of the Tree of Life is a macrocosmic Body of Light. Any exploration that we make within this wondrous universal glyph is also a discovery of ourselves. Figure 26 gives an idea of the rich correspondences it holds.

The Tree of Life has a total of twenty-two paths connecting it. The fact that the Hebrew alphabet has twenty-two letters and that the Tarot has twenty-two trumps has not gone unnoticed. The Hermetic Kabbalah ascribes the Tarot trumps to the paths of the Tree of Life. This correspondence, initiated by the Golden Dawn, provides a method of mediation that many can find fruitful. We must remember, however, that these ascriptions were laid down only a century or so ago. In *The Talking Tree* (200), W. G. Gray suggests a wholly different set of ascriptions that work just as well and can be used to understand the Tree of Life more deeply. Ultimately, the systems and symbols do not matter—it is what they stand for that is important. In working with such symbols, note that while they are realizations of what we may be, they are also powerhouses that should be used with care.

Apart from the constant circulation of planetary, solar, and cosmic energies through our astral body, we each have appropriated, out of the greater whole, enough astral energy to construct an individual and separate astral body, responsive to our own peculiar note and either limiting us or not according to our own point on the ladder of evolution (33).

We take what we need from these symbol systems, learning our theory of levels. It is the work of a lifetime. Their cumulative effect is to prepare us for the Great Work itself. Having looked outward at the heavens, the next chapter will have us looking within to find the balanced point. The pupil who receives force from his master on a higher plane for the purpose of transmission to the physical plane must be prepared to effect the transmutation of the corresponding amount of force in his own nature—to take it from a lower place to a higher place in order to preserve the necessary balance (160).

This is the work of the alchemist. In pursuit of the Great Work of transmutation, he does not retain the inner force and impression but transmutes that part of himself in order to transmit it to the mundane world. It is a reciprocal exchange: matter for spirit.

PRACTICES

◈ *16. The Caduceus of Hermes* ◈

> It is taught that there is a single light, in the form of a man, which radiates through all the four universes, Atzilut, Beryah, Yetzirah and Asiyah, reaching down to the physical elements. This light is bound to the lights of the Supernal Man, which are called the ten sefirot. These are clothed in this light, which is called the Light of the Quarry of Souls and in it are included all souls below. (308)

This description of Adam Kadmon is also a description of the Tree of Life, which forms the basis for this exercise. Our purposes here are to create an affinity with the macrocosmic body of the universe, to heal those souls that are included within it, and to maintain our unity within the Body of Light. It is not necessary to have any knowledge of the Kabbalah in order to perform this exercise, although if you are well read and practiced in the subject, you will be able to use this practice in more sophisticated ways.

Method

Sit in an upright chair, or stand, with your weight balanced equally on both feet. Then make a cross of light in the following manner to seal the aura and stabilize the subtle bodies. Say the following, accompanying each portion with the described action:

Between heights,	(touch the top of your forehead with the middle and index fingers of your right hand)
And depths,	(touch your solar plexus)
Between justice,	(touch your right shoulder)
And mercy,	(touch your left shoulder)
I am centered.	(cross your hands over your heart)

As you perform this, visualize a column of white light coming from above your head and descending into the earth beneath your feet and a band of light coming from beyond your left shoulder and extending beyond your right shoulder, crossing the column in the middle of your chest. If you so desire, at this point you may also put yourself under the protection of God using your own words. Establish your auric field through a steady circulation of breath: Visualize your breathing as a double band of light that outlines your body from your left ear to your left foot and back over your head, and from your forehead to your feet to the back of your head. There is no need to maintain this visualization once you have established a breathing pattern.

Your feet stand upon the physical earth of this world but your body is going to stretch through the worlds of inner space. Visualize the planet beneath you as it is seen from space: a sphere with landmasses and seas. Here your feet are firmly established on the ground while your body is stretching up through inner space until the moon—which you visualize as you know it in the night sky—is at the level of your genitals. Stretching farther, you travel on until the sun is at your heart and the bright star Sirius is at the level of your throat. Above your head is the primum mobile itself, the center where creation is endlessly effected, which you can visualize as a whirling white nebula (see fig. 27). It is very important that you do not equate these positions with the subtle centers of your etheric body.

When you have completed the stretching, see these five heavenly bodies arranged vertically in front of you. You are now indeed a giant. Your body and that of Adam Kadmon are aligned with each other. When you perform this practice for the first time, do not go beyond this point. Quietly reestablish a steady rhythm of breathing, if necessary, and very slowly reverse the instructions, coming gently back down to your own size and to your own place. Seal yourself off by repeating the words and gestures given above, write down any realizations, and then eat and drink to ensure that you are well earthed.

Once you have established this part of the practice, you may build the next part, which continues from where you have aligned to all five "planetary" positions. Your visualization helps align inner and outer space, macrocosm and microcosm. (Note: If you experience any dizziness or disorientation, make sure you reverse the procedure slowly and seal off completely.) As you proceed, you feel two great forces of polarized intensity, like two great poles of electrical current, rising at either side of your body from the earth beneath your feet. Breathe evenly and slowly. The energies, positive and negative forces, weave and grow around each of the spheres until they stop just below the primum mobile at the level of your ears (fig. 27). It is very important to note that the positive and negative streams of energy on the caduceus do not denote good and evil influences, but rather the reciprocal flow of life's energy current (179). Remember, the energy weaves around the spheres but not around your own body. You have now built the caduceus of Hermes upon the body of Adam Kadmon.

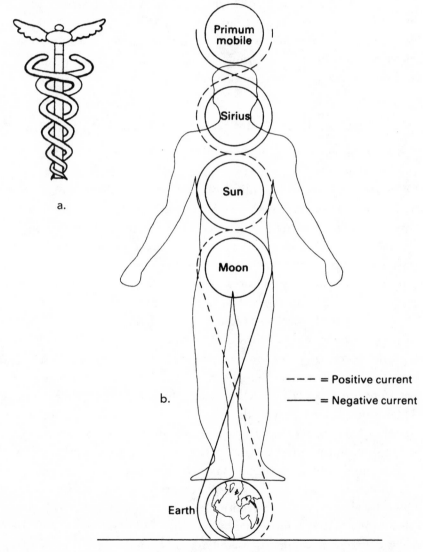

Fig. 27. The caduceus of Hermes (a) is formed on the body by the inhalation and exhalation of the practitioner, which creates a sacred continuum of energy (b).

Discovery

As you meditate, you will notice an exchange of energies between the two currents of the caduceus. Be aware of the cosmic unity of all life and of your own vocation as an instrument of the inner realm. Be especially aware that the wand you have built is also the symbol of Asclepios, the god of healing, as well as the staff of Hermes. It can bring healing to all who need it, for every divine spark within every human body comprises the Body of Light. Do not hold this visualization for long the first time—and do not attempt this if you are emotionally unbalanced or unstable on any level. If you observe commonsense measures, this exercise is cosmically beneficial, but it is a powerful one and should not be attempted often.

❖ 17. Otherworld Gateways and Symbols ❖

Working with symbol systems is a basic skill that all who walk between the worlds should acquire. There are many gateways to the Otherworld. Those who follow the Hermetic path may wish to visit actual sites associated with the Mysteries. Such place can sometimes serve as lenses that magnify and concentrate the will of the operator. For most, the skill and creative power of the imagination can help build doorways such as the Pylon Gate and the Cave of the Sibyl, to name only two of the many hundreds of entrance glyphs that enable us to project ourselves into the realms of the infinite.

Symbols in themselves hold no reality; they are constructs made up of the collective belief of those who work with them. Magically speaking, the esotericist takes these representations and, having externalized them, makes from them the gateways to an inner reality entirely different from the outer reality where he or she is contemplating the image. Thus infused with power, the symbol becomes a focal point for the operator's whole being and as such can be imbued with a kind of external reality that he or she can experience. In this way a guardian angel or elemental contact that may have no concrete reality (at least not in our dimension) assumes a symbolic reality—initially in the consciousness of the operator, but eventually outside his or her consciousness. This allows the angelic archetypes of the kind often mediated in kabbalistic magic to build up in pillars of textured color until, having received the impression of a reality outside our normal understanding, it is possible almost to taste and feel the hues.

The whole question of what we actually understand as real again comes into play here. It has been said that we spend a great deal of time and energy establishing perimeters of reality and in reaffirming them daily in order to protect ourselves from the madness that would result if we apprehended too much reality. In this instance we may see the work of the esotericist as establishing a bridge between two sides of reality, inner and outer, enabling others to pass from one to the other without fear. It is not difficult for us to envisage—perhaps even with geometric precision—invisible lines of force in the air around us. Most of the time we remain unaware of the existence of these vital links with the infinite, though they are really no different from the shining paths that connect the stone circles and standing hills of the native tradition. In ritual, when we draw a symbol of great power in the air with our finger or a wand, we are locking our own sign into the web of invisible force that surrounds us.

Such an understanding requires a radical alteration of our daily consciousness, and for this reason we use symbols and signs as visual keys. To the ancient mind, signs were of the greatest importance: They were efficacious representations of things that could not be seen with the naked eye but which could nonetheless be understood by the inner senses. "[A]ll things which the eye can see are mere phantoms and insubstantial outlines; but the things which the eye cannot see are the realities . . ." (35) This suggests a different order of reality harkening back to the synthemata (images of inexpressible symbolic power) of Iamblichus (263) or forward to the efficacy of signs such as those discussed by the artist David Jones (273).

Method

Once we understand the possible ways that a symbol might work within esoteric practice, we may develop our own individual systems of symbology by drawing, creating, or borrowing symbols and assigning meanings to them that are powerful keys in our practice. An example of a useful symbol is the drawing or model of a pyramid. The four faces of this figure can represent a number of things: north, south, east, and west; god forms; colors; names or archetypes. These can then be seen as meeting at the apex of the pyramid, which becomes the point where the powers interact and are balanced to produce an effect such as a flash of visionary insight or an opening of an entrance to another dimension.

Meditation upon such figures can bring into focus what before seemed hazy or insubstantial. All traditional images of this kind are the product of inner teaching. The Grail drawn as a cup, for instance, takes on the form of two triangles—one inverted and the other upright—and is particularly effective as a glyph of upward aspiration and downward energizing (fig. 28). The nexus between the two triangles stands for the point at which the initiate (the lower triangle) receives and transmits the downward-flowing energy of the gods (the upper triangle) as it meets his or her own mounting aspiration. Another example is the star, five pointed or otherwise, which we may see as the endless knot or pentacle, with each point representing a different aspect of deity, or as a symbol of force.

You may try different combinations of symbology until you feel you have developed a workable system, then use it for meditation for several days or even weeks, depending on the results you acheive.

Fig. 28. Two triangles—one inverted and one upright—form a glyph for the Grail.

Discovery

This system can also relate to the positioning of sacred objects in the temple or working area, or indeed to the places each participant takes in any ritual. It might also be related to star alignments or ley lines, cardinal positions in the ritual temenos, or aspects of deities assumed by the operators. If you have the skill, make three-dimensional representations of your chosen symbols. The physical creation of your symbols becomes a meditation in itself.

With the few examples provided here and others to be found in the works of Regardie, Gray, and Knight (see bibliography), it should be possible in a comparatively short space of time to accumulate a thorough working system of telesmatic imagery—the forms that spiritual powers use and inhabit and which are drawn mostly from the group mind of a culture. Magical groups and individuals gradually build upon and work with this imagery. Do not be concerned, however, if you get little immediate response; some people are better equipped to work with symbols than others. The use of images and symbols over long periods of study and meditation will help you find keys to otherworldly doors. It is well worthwhile pursuing the elusive moment when a chosen symbol will "click" into place in your consciousness. Once this step has been achieved, you will find that the rest follows naturally.

❧ *18. Honoring Our Spiritual Lineage* ❧

Our path to the present moment has been aided by many teachers of many traditions. These may have been earthly teachers, books of wisdom, spiritual contacts or allies that have accompanied us at different times and places. Whether you are still following these ways of wisdom or have changed allegiance to another path, it is important to honor all that have helped you on your way.

Method

In your first session, sit in meditation and contemplate the figures and influences that have shown you wisdom and accompanied you in your life. As they arise in your imagination, give each your blessing either in words of your own devising or by a sign. Bless everyone, even those who were not actually good influences but whose deviation from the way of service nevertheless revealed the way to you by their bad example. These are still your teachers. Note which teachers and ways of wisdom still have charge for you and which pathways you could have taken but chose not to. Return to the present time and write down each of those whom you acknowledged, what gift you were given, what door was opened to you, or how you were led to the next stepping-stone on your way.

In the next session, stand in your meditation space, allowing room behind and in front of you. Choosing one of those on your list whom you feel has given you the greatest help and encouragement, close your eyes and enter into meditation. Feel your chosen teacher behind you and build up his or her image and aspect, qualities, and gifts. Now step backward into the position of that teacher. As you breathe, feel what it is like to be your teacher and offer thanks for the inspiration and encouragement you have received. Step back into your own place and write down any realizations.

In the third session, repeat the working of session two, but rather than returning to your own place, remain standing in your teacher's place and begin to visualize your teacher's most important teacher and influence. Even though this may be unknown to you, allow impressions to form. What important gift of wisdom did your teacher's teacher impart? Bless the giver and the gift. Step back into the footsteps of your teacher's teacher. What is it like to be in this person's shoes? After you have experienced this fully, thank this teacher for aiding your teacher, then step back into your teacher's place and then into your own.

You may go back as far as you wish in each subsequent session. Eventually you will arrive at an inner teacher or influence of wisdom. The spiritual lineage may consist of a long line of physically incarnated teachers but you may soon find yourself in contact with a nonincarnate being such as Hermes, Thoth, Orpheus, Isis, Sophia, or Mnemosyne. If it feels appropriate and you are welcomed, step back briefly into the divine or spiritual form that heads your spiritual lineage. The most interesting question for this being is, "Who or what gave you or led you to wisdom?"

When you have gone as far back as you can, prepare to step forward in meditation in the next session. Feel before you the one who will follow you in this line of wisdom. What does he or she most ask of you? What wisdom can you bequeath? Step forward into the place where your successor stands. Feel what his or her need and desire might be. Find the answer by drawing on the wisdom of the long line behind you. If you cannot supply the answer, ask for help.

After stepping back into your own place, sit and contemplate the next step in your ritual and magical life.

Discovery

After you have explored your spiritual lineage, create a shrine that honors your teachers. Include something that represents the head of your spiritual lineage. For example, if you were led back to Dionysus, you could incorporate a pinecone, which is one of his symbols. Also include something that represents yourself and something that represents any who succeed you in acknowledgment that you are all part of a living spiritual tradition, just as you would place family photos on your mantelpiece to acknowledge your bonds and traditions. Before you perform any future working, light the shrine, offer incense, and re-create the bridge that connects you to all others who have walked this way before you. Meditate with, in, and through them regularly.

10

Alchemy:
The Fire-Tried Stone

*You should understand that alchemy is nothing but the
art which makes the impure into the pure through fire.*
— PARACELSUS

Matter is the last step on the path to God.
— RUDOLPH HAUSCHKA, *THE NATURE OF SUBSTANCE*

Hunting the Green Lion

"*M*atter cannot be created or destroyed," says the scientific
law of conservation. "But it can be transformed," replies
the alchemist. God's Great Work is the Creation itself and
sets in it the signatures and correspondences by which it may evolve.
Everything created has life—not human life, but a life according to its
proper nature. Alchemy has always treated matter as its *prima materia*
from which the divine spark can be kindled into awareness of matter's
potential. The alchemical process concentrates on isolating the prima
materia of creation so that the evolution of matter might ensue, for as
with matter, so with humanity. The whole chain of creation releasing its
divine sparks, rising through the planes of existence in a joyful return
to the primal unity—such is the vision of alchemy.

The philosopher's search is for wisdom and the alchemist's search is
for the philosopher's stone, the keystone of the earth's structure, the
*lapsit exilla*s (stone that was rejected) that fell from heaven and from
which all matter is formed. In this stone is encoded the cipher of life's

mysteries—the male and female components that are divided in the outer world but are joined in the inner realm. In the language of alchemy both wisdom and the philosopher's stone are described as "a gift and sacrament of God and a divine matter, which deeply and in diverse manners was veiled in images by the wise." (26) If such language seems unduly veiled, we must consider that our very existence is due to a genetic process of alchemical complexity. What is hidden under the sign of emblem and glyph within alchemy is scientifically discernible under the microscope as genes and chromosomes, the complex individualized DNA of all human beings. The real prima materia of humanity is the flesh. The way in which our bodies develop is partly encoded in us at birth and partly attributable to the physical conditions in which we grow up. But the primary potential of every human being resides within the genes and within the spiral of DNA. A strange alchemy dictates our transmutation from the fusion of ovum and sperm, through the cyclic metabolic renewal of our cell structure, to our eventual demise when our flesh joins the chain of matter through its physical decay. Physics had sought to comprehend this mystery and now medical science is striving to re-create the conditions in which the mystery of life can be transmitted and genetically altered—with who knows what possibilities? The fact remains, however, that though science may be able to produce crude DNA spirals and graft one life upon another, it has not discovered the hiding place of the spirit.

> *I behold how all things in the*
> *aether are mixed with pneuma.*
> *I see in spirit how all things*
> *are sustained by pneuma:*
> *Flesh hangs itself upon soul,*
> *Soul is upborne by air,*
> *Air hangs itself upon aether.*
> *Fruits rise up from the depth,*
> *A child is lifted from the womb.* (25)

The spirit is the inner corollative of the flesh and no life can be reproduced in our world without a corresponding ensoulment on the inner world.

The conception of a child is the mightiest alchemy, but while the birth of a child necessitates a "choice" between two opposites—a decision for one gender or another as a requirement of earthly life—the work of the alchemist, which is an attempt to be born on the inner world, necessitates the reconciliation of opposites within the philosopher's stone. The true secret of alchemy is that the operator becomes the stone.

But what is this stone and how do we become it? Its beginnings are obscure, black like the rich soil of the Nile Delta that gave its name to alchemy. (In Egyptian *keme* means "black earth.") The Greeks, who understood the symbology of color, knew that the inner tincture of black was really gold (333), so although Apollo was depicted with black hair, his locks were symbolically golden. The mystery of alchemy is also found in the cult of Isis: In the Hermetic document the *Kore Kosmou* (The Universal Maiden—314), Isis is given the secrets of alchemy, which are to be transmitted only to her son Horus. She receives "the gift of the Perfect Black,'" which, in the context of the text, we must see as Osiris himself, the consort with whom she is united in alchemical union. Yet Isis herself is both the black earth and the pupil of the eye of Osiris (410); she is the veiled mystery who appears outwardly as Black Isis but whose inner reality is the Bright Isis of the Stars.

Here is the kernel of the mystery that assigns feminine symbolism to matter and masculine symbolism to spirit. Isis and Osiris, Sophia and Logos, White Queen and Red King are syzygies whose union can be achieved only by the levels of the alchemical process. Nowhere is it stated or implied that matter is woman or spirit is man, nor should we seek to impose these meanings. It is the union of these complementary opposites of matter and spirit, queen and king that is the subject of this chapter.

Many insist that alchemy is merely the foundation upon which chemistry was established. Indeed, the history of alchemy includes proto-scientists and chemists as well as mystics and magicians. Of course, if we look at science from a contemporary standpoint, it is not easy to reconcile the application of both physics and metaphysics within one discipline.

Up to now this book has focused on the nature of the spirit, for only by understanding the eternal will we begin to perceive the temporal. For this reason we have left to last a discussion of matter. We can look upon matter neither with the fundamentalism of rational science nor with the disdain of the Manichaen. We must approach it with the compassionate perception of inner awareness and eternal correspondence. "Aristotle wrote of the *prima materia,* Plato of the *hyle,* Hermes of the *umbra horrenda,* Pythagoras of the 'Symbolical Unity,' and

Hippocrates of the 'deformed chaos,'"says Robert Fludd (538), show-ing how crucial matter was in relation to esoteric philosophy. The lan-guage of metaphysics was continuously applied to the realm of physics throughout the Western world up until the so-called Enlightenment.

Now the New Physics has come full circle in its understanding of science through its use of Eastern spiritual terminology: That which is inexplicable in mundane scientific language can be encapsulated within cosmic conceptualizations. We should cautiously herald this ironic turn of fate—that the once despised mythological paradigms have become the new currency of physics. What's more, the spiritual symbolism of mythology, now the stock-in-trade of the psychologist, may become the banner of the New Physics with as little justification and sense of guardianship. When the alchemists spoke in symbolic language, they at least knew the interior reality of the symbol; they subscribed to a sacred continuum in which matter and spirit were mixed together. There is a world of difference between the shaman and the psychologist and between the alchemist and the scientist.

Alchemy is spiritual chemistry, for although it is said to have devel-oped from physical experimentation to "soul alchemy," it has always been concerned with the reconciliation of opposites as described in the Emerald Tablet. We have already seen in chapter 9 how planetary cor-respondences were observed in all the manifestations of nature. Similarly, the subtle correspondences of the colors, shapes, sounds, smells, and tastes by which our senses tell us the story of any creation were first observed by alchemists in base matter: the metals, minerals, and compounds of matter that formed the foundation of the hierarchi-cal chain of being itself. Alchemy reasoned that if a metal could be transmuted, the chain of existence would be affected.

The creation of gold from lead can be looked upon as the Hermetic equivalent of bringing back faery gold from the Otherworld: It would be the transference of energy from the inner world to the outer world. Alchemists "understood that what they were working with was not so much the actual substances as spiritual properties concealed in the met-als." (489) We might say they attempted to bring out the inner poten-tial or divine spark within the metal. "Lead is gold fallen sick."(352) The metal of Saturn/Cronos no longer has the luster it once had in the Golden Age.

The alchemist stands in direct succession to the smith of the native tradition, who forged the first tools from the ores of the earth itself and who was held in superstitious regard as the guardian of a great mystery. The smith is the weapon maker of the Gods: Govannon, Wayland, Hephaistos—the blackened lame one. The alchemist seems to have shared the almost universal distrust that has been meted out to all metalworkers, tinkers, and miners since the time of Prometheus. The miner burrows into the womb of the earth, careful to propiate her, as we see from the finds excavated from the Neolithic mine at Grimes Graves, Norfolk, in England. The metalworker knows the mystery of fire's transmutation. The tinker and jobbing blacksmith know the mystery of metal and have the lingua franca or *shelta* of all smiths: the horseman's word—the means of controlling animals. Because such people were under the patronage of the goddess Brigid, the alchemist pays careful attention to the service of the Anima Mundi of Our Lady Earth.

The alchemist was both midwife and priest of transmutation: "[M]etals and minerals were born, grew, married, copulated, gave birth and died. Rocks and stones had bodies, souls, emotions and wants." (54) Entering into a real relationship with the metals and elements in his or her charge, the alchemist administered alchemical sacraments to these living children of the earth. Like the real midwife and priest, continence, sobriety, and watchfulness were necessary in the lying-in chamber—the *laboratory,* a word in which the Benedictine motto *"Laborare est orare"* ("To work is to pray") was made manifest.

We can see within alchemy the descent of the Western Way in microcosm: It arises in the cosmological speculations of native tradition; receives the tributaries of philosophy, Gnosticism, the Kabbalah, magic, and Rosicrucianism; and finally, within our own time, splits off into a complex meandering stream of chemistry and psychology—the studies of the physical and psychic constituents of creation, a subject about which we are still amazingly ignorant. The Hermetic texts drew upon knowledge of Egyptian alchemical techniques as well as upon the Hellenic scientific thought that subsequently informed both Platonic and Neoplatonic philosophy. The insights of Gnosticism, themselves derived from a variety of Middle Eastern sources, fructified the symbology of alchemy, as we shall see. By the time kabbalistic magic and Rosicrucian elements fed into this ever more powerful stream, the Western Way had received all the necessary nutrients to help it survive. Alchemy became the equivalent of the tantric and Varjayana path of the West.

We can trace the history of the transmission of this energetic path from many standpoints. Most commentators favor a straight scientific appraisal, ignoring the esoteric adjuncts as an embarrassing and medieval excess. But by taking this perspective, alchemy is robbed of its true meaning, which is nothing less than the marriage of macrocosm with microcosm. The contemporary distrust of science is rooted in this separation of matter and spirit. Yet up until the dawn of rational science, scientists and proto-scientists devoutly believed in the interelation of their studies with God; they harnessed their work with the yoke of prayer. This was especially important in the arts of metallurgy, herbal medicine, astronomy, and astrology, which, according to Hermetic tradition, were considered to have been imparted to humanity by the Fallen Angels (332).

Aristotle's theory of the four classical elements is the forerunner of the periodic table. The four elements, which were seen to be in a state of flux, changing from one into the other, underlie the basic alchemical process. A combination of air and fire results in heat, the combination of earth and water results in coldness. This schema gave rise to the theory of the four humors, by which individuals were judged to be phlegmatic, melancholic, sanguine, or choleric according to their elemental makeup (fig. 29). All the elements were seen to derive from the prima materia and indeed were subjected to the process that returned them to

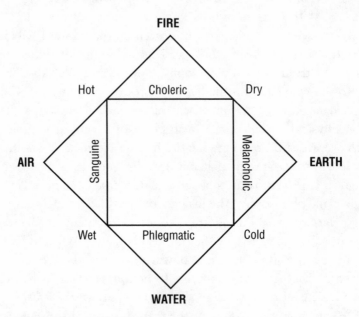

Fig. 29. The Aristotelian Table of Elements and Humors referred to in medieval medicine and philosophy

their prime condition. Yet the sum of the four elements was the *quintessentia*, or fifth element, a condition that alchemists sought by combining the elements in various processes. This can be seen in figure 30, which is a three-dimensional representation of the Great Work. When the elements are in balance, the quintessentia can result. The fifth element is itself a perfected mirror image of the prima materia from which the other four elements derive.

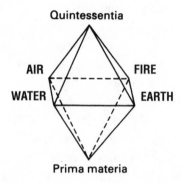

Fig. 30. The crystalline structure of the Great Work is created from the admixture of the elements with the prima material, leading to the quintessence, or fifth and highest element.

The numerous and lengthy processes alchemists used on the elements have been described in a number of ways both chemically and psychologically, as well as in mythological and symbolic terms. Here, however, we will consider these processes in terms of the Emerald Tablet itself. The many emblem books of the seventeenth century—notably *The Rosarium Philosophorum* (355) and the Mylius *Engravings* (434)—give a clear breakdown of the classical alchemical process.

The following meditation, which can serve as a means of focusing on the alchemical mysteries, is based upon a close reading of the Emerald Tablet and follows the process of alchemical transmutation. The prima materia was understood to have been "generated by fire, born of water, brought down from the sky by wind, and nourished by earth" (538)—matter balanced by the elements. Yet its essential core—its DNA—remains a secret. All things created derive from its substance, yet its perfection is the achievement of the Great Work. The prima materia must be given over to the "mother" to be shaped or "fixed." When the "child" is growing, it must be purged of its separate elements in order to grow strong. The soul and spirit of the prima materia mature. Next, the correspondences between microcosm and macrocosm must be comprehended: The "youth" is sent to its "father" for instruction in sublime matters. When the "youth" achieves comprehension, he returns to earth as an "adult" in order to practice this wisdom. The prima materia has been united with the quintessentia, which it mirrors, and discovers its adamantine purity and strength.

This is the process by which everything is created and, if imitated with wisdom, it can effect healing, long life, and illumination of the whole world. The guardian of this work is Hermes Trismegistos himself, the child of the philosophers and inheritor of their accumulated wisdom; the youthful initiate in the Mysteries of both mother and father, God and Goddess; and the mature guardian of the Mysteries, the Agathodaimon of all who seek to achieve the Great Work.

This extended metaphor and meditation upon the text of the Emerald Tablet is a model for those who wish to go further in this work. Alternatively, you may choose to work with the three primary constituents of the alchemy process—salt, sulfur, and mercury. These are not to be taken as merely physical or chemical substances, but, like so much in mystery work, must be considered as metaphors for body, soul, and spirit. You might also wish to use in your meditation the classical terms for the main alchemical processes: the *nigredo, albedo,* and *rubedo,* which we shall be investigating later in this chapter.

The metal of Hermes himself—Mercury—is a bridge between the chemical substances employed in alchemy. Of all the metals, quicksilver (mercury) "did not participate in the last stages of earth's densifying [but] remained a fluid" (236) in much the same way that Hermes Trismegistos does not remain anchored in one mythos but instead ranges as a messenger throughout the systems and mythologies of many cultures. We can best assimilate the mercurial powers of Hermes under his symbolic representation as the Green Lion of the alchemical processes. His continual shapeshifting connects the many levels and systems within the processes and produces a wealth of knowledge, as set forth in the Emerald Tablet:

The green lion is extremely agile
And blows forth the sun's colours

So that the reflection
May be seen on the plain. (8)

Hermes, as the Green Lion, explores the heights and depths: the heavens, the earth, and the waters beneath the earth. His example is the pattern the alchemist follows.

Fig. 31. The image of the Green Lion devouring the sun is an alchemical emblem of spiritual transformation.

Alchemy is the soul price of the cosmos: It teaches us to relate the infinite to the mundane, to find the presence of the Divine in the daily circle of being. Used by those who seek the philosopher's stone, the process is, like the Tree of Life, a spiritual code or system of correspondences through which to relate everything microcosmically and macrocosmically. The search for the philosopher's stone consists of refining the soul, purging it of elemental influences until all that remains is a single unit—a perfectly tuned microcosm reflecting the macrocosm. All matter is a mystery. The processes of alchemy are a ladder we can use to transcend time and space until we stand at the highest point of creation, which is God.

We have said that all is mysteriously alive. The "deepening of the plane" leading to the despiritualization of matter seems an ominous possibility in our own time, with its "black alchemy" of nuclear technology. The heavier radioactive elements stand in danger of being totally cut off from the spiritual world. "The descent of the spirit into matter has now reached a turning point in the earth and from now on it is man's task to recognise and release the spirit in matter. The descent of the spirit into matter reached a turning point at the element lead." (353) When science, which has contributed so much to the cause of mitigating human suffering, loses sight of its primal function within the cosmos, it loses faith with creation. Rudolf Steiner believed that the role of science could be crucial:

> The initiate-ruler, the philosopher of personality, the priestly reconciler of knowledge and faith are equally unable to rescue modern humanity from the fruit of its own attainments. Only a man trained in the scientific thinking motivating the technological research and developments of modern civilisation can discover those new elements which must enter human consciousness if mankind is not to fall victim of its own achievements. (564)

A bringing together of all the disciplines of art, science, and the spirit was the aim of the Rosicrucian manifestos. Francis Bacon's vision in the *New Atlantis* (1627 C.E.) and his *Great Instauration* (1582 C.E.) propounded "the universal and general reformation of the whole wide world through the renewal of all arts and sciences." Subsequently, the Royal Society was founded in 1660, but short of it being the "invisible college made manifest," after the Rosicrucian model, it soon became the cradle for rational science. Such "externalizations of the hierarchy" rarely result in anything unless they are truly spiritually contacted. Historically and in novels, contacts for such institutions have been not inner spiritual beings but the creations of proto-scientists. From Rabbi Judah Leib's golem in sixteenth-century Prague (542) to Dr. Frankenstein's monster is a long step—as far as Roger Bacon's Brazen Head is from the computer. The magician is credited with the creation of the *homunculus*—a genie in a bottle, possibly a wild fundamentalization of the creation of the Child of the Philosophers—yet what are we to make of the experimentation to which human flesh, with its divine spark, is currently subjected? Where does this stand in the alchemical canon? Human creations are to be serviceable machines, obedient to their masters. But can such creations ever be friends and counselors like the inner guardians? The ultimate materialism of the Great Work has hounded alchemy from the very beginning: The outer currency of mundane commerce, not the inner gold of the spirit, is demanded on request.

> All clamour aloud: "We want to be rich!" Rich! Yes, you desire wealth and say with Epicurus: "let us provide our bodies and leave our souls to take care of themselves. Even as Midas in the fable, we wish to turn all things to gold." So there are people who seek this gold in Antimony, but since they do not care for God, and have cast far away from them the love of their neighbour, they will look at the horse's teeth of Antimony forever without knowing a thing of its age and quality. Like the wedding guests at Cana, they may behold, but . . . know nothing.

So writes Basilius Valentinus in his *Triumphal Chariot of Antimony* (617).

Our search for the stone must continue. It promises healing, long life, and illumination, not earthly gold. "The Stone, the Light of the Earth, serves as a guide to all created things and makes hidden things manifest." (603) Yet what if it remains hidden? The only recourse is to take the path of the walkers between the worlds with wisdom as our guide.

The Wandering *Viaticum*

Those who follow the alchemical path of the Western Way travel by signs and stories, as all good travelers from the Canterbury Pilgrims to those in Italo Calvino's *Castle of Crossed Destinies* (73) have done. Those who want to make an alchemical excursion might first read accounts of such journeys for informative tips on how they are to proceed, only to find that they can make no sense of alchemical texts because they can be read only by means of symbolic keys. It take patience and determination to learn the symbolic language of the wise. Yet as Paracelsus says, "[R]esolute imagination can accomplish all things." (228) To keep going upon the road, we need the *viaticum*—the bread of the soul traveler.

To whom should we go for guidance? Faced with the numerous commentaries on this and that text, we students of alchemy may well falter. But we must remember that we are all alchemists to some degree, transmuting our bodies and natures into something else by the ingestion of food and ideas. Just as metabolism replaces all our cells so that we are physically reconstituted within seven years, so changes in our inner motivations and experience remake our consciousness. Our progress in alchemical exploration depends very much upon the ideas and experiences we receive. It is doubly important, then, that we study original texts when possible and carefully monitor what all commentators tell us. Though we once would have studied under earthly teachers and guardians of tradition, we must now learn to listen for the teachings of the inner guardians, who ensure that the Mysteries are transmitted, employing as much as we can the use of symbolic archetypes to aid this transmission.

We have already spoken of how symbolism must be grounded in firsthand understanding. So it is with the archetypes of the inner world—we cannot presume to work with them secondhand or relegate them to the unconscious. Such an understanding will help our reading of alchemical texts. The complex processes and strange symbolic beasts, kings, and androgynes of alchemy are the signature of those inner energies we call the gods, rather than abstractions or productions of our psyches working in some objective sense from a projected theater of memory. Their effect is real, not illusory. Hidden under many guises these inner energies come through us; they do not originate within us, as Jung himself acknowledged. The poet W. B. Yeats corroborates this understanding: "There are, indeed, personifying spirits that we had best call but Gates and Gatekeepers, because through their dramatic power they bring our souls to crisis, to Mask and Image. . . . They have but one purpose, to bring their chosen man to the greatest obstacle he may confront without despair." (658)

Without such encounters, our alchemical quest cannot be maintained, because without these gates and gatekeepers, we cannot find our way onward. The alchemical archetypes are our *neter*—the Egyptian term for "archetype" or "salt"—the prima materia of our search, the basis upon which the other elements work. Our archetypes are like those around us whom we call "the salt of the earth," whose daily intercourse leavens the lumpishness of life. Yet the *archai* —"principles" or "beginnings"—are "something more universal than the elements." (603)

We need careful preparation in order to work with them in full coop-eration. This is where the groundwork of correspondences comes in and where we can prepare the way for ourselves by the means suggested in chapter 9.

One way that we can prepare is by making a talisman—not a good-luck charm but a method of fine-tuning our resonance with the spiritual forms that are our working partners. A talisman is "a magical figure charged with the Force which it is intended to represent." (507) Israel Regardie's book *How to Make and Use Talismans* gives practical advice on their construction. Whether they are made of paper, virgin parchment, or precious metals, however, it is not the quality of the material but the quality of the meditation and concentration by which they are conse-crated that matters. The Egyptian sculptor imbued each statue in a similarly talismanic way, by concentrating the divine energy of the god por-trayed. The hieroglyph for sculptor meant "he-who-keeps-alive." (106)

Music provides another method of preparation. Its subtle corre-spondences activate the archai in a universal manner once the right har-monic permutations are discovered. Orpheus was able to change the nature of beasts and men by the permutation of the seven strings of his lyre. If you choose to work by means of music's alchemy, then he is the one to contact. Note, however, that recorded music cannot replace the music you make yourself:

> Remember that song is the most powerful imitator of all things. For it imitates the intentions and affections of the soul, and speech, and also reproduces bodily gestures, human movements, and moral characters, and imitates and acts everything so powerfully that it immediately provokes both the singer and hearer to imitate and perform the same things. (630)

Marcilio Ficino sought to reproduce planetary correspondences by means of his Hermetic hymns. Fabio Paolini, a professor of Greek in Venice in 1589 who wrote about the talismanic alchemy of music, also noted that although musicians in his own time were masterly skillful, "none has produced effects superior to Orpheus." (630)

For most people, the most immediate means of preparation will be reading the alchemical texts and contemplating alchemical emblems. These can have a deep inner effect, as Jung himself recorded in his psy-chological study of alchemy (282). Just as the architectural language of medieval symbolism presented books in stone in every cathedral, so the alchemical texts portrayed archetypes as emblems conveying initiatory clues. How shall we go about working with these? Gerhard Dorn (floreat 1565–1578 C.E.), a disciple of Paracelsus, offers advice on how to approach the Great Work: "Through study one acquires knowledge; through knowledge, love, which creates devotion; devotion creates repetition and by fixing repetition one creates in oneself experience, virtue and power, through which the miraculous work is done and the work in nature is of this quality." (623)

Marie-Louise von Franz speculates that the "study" spoken of above means the actual reading of the alchemical texts—that exposure to them can itself have an effect. Although the processes described verbally and pictorially within the texts correspond to the chemical admixture of various substances, they are also emblematic of the inner human condition—a central point of study of the psychological schools.

Such reading and contemplation is the start of the initiatory journey. In *The Chymical Wedding of Christian Rosenkreutz* (313), the hero, Rosenkreutz himself, describes his own initiation in such a way that only those who have themselves experienced initiation could understand. Yet if we meditate upon the hidden words and images—"fixing by repetition," as Dorn has it—we will find some of the keys we seek. In default of operational mystery schools and mystery guardians, we are left with the mystery stories, which we can explore only by meditating, by entering the story.

Alchemy is the most complete expression of the Western Way, being concerned with the transmutation and perfection of consciousness. The native tradition's guardians sought to effect the change from tribal to individual consciousness just as the Hermetic tradition's guardians have sought to transmute individual consciousness into cosmic consciousness. Both shaman and magician have tried to interrelate the microcosm to the macrocosm, in their different ways. Their roles have fragmented, their symbologies have varied with bewildering complexity, but we can trace the similarities and choose how we want to align our own inner journey toward the Great Work. The Foretime was motivated by a chthonic identification; its alchemy was effected by means of earth, wood, and stone. Later ages looked to the celestial hierarchies for their integration in the Body of Light, yet they still recognized the chthonic signatures of metals, the talismanic properties of all created things. The cauldron and alembic were both transformative vessels that ultimately met in the universal image of the Grail. Shaman and alchemist are connected by the same story involving the difficult inner world journey of the initiate, his quest for otherworldly guides and for the drink that will bring healing, long life, and illumination to his tribe.

Just as the Hermetic inner landscape harks back to the natural perfection of the native Otherworld, so transformative images find their roots in Paradise itself. The scenario in which the transformative symbol is sought varies little from story to story. In the apocryphal text the Apocalypse of Moses, dated to the early Christian era, we read how Seth, the inheritor of Adam's wisdom in Hermetic tradition, is sent by his father to obtain the oil of mercy from Eden. He is refused by the archangel Michael, but is promised that it shall be forthcoming "to the holy people at the end of time." (496) This oil of mercy is a healing oil that will restore Adam to his former wholeness, but although Seth does not obtain it for the healing of his father, he is promised that his line shall indeed produce a savior who will administer healing to Seth's descendants. This story and the discovery of the Emerald Tablet (chapter 6) point to a quest to be undertaken, a challenge to be answered. They are the archetypal myths of the Hermetic quest for the reunion of the divine spark with God in Paradise so that the world will be healed and there will be no more death or ignorance.

The story of the Grail from the native tradition is another of these archetypal myths embodying transformation, as are all of its precedents, the native myths that refer to the healing waters, springs, or fountains of the Otherworld that brought wisdom and healing and the stories that tell of the cauldron of transformation, which variously produced the food of one's desire, brought the dead to life, and healed the sick. The Wounded King will be made whole, the Wasteland—earth in disharmony with the cosmos—will be transformed, and Lady Sovereignty and the king will be joined once more in alchemical union.

Who can tell how many times this mystery has been expounded and in how many different ways? The dimension of the inner quest for the transformative symbol is further deepened by the admixture of native and Hermetic traditions at the nexus of Christianity. It was here that the native stories of the poet-singer became fused with the Hermetic craft of the alchemist and magician. Storyteller and artificer, troubadour and guildsman, master man and Kabbalist, Grail knight and Rosicrucian sage are caught up together in a marvelous exchange of material. Many of the exponents of the mystery schools had been subsumed into Christianity; eventually the Celtic hero became the medieval knight questing for the transformative vessel. The Grail legends became the healing lance of spiritual chivalry and the Grail itself became identified with the cup of the Last Supper or with the cruets in which Joseph of Arimathea caught the blood and water from the side of the crucified Lord. Seth's mighty descendant had returned to redeem his people and give them, at long last, the oil of mercy.

If the Grail legends are the epitome of Catholic Europe's inner Mysteries, then those of Christian Rosenkreutz are the underlying Mysteries of Protestant Europe after the Reformation. In the tradition of the Master Men of Celtic tradition, Rosenkreutz enters the mountain of the goddess and lifts her veil. He goes on a quest for inner wisdom and vouchsafes himself the champion of the ignorant, the sick, and the tormented. In *The Chymical Wedding* he unites king and queen and is himself united with Lady Venus, who represents inner wisdom. He can be identified with Hermes, Christ, and Perceval at the moment of their accomplishment of the philosopher's stone, the Redemption, and the Grail.

Both sets of legends—those of the Grail and of Christian Rosenkreutz—show a remarkable similarity in dedication to the Great Work. The company of Arthur's Round Table and the Congregation of the Rosicrucians each meet once a year, at Camelot during Pentecost and in the House of the Holy Spirit at Christmas, respectively. Both brotherhoods swear to do good service to all who ask of it, freely and without favor. While Arthur's knights subdue dragons and quell atavistic, evil customs in the land, Rosicrucians strive to heal the sick and counsel the ignorant. Evidently spiritual chivalry did not die at the Reformation and Renaissance (8, 311).

The storytellers, or *makars,* who had once enjoyed an honorable place in society, were able to return with the letters of learning after their names, having vindicated the Mysteries and brought them to a new generation. It was time to begin again physical participation in the Mysteries within the boundaries of alchemy and science. The fragmented shaman—smith, magician, astrologer, priest, poet, philosopher—was united in the person of the alchemist, once more under royal patronage to pursue the Great Work. It was a brief return of an ancient way of life that was to dissipate under the ignorance of the "new learning," which despised the emblematic processes of the alchemical story and looked upon them as childish allegories that only prefigured the glories of science. The transformative wisdom of the philosopher's stone was ignored in favor of a material end to all ills. The demise of alchemy's classical age was brought about by disbelief in its internalized mythological sequences. Both native and Hermetic traditions died back, to seed from the inner world in a later century, in our own time.

If the Foretime's wisdom is the natural resonance of the native tradition in our own time, then Alchemy is the current resonance of the Hermetic tradition. There is still much recovery work to be done among those who are committed to the survival of the Western Way. Yet whatever has been lost in the physical world is still recoverable by means of meditation and analeptic memory (see practice 2, Analeptic Memory).

We each have the potential to approach alchemy as our own study according to our individual talents, whether we are poets, singers, magicians, scientists, or craftsmen. Alchemy is crucially important to the future development of the West, which is still unable to see the connections and distinctions between physical sexuality and inner polarity, let alone discern the interpenetration of microcosm and macrocosm. We have yet to plumb the deepest mysteries of reconciliation: It is a path walked in darkness, illumined only by the lantern of love.

The Chymical Wedding

In an age concerned with revamping the old symbologies and archetypes, the rightful position of symbols of the Divine Masculine and the Divine Feminine has been much debated, just as there has been a great deal of debate about the respective roles of men and women. In the esoteric world such disputes are rare: The symbolism of Lord and Lady, God and Goddess are the everyday currency of the inner planes.

The Divine Masculine and the Divine Feminine are like a two-sided door. In terms of developing consciousness, we come through the door of the Goddess, for she is the primal image of our birth into the Mysteries. She stands at the entrance of the inward spiral of the native tradition and it is her wisdom that helps us navigate the labyrinth. The door on the reverse of the Goddess is the God, who stands at the end of the outward spiral of the Hermetic tradition. We cannot emerge without the assistance of his knowledge. These dual influences affect whole ages and cultures at different times and affect us too in our own life cycle when we encounter them at the appointed time. Our own parents inform us about mother and father; our own relationships teach us about wife and husband; our own children inform us about son and daughter. As we age physically, so our inner understanding appreciates the ever-youthening aspects of masculine and feminine. But this is merely one expression—the physical realization—of a complex set of polarities; there are those of the inner world as well.

Each man stands under the macrocosmic archetype of the Logos, or God, and is capable of mediating that force; each woman stands under the macrocosmic archetype of the Goddess, or Sophia, and is capable of mediating that force (see fig. 24, page 316). Man is able to experience the love of a woman as well as the inspiration of his inner companion—the Muse or sibyl—and can behold the macrocosmic beauty of the Divine Feminine. Likewise, woman is able to experience the love of a man, the inspiration of her inner companion—the daimon or prophet—and can behold the macrocosmic beauty of the Divine Masculine. Further, each polarity is able to mate on its own plane (i.e., man with woman, prophet with sibyl, God with Goddess). Each polarity can also mate at either of the other two levels. Finally, each of these polarities is mysteriously within us. In most modern relationships, couples are mated only on the physical plane; the other levels of union are not realized and thus remain unpolarized and unable to mate. The dilemma occurs when the honeymoon period has worn off and some time has passed. It is then that partners long for something more and are unable to bring this to or receive this from each other.

The alchemical understanding of the coniunctio is this mating on every plane, which produces the *rebus* or hermaphrodite of the Great Work—a reconciliation that prefigures the union of microcosm and macrocosm, the secret of the highest working of alchemy. The divine pair whose union represents the alchemical transmutation are known as the White Queen and the Red King, so named from the color resulting from the two final stages of the alchemical process. To assume the roles of the White Queen and the Red King is possible only if both partners are initiates within the Great Work: This is the reason for the alchemist's working with his *soror mystica* (sister/female partner in the Great Work), who is invariably his wife. Those who see the woman's role within the work merely as a conjuror's assistant are mistaken. The soror mystica is not a passive agent in the operation—and if the alchemist is female, she will require the assistance of a *frater mysticus* (brother/male partner in the Great Work).

*Fig. 32. The alchemical Red King and White Queen share their essence,
receiving the transformative gift of love.*

But where does this leave the initiate who has married a partner
who not only is ignorant of inner realities, but also positively refuses to
believe in their existence? It is customary for such an unpaired initiate
to work with a magical partner with whom he or she creates a broth-
erly or sisterly bond. Indeed, we may ask how any of us can achieve the
Great Work without tearing at the delicate webs of love that bind one
human being to another. The radical revisioning of male and female
roles in our time and the way in which genital sexuality, rather than
fully mated love, is now seen as the normative pattern for any relationship make it hard for us to approach the alchemical transformation and
apply it to our own time and place. But the mirror of the Mysteries has
been shattered if we cannot mate on the higher levels with our partner,
for the sacramental union of human beings is a touchstone of our
ability to fuse, transform, and re-create. "Only those who are rightly

married can go to the higher degrees," writes Dion Fortune in her study of the laws of sexuality and polarity (163). By "rightly married" she means a partnership that is divinely sanctioned and in balance in both physical expression and spiritual mediation.

Of course, this does not mean to say that partnerships should be abandoned when esoteric duty calls. The esoteric laws on this point are clear enough: Whatever contracts have been entered into must be abided by, especially when children are involved. The law regarding marriage reflects the understanding that marriage is a sacrament that one human being gives to another in the token of flesh.

The seemingly irreconcilable division of opposites has been the subject of many myths and legends. The traditional story about the incestuous love of the sun for the moon, his sister, is one that finds its home within the alchemical and Hermetic symbology. God sets sun and moon in the sky so that they follow each other around the heavens, never meeting except at the moment of eclipse, when they are seen to embrace. Yet the unsatisfied yearning of the sun and moon gives us light by day and night. "Life is poured into all things through the moon and sun, and therefore they are called by Orpheus the vivifying eyes of Heaven." (153) In an early Hermetic text Hermes is addressed as one "whose tireless eyes are sun and moon—that shine in the pupils of the eyes of men." Hermes, the child of sun and moon, mediates the imagery of God and Goddess within the symbology of all myths, so we perceive all things as partaking of these dual natures on many levels. Yet, in the

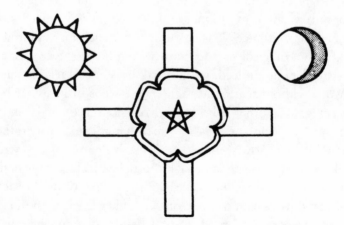

Fig. 33. Sun and moon shine upon the rose cross of the Great Work.

Revelation of Saint John (chapter 22), we are told that there shall be no need for sun or moon in the Holy City because the light of God will be shining in and through us. The need to steer by the celestial influences of either Divine Masculine or Divine Feminine will be over because we shall be the light itself.

We are still earthbound rather than spiritual beings, however, and the Neo-Pythagorean invocation to the Eternal Feminine is still appropriate to our needs: "Honour be to woman on earth, as in Heaven, and may she be sanctified, and help us mount to the Great Soul of the world who gives birth, preserves, and renews—the Divine Goddess who bears along all souls in her mantle of light." (525)

Those who wish to work with these archetypes of reconciliation can employ many different scenarios drawn from whatever tradition they find appropriate. One of these is the Gnostic apocatastasis, in which the bride, Sophia, is raised up to her bridegroom, the Logos. Together they form the gateway of the bridal chamber where they are to conjoin: Each holds out a curved hand, forming an O through which pass the created hierarchies—mineral, vegetable, animal, human, angelic, and so forth. When everything has passed within, their union takes place. Similarly, the reconciliation of the Shekinah with God can be visualized, after the kabbalistic Sabbath meditation of *yichudim*. The Assumption and Coronation of the Virgin can also be regarded as an icon of this reconciliation: Although her body and soul have been assumed to heaven, she is, with her Son, a bridge over which the whole of creation may enter into the final unity of Paradise.

Fig. 34. The interlinked sigils of alpha and omega form an emblem of reconciliation and eternal hope.

Alchemy ultimately answers the challenge of dualism by not passing up the challenge of duality. The "evil" nature of the flesh, a fear of which lay at the very heart of many of the classical mystery schools, was not resolved until alchemy became a working system. Here it was realized that the task of transmuting the fleshly envelope toward a higher spiritual plane of existence could begin while we were still living and that the effect of this transmutation could become a means of uniting the scattered Body of Light for the benefit of all creation. The unification of the alchemist and the soror mystica in the bridal chamber and of the elements within the furnace was a paradigm of this gathering-in. It is a reconciliation that takes place everywhere and in every time, not just at the end of time.

The alchemical processes vary considerably from text to text: Some relate the integration of two opposites, as in *The Rosary of the Philosophers* (357), where sun and moon go through two sets of processes. Others represent the elements as being subjected to seven stages, corresponding to the sevenfold planetary system. Some tell of the birth of the perfect Mercurius, who emerges only at the end of this sevenfold cycle of transmutations, through the nigredo (black), albedo (white), and rubedo (red) stages of the alchemical process. Hermes Trismegistos himself goes through the seven days of creation in reverse, to appear triumphant.

The black, white, and red stages are the archetypal pattern of both alchemy and native folk stories. Perfection is seen to reside in a combination of these three colors: The languishing prince or princess of the story can marry only one whose cheek is pale as the snow, whose lips are red as blood, whose hair is black as the raven's wing. This symbolic key is employed in a far more complex way in alchemy, where each stage has its own mythos.

In the nigredo, the Wounded King encounters the Wasteland, Christ enters the tomb, and Osiris is scattered by Set. The king of the alchemical process and his flesh are sundered and putrefaction sets in. In the albedo, a sevenfold bath is prepared, the bones of the scattered love are restored by Isis, the White Mass of the Holy Mother—in which the Virgin offers up her child—is celebrated, the Wounded King drinks from the Grail, and the heavenly dew of the planets is bestowed. In the rubedo the glorified body is resurrected, Isis joins with Osiris to produce Horus, the Grail knight succeeds his Wounded King and marries his master's daughter, and the philosopher's stone is achieved (147).

Just as the alchemical elements were separated, purified, changed, and reunited, so have the divine sparks of creation been separated from their source, changed by earthly experience, and purified by the trials they encountered. They will, like the elements, return to the primal unity. The figures of Adam Kadmon in the Kabbalah, the Gnostic anthropos, and the elusive Mercurius in alchemy are paradigms of the same esoteric truth. Our touchstone is always the symbol of the scattered Body of Light.

Alchemy is the philosophy that enables us to transcend the limitations of mortality: Our divine spark is transmuted into the elixir of life so that the physical vehicle becomes a temple in truth. To find and isolate the quintessentia—the undying part of ourselves—is the quest. Like the oyster that forms a pearl, we must learn to live with irritation and toil in order to achieve this quest. The transmutation of the earthly into the heavenly is, however, not the concern of just alchemy. In the daily transubstantiation of the Mass, bread is offered at the altar and mysteriously becomes the body of Christ. The moment of Redemption in which matter is given the potential of spiritual regeneration is offered for all by one who is the high priest of these Mysteries. Alchemy was able to claim that "the earthly philosopher's stone is the true image of the spiritual and heavenly stone, Jesus Christ." (105) This was neither blasphemous nor alien to the Hermetic tradition; all who follow the way to cosmic consciousness and regeneration of matter use the bridges tradition provides for us. Christ, partaking of both earthly and divine natures, was seen as such a bridge. His Resurrection and the Assumption of his Mother figure frequently in alchemical emblems as symbolic of the achieved Work. Significantly, the term Corpus Christi —the body of Christ—has three meanings: the glorified body of Christ, the consecrated bread upon the altar, and the community of believers who form the macrocosmic body of Christ.

In the mythos of Christ is seen the meeting of two traditions. As Dionysus is torn to pieces by the Titans or Orpheus by the Maenads within the native tradition—both paradigms of the ritual sacrifice in which the tribe partakes of the tortured body of John Barleycorn—so the Red King, part of the Hermetic tradition, dissolves in the alchemical bath of natron, which then turns to pure gold.

The foundation Mysteries of the native tradition speak of the apportioning of the body of the Goddess to form the world. Likewise, the foundation Mysteries of the Hermetic tradition are those of the scattered God. Their reunion has been celebrated from Sumeria to Ireland: from the ritual mating of the Goddess's representative with the King to the Gnostic bridal chamber (380). Red King and White Queen are God and Nature, Christ and Sophia, Mercury and Venus.

The lapsit exillas—the stone that was rejected, that fell from heaven—is matter personified by its guardian, the Anima Mundi or Sophia. Only when the quintessentia embraces the prima materia can the rejected stone become the keystone of creation. The Rosicrucian alchemists were correct in their appaisal of Christ as the philosopher's stone because he, of all created humanity, has achieved not only birth and death, but also resurrection in his created body.

We can only guess at the mysterious encounter of Christ in the depths of the Underworld before his Resurrection. He brought his heavenly light, like that Star of Bethlehem at the place of his birth, into the darkness of the tomb. As one in human flesh, he embraced the human condition of death and dissolution, making it his sister and bride. Thus the laws of nature were altered in an inapprehensible way. The Shroud of Turin bears the imprint of this mysterious encounter. Flesh was offered voluntarily for the redemption of all flesh: a sacrifice that could not be unacceptable. What Christ has done changes the laws of the created world forever (380). Word and wisdom, Logos and Sophia, have embraced, but our Anima Mundi cannot rest from "mantling the guilty globe" until the whole creation is returned to the primal unity.

The Golden Age Restored, an alchemical treatise, speaks of matter personified as the "pure and chaste virgin of whom Adam was formed and created." The alchemist, like Christ, must choose her and say, "[H]er garments are old, defiled, and foul; but I will purge them, and love her with all my heart." (538) Alchemical work is therefore of planetary service, for only by dedication to the whole earth and those living on it can the Great Work be achieved at last.

We have heard how the Emerald Tablet was found in the hands of Hermes Trismegistos, how the oil of mercy was eventually given to Adam's successors, how Adam passed to Seth the precious Pearl of gnosis—these are ultimately stories of the inheritance of an unworldly wisdom. Genetically we are part of the Body of Light; the two serpents on Hermes' caduceus rule our every cell with their encoded spirals of DNA. The cup of gnosis waits to be held to our lips at the end of the quest. These are the esoteric paradigms of the Hermeticist—the same stories that our ancestral shamans once told and which have been reshaped by successive generations of travelers on the Western Way. They are the stories that will be told until the sigh of the last blade of grass, when creation will run backward, a succession of brilliant sparks in the darkness, into the abode of light.

PRACTICES

❖ 19. The Shepherd of Stars ❖

"The ultimate ideal is for every human being is to be psychically androgynous." (127) The meaning of this dictum can be realized within the following exercise. In practice 16, The Caduceus of Hermes, you experienced the elements and learned to integrate them. In this practice you will learn to balance the male and female halves of your inner nature.

Method

Seated in meditation, you visualize that you are standing at the edge of the world. Before you are the two equilibrated pillars. To your left is the white pillar, the Pillar of Mercy on the Tree of Life, denoting the Divine Masculine energy, which is positive and outer in its effect. To your right is the black pillar, the Pillar of Justice on the Tree of Life, denoting the power of the Divine Feminine, which is negative and inner in its effect. (Note that these currents of positive and negative are not at all related to "evil" and "good." They are merely the powers of life that give and take, flow and ebb.) Behind the pillars is a vast night sky of deep indigo in which you see the stars and planets. The heavenly bodies appear both to have eternal stillness and to spin on their axes at the same time.

Begin by concentrating on the individual force of the pillars. If it helps, bring to mind the symbolism of a mythos you feel at home with and transfer its energy to the pillars in order to focus on their effect. Do not hurry; allow the polarized forces to rise. Without touching either pillar, feel their interlocking energies as a magnetic field that is almost tangible. When it is stabilized and firmly established, visualize the power of each pillar emanating as a ray, like the beam of a spotlight, into the heavens beyond you. At the point where the rays intersect, a naked figure stands in an oval of polarized light. It is an androgyne, half female and half male, formed of the dual energies—one side of its body is composed of a perfect man and the other of a perfect woman. The figure is beautiful, with the power and purity of an angel. It is the sum of the pillars' energies in human form. A rainbow scarf swathes the body lightly.

You may end the practice here or go a stage further: The androgyne that stands behind the pillars is your potential self, perfected and balanced. When the time is ripe, and you feel prepared, step between the pillars and stand in the twin rays. You are identifying with the potential and essential nature of the whole earth, representing its place in the cosmos as a balanced and thriving unit. As you stand in the starry vault, receiving the power of both pillars, the Shepherd of Stars, the guardian of the soul flocks, appears before you. He says, "I am Alpha and Omega, the Guardian of the Gates, the Keeper of the Keys of Time." Meditate upon his words and listen to any other words he may have to tell you. You may not go beyond this point. Visualize yourself back before the pillars. Feel the power returning to the pillars and their force shutting down for this time. Seal off in your usual way, making sure you are well earthed.

Discovery

If you have a traditional Tarot deck, you may find it helpful to contemplate Trump twenty-one, the World, on which the androgyne appears. The Shepherd of Stars will appear in whatever shape is appropriate to your needs—after all, he has appeared as Thoth, Hermes, Orpheus, Aeon, and Christ, among others.

❧ 20. Revitalizing Your Roots ❧

If you have consistently worked the practices in this book, you will have begun to walk the Western Way. Perhaps you have set yourself a regular routine of meditation or practical work. You will then have discovered how, from time to time, your energy becomes depleted. While this is to be expected frequently if you are new to working in this way, everyone, from neophyte to adept, experiences this depletion at some time or another—especially after prolonged periods of work or if his or her studies have been very theoretical. In addition, it has been the practice of many Hermetic practitioners to remain in their study and avoid much contact with the outside world. Indeed, many schools of the Hermetic tradition fail to stress the importance of the natural world and our place within it, being concerned with training students in mental and visualizing tasks that ignore their physical well-being. In neglecting your own native tradition and the spirits of the location where you are living, it is possible to become unbalanced and physically devitalized.

Any period of prolonged exhaustion is dangerous and can leave you open to illness. If your energy is seriously depleted, a long vacation from inner work is indicated—and that means a complete break. To avoid depletion, ensure that you are never too mentally elevated or physically remote from nature. Regularly take a simple walk in nature, acknowledging the earth on which you live, sharing its energy as you breathe and sharing the wisdom and love that you have found in your work with the earth. The following practice is designed to help generate vitality. Use it when you need to revitalize yourself, remembering also to give yourself normal rest and refreshment.

The great tree of tradition on which you found your clan totem in practice 1, Finding Your Clan Totem, is the axile tree of the Western Way, the central landmark that intersects all levels of tradition. It is an image that can be fruitfully meditated upon and worked with in many ways, but in this practice we are going to draw on its vitality. There is no need to travel down the central bole of the trunk. If you have already worked practice 1, you should be able to visualize the tree and be there instantly. Take your personal totem with you as your passport and strength.

Method

Sit, relax, and establish an easy rhythm of breathing. This is particularly important if you are tired and tense. Five minutes of regular breathing will start to revitalize you. Visualize the tree before you. It is a beautiful day—just the kind of weather you like best. The earth is springy under your feet. Lay your hand on the trunk of the tree and feel the green strength running beneath the warm bark. Acknowledge your belonging to the tree of tradition.

Turn and look around you. If you have traveled extensively in the Otherworld, you may recognize certain features of the landscape. Beside the tree, sitting on a low mound, is the guardian of tradition. You may not have met him before. You will see him according to your ancestral alignment—there is no one way of seeing him. He is guardian of both the tree and a natural spring that rises nearby next to a slab of greenish stone. In his hands is a drinking horn.

Greet the guardian and request to drink from the spring. He may challenge you and ask by what right you come to drink. In this case, show your totem of belonging. If he accepts you—and he has the right to refuse you if he feels you are not true to the tradition—he will dip the horn into the spring and hand it to you. As you drink, you are deeply refreshed. The waters of the spring rise under the roots of the tree itself, coming from the very depths of the Underworld. Return the horn with thanks and go back to the tree. Sit with your back against its trunk, leaning in to share its pulsing vitality. Feel the strength seeping back into you. Enjoy this feeling of well-being, thank the guardian, and then return to your own time and place.

Discovery

Certain kinds of devitalization occur due to the type of inner tide that is running. The waning phases of the moon, the autumn and winter tides, and personal bodily rhythms need to be taken into account—especially at the onset of menstruation or of menopause. You should not attempt inner work other than very general meditation if you are pregnant. At that time all your physical and psychic energies should be engaged in nourishing the growing child. While male bodily rhythms are not as marked as female ones, men should likewise record and plot their own rhythms.

❖ 21. *Guardians of* Anima Mundi ❖

At this point in your work, you have learned many things from the spirits and guardians of the Otherworld in your meditations. This exercise encourages you to give something back. It is a meditation practice that can be performed before you go to sleep or incorporated into your prayers.

Method

As you lie down to sleep, visualize the four elemental guardians around your bed. They may be seen as the great archons of practice 15, The Foursquare Citadel, or as angels or as faery beings. Each of them bears an emblem of the element it guards. In the east is the guardian of air with the sword of life. In the south is the guardian of fire with the spear of light. In the west is the guardian of water with the grail of love. In the north is the guardian of earth with the stone of law.

These are the powerful defenders of our planet and all that live upon it. As you acknowledge them, one by one, experience your own connection with the guardians by feeling within your body the corresponding element of each—the air in your lungs, the fire in your blood, the water in your body, the physical substance of your frame—and say, in turn:

Blessed be the precious and preserving air, by which we are given life.
Blessed be the precious and preserving fire, by which we are warmed.
Blessed be the precious and preserving water, by which we are cleansed.
Blessed be the precious and preserving earth, by which we are sustained.

Be aware also of the mighty spirit that surrounds the planet, Anima Mundi herself, the Spirit of Earth, and acknowledge the protection that she gives us all. At the same time, be aware of the spirit that is within you and say:

Blessed be the precious and preserving spirit that is within and
around me.

When this meditation is established—and it will build speedily with continual practice—become aware of the zone of Anima Mundi, a belt of starry atmosphere that rings our planet. Now send up your deepest aspirations for the good of the planet in a prayer of loving intention.

Discovery

If you perform this practice nightly, sending up your prayers for the world's good to this boundary of the earth's soul, then all beings will imbibe, dream, and be nourished by the common pool of loving thoughts gathered there. When you awake, be aware of the elements first thing and throughout the day, blessing each as you use it: when you first consciously breath the air upon leaving the house, when you light the fire or turn on the stove or kettle, when you wash your hands, when you step out on the ground. The more you repeat this practice, the more you will be aware of the messages of your body. As you become a conscious earth walker in your daily life, you also become a soul defender of Anima Mundi.

Epilogue

Tomorrow's Tradition

Ultima Cumaei venit jam carminis aetas;
Magnus ab integro saeclorum pascitur ordo.
lam redit et virgo, redeunt Saturnia regna,
lam nova progenies caelo demittitur alto.

Now comes the last age according to the oracle at Cumae:
the great series of lifetimes is renewed. Now comes the
Virgin goddess once again, the golden days of Saturn's
reign return and a new race descends from heaven.
—Virgil, Eclogues

The sleeping place of the Age of Gold is in the depths of
every human heart.
—J. C. Powys, Morwyn

We have come a long way in space and time since we set out on a journey with our guide at the beginning of part 1. Like the Fool in the Tarot we have journeyed through the sequence of twenty-one practices, each of which has revealed some of the secrets of the major arcana from Magician to World. We have explored the inward spiral of the native tradition, visited ancient places, performed meditations and visualizations, found an inner guide and teacher, faced the guardians of the road, and passed beyond them through doors into inner worlds. There, perhaps, you have begun to map out your own inner landscape, to seek the answers to questions that have disturbed or fascinated you in your daily life. In following the outward spiral of the Hermetic tradition, we have perhaps discovered that the place of arrival is no longer the same as the place of departure.

390

Just as we cannot step twice into the same river, so we cannot expect to find the same old traditions in our own time and place. Traditions must transform in order to move on. We stand on the verge of a new beginning that is neither the fulfillment of a millennial apocalypse nor the blossoming of a lost Golden Age, but rather a nexus of traditions. What is the next likely step on this road we have been following from Foretime to future?

We are at a time when the wisdom from all paths and disciplines is meeting, pouring into one great river that empties into the sea. In the first edition of this book, back in the early 1980s, we predicted that "a universal development of the power to communicate over vast distances may not be so far off." Despite the caution of governments and regimes that have sought to limit use of the Worldwide Web, the surface of the earth has indeed been connected by global communication. The dissemination of knowledge is no longer in the hands of the experts. The Internet as a forum for the sharing of knowledge, as a meeting place for the like-minded, is acting as a leveler and balancer around the world. But knowledge is still not wisdom.

When wisdom from many streams comes together, then the mind has no limits; it can reach out beyond any boundaries of time and space we care to set. Above all, we must recognize that there are no limits to what we can achieve other than those we set ourselves, and there are no bolts and bars between the worlds except those we have personally hammered in place.

The ancients were right to attach so much importance to the idea of the vital spark within each of us, but by seeing it as trapped in flesh, they laid the foundation of a false teaching that eventually caused many to despise the body. But we must now realize that our physical selves are of the utmost value. From safe harbor of the body we depart on voyages of discovery and to it we return, to the welcome of home.

The soul too has looked to be welcomed home. Its longing for the place of its origin has impelled, through the ages, the search for the promised land, for a return to the paradisal home—whether the native tradition's earthly paradise of the ancestors or the Hermetic tradition's celestial heaven—from our state of seeming exile. Already in our time, though, the search for an endpoint to the soul's journey seems less relevant.

Now we have a more holistic view of the universe. From this perspective the alchemical path seems increasingly relevant: We no longer quest for a spiritual elevation that leaves the body behind. Instead we seek a balanced integration of mind, emotions, body, and spirit. Rather than flying blind toward whatever infinite realm we are seeking, we now aim, in a measured way, to be in tune with ourselves as well as with the infinite.

As the membership of institutional religions has waned, the quest for personal spirituality has flourished. There are now many unaffiliated "people of spirit" pursuing their own way. In abandoning the old tribal consciousness—which has survived well within institutions—in favor of individual consciousness, they have taken an evolutionary step. But the step ahead of us is an even greater one—from individual consciousness to cosmic consciousness, where the well-being of the secret commonwealth of all living beings will be the central concern. For now, we exist in an era in which individual consciousness inspires us with its advances and appalls us with its loveless selfishness. Not all people are "people of spirit"—many have abandoned belief in or involvement with spiritual life. For the first time in the history of the planet a great number of people believe that this present life is all there is and that the soul does not survive the body. Among the consequences of this belief are a mentality based on the short-term, a failure to understand cause and effect, a neglect of responsibility to our descendants, and personal behavior that can plummet to the depth of carelessness and even barbarity. As secularism and consumer-minded selfishness battle with personal integrity and world responsibility, this is certainly no time for complacency. One boon to remember is that in the heart of the labyrinth, compassion, wisdom, and truth may always be found, and we must seek them out if we are to continue evolving.

The sacred continuum of microcosm is part of the macrocosm. When we deny this, we lose our wisdom. How we each maintain our connection to both sides of reality, understanding them as two parts of the garment of life, matters very much. As Dion Fortune said, "Life is God made manifest and is sacred, and unless you have respect for life in a man you cannot approach him . . . for it is the deeper healing . . . of the soul itself which builds the body." (166)

The reemergence of the Divine Feminine and the balancing of masculine and feminine energies are signs of hope marking the road ahead, as is a new understanding of the multiplicity of roads that have brought us to this place. At last the division of the paths is ending and some are beginning to realize that there has only ever been one goal, even though there have always been many ways to reach it. Those who walk the

Fig. 35. Wisdom shines gloriously, enthroned in the center of the soul.

Way must learn to think differently from those people who are still at war. We must relearn whatever we have forgotten since the Foretime and fashion a new way of being, a new possibility of realizing the truth of our place in the cosmos.

This book is by no means a complete course in the traditions of the Western Mysteries. If your soul has been kindled here, then you will no doubt find that you have been walking the Way for some time already. You may wish to make more regular your practice of its wisdom by joining a mystery school or magical group, or you may want to continue mapping your own way or participate in one of the living spiritual traditions in which your spirit finds freedom. Much of what lies on these pages is worthwhile only if it is applied to your own life on a daily basis. The Way must be lived or it will remain a dusty, abstract study in your hands, a concept rather than a real, multidimensional path. Our hope is that you will find useful ways of improving your perceptions, deepening your connection to your allies and guardians—and marking the way for others.

It is said that the teacher and the taught comprise the teaching between them. The teaching is different for everyone: It is the individual reaction to it that reflects the abiding wisdom of a tradition from one generation to the next. With this in mind, create your own program of study, meditation, and practice, for it is these three disciplines that form the basic components of an esoteric way of life. Study gives us the material to work with, meditation shows us new approaches to the work and helps fix our individual response in a symbolic way, and practice grounds our inner experiences in outer reality. It is often the last of these that students of the Western Mysteries find most difficult. What we aim to mediate through ritual working is inevitably going to affect our mundane lives in the home, in the office, and in relationships. Everyday life is the best training ground of all. To test this out, try to live one whole day in accordance with your esoteric principles: Eat and drink with total attention to the items being consumed—their taste, the goodness being derived from their digestion. See everyone you meet as possessing the divine spark, see each being as someone as deserving as yourself. Perform your daily tasks with total attention to the principle involved: Cleaning the house, for instance, is really an extension of self-clarification and is itself a reflection of macrocosmic order. When faced with sudden decisions, try to see the choices before you not only as they affect you, but also as they affect others and as they affect the cosmos. Be attentive to your moments of relaxation: Work hard, but also rest well; feel the cessation of work as the commencement of a creative stillness that will rejuvenate your work. At the end of one day spent in this way, write down your realizations. You may then begin to understand just what is involved in the word *practice*.

Whatever path you choose for your study and work, always include your own perceptions and realizations. Trust your instincts, have faith in the journey, find encouragement in those who walk with you, and be resolute and loving as you find your way.

God said to man: I have placed you in the world that you may more readily see what you are. I have made you neither earthly nor heavenly, neither a mortal nor an immortal being, in order that you, as your own sculptor, may carve features for yourself. You may degenerate into an animal, but by using your free will you may also be reborn as a god-like being. (127)

We have taken many things for granted in this book—for example, the belief in other states of being, other worlds, and other orders of creation above and beyond what we recognize in our normal functioning state. We have stated that humankind has a future, that it is not necessarily doomed to extinction, even that it may in fact be on the verge of a wholly new development.

None of the gods of heaven will ever quit heaven, and pass its boundary, and come down to earth; but man ascends even to heaven, and measures it; and what is more than all beside, he mounts to heaven without quitting the earth; so vast a distance can he put forth his power. We must not shrink then from saying that a man on earth is a mortal god, and that god in heaven is a mortal man. (533)

Toward this end we have offered practices and techniques aimed at connecting us to the infinite worlds around us and to bringing back to our own dimension the wisdom of the Otherworld and the inner realm and making it a lasting part of our own eternal becoming. The techniques on their own mean nothing without the commitment to the truths that stand behind them. To some, the esoteric philosophy of the Western Mysteries is but a framework on which to hang the stuff of wonder, but how much more wonderful to be clothed in its wisdom! The truths to which we each dedicate ourselves as walkers between the worlds become at last the shining robe of the initiate.

In looking to the future, we have much to keep in mind and a great deal to consider and meditate upon. A long line of teachers stands behind us; another line stretches out ahead. We are all links in a chain of transmission. All of us together make up solar systems, even whole cosmologies with fixed stars and wandering planets. There are no known limits to where we may go or how far we may travel. We stand with map and compass in hand, ready to begin traveling, in the company of the guardians and co-walkers, into worlds that are strangely very familiar. All we have to do is step forth. The path awaits you, in your own time and in your own way. May your journey be as fruitful and joyful as ours has been, and may you always return safely!

> Hermes, offspring of Dionysos who revels in the dance
> and of Aphrodite, the Paphian maiden of the fluttering eyelids,
> you frequent the sacred house of Persephone
> as guide through the earth of ill-fated souls
> which you bring to their haven when their time has come,
> charming them with your sacred wand and giving them sleep
> from which you rose them again. To you indeed Persephone
> gave the office, throughout wide Tartaros,
> to lead the way for the eternal souls of men.
> But, blessed one, grant a good end for the initiate's work. (22)

Resources

The following groups and organizations offer training courses or contacts with local groups. For more details, please visit their Web sites, where you will also find contact information. If you choose to write to any, please include a large, self-addressed, stamped envelope (if you are in the country of addressee) or two international reply-paid coupons (for those overseas).

Native Traditions

Covenant of the Goddess
P.O. Box 1226, Berkeley, CA 94701, USA
www.cog.org
An international organization of cooperating and autonomous Wiccan congregations.

Foundation for Inspirational and Oracular Studies (FIOS)
BCM Hallowquest, London WC1N 3XX, England
www.hallowquest.org.uk
Founded by Caitlín and John Matthews with Felicity Wombwell, FIOS offers progressive training courses in Celtic and ancestral shamanism and hosts other courses in the Western Mysteries. FIOS encourages the oral and sacred traditions, presenting a series of master classes with living exemplars of these traditions. For membership or to purchase a recording of meditations, write to the address above or visit their Web site.

Foundation for Shamanic Studies
P.O. Box 1937, Mill Valley, CA 94942, USA
www.shamanism.org
Founded by Michael Harrier, this organization offers training in core (noncultural) shamanic techniques worldwide.

Order of Bards, Ovates, and Druids
P.O. Box 1333, Lewes, E. Sussex BN7 3ZG, England
www.druidry.org
Founded by Philip Carr-Gomm, this druidic order is rooted in the Celtic Mysteries, offering experiential training and correspondence courses in druidry. It maintains groups worldwide.

Pagan Federation
B.M. Box 7097, London WC1N 3XX, England
www.paganfed.demon.co.uk
Promotes contact between Pagan groups and genuine seekers, promotes international Pagan contact, and provides information about Paganism to the public.

R. J. Stewart
www.dreampower.com
Trained by magician W. G. Gray, R. J. Stewart works in a broad spectrum within the Western Mysteries, from the ancestral to the kabbalistic traditions. For information about his workshops, concerts, events, and books, visit his Web site.

Scandinavian Centre for Shamanic Studies
Artillerivei 63, Lejl 140, DK 2300 Copenhagen, Denmark
www.shamanism.dk
Courses in Europe are led by Jonathan Horwitz and Annette Horst in core (noncultural) and Scandinavian shamanic techniques.

Hermetic, Gnostic, and Mystical Traditions

Alchemy Web Site
www.levity.com/alchemy
Provides information on alchemy, alchemical emblems, methods, publications, and traditions as well as details of an alchemical training course by Adam McLain.

Builders of the Adytum
5010 North Figueroa St., Los Angeles, CA 90042, USA
www.bota.org
European address: 3 avenue des Palmiers, 6600 Perpignan, France
Offers correspondence courses on the Kabbalah, alchemy, and the Tarot.

Fellowship of Isis
Clonegal Castle, Enniscorthy, County Wexford, Ireland
www.fellowshipofisis.com
International nonsectarian association for all who venerate the Goddess.
Training courses and ordination in mysteries of the Goddess are offered
by groups worldwide.

The House of Life
www.thehouseoflife.co.uk
also www.naomiozaniec.co.uk for information on the role of the priestess,
past and present
Founded by Naomi Ozanied, this contemporary mystery school has been
established in the Western Mystery tradition.

Kabbalah Society
30a Greencroft Gdns., London NW6 3LT, England
www.kabbalahsociety.org
Courses and training by Z'ev Ben Shimon Halevi (Warren Kenton) in
practical Kabbalah from the Toledano tradition of medieval Spain.
Conferences, workshops, and study groups worldwide.

Servants of the Light
P.O. Box 215, St. Helier, Jersey, Channel Islands, UK
www.servantofthelight.org
A mystery school offering a supervised correspondence course and training events based on the Kabbalah and the Western Mysteries.

Society of the Inner Light
38 Steele's Rd., London NW3 4RG, England
www.innerlight.org
A mystery school founded by Dion Fortune, offering correspondence
courses on the Kabbalah.

Bibliography

1. Abulafia, A. *The Path of the Names.* Berkeley, Calif.: Trigram, 1976.

2. Adams, H. *Mont-Saint-Michel and Chartres.* London: Hamlyn, 1980.

3. Adler, M. *Drawing Down the Moon.* Boston: Beacon Press, 1979.

4. Agrippa, C. *Occult Philosophy.* Wellingborough, U.K.: Aquarian Press, 1975.

5. Ahern, G. *Sun at Midnight.* Wellingborough, U.K.: Aquarian Press, 1984.

6. Ainsworth, W. H. *Windsor Castle.* London: Collins, 1973.

7. Albertus, Frater. *Alchemist's Handbook.* London: Routledge and Kegan Paul, 1976.

8. Allen, P. M., ed. *A Christian Rosenkreutz Anthology.* New York: Rudolf Steiner, 1968.

9. Allen, R. H. *Star Names: Their Lore and Meaning.* New York: Dover Books, 1963.

10. Anderson, W. *Open Secrets: A Western Guide to Tibetan Buddhism.* Harmondsworth, Middlesex, U.K.: Penguin, 1980.

11. ———. *Holy Places in the British Isles.* London: Ebury Press, 1983.

12. Anonymous. *Meditations on the Tarot: A Journey into Christian Hermeticism.* New York: Amity House, 1975.

13. Apocryphal New Testament. Translated by M. R. James. Oxford: Oxford University Press, 1924.

14. Apuleius, Lucius. *The Golden Ass.* Translated by Robert Graves. Harmondsworth, Middlesex, U.K.: Penguin Books, 1950.

15. Ashcroft-Nowicki, D. *The Shining Paths.* Wellingborough, U.K.: Aquarian Press, 1983.

16. Ashe, G. *The Ancient Wisdom.* London: Macmillan, 1977.

17. ———. *Avalonian Quest.* London: Methuen, 1982.

18. ———. *Camelot and the Vision of Albion.* London: Heinemann, 1971.

19. ———. *Finger and the Moon.* London: Heinemann, 1973.

20. Assagioli, R. *Psychosynthesis.* Wellingborough, U.K.: Turnstone Press, 1975.

21. Assembly of Rabbis of the Reform Synagogues of Great Britain, eds. *Forms of Prayer for Jewish Worship*. London: Assembly of Rabbis of the Reform Synagogues of Great Britain, 1977.

22. Athanassakis, A. N., trans. *The Orphic Hymns*. Missoula, Mont.: Scholars Press, 1977.

23. Aubrey, J. *Monumenta Britannica*. Boston: Little Brown and Co., 1980.

24. Saint Augustine. *The City of God*. Harmondsworth, Middlesex, U.K.: Penguin Books, 1972.

25. Aurora Consurgens, ed. *M.-L. von Franz*. New York: Pantheon Books, 1966.

26. Bachofen, J. J. *Myth, Religion and Mother Right*. Princeton, N.J.: Bollingen, Princetown University Press, 1967.

27. Bacon, F. *Advancement of Learning and New Atlantis*. London: Oxford University Press, 1906.

28. *The Bahir*. Translated by A. Kaplan. New York: Weiser, 1979.

29. Baigent, M., H. Lincoln, and R. Leigh. *Holy Blood, Holy Grail*. London: Cape, 1982.

30. Bailey, A. A. *The Externalization of the Hierarchy*. London: Lucis Press, 1957.

31. ———. *From Intellect to Intuition*. London: Lucis Press, 1932.

32. ———. *Glamour: A World Problem*. London: Lucis Press, 1950.

33. ———. *The Rays and the Initiations*. London: Lucis Press, 1960.

34. ———. *A Treatise on White Magic*. London: Lucis Press, 1934.

35. Bamford, C. "Natureworld: The Hermetic Tradition and Today." In Schwaller de Lubicz, R. A. *Natureworld*. Great Barrington, Mass.: Lindisfarne Press, 1982.

36. Banks, N. N. *The Golden Thread*. London: Lucis Press, 1963.

37. Barbault, A. *Gold of a Thousand Mornings*. London: Neville Spearman, 1975.

38. Barber, R. *The Arthurian Legends*. Woodbridge, Suffolk, U.K.: Boydell and Brewer, 1979.

39. Barker, B. *Symbols of Sovereignty*. Newton Abbot, U.K.: Westbridge Books, 1979.

40. Bates, B. *The Real Middle Earth*. London: Sidgewick and Jackson, 2002.

41. Bausch, W. J. *Storytelling: Imagination and Faith*. Mystic, Conn.: Twenty-Third Publishers, 1984.

42. Bellamy, H. S. *Moons, Myths and Man*. London: Faber and Faber, 1949.

43. Bentov, L. *Stalking the Wild Pendulum*. Rochester, Vt.: Destiny Books, 1988.

44. Berlin, S. *Amergin: An Enigma of the Forest*. Devon, U.K.: David and Charles, 1978.

45. The Bible (Revised Standard Version). London: Nelson, 1966.

46. Blake, W. *Poetry and Prose*. Edited by G. Keynes. London: Nonesuch Library, 1975.

47. Blakeley, J. D. *Mystical Tower of the Tarot*. London: Watkins, 1974.

48. Blavatsky, H. P. *The Secret Doctrine*. London: Theosophical Publishing House, 1970.

49. ———. *Studies in Occultism*. London: Sphere Books, 1974.

50. Bolton, J. D. P. *Aristaeus of Proconnesus*. London: Oxford University Press, 1962.

51. Book of Enoch. Translated by R. H. Charles. London: SPCK, 1982.

52. Bord, J., and C. Bord. *Earth Rites*. London: Granada, 1982.

53. Bradbury, R. *Fahrenheit 451*. London: Hart-Davis, 1954.

54. Branston, B. *Gods of the North*. London: Thames and Hudson, 1955.

55. ———. *Lost Gods of England*. London: Thames and Hudson, 1957.

56. Brennan, M. *The Stars and the Stones*. London: Thames and Hudson, 1983.

57. Briggs, K. *A Dictionary of Fairies*. London: Allan Lane, 1976.

58. Bronstein, H. *A Passover Haggadah*. Harmondsworth, Middlesex, U.K.: Penguin, 1974.

59. Brown, A. C. L. *Origin of the Grail Legend*. Cambridge, Mass.: Harvard University Press, 1943.

60. Brown, T. *The Fate of the Dead*. Woodbridge, Suffolk, U.K.: Boydell and Brewer, 1979.

61. Bruno, G. *The Expulsion of the Triumphant Beast*. Translated by A. D. Imerti. New Brunswick, N.J.: Rutgers University Press, 1964.

62. Budge, E. A. W. *Osiris: The Egyptian Religion of Resurrection*. New York: University Books, 1961.

63. Burckhardt, T. *Alchemy: Science of the Cosmos, Science of the Soul*. Translated by W. Stoddart. London: Stuart and Watkins, 1967.

64. Burl, A. *Rites of the Gods*. London: J. M. Dent, 1981.

65. Burland, C. A. *Myths of Life and Death*. London: Macmillan, 1974.

66. Button, U., and J. Dolley. *Christian Evolution: Moving Towards a Global Spirituality*. Wellingborough, U.K.: Turnstone, 1984.

67. Butler, E. M. *The Myth of the Magus*. Cambridge: Cambridge University Press, 1979.

68. ———. *Ritual Magic*. Cambridge: Cambridge University Press, 1979.

69. Butler, W. E. *Apprenticed to Magic*. Wellingborough, U.K.: Aquarian Press, 1962.

70. Cade, C. M., and N. Coxhead. *The Awakened Mind.* London: Wildwood House, 1979.

71. Caesar. *De Bello Gallico.* Harmondsworth, Middlesex, U.K.: Penguin Books, 1953.

72. Caldecott, S. "The Treasures of Tradition." In *Resurgence,* no. 102, January/February 1984.

73. Calvino, I. *The Castle of Crossed Destinies.* London: Secker, 1977.

74. Campbell, J. *Flight of the Wild Gander.* South Bend, Ind.: Gateway Editions, n.d.

75. ———. *The Masks of God.* London: Souvenir Press, 1968–69.

76. ———. *The Mythic Image.* Princeton, N.J.: Princeton University Press, 1974.

77. ———. *Myths to Live By.* London: Souvenir Press, 1973.

78. Carmichael, A. *Carmina Gadelica.* Edinburgh: Scottish Academic Press, 1928.

79. Carter, F. *The Dragon of the Alchemists.* London: Elkin Matthews, 1926.

80. Carylon, R. *Guide to the Gods.* London: Heinemann/Quixote Press, 1981.

81. Casaubon, M. *A True and Faithful Relation of What Passed for Many Years Between Dr. John Dee and Some Spirits.* Glasgow: Antonine with Golden Dragon Press, 1974.

82. Castledown, R. *The Wilmington Giant.* Wellingborough, U.K.: Turnstone Press, 1983.

83. Catherine of Siena. *The Dialogues.* London: SPCK, 1980.

84. Cavendish, R. *King Arthur and the Grail.* London: Weidenfeld and Nicolson, 1978.

85. ———. *Legends of the World.* London: Orbis, 1982.

86. Chant, J. *The High Kings.* London: Allen and Unwin, 1983.

87. Chapman, V. *Bladdud the Birdman.* London: Rex Collings, 1978.

88. ———. *The Three Damosels.* London: Gollancz, 1996.

89. *The Charlemagne Cycle: Huon of Bordeaux, Chanson de Roland.* Translated by D. L. Sayers. Harmondsworth, Middlesex, U.K.: Penguin Books, 1957.

90. Charon, J. *The Unknown Spirit.* London: Coventure, 1983.

91. Chesterton, G. K. *Collected Poems.* London: Methuen, 1936.

92. Chevalier, G. *The Sacred Magician: A Ceremonial Diary.* London: Hart-Davis MacGibbon, 1976.

93. Child, F. J. *English and Scottish Popular Ballads.* New York: Dover, 1965.

94. Chrétien de Troyes. *Arthurian Romances.* Translated by W. W. Comfort. London: J. M. Dent, 1914.

95. ———. *Conte du Graal.* Translated by R. W. Linker. Chapel Hill: University of North Carolina Press, 1952.

96. Christian, P. *The History and Practice of Magic.* London: Forge Press, 1952.

97. Christie-Murray, D. *A History of Heresy.* London: New English Library, 1976.

98. *El Cid.* Translated by L. B. Simpson. Berkeley: University of California Press, 1957.

99. Claremont de Castillejo, L. *Knowing Woman: A Feminine Psychology.* New York: G. P. Putnam, 1973.

100. Cohn, N. *The Pursuit of the Millennium.* London: Paladin, 1970.

101. Colquhoun, L. *The Sword of Wisdom: MacGregor Mathers and the Golden Dawn.* London: Neville Spearman, 1975.

102. Coomaraswamy, R. P. *The Destruction of the Christian Tradition.* London: Perennial Books, 1981.

103. Cooper, J. C. *An Illustrated Encyclopaedia of Traditional Symbols.* London: Thames and Hudson, 1978.

104. Corbin, H. *The Man of Light in Iranian Sufism.* Boulder, Colo.: Shambhala, 1978.

105. Coudert, A. *Alchemy: The Philosophers' Stone.* London: Wildwood, 1980.

106. Court, S. *The Meditators' Manual.* Wellingborough, U.K.: Aquarian Press, 1984.

107. Craighead, Meinrad. *The Sign of the Tree.* London: Mitchell Beazley, 1979.

108. Critchlow, K. "Temenos and Temple." In *Temenos Review* 1, 1981.

109. Crossley-Holland, K. *The Norse Myths.* London: Andre Deutsch, 1980.

110. Crowley, A. *777.* Privately printed by Ordo Templi Orientis, n.d.

111. Crowley, J. *Little, Big.* London: Gollancz, 1982.

112. Cumont, F. *The Mysteries of Mithras.* New York: Dover, 1956.

113. Currer-Briggs, N. and R. Gambier. *Debrett's Family Historian.* 1981.

114. Daly, M. *Beyond God the Father.* Boston: Beacon Press, 1973.

115. Daniélou, A. *Shiva and Dionysus.* Rochester, Vt.: Inner Traditions, 1984.

116. Dante. *The Divine Comedy.* Translated by L. Binyon. London: Agenda, 1979.

117. Dart, J. *The Laughing Savior.* New York: Harper and Row, 1976.

118. Davidson, G. *A Dictionary of Angels.* New York: Free Press with Collier-Macmillan, 1967.

119. Davies, W. D., and L. Finkelstein, eds. *The Persian Period.* Cambridge History of Judaism, vol. 1. Cambridge: Cambridge University Press, 1984.

120. de Boron, R. *Merlin and the Grail: Joseph of Arimathea, Merlin, Perceval: The Trilogy of Prose Romances Attributed to Robert de Boron.* Translated by Nigel Bryant. Woodbridge, Suffolk, U.K.: D. S. Brewer, 2001.

121. de Chardin, Teilhard. *Hymn of the Universe*. London: Collins, 1965.

122. ———. *Towards the Future*. London: Collins, 1975.

123. De Jong, H. M. E. *Michael Maier's Atalanta Fugiens: Sources of an Alchemical Book of Emblems*. Leiden: E. J. Brill, 1969.

124. de Jubainville, F. *Irish Mythological Cycle and Celtic Mythology*. Dublin: O'Donoghue, 1903.

125. Deacon, R. *John Dee*. London: Frederick Muller, 1968.

126. Dee, J. *The Hieroglyphic Monarch*. New York: Weiser, 1975.

127. della Mirandola, P. *On the Dignity of Man, On Being and the One, Heptaplus*. Indianapolis: Bobbs-Merrill, 1965.

128. Denning, M., and O. Phillips. *The Magical Philosophy* (5 volumes). St. Paul: Llewellyn, 1974–81.

129. Devereux, P., and Ian Thompson. *The Ley Hunter's Companion*. London: Thames and Hudson, 1979.

130. Diodorus Siculus. *The Library of History*. Translated by C. H. Oldfather. London: Heinemann/Harvard University Press, 1935.

131. Dionysius the Areopagite. *The Divine Names and the Mystical Theology*. Translated by C. E. Rolt. London: SPCK, 1940.

132. ———. *The Mystical Theology and the Celestial Hierarchies*. Translated and edited by the Shrine of Wisdom. Fintry, Scotland: Shrine of Wisdom, 1949.

133. *Dream of Scipio*. Translated by R. Bullock. Wellingborough, U.K.: Aquarian, 1983.

134. Drower, E. S. *The Secret Adam: A Study of Nasoraean Gnosis*. Oxford: Oxford University Press, 1960.

135. Drury, N. *Don Juan, Mescalito and Modern Magic*. London: Routledge and Kegan Paul, 1978.

136. ———. *The Shaman and the Magician*. London: Routledge and Kegan Paul, 1982.

137. Duggan, A. *The Devil's Brood*. London: Faber and Faber, 1937.

138. Durdin-Robertson, L. *Goddesses of Chaldea, Syria and Egypt*. Enniscothy, Eire: Cesara, 1973.

139. Durrell, L. *The Alexandria Quartet*. London: Faber and Faber, 1968.

140. Eliade, M. *A History of Religious Ideas: From the Stone Age to the Eleusinian Mysteries*. London: Collins, 1979.

141. ———. *A History of Religious Ideas: From Gautama Buddha to the Triumph of Christianity*. Chicago: University of Chicago Press, 1982.

142. Eliot, T. S. *Collected Poems*. London: Faber and Faber, 1969.

143. Ellwood, R. S. *Religious and Spiritual Groups in Modern America*. Englewood Cliffs, N.J.: Prentice Hall, 1973.

144. Ellwood Post, W. *Saints, Signs and Symbols.* London: SPCK, 1962.

145. Epstein, P. *Kabbalah: The Way of the Jewish Mystic.* New York: Weiser, 1978.

146. Every, G. *Christian Mythology.* London: Hamlyn, 1970.

147. Fabricius, J. *Alchemy.* Copenhagen: Rosenkilde and Bagger, 1976.

148. Ferguson, J. *Illustrated Encyclopaedia of Mysticism and the Mystery Religions.* London, Thames and Hudson, 1976.

149. ———. *Jesus in the Tide of Time.* London: Routledge and Kegan Paul, 1980.

150. Ferguson, M. *The Aquarian Conspiracy.* London: Routledge and Kegan Paul, 1981.

151. Ferrucci, P. *What We May Be.* Wellingborough, U.K.: Turnstone Press, 1982.

152. Ficino, M. *The Letters of Marsilio Ficino,* vols. 1–5. London: Shepheard Walwyn, 1975.

153. Figulus, B. *A Golden and Blessed Casket of Nature's Marvels.* London: Vincent Stuart, 1963.

154. Fleming, D. L. *Contemporary Reading of the Spiritual Exercises.* St. Louis: Institute of Jesuit Sources, 1980.

155. Fludd, R. *The Origin and Structure of the Cosmos.* Edinburgh: Magnum Opus Hermetic Sourceworks, 1982.

156. Fontenrose, J. *Python.* Berkeley: University of California Press, 1959.

157. Fortune, D. *Applied Magic.* Wellingborough, U.K.: Aquarian Press, 1962.

158. ———. *Aspects of Occultism.* Wellingborough, U.K.: Aquarian Press 1973.

159. ———. *Avalon of the Heart.* Wellingborough, U.K.: Aquarian Press, 1971.

160. ———. *The Cosmic Doctrine.* Wellingborough, U.K.: Aquarian Press, 1976.

161. ———. *Esoteric Orders and Their Work.* St. Paul: Llewellyn, 1978.

162. ———. *Esoteric Philosophy of Love and Marriage.* Wellingborough, U.K.: Aquarian Press, 1970.

163. ———. *The Goat-Foot God.* London: Star Books, 1976.

164. ———. *Moon Magic.* Wellingborough, U.K.: Aquarian Press, 1956.

165. ———. *The Mystical Qabalah.* London: Ernest Benn, 1976.

166. ———. *Principles of Esoteric Healing.* Edited by Gareth Knight. Oceanside, Calif.: Sun Chalice Books, 2000.

167. ———. *The Sea Priestess.* Wellingborough, U.K.: Aquarian Press, 1957.

168. ———. *The Secrets of Dr. Taverner.* St. Paul: Llewellyn, 1979.

169. ———. *The Training and Work of an Initiate.* Wellingborough, U.K.: Aquarian Press, 1930.

170. Fouquet, J. *The Hours of Etienne Chevalier.* London: Thames and Hudson, 1972.

171. *Four Ancient Books of Wales.* Translated by W. F. Skene. Edinburgh, Edmonston and Douglas, 1968.

172. French, R. M. *The Way of the Pilgrim.* London: SPCK, 1930.

173. Gadal, A. *Sur le Chemin du Saint-Graal.* Haarlem: Rozekruis Pers, 1960.

174. Gardner, G. *The Meaning of Witchcraft.* Wellingborough, U.K.: Aquarian Press, 1959.

175. ———. *Witchcraft Today.* London: Rider, 1954.

176. Garner, A. *The Owl Service.* London: Collins, 1967.

177. Garrison, J. *The Darkness of God: Theology after Hiroshima.* London: SCM, 1982.

178. Geoffrey of Monmouth. *Historia Regum Britannia.* Translated by L. Thorpe. Harmondsworth, Middlesex, U.K.: Penguin Books, 1966.

179. Gill, E. *Holy Tradition of Working.* Edited by Brian Keeble. Ipswich, U.K.: Brian Keeble, 1983.

180. Ginzburg, C. *The Night Battles.* London: Routledge and Kegan Paul, 1983.

181. Giraldus Cambrensis. *The Journey through Wales.* Translated by L. Thorpe. Harmondsworth, Middlesex, U.K.: Penguin, 1978.

182. *The Gododdin.* Translated by D. O'Grady. Dublin: Dolmen Press, 1977.

183. Godwin, J. *Athanasius Kircher.* London: Thames and Hudson, 1979.

184. ———. "The Golden Chain of Orpheus." In *Temenos Review* 4 and 5, 1984.

185. ———. *Mystery Religions and the Ancient World.* London: Thames and Hudson, 1981.

186. ———. *Robert Fludd.* London: Thames and Hudson, 1979.

187. Golding, W. *The Inheritors.* London: Faber and Faber, 1955.

188. Gordon, S. *Suibne and the Crow God.* London: New English Library, 1975.

189. Gorman, P. *Pythagoras.* London: Routledge and Kegan Paul, 1979.

190. Gorres, I. F. *Broken Lights.* London: Burns and Oates, 1964.

191. Grant, F. C. *Hellenistic Religions: The Age of Syncretism.* New York: Bobbs-Merrill, 1953.

192. Graves, R. *Greek Myths.* London: Cassell, 1958.

193. ———. *Seven Days in New Crete.* London: Cassell, 1949.

194. ———. *The White Goddess.* London: Faber and Faber, 1948.

195. Graves, R., and R. Patai. *Hebrew Myths.* London: Cassell, 1963.

196. Graves, W. *Adam's Rib.* London: Trianon Press, 1955.

197. Gray, W. G. *Inner Traditions of Magic.* London: Aquarian Press, 1970.

198. ———. *The Ladder of Lights.* Toddington, Gloucestershire, U.K.: Helios Books, 1975.

199. ———. *Magical Ritual Methods*. Toddington, Gloucestershire, U.K.: Helios, 1971.

200. ———. *The Talking Tree*. New York: Weiser, 1977.

201. ———. *Western Inner Workings*. New York: Weiser, 1983.

202. Green, M. *Experiments in Aquarian Magic*. Wellingborough, U.K.: Aquarian, 1985.

203. ———. *A Harvest of Festivals*. London: Longmans, 1980.

204. ———. *Magic in the Aquarian Age*. Wellingborough, U.K.: Aquarian Press, 1983.

205. Greene, B., and V. Gollancz. *God of a Hundred Names*. London: Gollancz, 1962.

206. Greer, M. K. *Tarot for Your Self: A Workbook for Personal Transformation*. North Hollywood, Calif.: Newcastle, 1984.

207. ———. *Women of the Golden Dawn*. Rochester, Vt.: Park Street Press, 1995.

208. Grimm, J., and W. Grimm. *Grimm's Tales for Young and Old*. Translated by R. Manheim. London: Gollancz, 1979.

209. Grossinger, R. *The Alchemical Tradition*. Berkeley, Calif.: North Atlantic Books, 1983.

210. Grossinger, R. *The Night Sky*. San Francisco: Sierra Club, 1981.

211. Gruffydd, W. J. *Math ab Mathonwy*. Cardiff: University of Wales Press, 1928.

212. Guénon, R. *Crisis of the Modern World*. London: Luzac, 1975.

213. ———. *Symboles fondamentaux de la science sacré*. Paris: Gallimard, 1962.

214. Guirdham, A. *The Great Heresy*. Jersey, U.K.: Neville Spearman, 1977.

215. Guthrie, W. K. C. *Orpheus and Greek Religion*. New York: W. W. Norton, 1966.

216. Guyot, C. *The Legend of the City of Ys*. Amherst: University of Massachusetts Press, 1979.

217. Hadingham, E. *Ancient Carvings in Britain: A Mystery*. London: Garnstone, 1974.

218. Halevi, Z. *Adam and the Kabbalistic Tree*. London: Rider, 1974.

219. ———. *Kabbalah: Tradition of Hidden Knowledge*. London: Thames and Hudson, 1979.

220. ———. *A Kabbalistic Universe*. London: Rider, 1977.

221. ———. *The Work of the Kabbalist*. London: Gateway, 1985.

222. Halifax, J. *Shaman: The Wounded Healer*. London: Thames and Hudson, 1982.

223. ———. *Shamanic Voices*. London: Penguin Books, 1980.

224. Hall, M. P. *The Adepts in the Western Esoteric Tradition*. Los Angeles: Philosophical Research Society, 1949.

225. ———. *Magic*. Los Angeles: Philosophical Research Society, 1978.

226. ———. *The Secret Teachings of All Ages*. Los Angeles: Philosophical Research Society, 1975.

227. Harding, M. E. *Women's Mysteries: Ancient and Modern*. London: Rider, 1935.

228. Hargrave, J. *The Life and Soul of Paracelsus*. London: Gollancz, 1951.

229. Harner, M. *The Way of the Shaman*. New York: Harper and Row, 1980.

230. Harris, R. *The Lotus and the Grail: Legends from East to West*. London: Faber and Faber, 1974.

231. Harrison, M. *The Roots of Witchcraft*. London: Frederick Muller, 1973.

232. Hartley, C. *Western Mystery Tradition*. London: Aquarian Press, 1968.

233. Hauck, D. W. *The Emerald Tablet: Alchemy for Personal Transformation*. New York: Penguin, 1999.

234. Haughton, R. *The Catholic Thing*. Dublin: Villa, 1979.

235. ———. *Tales from Eternity: The World of Faeries and the Spiritual Search*. London: Allen and Unwin, 1973.

236. Hauschka, R. *The Nature of Substance*. London: Rudolf Steiner, 1983.

237. Hawkridge, R. *The Wisdom Tree*. New York: Houghton Mifflin, 1945.

238. Hayles, B. *The Moon Stallion*. London: Mirror Books, 1978.

239. Head, J., and S. L. Cranston. *Reincarnation: The Phoenix-Fire Mystery*. New York: Julian Press/Crown, 1977.

240. Heller, A. *Renaissance Man*. London: Routledge and Kegan Paul, 1978.

241. Henderson, J. *The Wisdom of the Serpent*. New York: George Brazillier, 1963.

242. Hesiod. *Works and Days*. Translated by R. Lattimore. Ann Arbor: University of Michigan Press, 1973.

243. Hesse, H. *The Glass Bead Game*. London: Cape, 1970.

244. Hildegard of Bingen. *Meditations*. Translated by G. Uhlein. Santa Fe: Bear and Co., 1983.

245. Hitchins, F. *Earth Magic*. London: Cassell, 1976.

246. Hoban, R. *Ridley Walker*. London: Cape, 1980.

247. Hoeller, S. A. *The Gnostic Jung and the Seven Sermons to the Dead*. Wheaton, Ill.: Theosophical Publishing, 1982.

248. Hoffman, E. *The Way of Splendor: Jewish Mysticism and Modern Psychology*. Boulder, Colo.: Shambhala, 1981.

249. Holt, J. C. *Robin Hood*. London: Thames and Hudson, 1972.

250. "Homage to Pythagoras." In *Lindisfarne Newsletter*. Great Barrington, Mass.: 1981.

251. Homer. *Homeric Hymns*. Translated by A. Athanassakis. Baltimore: John Hopkins University Press, 1976.

252. Hope, M. *Practical Egyptian Magic*. Wellingborough, U.K.: Aquarian Press, 1984.

253. ———. *Practical Techniques of Psychic Self-Defence*. Wellingborough, U.K.: Aquarian, 1983.

254. Houselander, C. *Letters*. London: Sheed and Ward, 1965.

255. Howey, M. O. *The Encircled Serpent*. London: Rider, n.d.

256. Huizinga, J. *The Waning of the Middle Ages*. Harmondsworth, Middlesex, U.K.: Penguin, 1955.

257. Hutton, R. *The Pagan Religions of the Ancient British Isles*. Oxford: Blackwell, 1991.

258. ———. *Rise and Fall of Merry England*. Oxford: Oxford University Press, 2001.

259. ———. *Stations of the Sun*. Oxford: Oxford University Press, 2001.

260. ———. *Triumph of the Moon*. Oxford: Oxford University Press, 2001.

261. Huxley, A. *The Perennial Philosophy*. London: Chatto and Windus, 1946.

262. Iamblichus. *On the Mysteries*. Translated by T. Taylor. San Diego: Wizard's Bookshelf, 1984.

263. ———. *On the Mysteries of the Egyptians*. Translated by T. Taylor. London: Bertram Dobell, 1895.

264. Jackson Knight, W. F. *Elysion*. London: Rider, 1970.

265. ———. *Vergil: Epic and Anthropology*. London: Allen and Unwin, 1967.

266. Jacobs, R. *Jewish Mystical Testimonies*. New York: Schoken Books, 1976.

267. Jarman, A. *Legend of Merlin*. Cardiff: University of Wales Press, 1976.

268. Jefferies, R. *Story of My Heart*. London: Longmans, Green and Co., 1883.

269. Saint John of the Cross. *Four Poems*. Translated by Y. Orta. Oxford: Carmelite Priory, Boar's Hill, 1984.

270. Johnston, W. *Christian Mysticism Today*. London: Collins, 1984.

271. Jonas, H. *The Gnostic Religion: The Message of the Alien God and the Beginnings of Christianity*. Boston: Beacon Press, 1963.

272. Jones, D. *The Anathemata*. London: Faber and Faber, 1952.

273. ———. *Epoch and Artist*. London: Faber and Faber, 1959.

274. ———. *The Sleeping Lord*. London: Faber and Faber, 1974.

275. Jones P., and C. Matthews. *Voices From the Circle*. Wellingborough, U.K.: Thorsons, 1990.

276. Jones, P., and N. Pennick. *History of Pagan Europe*. London: Routledge, 1995.

277. Jones, P. *Physics as Metaphor*. London: Wildwood, 1983.

278. Julian of Norwich. *Revelations of Divine Love*. Wheathampstead, U.K.: Anthony Clarke, 1973.

279. Jung, C. G. *Answer to Job*. London: Routledge and Kegan Paul, 1954.

280. ———. *Archetypes and the Collective Unconscious*. London: Routledge and Kegan Paul, 1968.

281. ———. *Memories, Dreams and Reflections*. London: Collins/Routledge and Kegan Paul, 1963.

282. ———. *Psychology and Alchemy*. London: Routledge and Kegan Paul, 1968.

283. ———. *Word and Image*. Edited by A. Jaffe. Princeton, N.J.: Princeton University Press, 1979.

284. Jung, C. G., and C. Kerényi. *Introduction to a Science of Mythology*. London: Routledge and Kegan Paul, 1951.

285. Jung, E., and M.-L. von Franz. *The Grail Legends*. London: Hodder, 1956.

286. *Kalevala*. Compiled and translated by E. Lonnrot. Cambridge, Mass.: Harvard University Press, 1963.

287. Kaplan, A. *Meditation and the Bible*. York Beach, Maine: Weiser, 1978.

288. ———. *Meditation and Kabbalah*. York Beach, Maine: Weiser, 1982.

289. Kaplan, S. R. *Tarot Classic*. New York: Grosset and Dunlap, 1972.

290. Keen, M. *Chivalry*. New Haven, Conn.: Yale University Press, 1984.

291. Kempis, T. *The Imitation of Christ*. Translated by R. Dudley. Wheathampstead, U.K.: Anthony Clarke, 1980.

292. Kerényi, K. *Dionysus*. London: Routledge and Kegan Paul, 1976.

293. ———. *Eleusis*. London: Routledge and Kegan Paul, 1967.

294. ———. *Gods of the Greeks*. London: Thames and Hudson, 1951.

295. ———. *Hermes: Guide of Souls*. Zurich: Spring Books, 1976.

296. ———. *Apollo*. Dallas: Spring Publications, 1983.

297. ———. *Asklepios*. New York: Pantheon Books, 1959.

298. ———. *The Heroes of the Greeks*. London: Thames and Hudson, 1959.

299. Kern, H. *Through the Labyrinth*. London: Prestell, 2000.

300. Kierkegaard, S. *For Self-Examination and Judge for Yourselves*. Translated by W. Lowrie. Oxford: Oxford University Press, 1941.

301. Kirk, R. *The Secret Commonwealth*. Cambridge, U.K.: D. S. Brewer, 1976.

302. Klibansky, R. *Continuity of the Platonic Tradition*. London: Warburg Institute, 1939.

303. Knight, G. *Dion Fortune and the Inner Light*. Loughborough, U.K.: Thoth, 2000.

304. ———. *Experience of Inner Worlds*. Toddington, U.K.: Helios, 1975.

305. ———. *A History of White Magic*. London: Mowbrays, 1978.

306. ———. *The Magical World of the Inklings*. Shaftesbury, U.K.: Element, 1994.

307. ———. *Occult Exercises and Practices*. Wellingborough, U.K.: Aquarian Press, 1982.

308. ———. *A Practical Guide to Qabalistic Symbolism*. Toddington, U.K.: Helios, 1965.

309. ———. *The Practice of Ritual Magic*. Wellingborough, U.K.: Aquarian Press, 1979.

310. ———. *The Rose Cross and the Goddess*. Wellingborough, U.K.: Aquarian Press, 1985.

311. ———. *The Secret Tradition in Arthurian Legend*. Wellingborough, U.K.: Aquarian Press, 1984.

312. ———. "The Work of a Modern Occult Fraternity." In Fortune, Dion, *The Secrets of Dr. Taverner*. St. Paul: Llewellyn, 1978.

313. Knight, G., and A. McLean. *Commentary on the Chymical Wedding of Christian Rosenkreutz*. Edinburgh: Magnum Opus Hermetic Sourceworks, 1984 .

314. *Kore Kosmou*. Translated by A. Kingsford and E. Maitland. Minneapolis: Wizard's Bookshelf, 1977.

315. Lacarriere, J. *The Gnostics*. London: Peter Owen, 1977.

316. Lambert, M. D. *Medieval Heresy*. London: Edward Arnold, 1977.

317. Lang-Sims, L. *The Christian Mystery*. London: Allen and Unwin, 1980.

318. Larsen, S. *The Shaman's Doorway*. Rochester, Vt.: Inner Traditions, 1998.

319. Layard, J. *The Celtic Quest*. Zurich: Spring Publications, 1975.

320. Le Roy Ladurie, E. *Montaillou*. London: Scolar Press, 1978.

321. *Lebor Gabala Erenn* (Book of Invasions). Edited by R. A. S. Macalister. Dublin: Irish Texts Society, 1938–35.

322. *Lenten Triodion*. Translated by Mother Mary and Archimandrite K. Ware. London: Faber and Faber, 1977.

323. Léon-Portilla, M. *Native Mesoamerican Spirituality*. London: SPCK, 1980.

324. Lethbridge, T. C. *Gogmagog*. London: Routledge and Kegan Paul, 1957.

325. Levy, G. R. *Gate of Horn*. London: Faber and Faber, 1943.

326. Lewis, C. S. *Abolition of Man*. London: Collins, 1978.

327. ———. *The Business of Heaven*. London: Fount, 1984.

328. ———. *The Chronicles of Narnia*. London: Geoffrey Bless, 1950–59.

329. ———. *The Cosmic Trilogy.* London: Bodley Head, 1990.

330. ———. *The Discarded Image.* Cambridge: Cambridge University Press, 1964.

331. ———. *Till We Have Faces.* London: Fount, 1978.

332. Lievegoed, B. C. J. *Mystery Streams in Europe and the New Mysteries.* New York: Anthroposophic Press, 1982.

333. Lindsay, J. *The Origins of Alchemy in Graeco-Roman Egypt.* London: Frederick Muller, 1970.

334. ———. *The Troubadours.* London: Frederick Muller, 1976.

335. Lionel, F. *The Seduction of the Occult Path.* Wellingborough, U.K.: Turnstone, 1983.

336. Loomis, R. S., ed. *Arthurian Literature in the Middle Ages.* Oxford: Oxford University Press, 1959.

337. Lossky, V. *The Mystical Theology of the Eastern Church.* Cambridge: James Clarke and Co., 1957.

338. Love, J. *The Quantum Gods.* Tisbury, Wiltshire, U.K.: Compton Russell/Element, 1976.

339. Lucian. *The Syrian Goddess.* London: Constable, 1913.

340. Luhrman, T. M. *Persuasions of the Witch's Craft.* Oxford: Blackwell, 1989.

341. Luke, H. M. *Woman, Earth and Spirit.* New York: Crossroad, 1981.

342. Lurker, M. *Gods and Symbols of Ancient Egypt.* Thames and Hudson, 1974.

343. *The Mabinogion.* Translated by J. Gantz. Harmondsworth, Middlesex: U.K.: Penguin Books, 1976.

344. MacCana, P. *Celtic Mythology.* London: Hamlyn, 1970.

345. Macdonald, G. *The Princess and the Goblin.* Harmondsworth, Middlesex: Puffin, 1964.

346. MacGregor, G. *Reincarnation as a Christian Hope.* London: Macmillan, 1982.

347. Mackenzie, D. A. *Scottish Folk-Lore and Folk-Life.* Edinburgh: Blackie, 1935.

348. Mackie, E. *Megalith Builders.* Oxford: Phaidon, 1977.

349. McClain, E. G. *The Pythagorean Plato.* Stony Brook, N.Y.: Nicholas Hays, 1978.

350. McGregor-Mathers, S. L. *The Book of the Sacred Magic of AbraMelin the Mage.* Wellingborough, U.K.: Thorsons, 1976.

351. McGuinn, B., ed. and trans. *Apocalyptic Spirituality.* London: SPCK, 1979.

352. Mcintosh, C. *Rosy Cross Unveiled.* Wellingborough, U.K.: Aquarian Press, 1980.

353. McLean, A. *A Compendium on the Rosicrucian Vault.* Edinburgh: Hermetic Research Series, 1985.

354. ———. "A Hermetic Origin of the Tarot Cards?" In *Hermetic Journal* 21, Autumn 1983.

355. ———. *Journal of Rosicrucian Studies* 1, Autumn 1983.

356. ———. "Robert Fludd's Great Treatise of Rosicrucian Science." In *Hermetic Journal* 17, Autumn 1982.

357. ———., ed. *The Rosary of the Philosophers*. Edinburgh: Magnum Opus Hermetic Sourceworks, 1980.

358. ———. "A Rosicrucian Alchemical Mystery Centre in Scotland." In *Hermetic Journal* 4, Summer 1979.

359. ———. *The Western Mandala*. Edinburgh: Hermetic Research Series, 1983.

360. McMann, J. *Riddles of the Stone Age*. London: Thames and Hudson, 1980.

361. McWaters, B. *Conscious Evolution*. Wellingborough, U.K.: Turnstone Press, 1983.

362. Macrobius. *Commentary on the Dream of Scipio*. New York: Columbia University Press, 1952.

363. Malinowski, B. *Magic, Science and Religion and Other Essays*. New York: Free Press, 1948.

364. Malory, Sir T. *Le Mort d'Arthur*. Edited by J. Matthews. London: Cassell, 2000.

365. Maltwood, K. *Enchantments of Britain*. Cambridge, U.K.: James Clarke, 1982.

366. Markale, J. *Celtic Civilization*. London: Gordon and Cremonesi, 1978.

367. ———. *The Druids*. Rochester, Vt.: Inner Traditions, 1999.

368. ———. *The Grail*. Rochester, Vt.: Inner Traditions, 1999.

369. ———. *Merlin: Priest of Nature*. Rochester, Vt.: Inner Traditions, 1995.

370. ———. *Women of the Celts*. Rochester, Vt.: Inner Traditions, 1986.

371. Massingham, H. *Downland Man*. London: Jonathan Cape, 1926.

372. Matthews, C. *The Blessing Seed*. Bath, U.K.: Barefoot Books, 1998.

373. ———. *The Celtic Book of the Dead*. London: Connections, 2002.

374. ———. *Celtic Devotional*. Alresford, U.K.: Godsfield Press, 2004.

375. ———. *Celtic Memory*. Bath, U.K.: Barefoot Books, 2003.

376. ———. *Celtic Spirit*. New York: HarperCollins, 1999.

377. ———. *In Search of Woman's Passionate Soul*. Shaftesbury, U.K.: Element Books, 1997.

378. ———. *King Arthur and the Goddess of the Land*. Rochester, Vt.: Inner Traditions, 2002.

379. ———. *Mabon and the Guardians of Celtic Britain*, Rochester, Vt.: Inner Traditions, 2002.

380. ———. "The Rosicrucian Vault as Vessel of Transformation." In *At the Table of the Grail*. Edited by J. Matthews. London: Watkins Books, 2002.

381. ———. *Singing the Soul Back Home*. London: Connections, 2002.

382. ———. "Sophia as Companion on the Quest." In *At the Table of the Grail*. Edited by J. Matthews. London: Watkins Books, 2002.

383. ———. *Sophia, Goddess of Wisdom*. Wheaton, Ill.: Quest Books, 2001.

384. ———. *Voices of the Goddess*. London: Aquarian Press, 1990.

385. ———. *The Way of Celtic Tradition*. London: Element Books, 2002.

386. Matthews, C., and J. Matthews. *The Arthurian Tarot*. London: Element, 2002.

387. ———. *The Encyclopaedia of Celtic Myth and Legend*. London: Rider, 2003.

388. ———. *The Encyclopaedia of Celtic Wisdom*. London, Rider, 2001.

389. ———. *Ladies of the Lake*. London: Thorsons, 1994.

390. Matthews, J. *At the Table of the Grail*. London: Watkins Books, 2002.

391. ———. *Bardic Source Book*. London: Cassell, 1998.

392. ———. *The Book of Arthur*. London: Vega, 2002.

393. ———. *Celtic Seers' Source Book*. London: Cassell, 1999.

394. ———. *Celtic Shaman*. London: Rider, 2001.

395. ———. *The Druid Source Book*. London: Cassell, 1996.

396. ———. *The Grail: Quest for the Eternal*. London: Thames and Hudson, 1981.

397. ———. *Quest for the Green Man*. Alresford, U.K./Wheaton, Ill.: Godsfield Press/Quest, 1999.

398. ———. *Sir Gawain: Knight of the Goddess*. Rochester, Vt.: Inner Traditions, 2003.

399. ———. *Sources of the Grail*. Edinburgh: Floris Books, 1996.

400. ———. *Summer Solstice*. Wheaton, Ill.: Quest, 2002.

401. ———. *Winter Solstice*. Wheaton, Ill.: Quest, 2000.

402. ———. Wizards: *From the Shaman to Harry Potter*. New York: Barrons, 2003.

403. Matthews, J., and M. Green. *The Grail Seeker's Companion*. Loughborough, U.K.: Thoth Books, 2003.

404. Matthews, J., and C. Matthews. *Taliesin: The Last Celtic Shaman*. Rochester, Vt.: Inner Traditions, 2002.

405. Mead, G. R. S. *Apollonius of Tyana*. New York: University Books, 1966.

406. ———. *Fragments of a Faith Forgotten*. New York: University Books, 1960.

407. ———. *Mysteries of Mithras*. London: Theosophical Publishing Society, 1907.

408. ———. *Vision of Aridaeus*. London: Theosophical Publishing Society, 1907.

409. ———. *Orpheus*. London: Watkins, 1965.

410. ———. *Thrice Greatest Hermes*. London: Watkins, 1964.

411. Meltzer, D., ed. *Birth: An Anthology of Ancient Texts*. San Francisco: North Point, 1981.

412. ———. *Six*. Santa Barbara, Calif.: Black Sparrow, 1976.

413. Menahern Nahum of Chernobyl. *Upright Practices*. New York: Paulist Press, 1982.

414. Merry, E. *I Am: The Ascent of Mankind*. London: Rider, 1944.

415. Merton, T. *Seven Story Mountain*. London: Sheldon Press, 1975.

416. Meyer, K., and A. Nutt. *The Voyage of Bran, Son of Febal*. London: David Nutt, 1895.

417. Meyer, T. *The Umbrella of Aesculapius*. Winston-Salem, N.C.: Jargon Society, 1975.

418. Michell, J. *Megalithomania*. London: Thames and Hudson, 1982.

419. ———. *New View Over Atlantis*. London: Thames and Hudson, 1983.

420. Miller, R. *Continents in Collision*. Amsterdam, the Netherlands: Time-Life, 1983.

421. Milton, J. *Complete Poetry*. New York: Anchor Books, 1971.

422. Mol, H. *The Firm and the Formless*. London: Wilfrid Press, 1982.

423. Monaco, R. *Runes*. New York: Ace Fantasy Books, 1984.

424. Moncreiffe of That Ilk and D. Hicks. *The Highland Clans*. London: Barrie and Rockliff, 1967.

425. Moore, V. *The Unicorn: William Butler Yeats's Search for Reality*. New York: Macmillan, 1954.

426. Moore, T. *The Planets Within*. West Stockbridge, Mass.: Lindisfarne, 1990.

427. Morris, J. *The Age of Arthur*. London: Weidenfeld and Nicolson, 1973.

428. Mottram, E. *The Book of Herne*. Colne, Lancashire, U.K.: Arrowspire Press, 1982.

429. Mountford, C. P. *Winbaraku and the Myth of Jarapiri*. Adelaide: Rigby, 1968.

430. Muir, W. *Living with Ballads*. London: Hogarth Press, 1965.

431. *Munificentissimus Deus*. Papal encyclical, Pope Pius XII. Derby, N.Y.: Daughters of Saint Paul, 1950.

432. Murray, M. *The Divine King in England*. London: Faber and Faber, 1954.

433. ———. *The God of the Witches*. London: Sampson Low, 1931.

434. Mylius, J. D. *Alchemical Engravings*. Translated by P. Tahta. Edinburgh: Magnum Opus Hermetic Sourceworks, 1984.

435. *Nag Hammadi Library.* Translated by J. M. Robinson. Leiden: E. J. Brill, 1977.

436. Nahman of Bratislav. *The Tales.* New York: Paulist Press, 1978.

437. Nash, D. W. *Taliesin, or the Bards and Druids of Britain.* London: John Russel Smith, 1858.

438. Needleman, J. *Lost Christianity.* New York: Doubleday, 1980.

439. ———. *Sense of the Cosmos.* New York: Dutton, 1965.

440. ———, ed. *Sword of Gnosis.* Baltimore: Penguin Books, 1974.

441. Neihardt, J. G. *Black Elk Speaks.* New York: Pocket Books, 1972.

442. Nennius. *British History and the Welsh Annals.* London, Phillimore, 1980.

443. Neubecker, O. *Guide to Heraldry.* London: Cassell, 1979.

444. Neumann, E. *The Great Mother.* Princeton, N.J.: Princeton University Press, 1963.

445. ———. *Origins and History of Consciousness.* Princeton, N.J.: Princeton University Press, 1954.

446. Newman, J. H. *The Arians of the 4th Century.* London: E. Lumley, 1871.

447. Newman, P. *Hill of the Dragon.* London: Kingsmead Press, 1979.

448. Newstead, H. *Bran the Blessed in Arthurian Romance.* New York: Columbia University Press, 1939.

449. *Nibelungenlied.* Translated by A. T. Hatto. Harmondsworth, Middlessex, U.K.: Penguin, 1965.

450. Nicholas of Cusa. *The Vision of God.* New York: Ungar, 1960.

451. North, F. J. *Sunken Cities.* Cardiff: University of Wales Press, 1957.

452. O'Brien, C. *The Megalithic Odyssey.* Wellingborough, U.K.: Turnstone, 1973.

453. Origen. *An Exhortation to Martyrdom and Other Writings.* Translated by M. Gasser. London: SPCK, 1979.

454. *Orphic Hymns.* Translation and notes by A. M. Athanassakis. Missoula, Mont.: Scholars Press, 1977.

455. Otto, W. X. *Dionysus: Myth and Cult.* Bloomington: Indiana University Press, 1965.

456. Ovid. *Metamorphoses.* Translated by M. M. Innes. Harmondsworth, Middlesex, U.K.: Penguin Books, 1955.

457. *Oxford Classical Dictionary.* Edited by N. G. K. Hammond and H. H. Scullard. London: Oxford University Press, 1970.

458. *Oxford Dictionary of the Christian Church.* Edited by F. L. Cross and E. A. Livingston. London: Oxford University Press, 1957.

459. *Oxford Dictionary of Nursery Rhymes.* Edited by I. and P. Opie. London: Oxford University Press, 1951.

460. *Oxford Dictionary of Saints*. Edited D. H. Farmer. Oxford: Oxford University Press, 1978.

461. Paracelsus. *The Archidoxes of Magic*. London: Askin, 1975.

462. ———. *Selected Writings*. Edited by J. Incubi. Princeton, N.J.: Princeton University Press, 1951.

463. Patai, R. *The Hebrew Goddess*. New York: Avon Books, 1978.

464. Pausanius. *Guide to Greece*. Translated by P. Levi. Harmondsworth, Middlesex, U.K.: Penguin Books, 1971.

465. Pegg, B. *Folk: A Portrait of English Traditional Music, Musicians and Customs*. London: Wildwood, 1976.

466. Pelikan, J. *Vindication of Tradition*. New Haven, Conn.: Yale University Press, 1984.

467. Pennick, N. *The Ancient Science of Geomancy*. London: Thames and Hudson, 1979.

468. ———. *Practical Magic in the Northern Traditions*. Loughborough, U.K.: Thoth Publications, 1989.

469. Pepper, E., and J. Willock. *Magical and Mystical Sites: Europe and the British Isles*. London: Weidenfeld, 1976.

470. Perera, S. B. *Descent to the Goddess: A Way of Initiation for Women*. Toronto: Inner City Books, 1981.

471. *Perlesvaus: The High History of the Holy Grail*. Translated by S. Evans. London: J. M. Dent, 1911.

472. Perry, M. *Psychic Studies*. Wellingborough, U.K.: Aquarian Press, 1984.

473. Perry, W. N. *A Treasury of Traditional Wisdom*. Louisville, Ky.: Fons Vitae, 2001.

474. Petry, M. J. *Herne the Hunter: A Berkshire Legend*. Reading, U.K.: William Smith, 1972.

475. Philo of Alexandria. *The Contemplative Life*. London: Paulist Press, 1981.

476. Pindar. *The Odes*. Translated by C. M. Bowra. Harmondsworth, Middlesex, U.K.: Penguin Books, 1969.

477. Piske, L. *The Actor and His Body*. London: Harrap, 1975.

478. Plato. *The Collected Dialogues of Plato*. Edited by E. Hamilton. Princeton, N.J.: Princeton University Press, 1973.

479. ———. *The Republic*. Translated by D. Lee. Harmondsworth, Middlesex, U.K.: Penguin Books, 1955.

480. ———. *Timaeus and Critias*. Translated by D. Lee. Harmondsworth, Middlesex, U.K.: Penguin Books, 1965.

481. Plotinus. *The Enneads*. Translated by S. Mackenna. London: Faber and Faber, 1956.

482. ———. *Enneads*. Translated by Stanbrook Abbey. Callow End, Worcester, U.K.: Stanbrook Abbey, n.d.

483. Plumb, J. H. *The Death of the Past*. London: Macmillan, 1969.

484. Plutarch. *Moralia V: Isis and Osiris*. Translated by F. C. Babbitt. Cambridge, Mass.: Harvard University Press, 1957.

485. ———. *Moralia VI: On the Sign of Plato*. Translated by P. H. De Lacy and B. Einarson. Cambridge Mass.: Harvard University Press, 1968.

486. "Poetry and Prophecy." In *Lindisfarne Newsletter 9*. Great Barrington, Mass.: 1979.

487. Pollack, Rachel. *The Forest of Souls: A Walk Through the Tarot*. St. Paul: Llewellyn, 2002.

488. Ponce, C. *The Game of Wizards*. New York: Penguin Books, 1975.

489. ———. *Papers Towards a Radical Metaphysics: Alchemy*. Berkeley, Calif.: North Atlantic Books, 1983.

490. Potok, C. *The Book of Lights*. London: Heinemann, 1982.

491. ———. *The Chosen*. Harmondsworth, Middlesex, U.K.: Penguin Books, 1970.

492. Powys, J. C. *Morwyn or the Vengeance of God*. London: Village Press, 1974.

493. Pullman, P. *His Dark Materials Trilogy: Northern Lights, The Subtle Knife, The Amber Spyglass*. London: Scholastic, 2001.

494. Pythagoreans. *Golden Verses of the Pythagoreans*. Translated and edited by the Shrine of Wisdom. Fintry, Scotland: Shrine of Wisdom, n.d.

495. *Quest of the Holy Grail*. Translated by P. Metarasso. Harmondsworth, Middlesex, U.K.: Penguin Books, 1969.

496. Quinn, E. C. *The Quest of Seth*. Chicago: University of Chicago Press, 1962.

497. Quispel, G. *Secret Book of Revelation*. London: Collins, 1979.

498. Raine, K. *Defending Ancient Springs*. Oxford: Oxford University Press, 1967.

499. Rakoczi, B. I. *Fortune Telling*. London: MacDonald, 1970.

500. Rank, O. *The Myth of the Birth of the Hero*. New York: Knopf, 1959.

501. Reader's Digest. *Folklore, Myths, and Legends of Britain*. London: Reader's Digest, 1973.

502. Rees, A., and B. Rees. *Celtic Heritage*. London: Thames and Hudson, 1961.

503. Reeves, M. J. *Joachim of Fiore and the Prophetic Future*. London: SPCK, 1976.

504. Regardie, I. *The Complete Golden Dawn System of Magic*. Phoenix: Falcon Press, 1984.

505. ———. *Foundation and Practice of Magic*. Wellingborough, U.K.: Aquarian, 1979.

506. ———. *The Golden Dawn*. St. Paul: Llewellyn, 1971.

507. ———. *How to Make and Use Talismans*. Wellingborough, U.K.: Aquarian Press, 1981.

508. Reyner, K. *This Holiest Erthe*. London: Perennial, 1974.

509. Robertson, S. M. *Rosegarden and Labyrinth*. London: Routledge and Kegan Paul, 1963.

510. Ross, A. *Pagan Celtic Britain*. London: Routledge and Kegan Paul, 1967.

511. Roszak, T. *Person Planet*. London: Granada, 1981.

512. Rudolph, K. *Gnosis*. Edinburgh: T. and T. Clark, 1983.

513. Russell, G. "The Glastonbury Tor Maze." In *Glastonbury: A Study in Patterns*. Edited by M. Williams. London: Research into Lost Knowledge Organisation (RILKO), 1969.

514. Russell, G. W. ("A. E."). *A Candle of Vision*. New York: Theosophical Publishing, 1974.

515. ———. *The Song of Its Fountains*. London: Macmillan, 1932.

516. Russell, J. B. *A History of Witchcraft*. London: Thames and Hudson, 1980.

517. Russell, R. *The Awakening Earth: Our Next Evolutionary Leap*. London: Routledge and Kegan Paul, 1982.

518. Salinger, J. D. *Franny and Zooey*. London: Heinemann, 1962.

519. Saurat, D. *Literature and Occult Tradition*. London: Bell and Sons, 1930.

520. Sawyer, R. *The Way of the Storyteller*. London: Harrap, 1944.

521. Schaya, L. *Universal Meaning of the Kabbalah*. London: Allen and Unwin, 1971.

522. Schnapper, E. *The Inward Odyssey*. London: Allen and Unwin, 1965.

523. Scholem, G. G. *Major Trends in Jewish Mysticism*. New York: Schoken Books, 1961.

524. Schuon, F. *Esotericism As Principle and As Way*. Bedfordshire, U.K.: Perennial, 1981.

525. Schure, E. *The Great Initiates*. New York: Mackay, 1913.

526. Schwaller de Lubicz, R. A. *Nature Word*. Great Barrington, Mass.: Lindisfarne Press, 1982.

527. Schwaller de Lubicz, Isha. *The Opening of the Way*. Rochester, Vt.: Inner Traditions, 1981.

528. Schwaller de Lubicz, R. A. *Sacred Science*. Rochester, Vt.: Inner Traditions, 1982.

529. ———. *Symbol and the Symbolic*. Rochester, Vt.: Inner Traditions, 1978.

530. Schwartz-Bart, A. *The Last of the Just*. Harmondsworth, Middlesex, U.K.: Penguin, 1984.

531. Schweighardt, T. "The Mirror of Wisdom." Translated by D. McLean. In *Hermetic Journal* 25.

532. Scott, M. *Kundalini in the Physical World.* London: Routledge and Kegan Paul, 1983.

533. Scott, W. *Hermetica,* vols. 1–4, Boulder, Colo.: Hermes House, 1982.

534. Screeton, P. *Quicksilver Heritage.* Wellingborough, U.K.: Turnstone, 1974.

535. Scruton, R. *From Descartes to Wittgenstein.* London: Routledge and Kegan Paul, 1981.

536. Senior, M. *Myths of Britain.* London: Orbis, 1979.

537. Shaw, M. F. *Folksongs and Folklore of South Uist.* London: Routledge and Kegan Paul, 1955.

538. Shumaker, W. *The Occult Sciences in the Renaissance.* Berkeley: University of California Press, 1972.

539. Silverberg, R. *The Mound Builders.* New York: New York Graphic Society, 1970.

540. ———. *The Realm of Prester John.* New York: Doubleday, 1972.

541. Sinclair, J. R. *The Alice Bailey Inheritance.* Wellingborough, U.K.: Turnstone Press, 1984.

542. Singer, I. B. *The Golem.* London: Deutsch, 1983.

543. *Sir Gawain and the Green Knight.* Translated by J. R. R. Tolkien. London: Allen and Unwin, 1975.

544. Sjoestedt, M.-L. *Gods and Heroes of the Celts.* Berkeley, Calif.: Turtle Island Foundation, 1982.

545. Skelton, R. *Spellcraft: A Manual of Verbal Magic.* London: Routledge and Kegan Paul, 1978.

546. Slade, H. *Contemplative Meditation.* London: Darton Longman and Todd, 1977.

547. Smith, M. *Jesus the Magician.* London: Gollancz, 1978.

548. Society of the Inner Light Study Course. 38 Steele's Road, London NW3.

549. Solomon, J. *The Structure of Matter.* Newton Abbot, Devon, U.K.: David and Charles, 1973.

550. Sorabi, R. *Time, Creation and the Continuum.* London: Duckworth, 1983.

551. Southwell, R. *Poetical Works.* London: John Russell Smith, 1856.

552. Spence, L. *Fairy Tradition in Britain.* London: Rider, 1948.

553. ———. *The History of Atlantis.* London: Rider, 1930.

554. ———. *The Magical Arts in Celtic Britain.* Wellingborough, U.K.: Aquarian Press, 1970.

555. ———. *The Mysteries of Britain.* Wellingborough, U.K.: AquarianPress, 1970.

556. ———. *Myths of the American Indians.* London: Harrap, 1918.

557. ———. *Occult Sciences in Atlantis*. London: Aquarian Press, 1970.

558. Spiegelman, J. *The Tree: Tales in Psycho-Mythology*. Phoenix: Falcon Press, 1982.

559. Starhawk. *Dreaming the Dark*. Boston: Beacon Press, 1982.

560. ———. *The Spiral Dance: A Rebirth of the Ancient Religion of the Great Goddess*. San Francisco: Harper and Row, 1979.

561. Steinbeck, J. *Acts of King Arthur and His Noble Knights*. London: Heinemann, 1976.

562. Steinbrecher, E. *The Inner Guide Meditation*. Santa Fe: Blue Feather Press, 1978.

563. Steiner, R. *Atlantis and Lemuria*. New York: Anthroposophical Publications, 1923.

564. ———. *The Course of My Life*. New York: Steiner Books, 1977.

565. ———. *Evolution and Consciousness*. London: Rudolf Steiner, 1979.

566. ———. *Mystery Knowledge and Mystery Centres*. London: Rudolf Steiner, 1973.

567. ———. *Occult Science: An Outline*. London: Rudolf Steiner, 1979.

568. ———. *The Occult Significance of Blood*. London: Rudolf Steiner, 1967.

569. Stewart, R. J. *Advanced Magical Arts*. Shaftesbury, Dorset, U.K.: Element, 1992.

570. ———. *Earth Light*. Shaftesbury, Dorset, U.K.: Element, 1992.

571. ———. *Living Magical Arts*. Poole, Dorset, U.K.: Blandford, 1987.

572. ———. *The Miracle Tree: Deciphering the Qabala*. Franklin Lakes, N.J.: New Page Books, 2003.

573. ———. *The Mystic Life of Merlin*. London: Arkana, 1990.

574. ———. *Power Within the Land*. Shaftesbury, Dorset, U.K.: Element Books, 1992.

575. ———. *The Underworld Initiation*. Wellingborough, U.K.: Aquarian Press, 1985.

576. ———. *The Waters of the Gap*. Bath, U.K.: Bath City Council, 1981.

577. ———. *Where Is St. George?* Bradford-on-Avon, U.K.: Moonraker Press, 1977.

578. Stewart, R. J. and J. Matthews, eds. *Merlin Through the Ages: A Chronological Anthology and Source Book*. London: Blandford, 1995.

579. Storms, G. *Anglo-Saxon Magic*. The Hague: Martinus Nyhoff, 1948.

580. Stukeley, W. *Itinerarium Curiosum*, Hampshire, U.K.: Greg International, 1969.

581. Sullivan. C. W. III. *The Mabinogi: A Book of Essays*. New York: Garland, 1996.

582. Summerfield, H. *That Myriad-Minded Man: A Biography of G. W. Russell—"A. E."* Gerrards Cross, Hertfordshire, U.K.: Colin Smythe, 1975.

583. Sutcliff, R. *High Deeds of Finn MacCool.* London: Bodley Head, 1967.

584. ———. *The Hound of Ulster.* London: Bodley Head, 1963.

585. Szekeley, E. B. *The Gospel of the Essenes.* London: C. W. Daniel, 1976.

586. Tacitus. *The Agricola and the Germania.* Harmondsworth, Middlesex, U.K.: Penguin, 1970.

587. Tahta, P. *Alchemical Engravings: Magnum Opus.* Translated by J. D. Mylius. Edinburgh: Hermetic Sourceworks, 1984.

588. *Táin Bó Cúalnge* (The Cattle Raid of Cooley). Translated by T. Kinsella. Dublin: Dolmen Press, 1970.

589. Taylor, T. *Selected Writings.* Edited by K. Raine. Princeton, N.J.: Princeton University Press, 1969.

590. *Temenos Review.* Edited by K. Raine. L. 1981 et seq.

591. Temple, R. *Conversations with Eternity.* London: Rider, 1984.

592. Tennyson, A. *Idylls of the King.* Harmondsworth, Middlesex, U.K.: Penguin, 1983.

593. Thom, A. *Megalithic and Luna Observatories.* Oxford: Oxford University Press, 1971.

594. ———. *Megalithic Sites in Britain.* Oxford: Oxford University Press, 1967.

595. Tillyard, E. M. W. *The Elizabethan World Picture.* London: Chatto and Windus, 1943.

596. Tolkien, J. R. R. *The Lord of the Rings.* London: George Allen and Unwin, 1954.

597. ———. *The Monsters and the Critics and Other Essays.* London: George Allen and Unwin, 1983.

598. Tolstoy, N. *The Quest for Merlin.* London: Hamish Hamilton, 1985.

599. Traherne, T. *Poetical Works.* London: P. J. and A. E. Dobell, 1932.

600. Treece, H. *The Golden Strangers.* London: Bodley Head, 1956.

601. ———. *The Green Man.* London: Bodley Head, 1966.

602. *Trioedd ynys Prydein* (The Welsh Triads). Edited by R. Bromwich. Cardiff: University of Wales Press, 1961.

603. Trinick, J. *The Fire-Tried Stone.* London: Stuart and Watkins, 1967.

604. Underhill, E., ed. *Cloud of Unknowing.* London: Stuart and Watkins, 1970.

605. ———. *Mysticism.* New York: Dutton and Colne, 1961.

606. Underwood, G. *The Patterns of the Past.* London: Abacus, 1972.

607. Unterman, A. *The Jews: Their Religious Beliefs and Practices.* London: Routledge and Kegan Paul, 1981.

608. Urmson, J. O. *Concise Encyclopaedia of Western Philosophy and Philosophers.* London: Hutchinson, 1960.

609. Valiente, D. *ABC's of Witchcraft.* London: Hale, 1984.

610. ———. *Witchcraft for Tomorrow.* London: Hale, 1978.

611. Vansittart, P. *The Death of Robin Hood.* London: Peter Owen, 1982.

612. ———. *Worlds and Underworlds.* London: Peter Owen, 1974.

613. Vaughan, H. *The Complete Poems.* Edited by A. Rudrum. Harmondsworth, Middlesex, U.K.: Penguin, 1976.

614. Vaughan, T. *The Works of Thomas Vaughan.* New York: University Books, 1968.

615. Vermaseren, M. J. *Cybele and Attis.* London: Thames and Hudson, 1977.

616. ———. *Mithras: The Secret God.* London: Chatto and Windus, 1963.

617. Versluis, A. *The Philosophy of Magic.* London: Routledge and Kegan Paul, n.d.

618. Vidal, G. *Julian.* London: Heinemann, 1964.

619. Vigars, D. *Atlantis Rising.* London: Andrew Dakers, 1944.

620. Virgil. *The Eclogues.* Harmondsworth, Middlesex, U.K.: Penguin, 1980.

621. *Vita Merlini.* Edited by J. J. Parry. Urbana: University of Illinois Press, 1925.

622. Von Eschenbach, W. *Parzival.* Translated by A. T. Hatto. Harmondsworth, Middlesex, U.K.: Penguin, 1980.

623. von Franz, M.-L. *Alchemical Active Imagination.* Zurich: Spring Books, 1979.

624. ———. *Alchemy.* Toronto: Inner City Books, 1980.

625. ———. *C. G. Jung: His Myth in Our Time.* London: Hodder and Stoughton, 1975.

626. Waddell, H. *Songs of the Wandering Scholars.* London: Folio Society, 1982.

627. Waite, A. E. *The Brotherhood of the Rosy Cross.* New York: University Books, 1961.

628. ———. *The New Encyclopedia of Freemasonry.* New York: Weathervane Books, 1970.

629. Walker, B. *Gnosticism.* Wellingborough, U.K.: Aquarian Press, 1983.

630. Walker, D. P. *Spiritual and Demonic Magic.* London: University of Notre Dame Press, 1969.

631. Walton, E. *The Mabinogion Tetrology.* New York: Overlook Press, 2002.

632. Wang, R. *The Qabalistic Tarot.* York Beach, Maine: Weiser, 1983.

633. Warden, J. *Orpheus: The Metamorphosis of a Myth.* Toronto: University of Toronto Press, 1982.

634. Ware, T. *The Orthodox Church*. Harmondsworth, Middlesex, U.K.: Penguin, 1963.

635. Ware, K. *The Orthodox Way*. London: Mowbrays, 1979.

636. Wasson, R. G. *The Road to Eleusis*. New York: Harcourt Brace Jovanovitch, 1978.

637. Watt, R. E. *Isis in the Graeco-Roman World*. London: Thames and Hudson, 1971.

638. Waters, F. *Book of the Hopi*. Harmondsworth, Middlesex, U.K.: Penguin Books, 1977.

639. Watkins, A. *The Old Straight Track*. London: Garnstone Press, 1970.

640. *Way of Hermes* (Corpus Hermeticum). Translated by C. Salaman, D. von Oyen, and W. D. Wharton. London: Duckworth, 1999.

641. Weaver, H. *Dowsing the Primary Sense*. London: Routledge and Kegan Paul, 1978.

642. Wentz, W. Y. Evans. *The Fairy-faith in Celtic Countries*. New York: Lemma, 1973.

643. West, M. L. *The Orphic Poems*. Oxford: Clarendon Press, 1984.

644. Whitman, W. *Complete Poetry, Selected Prose and Letters*. London: Nonesuch, 1938.

645. Whitmont, E. *Return of the Goddess*. London: Routledge and Kegan Paul, 1983.

646. Whitson, R. E. *The Shakers*. London: SPCK, 1983.

647. Whone, H. *Church, Monastery, Cathedral*. Tisbury, U.K.: Compton Russell and Element, 1977.

648. Wilber, K. *Up from Eden*. London: Routledge and Kegan Paul, 1983.

649. Wilby, B. *New Dimensions Red Book*. Toddington, U.K.: Helios Books, 1968.

650. Wilkins, E. *The Rose Garden Game*. London: Gollancz, 1969.

651. Williams, C., and C. S. Lewis. *Arthurian Torso*. Oxford: Oxford University Press, 1948.

652. Williamson, T., and L. Bellamy. *Ley Lines in Question*. London: Worlds Work, 1983.

653. Wilson, P. L. *Angels*. London: Thames and Hudson, 1980.

654. Yates, F. *Giordano Bruno and the Hermetic Tradition*. London: Routledge and Kegan Paul, 1971.

655. ———. *The Rosicrucian Enlightenment*. London: Routledge and Kegan Paul, 1972.

656. ———. *The Art of Memory*. London: Routledge and Kegan Paul, 1966.

657. ———. *Occult Philosophy in the Elizabethan Age*. London: Routledge and Kegan Paul, 1979.

658. Yeats, W. B. *Autobiography*. New York: Collier-Macmillan, 1974.

659. ———. *Collected Plays*. London: Macmillan, 1952.

660. Zoroaster. *The Chaldean Oracles*. Wellingborough, U.K.: Aquarian Press, 1983.

Index